MY HERO ACADEMIA
VIGILANTES

6

Writer / Letterer
Hideyuki Furuhashi

Penciller / Colorist
Betten Court

Original Concept
Kohei Horikoshi

【team up】

verb | team up
: when multiple individuals work toward a
common goal

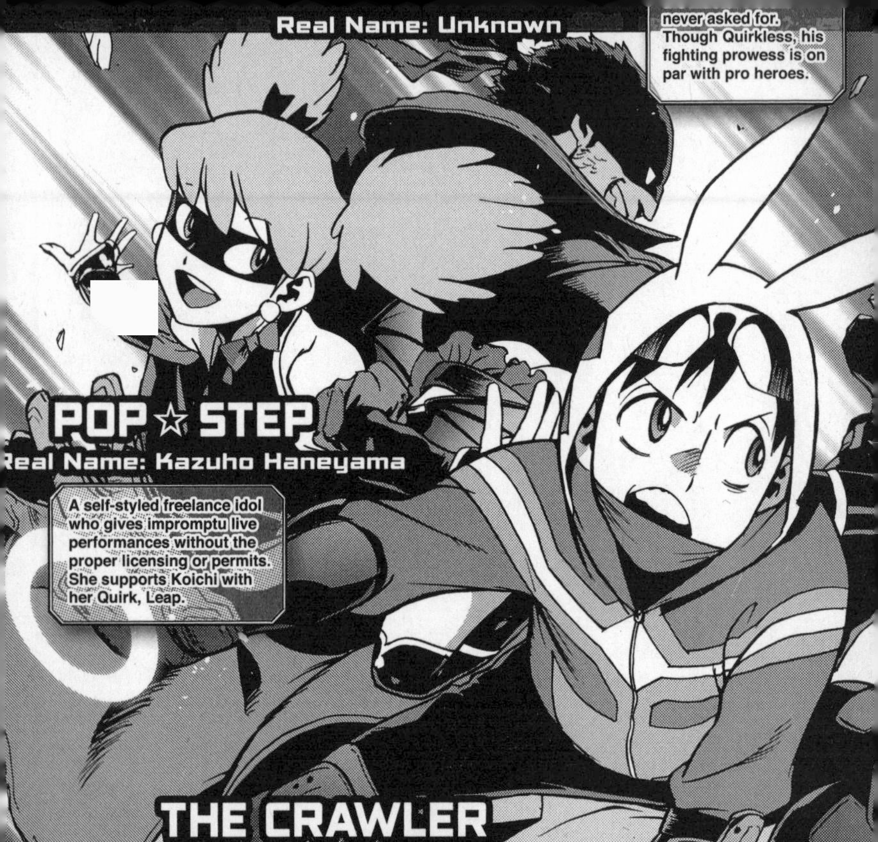
never asked for. Though Quirkless, his fighting prowess is on par with pro heroes.
Real Name: Unknown
POP☆STEP
Real Name: Kazuho Haneyama
A self-styled freelance idol who gives impromptu live performances without the proper licensing or permits. She supports Koichi with her Quirk, Leap.
THE CRAWLER
Real Name: Koichi Haimawari
A college freshman. With his Slide and Glide Quirk, this good-natured young man initially delved into the world of vigilantism under the moniker "Nice Guy."

STORY

What is "justice" anyway? Get ready for a PLUS ULTRA spin-off set in the world of *My Hero Academia*!!

Heroes. The chosen ones who, with explicit government permission, use their natural talents, or Quirks, to aid society. However, not everyone can be chosen, and some take action of their own accord, becoming illegal heroes. What does justice mean to them? And can we really call them heroes? This story takes to the streets in order to follow the exploits of those known as *vigilantes*.

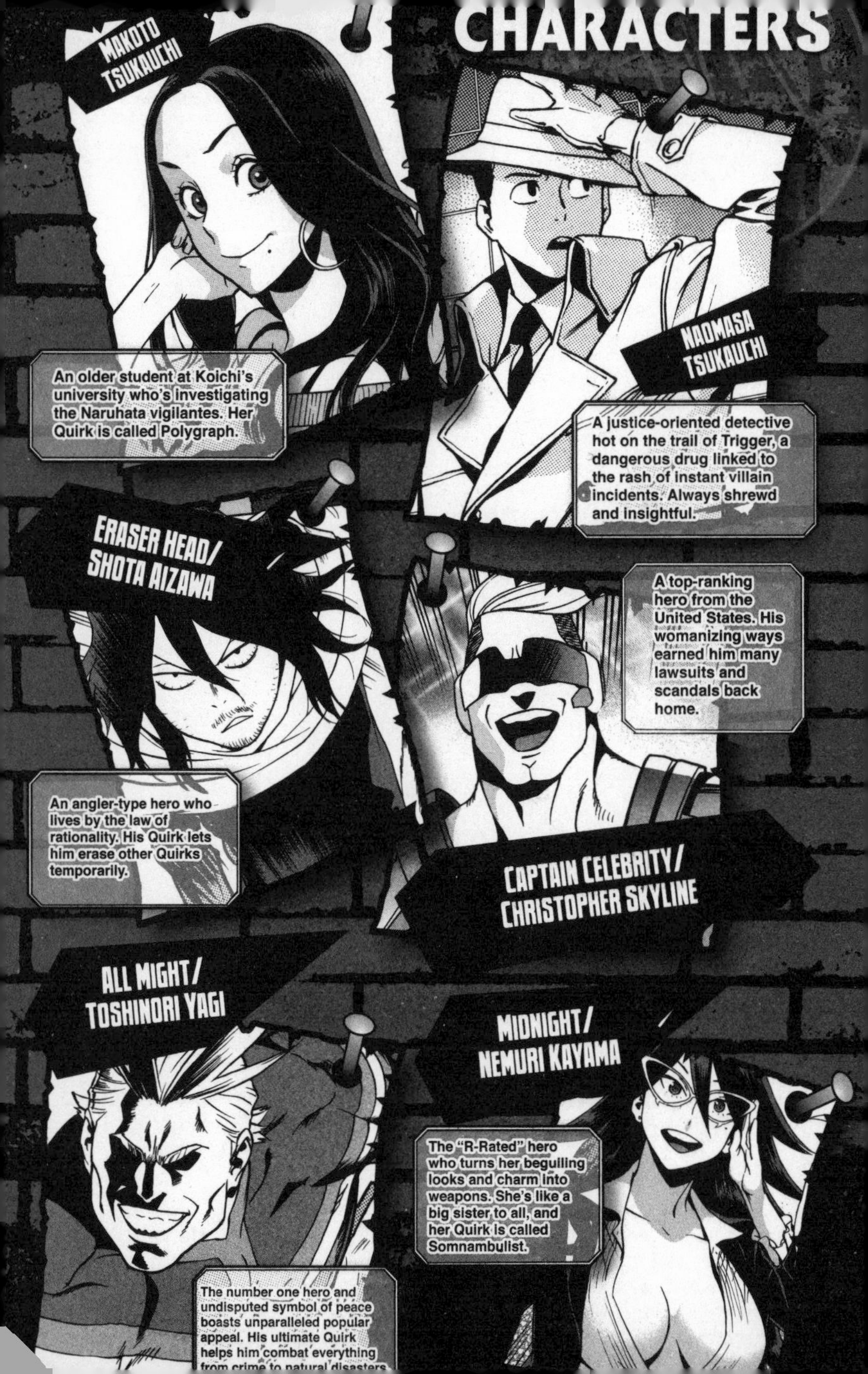
CHARACTERS
NAOMASA TSUKAUCHI
A justice-oriented detective hot on the trail of Trigger, a dangerous drug linked to the rash of instant villain incidents. Always shrewd and insightful.
MAKOTO TSUKAUCHI
An older student at Koichi's university who's investigating the Naruhata vigilantes. Her Quirk is called Polygraph.
CAPTAIN CELEBRITY/ CHRISTOPHER SKYLINE
A top-ranking hero from the United States. His womanizing ways earned him many lawsuits and scandals back home.
ERASER HEAD/ SHOTA AIZAWA
An angler-type hero who lives by the law of rationality. His Quirk lets him erase other Quirks temporarily.
MIDNIGHT/ NEMURI KAYAMA
The "R-Rated" hero who turns her beguiling looks and charm into weapons. She's like a big sister to all, and her Quirk is called Somnambulist.
ALL MIGHT/ TOSHINORI YAGI
The number one hero and undisputed symbol of peace boasts unparalleled popular appeal. His ultimate Quirk helps him combat everything from crime to natural disasters.

MY HERO ACADEMIA VIGILANTES

6

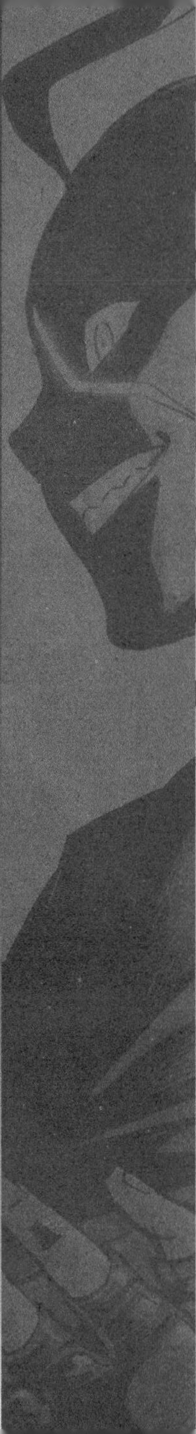

CONTENTS

EP. 36 - MUST-HAVE MERCHANDISE

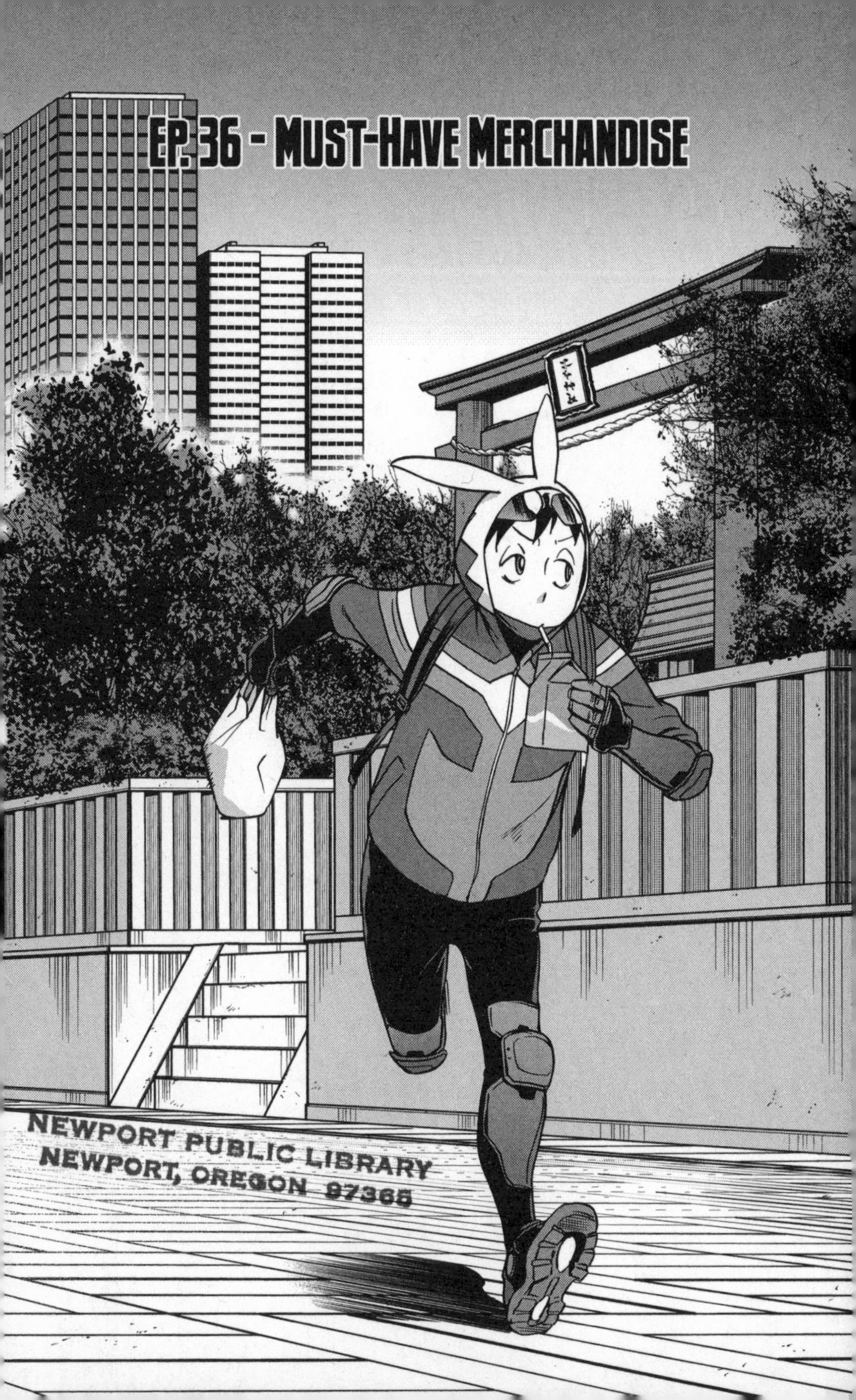

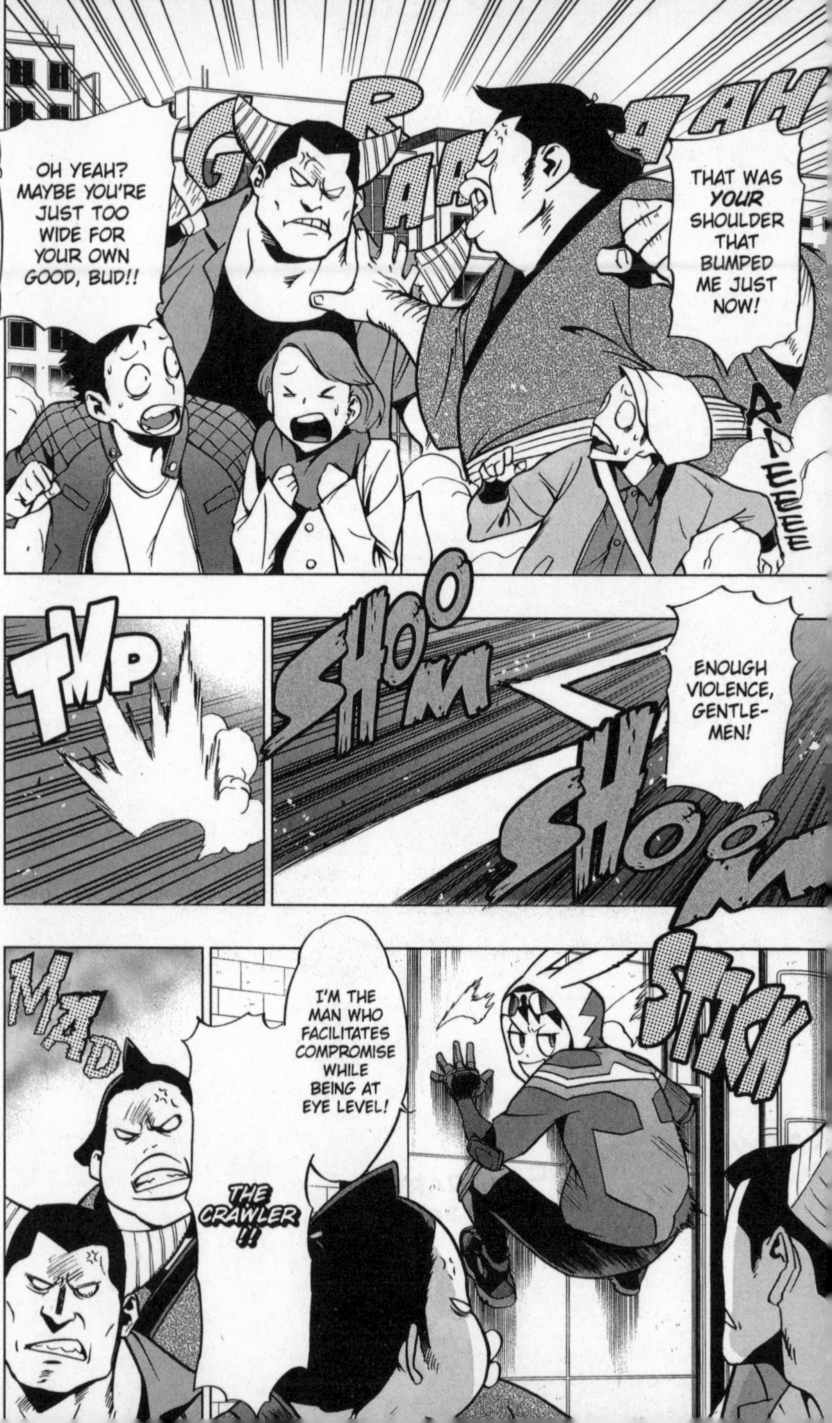
THAT WAS YOUR SHOULDER THAT BUMPED ME JUST NOW!
OH YEAH? MAYBE YOU'RE JUST TOO WIDE FOR YOUR OWN GOOD, BUD!!
AIEEEE
ENOUGH VIOLENCE, GENTLE-MEN!
SHOOOM
SHOOOM
TMP
STICK
I'M THE MAN WHO FACILITATES COMPROMISE WHILE BEING AT EYE LEVEL!
THE CRAWLER!!
MAD

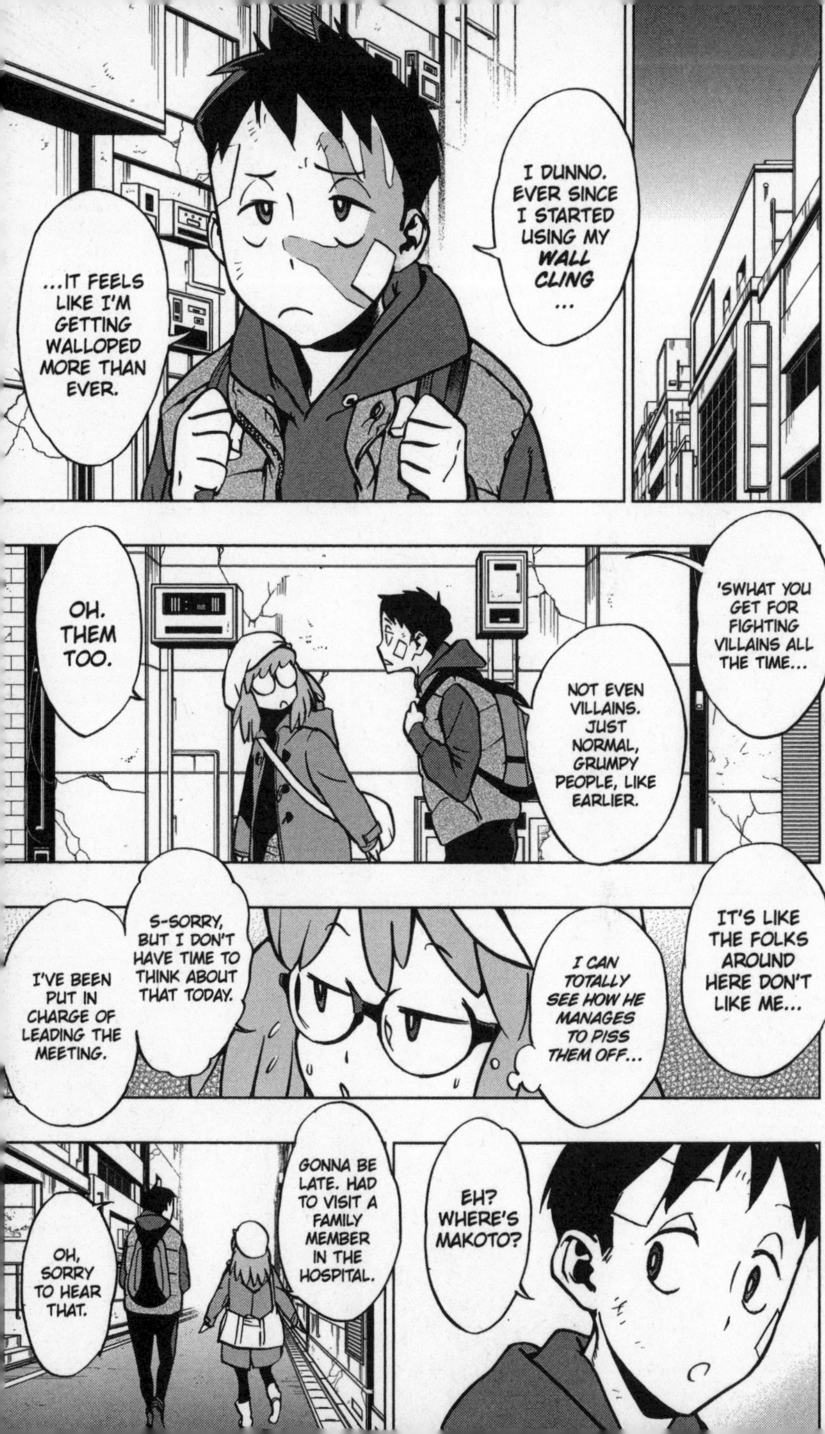
I DUNNO. EVER SINCE I STARTED USING MY *WALL CLING* ...
...IT FEELS LIKE I'M GETTING WALLOPED MORE THAN EVER.
'SWHAT YOU GET FOR FIGHTING VILLAINS ALL THE TIME...
NOT EVEN VILLAINS. JUST NORMAL, GRUMPY PEOPLE, LIKE EARLIER.
OH. THEM TOO.
IT'S LIKE THE FOLKS AROUND HERE DON'T LIKE ME...
I CAN TOTALLY SEE HOW HE MANAGES TO PISS THEM OFF...
S-SORRY, BUT I DON'T HAVE TIME TO THINK ABOUT THAT TODAY.
I'VE BEEN PUT IN CHARGE OF LEADING THE MEETING.
EH? WHERE'S MAKOTO?
GONNA BE LATE. HAD TO VISIT A FAMILY MEMBER IN THE HOSPITAL.
OH, SORRY TO HEAR THAT.

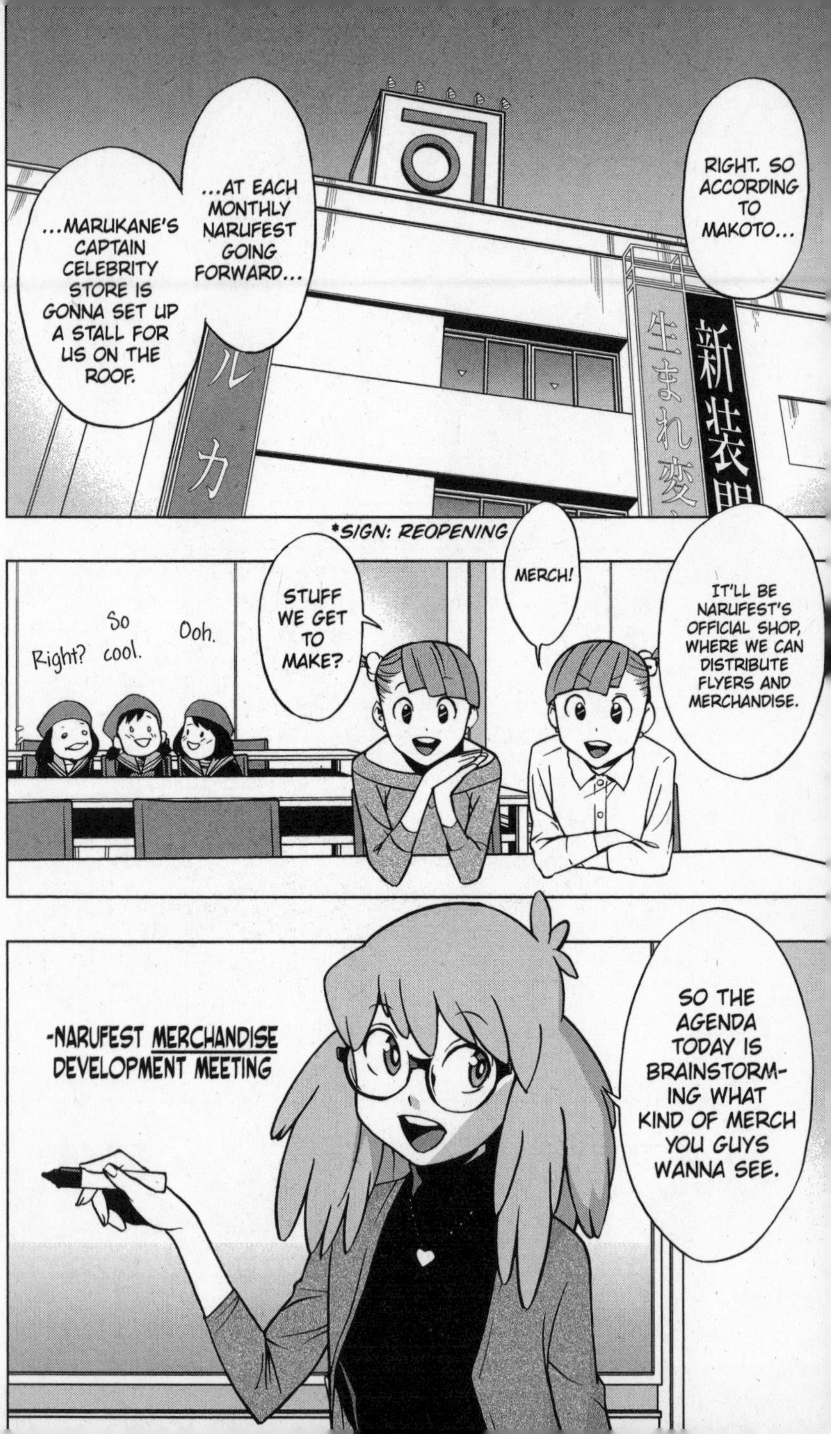
RIGHT. SO ACCORDING TO MAKOTO...
...AT EACH MONTHLY NARUFEST GOING FORWARD...
...MARUKANE'S CAPTAIN CELEBRITY STORE IS GONNA SET UP A STALL FOR US ON THE ROOF.
*SIGN: REOPENING
IT'LL BE NARUFEST'S OFFICIAL SHOP, WHERE WE CAN DISTRIBUTE FLYERS AND MERCHANDISE.
MERCH!
STUFF WE GET TO MAKE?
Ooh.
So cool.
Right?
SO THE AGENDA TODAY IS BRAINSTORMING WHAT KIND OF MERCH YOU GUYS WANNA SEE.
-NARUFEST MERCHANDISE DEVELOPMENT MEETING

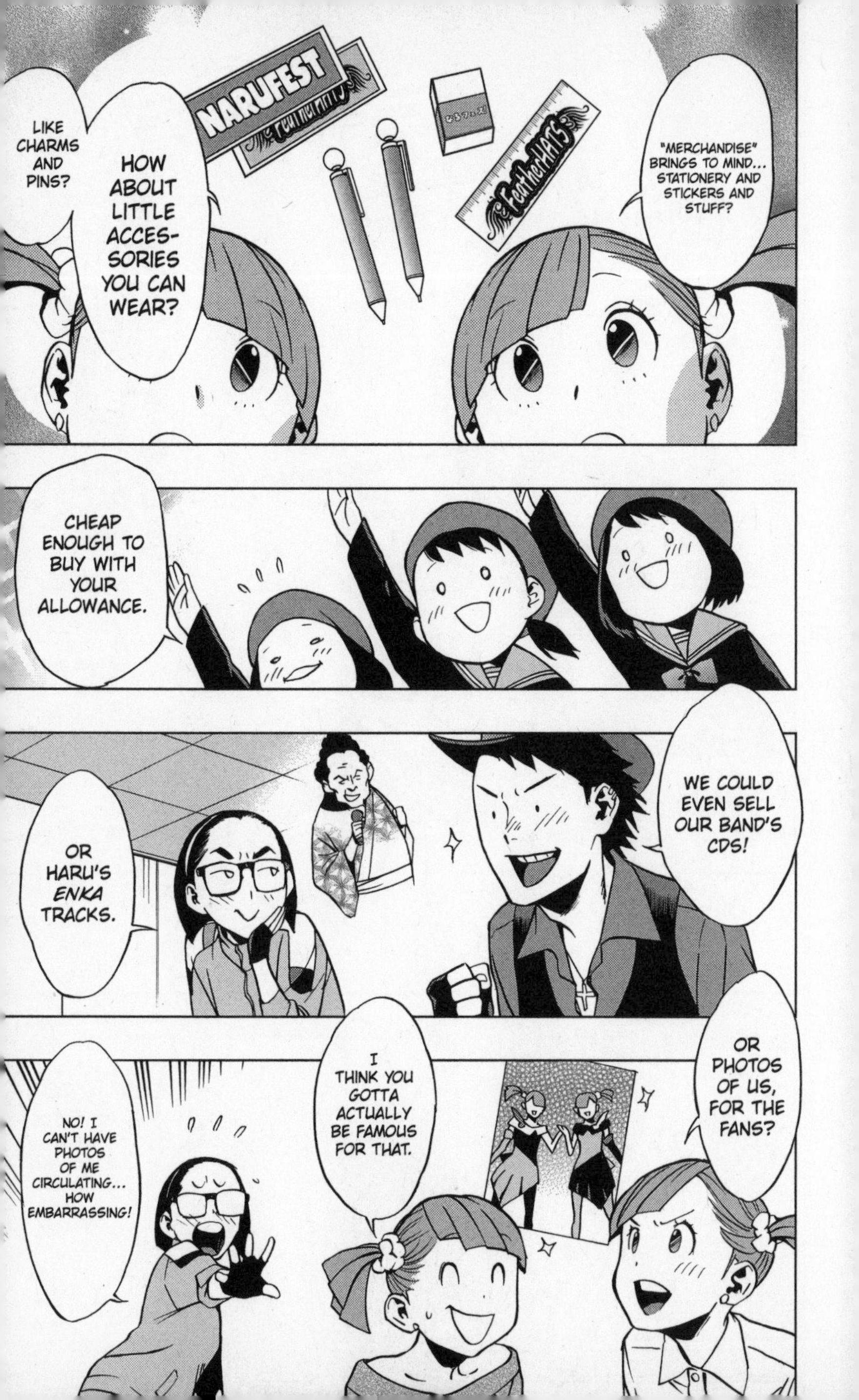
NARUFEST
FeatherHATS
"MERCHANDISE" BRINGS TO MIND... STATIONERY AND STICKERS AND STUFF?
HOW ABOUT LITTLE ACCES-SORIES YOU CAN WEAR?
LIKE CHARMS AND PINS?
CHEAP ENOUGH TO BUY WITH YOUR ALLOWANCE.
WE COULD EVEN SELL OUR BAND'S CDS!
OR HARU'S *ENKA* TRACKS.
OR PHOTOS OF US, FOR THE FANS?
I THINK YOU GOTTA ACTUALLY BE FAMOUS FOR THAT.
NO! I CAN'T HAVE PHOTOS OF ME CIRCULATING... HOW EMBARRASSING!

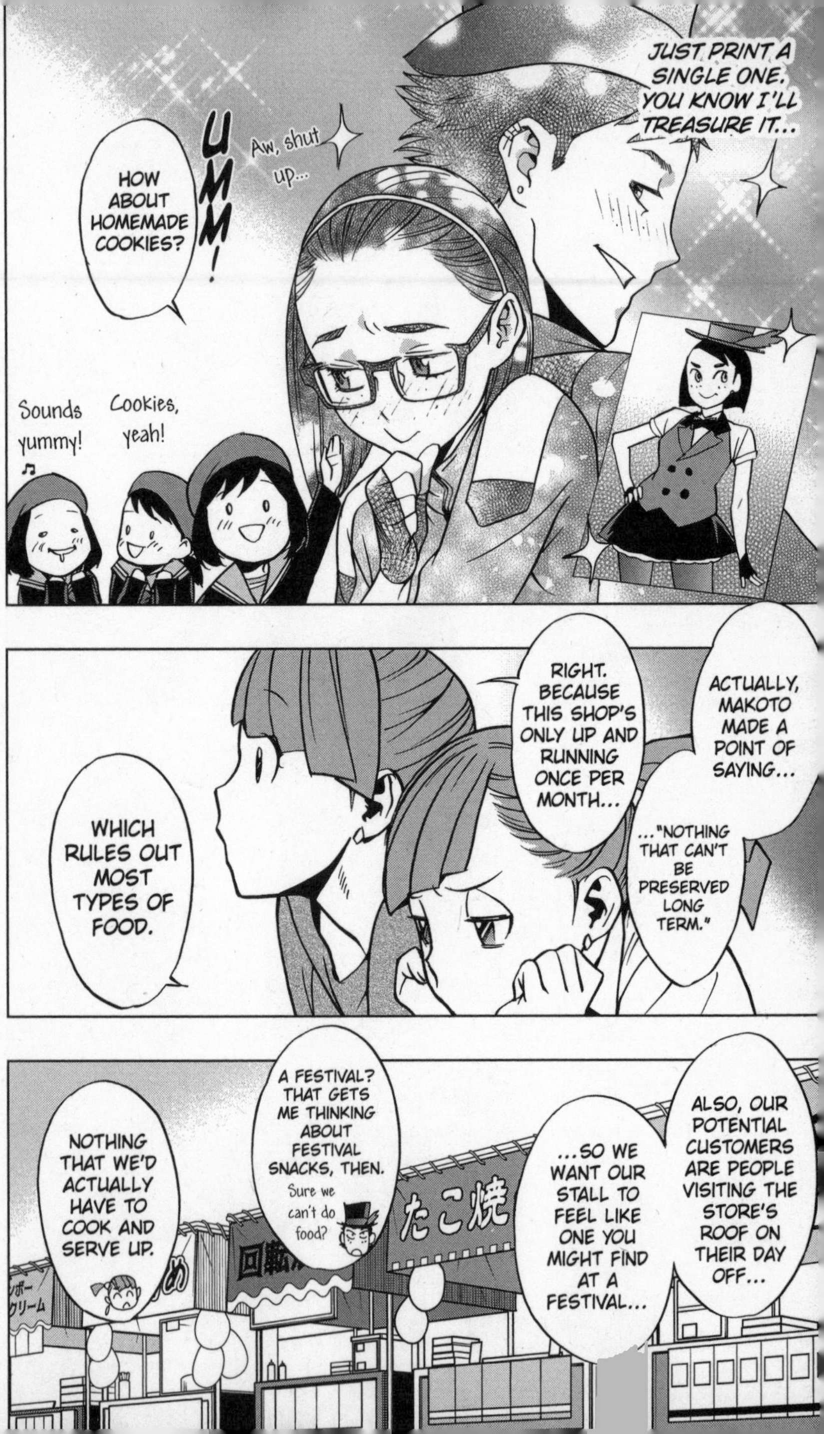
JUST PRINT A SINGLE ONE. YOU KNOW I'LL TREASURE IT...
Aw, shut up...
UMM!
HOW ABOUT HOMEMADE COOKIES?
Cookies, yeah!
Sounds yummy! ♫
ACTUALLY, MAKOTO MADE A POINT OF SAYING...
..."NOTHING THAT CAN'T BE PRESERVED LONG TERM."
RIGHT. BECAUSE THIS SHOP'S ONLY UP AND RUNNING ONCE PER MONTH...
WHICH RULES OUT MOST TYPES OF FOOD.
ALSO, OUR POTENTIAL CUSTOMERS ARE PEOPLE VISITING THE STORE'S ROOF ON THEIR DAY OFF...
...SO WE WANT OUR STALL TO FEEL LIKE ONE YOU MIGHT FIND AT A FESTIVAL...
たこ焼
A FESTIVAL? THAT GETS ME THINKING ABOUT FESTIVAL SNACKS, THEN.
Sure we can't do food?
NOTHING THAT WE'D ACTUALLY HAVE TO COOK AND SERVE UP.

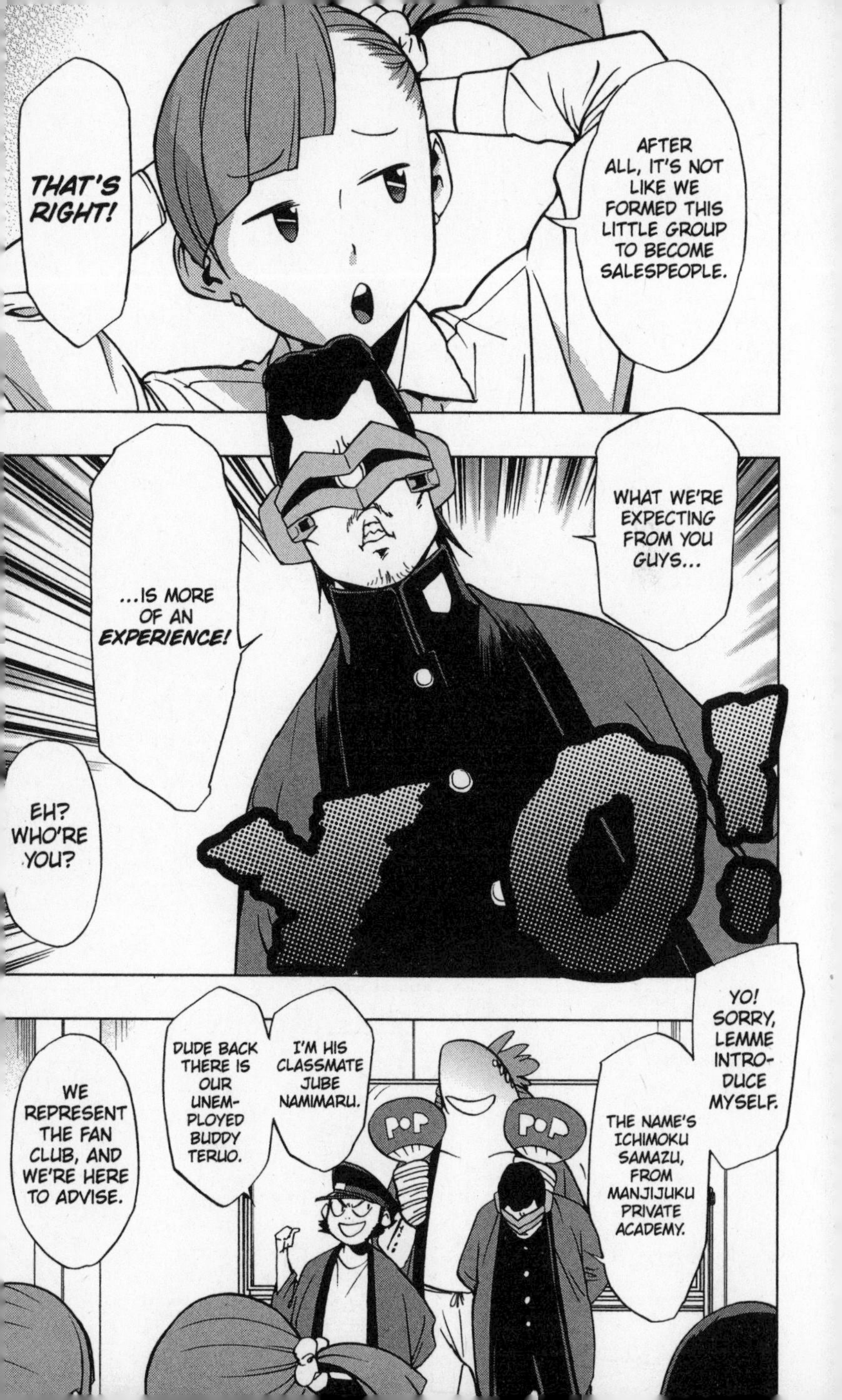
AFTER ALL, IT'S NOT LIKE WE FORMED THIS LITTLE GROUP TO BECOME SALESPEOPLE.
THAT'S RIGHT!
WHAT WE'RE EXPECTING FROM YOU GUYS...
...IS MORE OF AN EXPERIENCE!
YO!
EH? WHO'RE YOU?
YO! SORRY, LEMME INTRO-DUCE MYSELF.
THE NAME'S ICHIMOKU SAMAZU, FROM MANJIJUKU PRIVATE ACADEMY.
I'M HIS CLASSMATE JUBE NAMIMARU.
DUDE BACK THERE IS OUR UNEM-PLOYED BUDDY TERUO.
WE REPRESENT THE FAN CLUB, AND WE'RE HERE TO ADVISE.

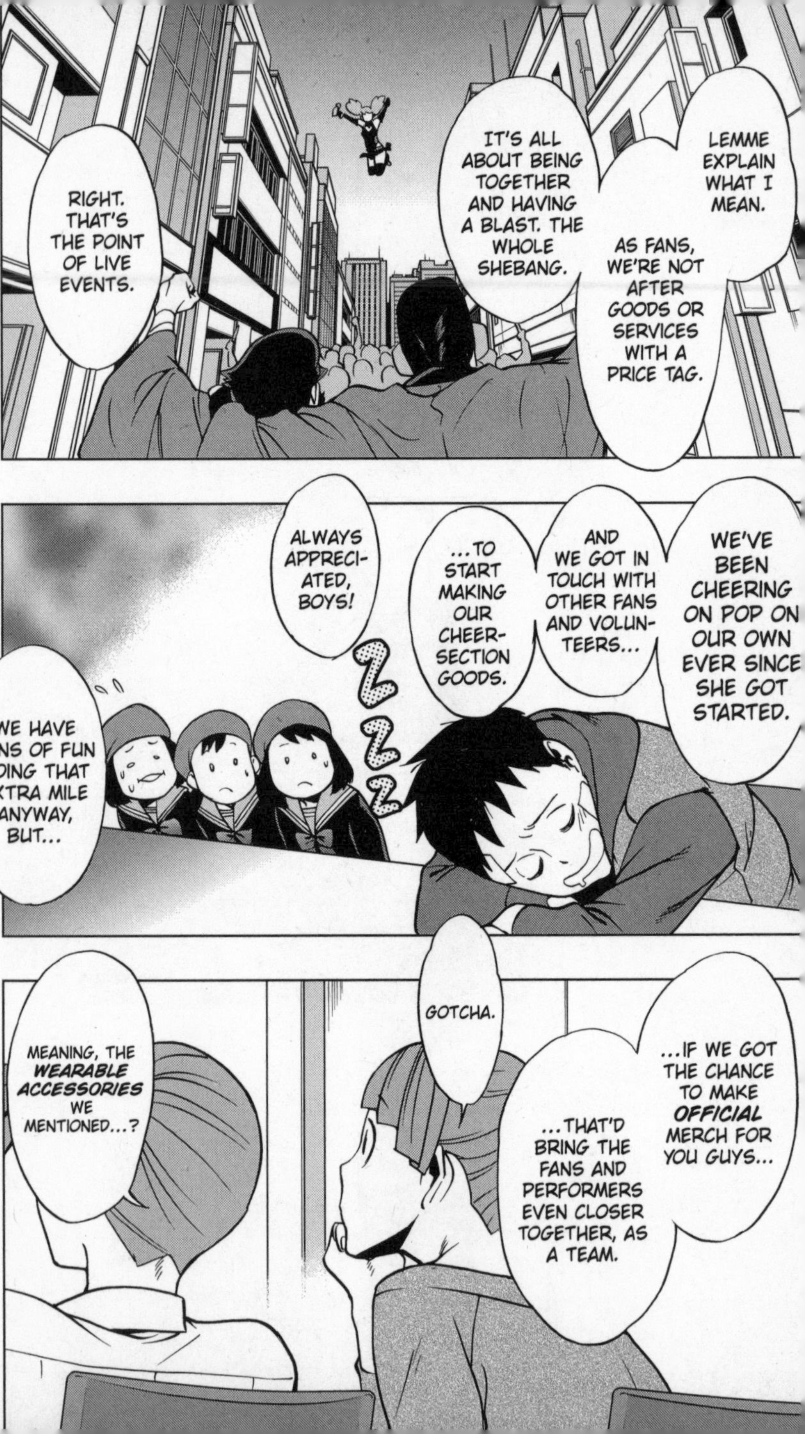
LEMME EXPLAIN WHAT I MEAN.
AS FANS, WE'RE NOT AFTER GOODS OR SERVICES WITH A PRICE TAG.
IT'S ALL ABOUT BEING TOGETHER AND HAVING A BLAST. THE WHOLE SHEBANG.
RIGHT. THAT'S THE POINT OF LIVE EVENTS.
WE'VE BEEN CHEERING ON POP ON OUR OWN EVER SINCE SHE GOT STARTED.
AND WE GOT IN TOUCH WITH OTHER FANS AND VOLUNTEERS...
...TO START MAKING OUR CHEER-SECTION GOODS.
ALWAYS APPRECIATED, BOYS!
ZZZ
WE HAVE TONS OF FUN GOING THAT EXTRA MILE ANYWAY, BUT...
...IF WE GOT THE CHANCE TO MAKE *OFFICIAL* MERCH FOR YOU GUYS...
...THAT'D BRING THE FANS AND PERFORMERS EVEN CLOSER TOGETHER, AS A TEAM.
GOTCHA.
MEANING, THE *WEARABLE ACCESSORIES* WE MENTIONED...?

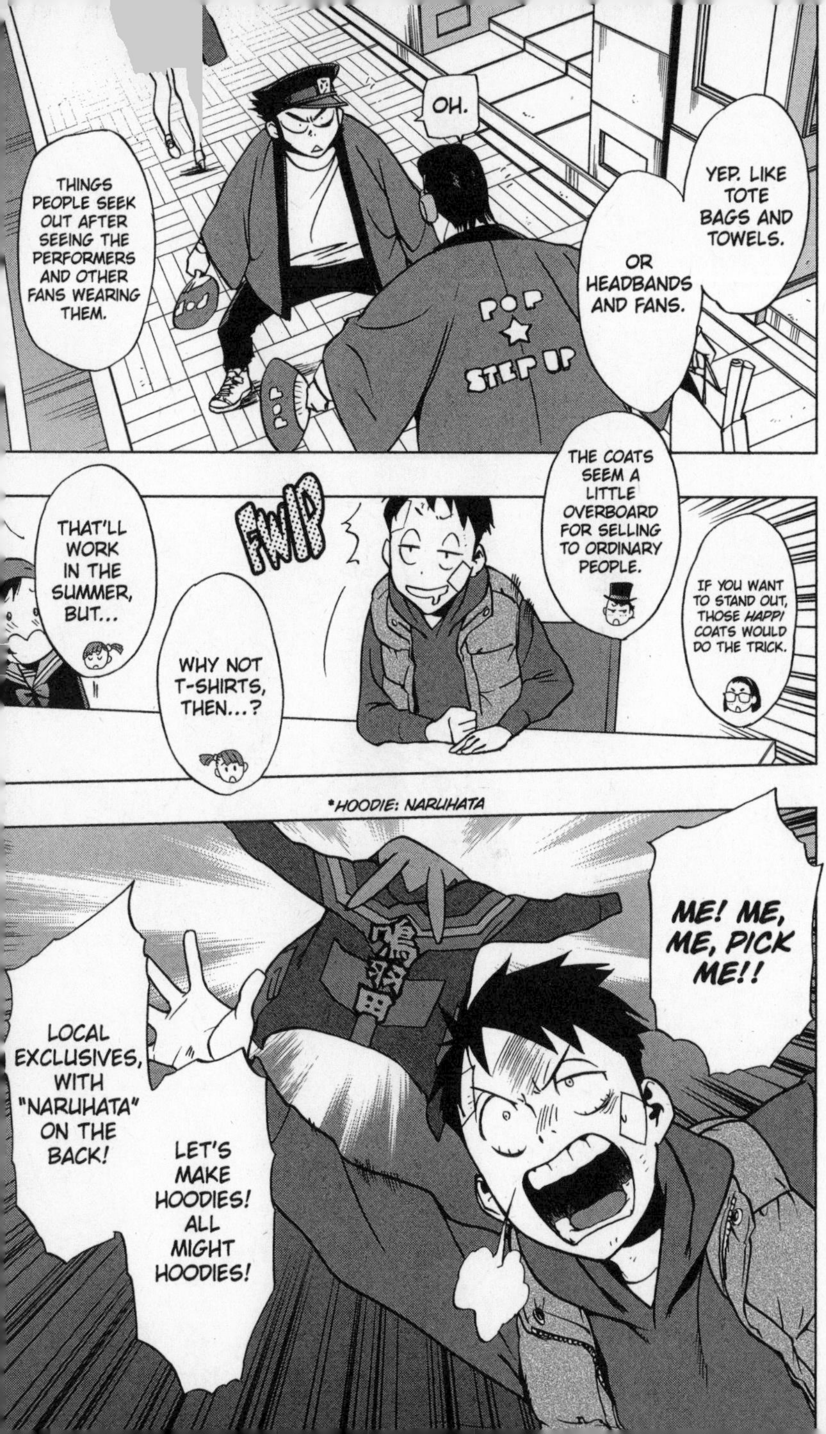
YEP. LIKE TOTE BAGS AND TOWELS.
OR HEADBANDS AND FANS.
OH.
THINGS PEOPLE SEEK OUT AFTER SEEING THE PERFORMERS AND OTHER FANS WEARING THEM.
POP ☆ STEP UP
IF YOU WANT TO STAND OUT, THOSE *HAPPI* COATS WOULD DO THE TRICK.
THE COATS SEEM A LITTLE OVERBOARD FOR SELLING TO ORDINARY PEOPLE.
FWIP
WHY NOT T-SHIRTS, THEN...?
THAT'LL WORK IN THE SUMMER, BUT...
*HOODIE: NARUHATA
ME! ME, ME, PICK ME!!
LET'S MAKE HOODIES! ALL MIGHT HOODIES!
LOCAL EXCLUSIVES, WITH "NARUHATA" ON THE BACK!

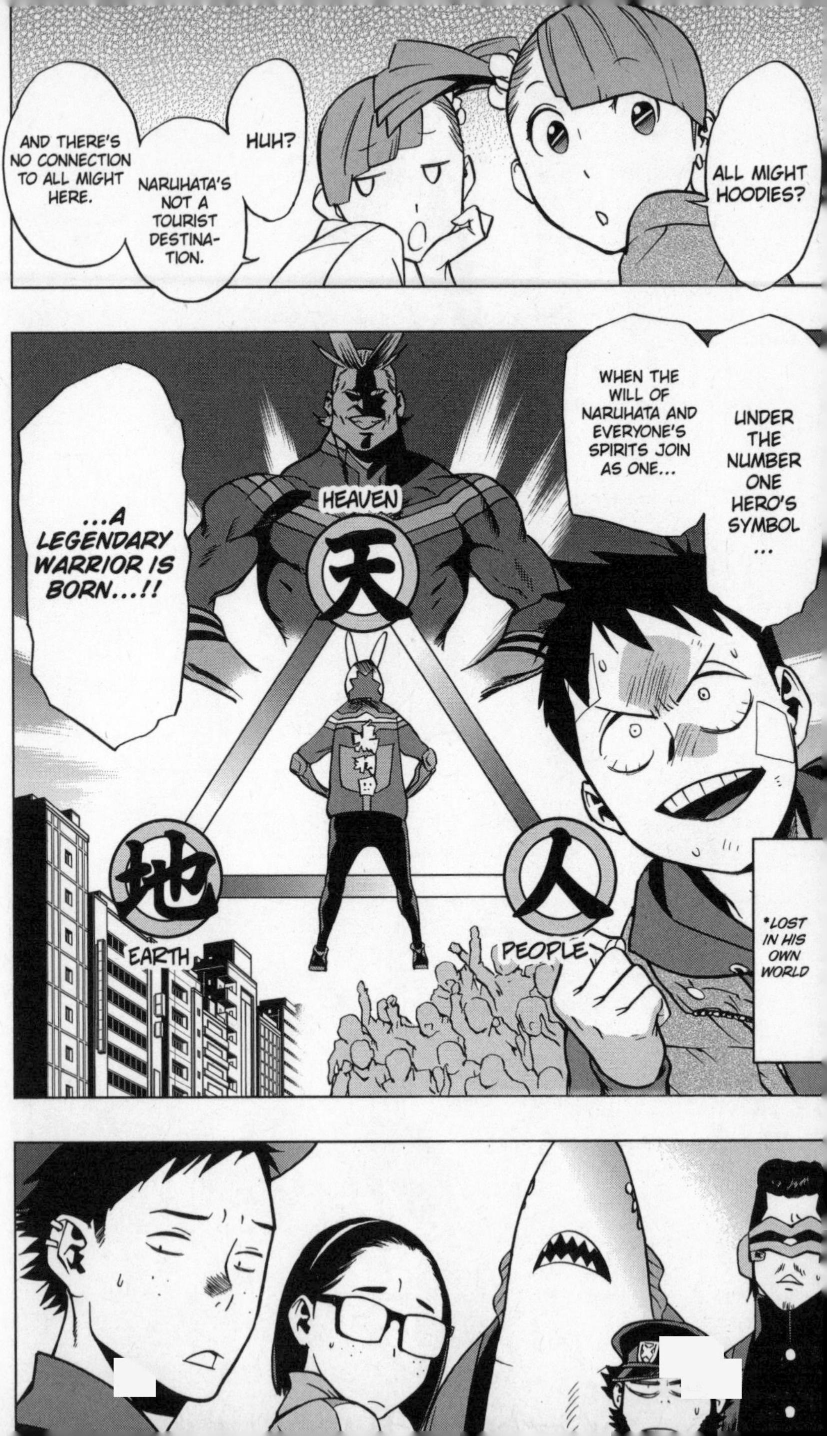
ALL MIGHT HOODIES?
HUH?
NARUHATA'S NOT A TOURIST DESTINATION.
AND THERE'S NO CONNECTION TO ALL MIGHT HERE.
*LOST IN HIS OWN WORLD
UNDER THE NUMBER ONE HERO'S SYMBOL...
WHEN THE WILL OF NARUHATA AND EVERYONE'S SPIRITS JOIN AS ONE...
HEAVEN
天
人
PEOPLE
地
EARTH
...A LEGENDARY WARRIOR IS BORN...!!

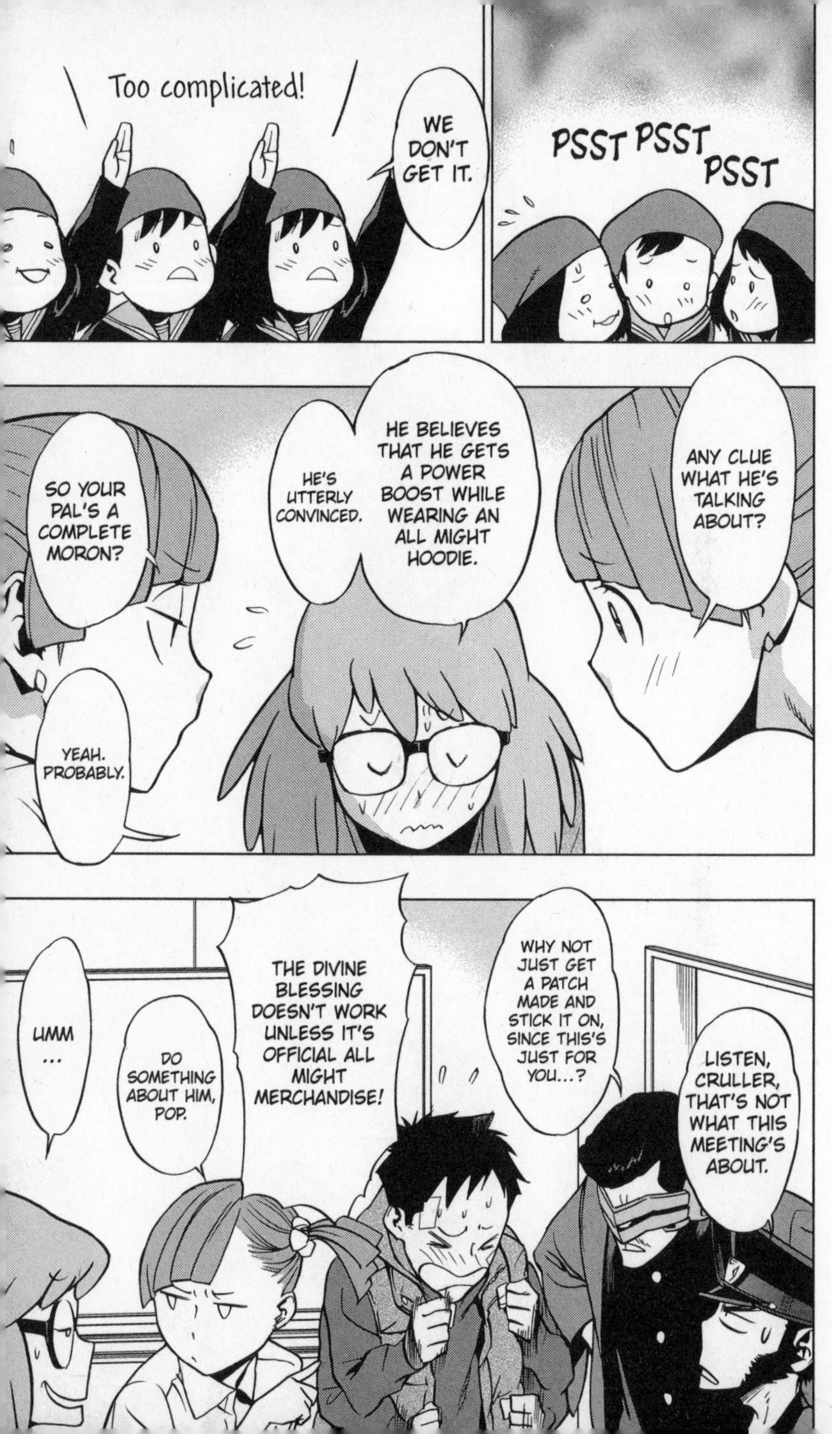
PSST PSST PSST
WE DON'T GET IT.
Too complicated!
ANY CLUE WHAT HE'S TALKING ABOUT?
HE BELIEVES THAT HE GETS A POWER BOOST WHILE WEARING AN ALL MIGHT HOODIE.
HE'S UTTERLY CONVINCED.
SO YOUR PAL'S A COMPLETE MORON?
YEAH. PROBABLY.
LISTEN, CRULLER, THAT'S NOT WHAT THIS MEETING'S ABOUT.
WHY NOT JUST GET A PATCH MADE AND STICK IT ON, SINCE THIS'S JUST FOR YOU...?
THE DIVINE BLESSING DOESN'T WORK UNLESS IT'S OFFICIAL ALL MIGHT MERCHANDISE!
DO SOMETHING ABOUT HIM, POP.
UMM ...

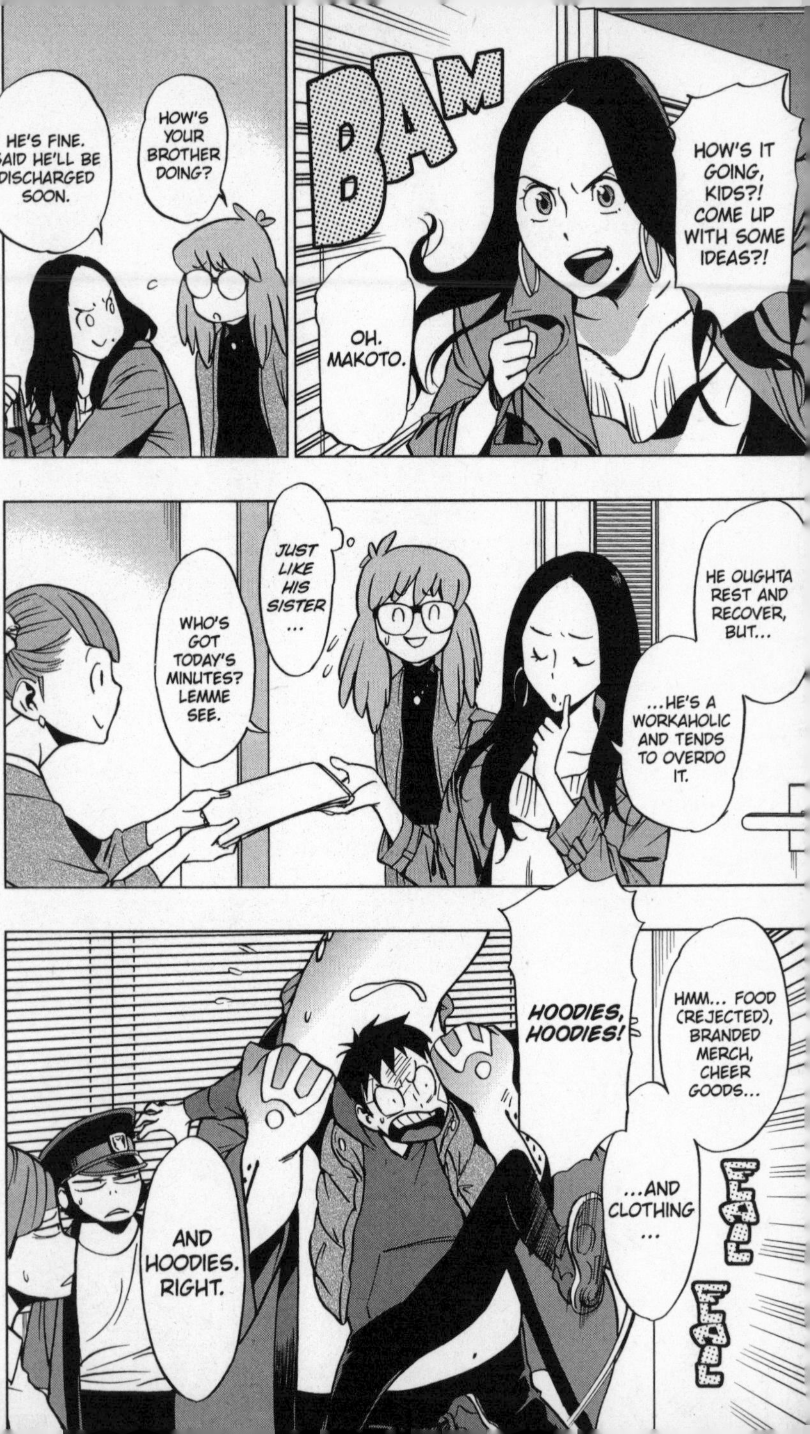
BAM
HOW'S IT GOING, KIDS?! COME UP WITH SOME IDEAS?!
OH. MAKOTO.
HOW'S YOUR BROTHER DOING?
HE'S FINE. SAID HE'LL BE DISCHARGED SOON.
HE OUGHTA REST AND RECOVER, BUT...
...HE'S A WORKAHOLIC AND TENDS TO OVERDO IT.
JUST LIKE HIS SISTER...
WHO'S GOT TODAY'S MINUTES? LEMME SEE.
HMM... FOOD (REJECTED), BRANDED MERCH, CHEER GOODS...
...AND CLOTHING...
HOODIES, HOODIES!
AND HOODIES. RIGHT.

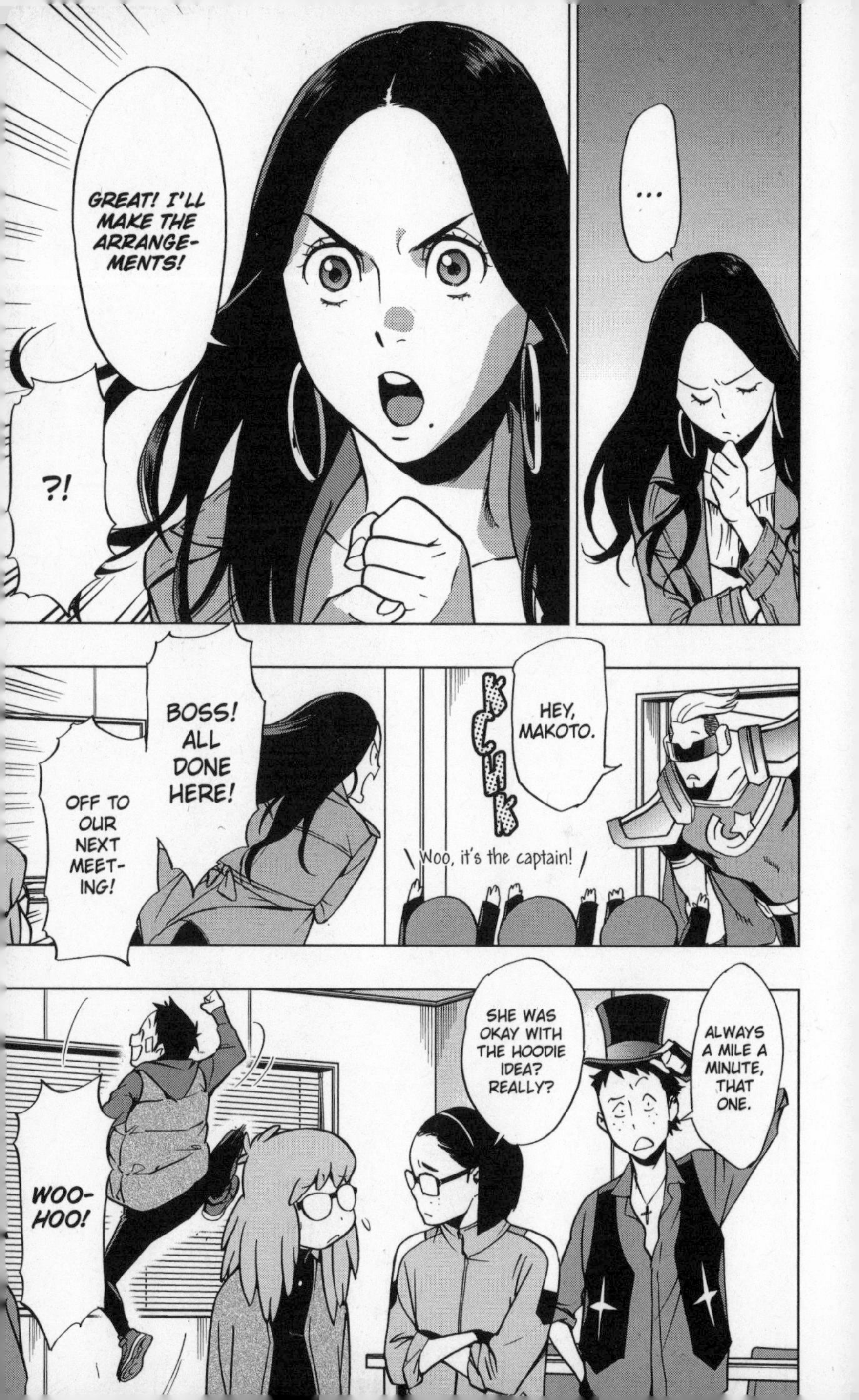
...
GREAT! I'LL MAKE THE ARRANGE-MENTS!
?!
HEY, MAKOTO.
KCHK
Woo, it's the captain!
BOSS! ALL DONE HERE!
OFF TO OUR NEXT MEET-ING!
ALWAYS A MILE A MINUTE, THAT ONE.
SHE WAS OKAY WITH THE HOODIE IDEA? REALLY?
WOO-HOO!

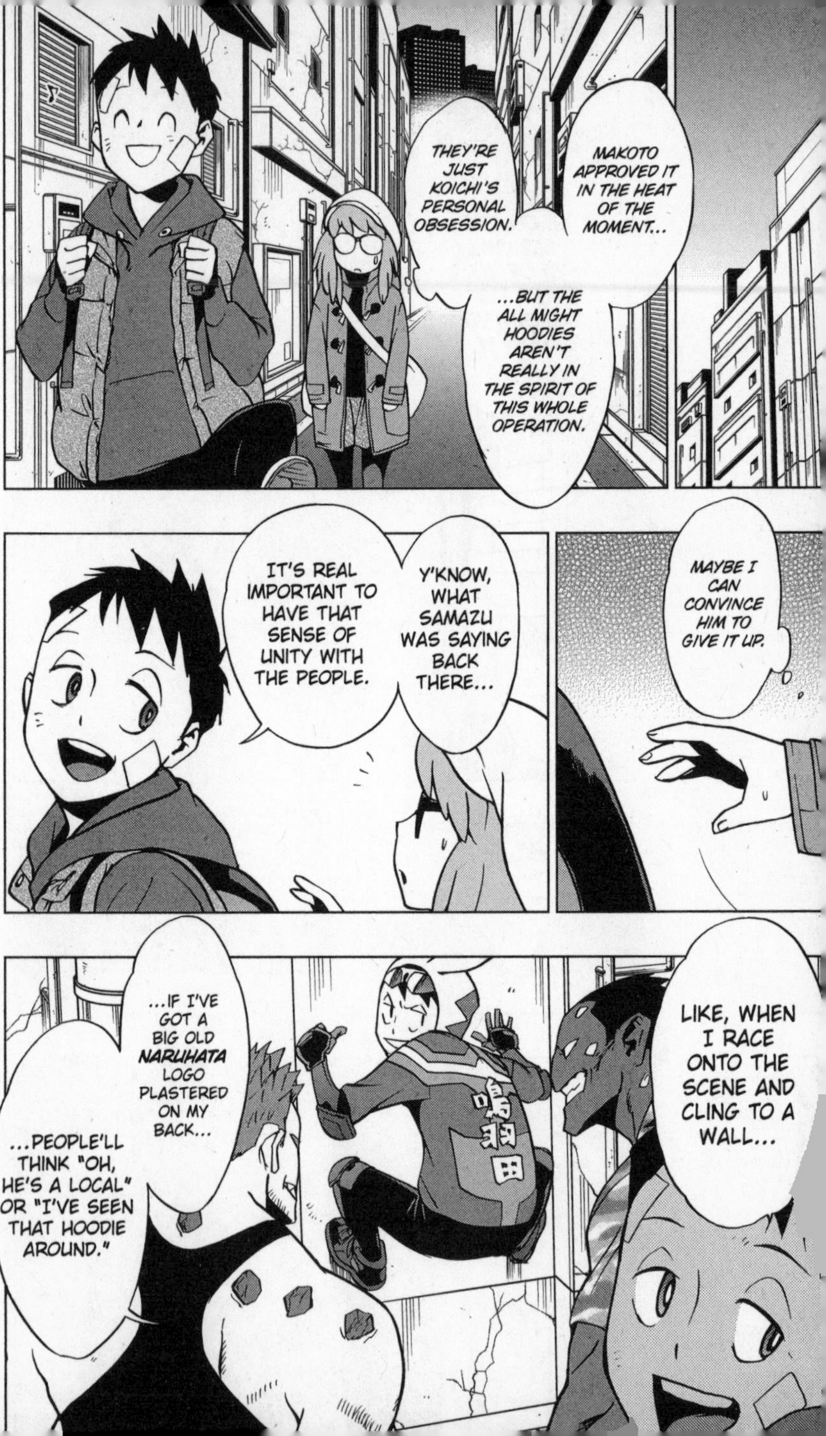
MAKOTO APPROVED IT IN THE HEAT OF THE MOMENT...
...BUT THE ALL MIGHT HOODIES AREN'T REALLY IN THE SPIRIT OF THIS WHOLE OPERATION.
THEY'RE JUST KOICHI'S PERSONAL OBSESSION.
MAYBE I CAN CONVINCE HIM TO GIVE IT UP.
Y'KNOW, WHAT SAMAZU WAS SAYING BACK THERE...
IT'S REAL IMPORTANT TO HAVE THAT SENSE OF UNITY WITH THE PEOPLE.
LIKE, WHEN I RACE ONTO THE SCENE AND CLING TO A WALL...
...IF I'VE GOT A BIG OLD **NARUHATA** LOGO PLASTERED ON MY BACK...
...PEOPLE'LL THINK "OH, HE'S A LOCAL" OR "I'VE SEEN THAT HOODIE AROUND."

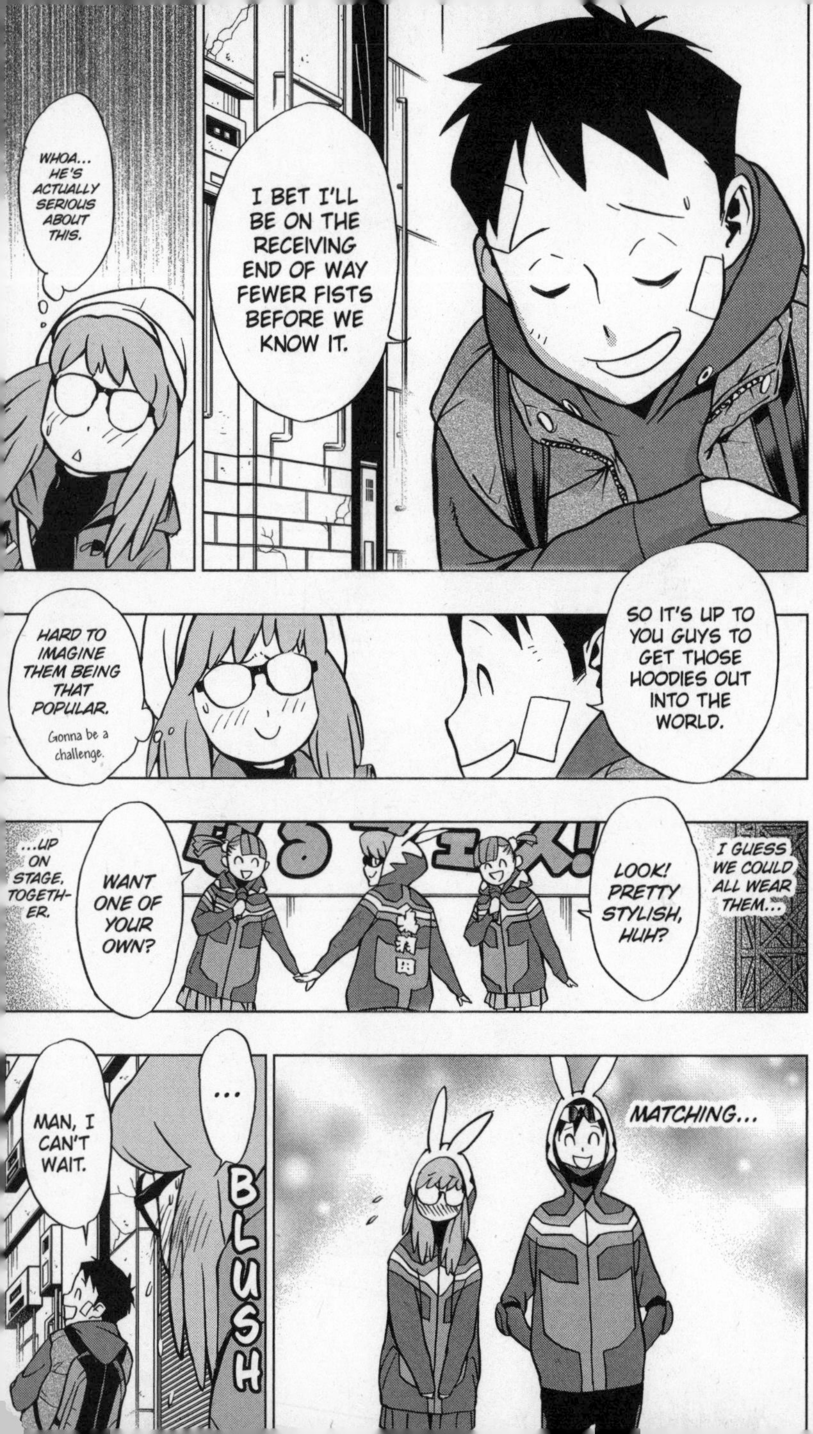
I BET I'LL BE ON THE RECEIVING END OF WAY FEWER FISTS BEFORE WE KNOW IT.
WHOA... HE'S ACTUALLY SERIOUS ABOUT THIS.
SO IT'S UP TO YOU GUYS TO GET THOSE HOODIES OUT INTO THE WORLD.
HARD TO IMAGINE THEM BEING THAT POPULAR.
Gonna be a challenge.
I GUESS WE COULD ALL WEAR THEM...
LOOK! PRETTY STYLISH, HUH?
WANT ONE OF YOUR OWN?
...UP ON STAGE, TOGETHER.
MATCHING...
...
BLUSH
MAN, I CAN'T WAIT.

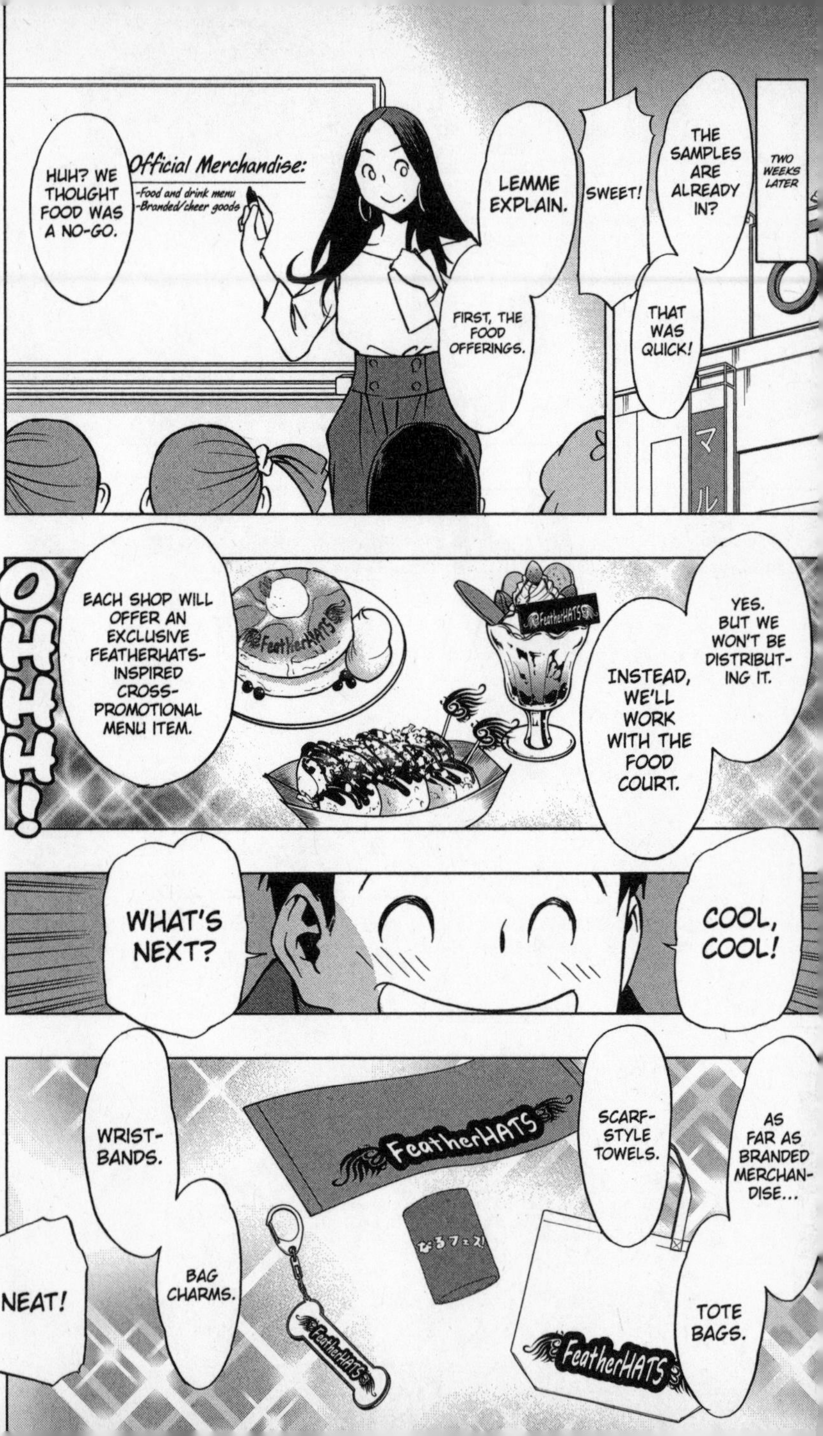
TWO WEEKS LATER
THE SAMPLES ARE ALREADY IN?
SWEET!
THAT WAS QUICK!
LEMME EXPLAIN.
FIRST, THE FOOD OFFERINGS.
Official Merchandise:
-Food and drink menu
-Branded/cheer goods
HUH? WE THOUGHT FOOD WAS A NO-GO.
YES. BUT WE WON'T BE DISTRIBUT-ING IT.
INSTEAD, WE'LL WORK WITH THE FOOD COURT.
FeatherHATS
FeatherHATS
EACH SHOP WILL OFFER AN EXCLUSIVE FEATHERHATS-INSPIRED CROSS-PROMOTIONAL MENU ITEM.
OHHH!
COOL, COOL!
WHAT'S NEXT?
AS FAR AS BRANDED MERCHAN-DISE...
SCARF-STYLE TOWELS.
FeatherHATS
TOTE BAGS.
FeatherHATS
WRIST-BANDS.
BAG CHARMS.
FeatherHATS
NEAT!

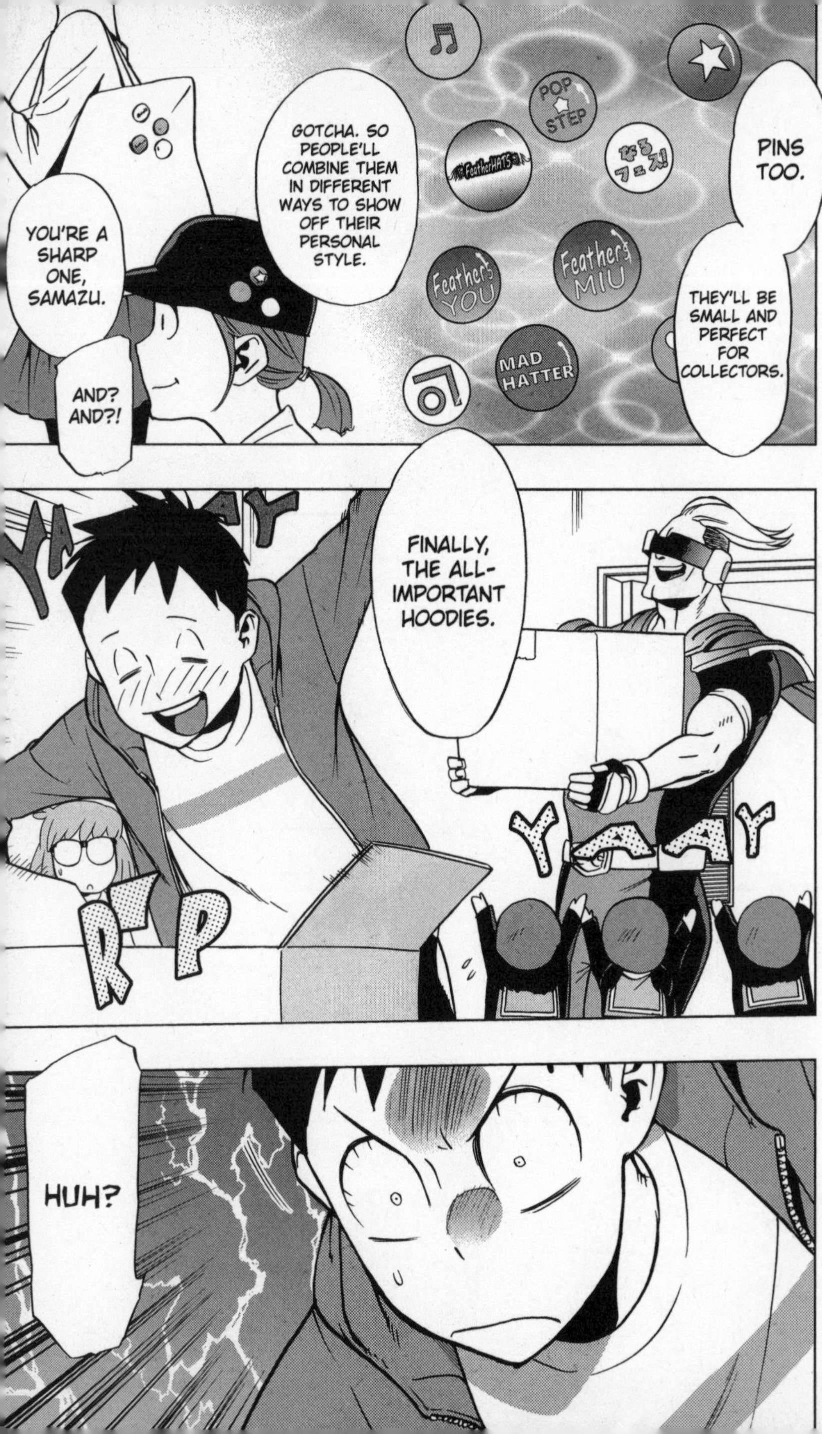
PINS TOO.
THEY'LL BE SMALL AND PERFECT FOR COLLECTORS.
POP STEP
FeatherHATS
Feathers MIU
Feathers YOU
MAD HATTER
GOTCHA. SO PEOPLE'LL COMBINE THEM IN DIFFERENT WAYS TO SHOW OFF THEIR PERSONAL STYLE.
YOU'RE A SHARP ONE, SAMAZU.
AND? AND?!
FINALLY, THE ALL-IMPORTANT HOODIES.
YAY
YAY
RIP
HUH?

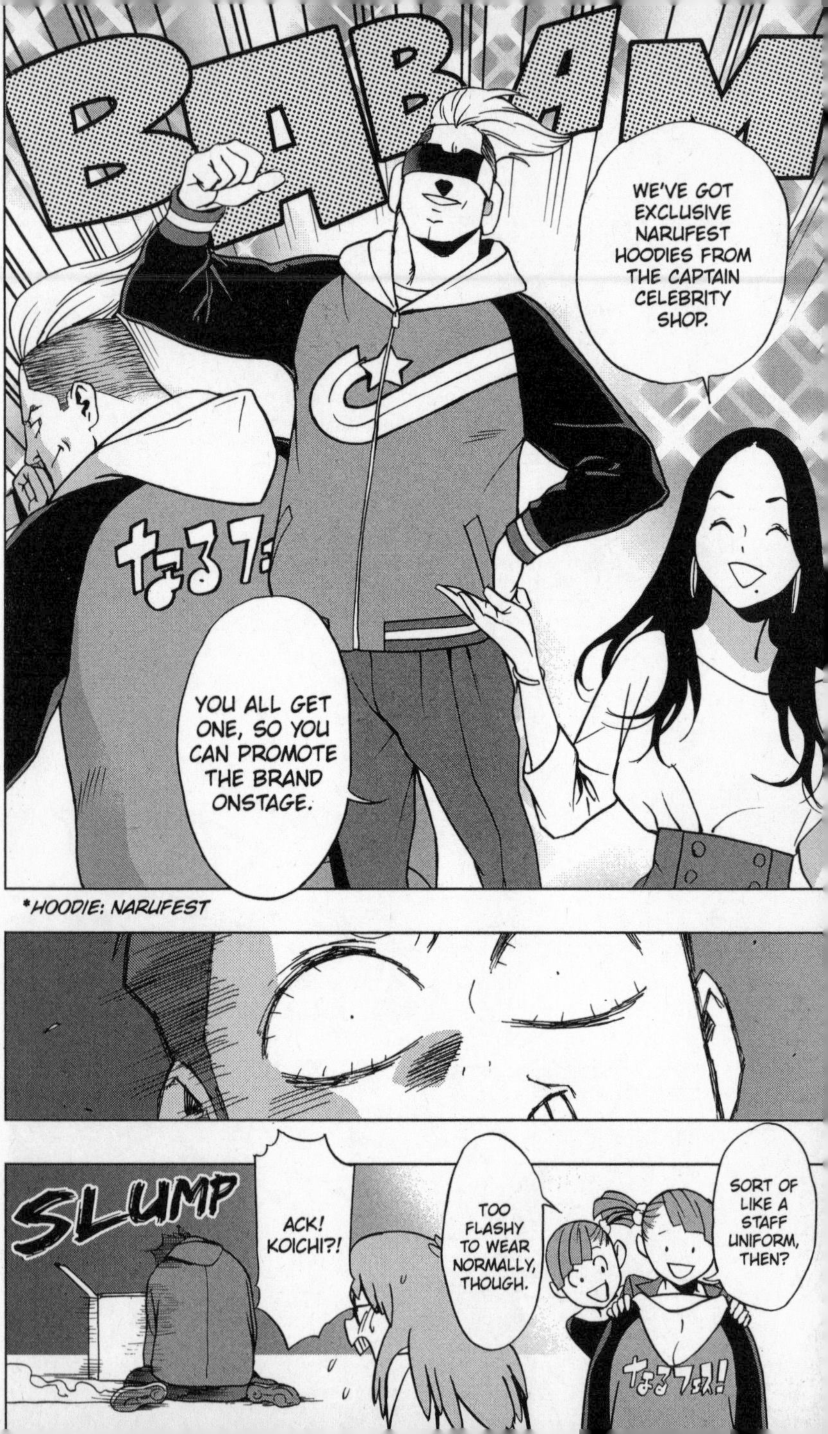
BABAM
WE'VE GOT EXCLUSIVE NARUFEST HOODIES FROM THE CAPTAIN CELEBRITY SHOP.
YOU ALL GET ONE, SO YOU CAN PROMOTE THE BRAND ONSTAGE.
*HOODIE: NARUFEST
SORT OF LIKE A STAFF UNIFORM, THEN?
TOO FLASHY TO WEAR NORMALLY, THOUGH.
なるフェス!
ACK! KOICHI?!
SLUMP

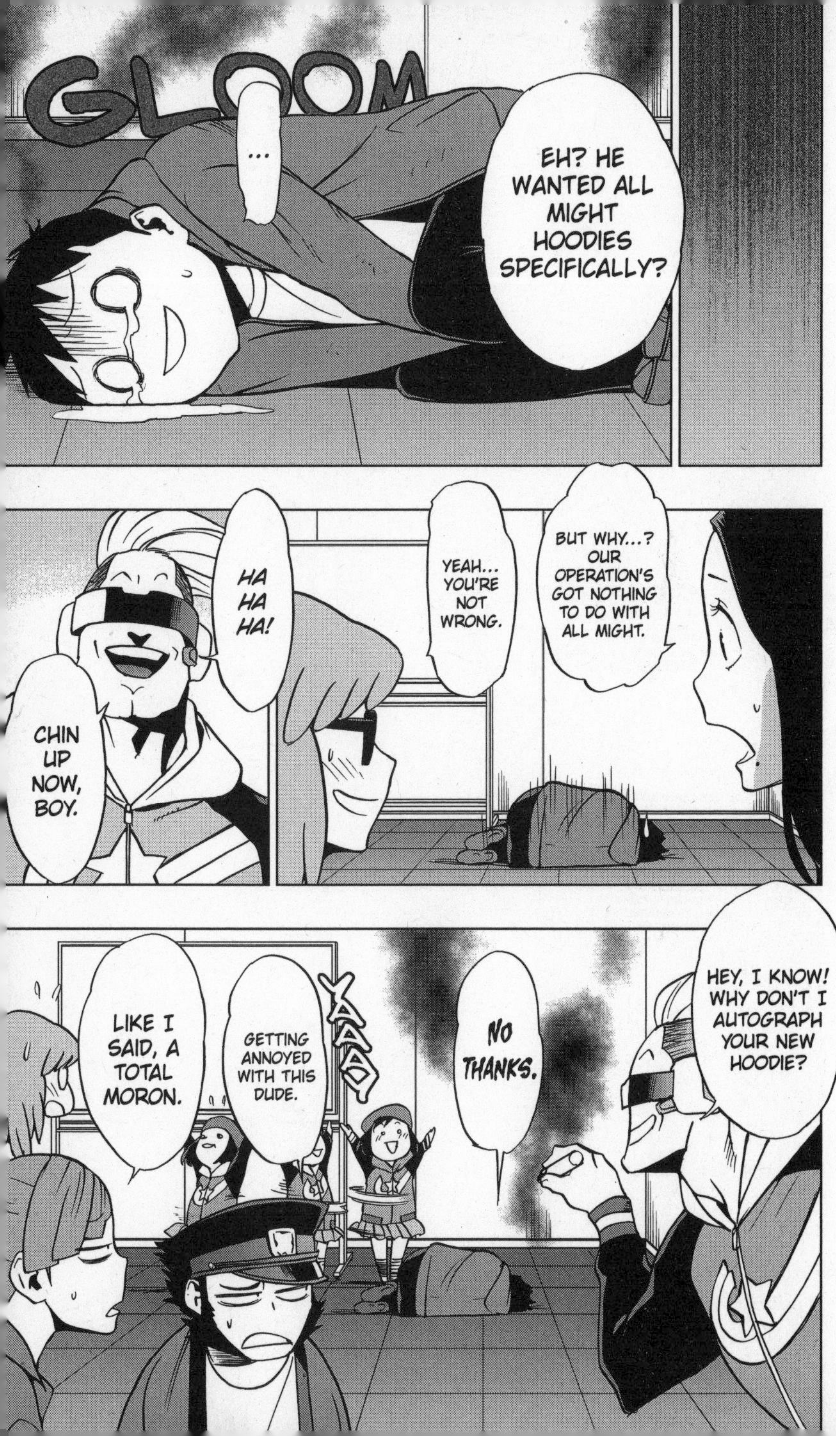
EH? HE WANTED ALL MIGHT HOODIES SPECIFICALLY?
...
GLOOM
BUT WHY...? OUR OPERATION'S GOT NOTHING TO DO WITH ALL MIGHT.
YEAH... YOU'RE NOT WRONG.
HA HA HA!
CHIN UP NOW, BOY.
HEY, I KNOW! WHY DON'T I AUTOGRAPH YOUR NEW HOODIE?
NO THANKS.
YAAAY
GETTING ANNOYED WITH THIS DUDE.
LIKE I SAID, A TOTAL MORON.

THE COLUMN

MIU AND YU

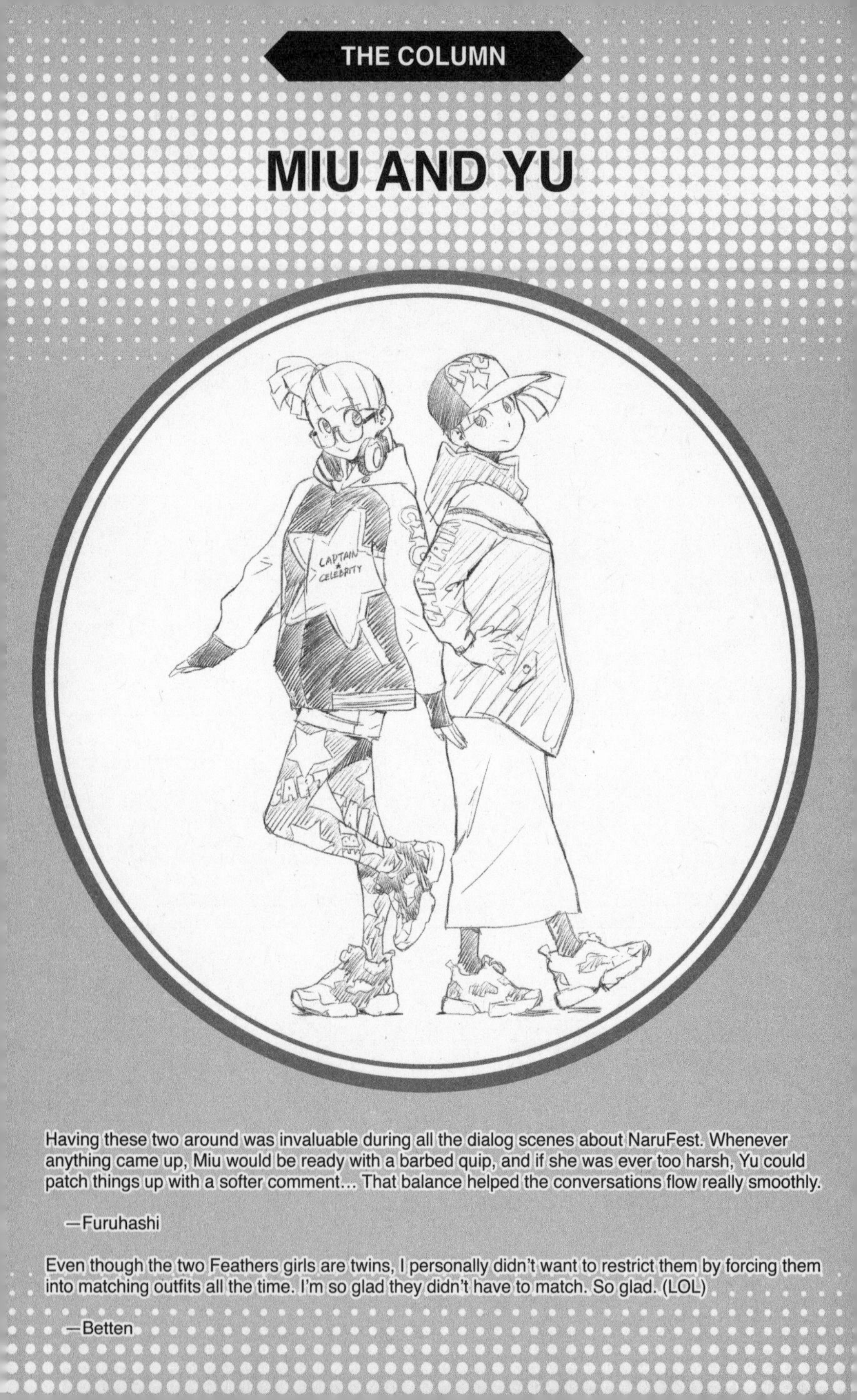
CAPTAIN
★
CELEBRITY

Having these two around was invaluable during all the dialog scenes about NaruFest. Whenever anything came up, Miu would be ready with a barbed quip, and if she was ever too harsh, Yu could patch things up with a softer comment... That balance helped the conversations flow really smoothly.

—Furuhashi

Even though the two Feathers girls are twins, I personally didn't want to restrict them by forcing them into matching outfits all the time. I'm so glad they didn't have to match. So glad. (LOL)

—Betten

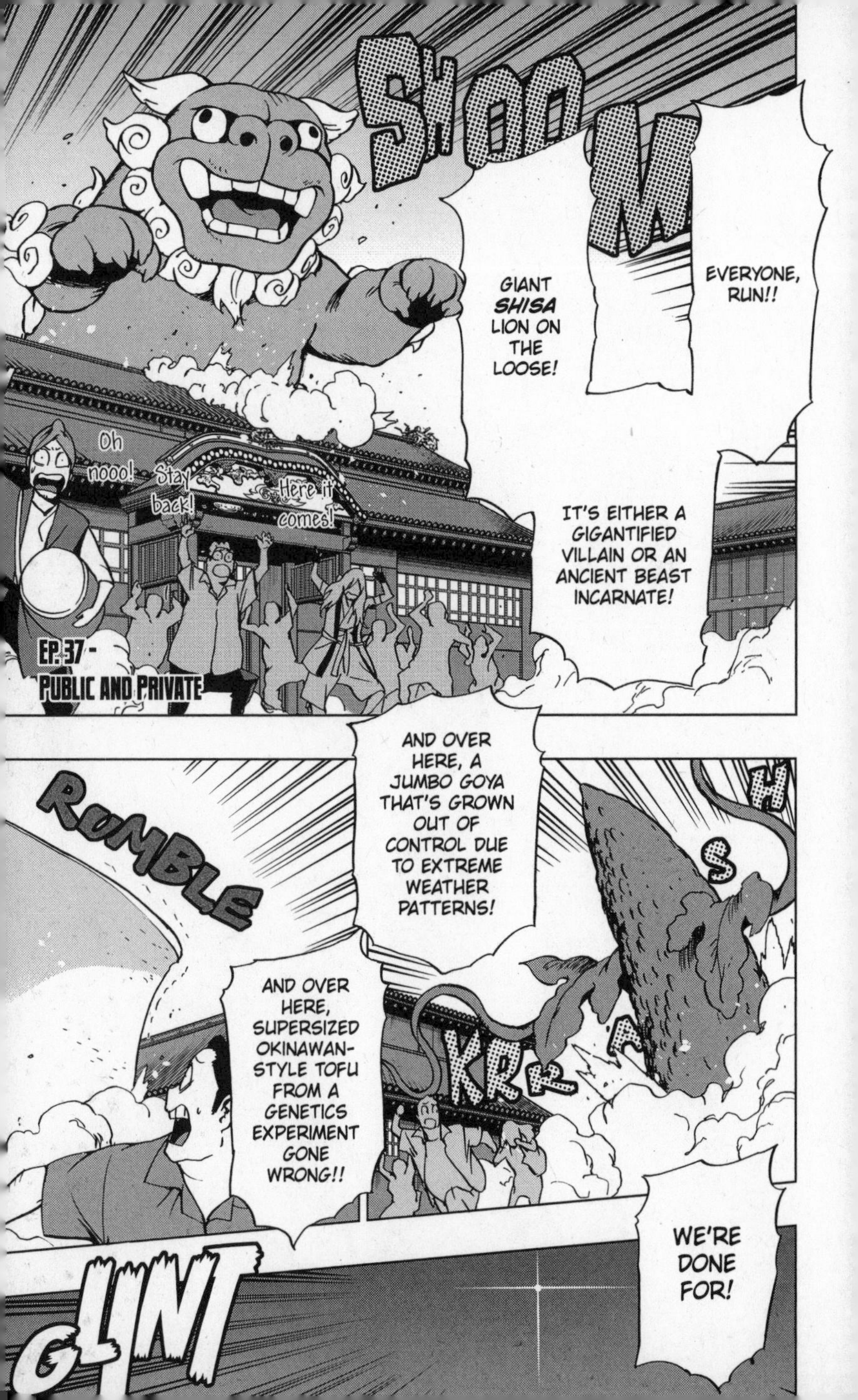
SHOOM
EVERYONE, RUN!!
GIANT *SHISA* LION ON THE LOOSE!
IT'S EITHER A GIGANTIFIED VILLAIN OR AN ANCIENT BEAST INCARNATE!
Here it comes!
Stay back!
Oh nooo!
EP. 37 - PUBLIC AND PRIVATE
KRR
AND OVER HERE, A JUMBO GOYA THAT'S GROWN OUT OF CONTROL DUE TO EXTREME WEATHER PATTERNS!
RUMBLE
AND OVER HERE, SUPERSIZED OKINAWAN-STYLE TOFU FROM A GENETICS EXPERIMENT GONE WRONG!!
WE'RE DONE FOR!
GLINT

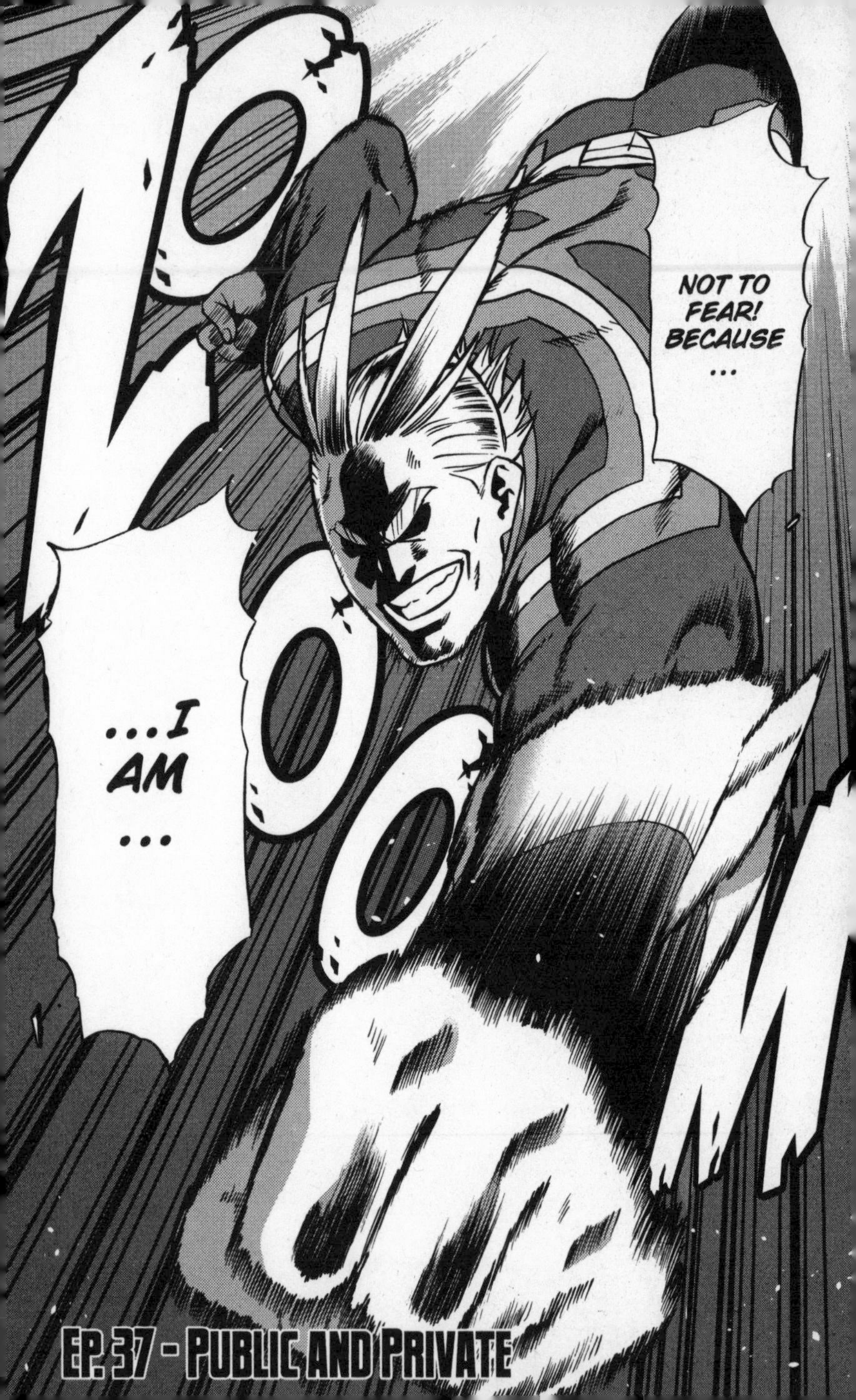
NOT TO FEAR! BECAUSE ...
...I AM ...

EP. 37 - PUBLIC AND PRIVATE

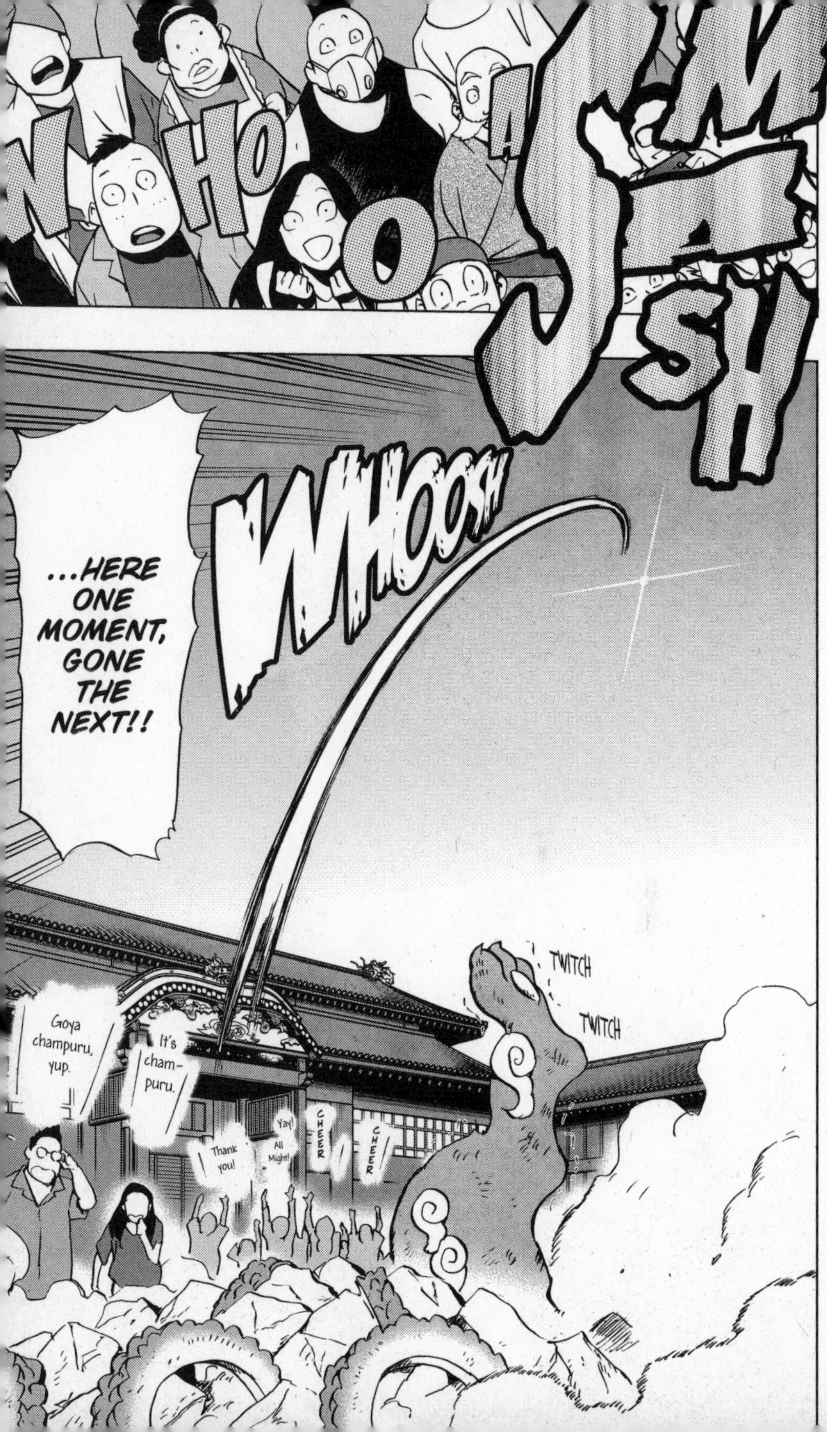
SMASH
WHOOSH
...HERE ONE MOMENT, GONE THE NEXT!!
TWITCH
TWITCH
CHEER
CHEER
Yay! All Might!
Thank you!
It's cham-puru.
Goya champuru, yup.

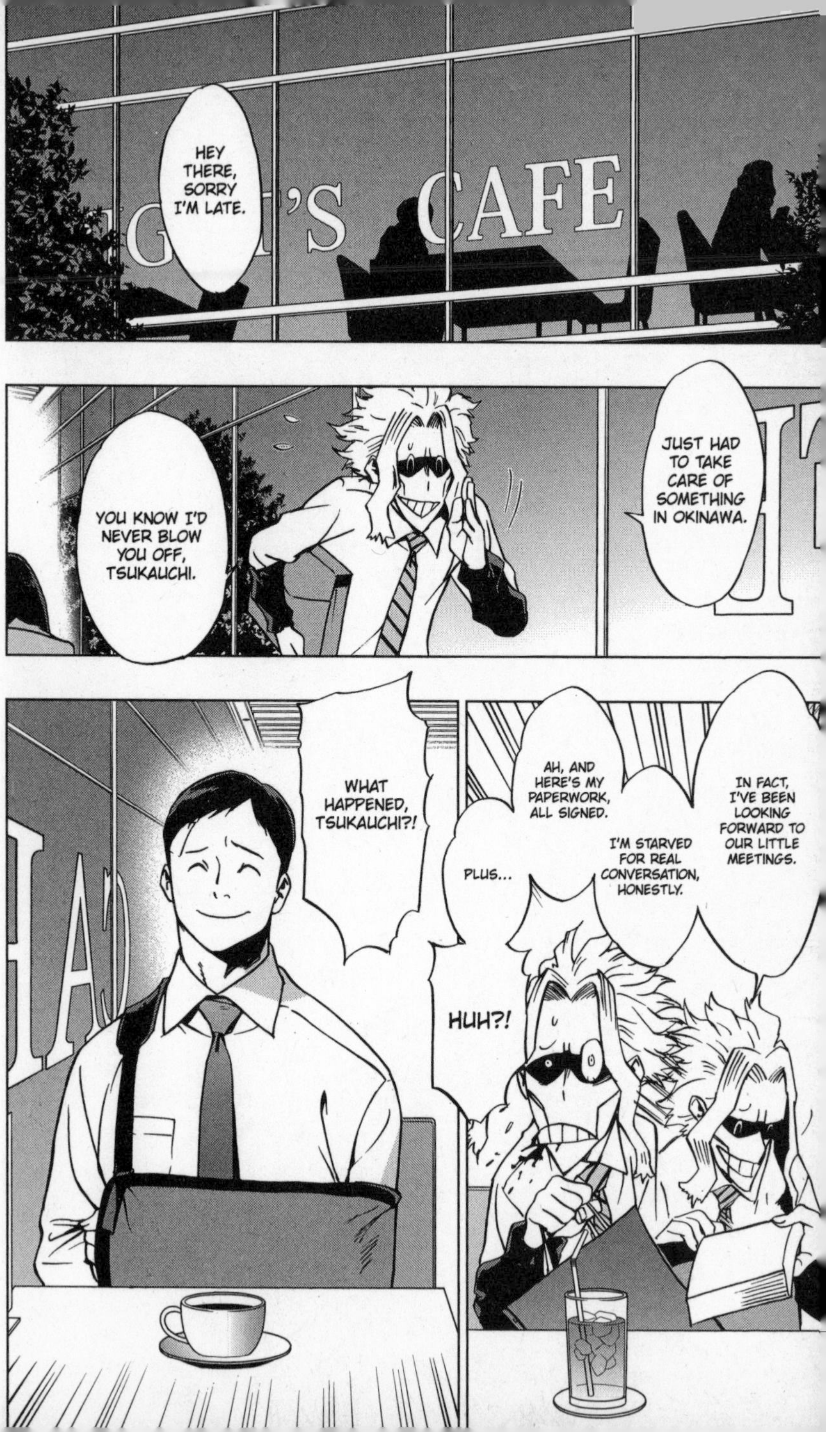
HEY THERE, SORRY I'M LATE.
JUST HAD TO TAKE CARE OF SOMETHING IN OKINAWA.
YOU KNOW I'D NEVER BLOW YOU OFF, TSUKAUCHI.
IN FACT, I'VE BEEN LOOKING FORWARD TO OUR LITTLE MEETINGS.
I'M STARVED FOR REAL CONVERSATION, HONESTLY.
AH, AND HERE'S MY PAPERWORK, ALL SIGNED.
PLUS...
HUH?!
WHAT HAPPENED, TSUKAUCHI?!

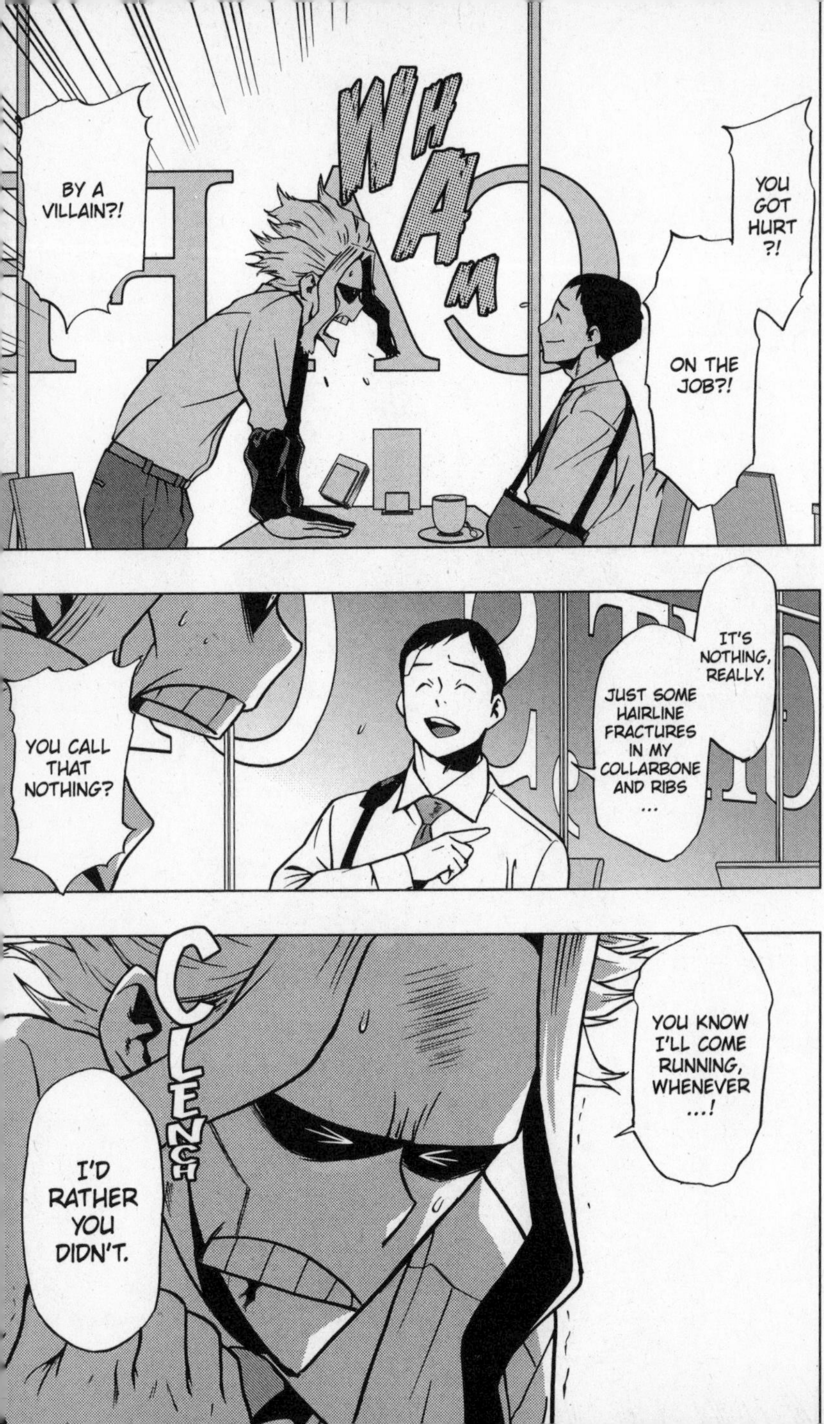
YOU GOT HURT ?!
ON THE JOB?!
WHAM
BY A VILLAIN?!
IT'S NOTHING, REALLY.
JUST SOME HAIRLINE FRACTURES IN MY COLLARBONE AND RIBS ...
YOU CALL THAT NOTHING?
YOU KNOW I'LL COME RUNNING, WHENEVER ...!
CLENCH
I'D RATHER YOU DIDN'T.

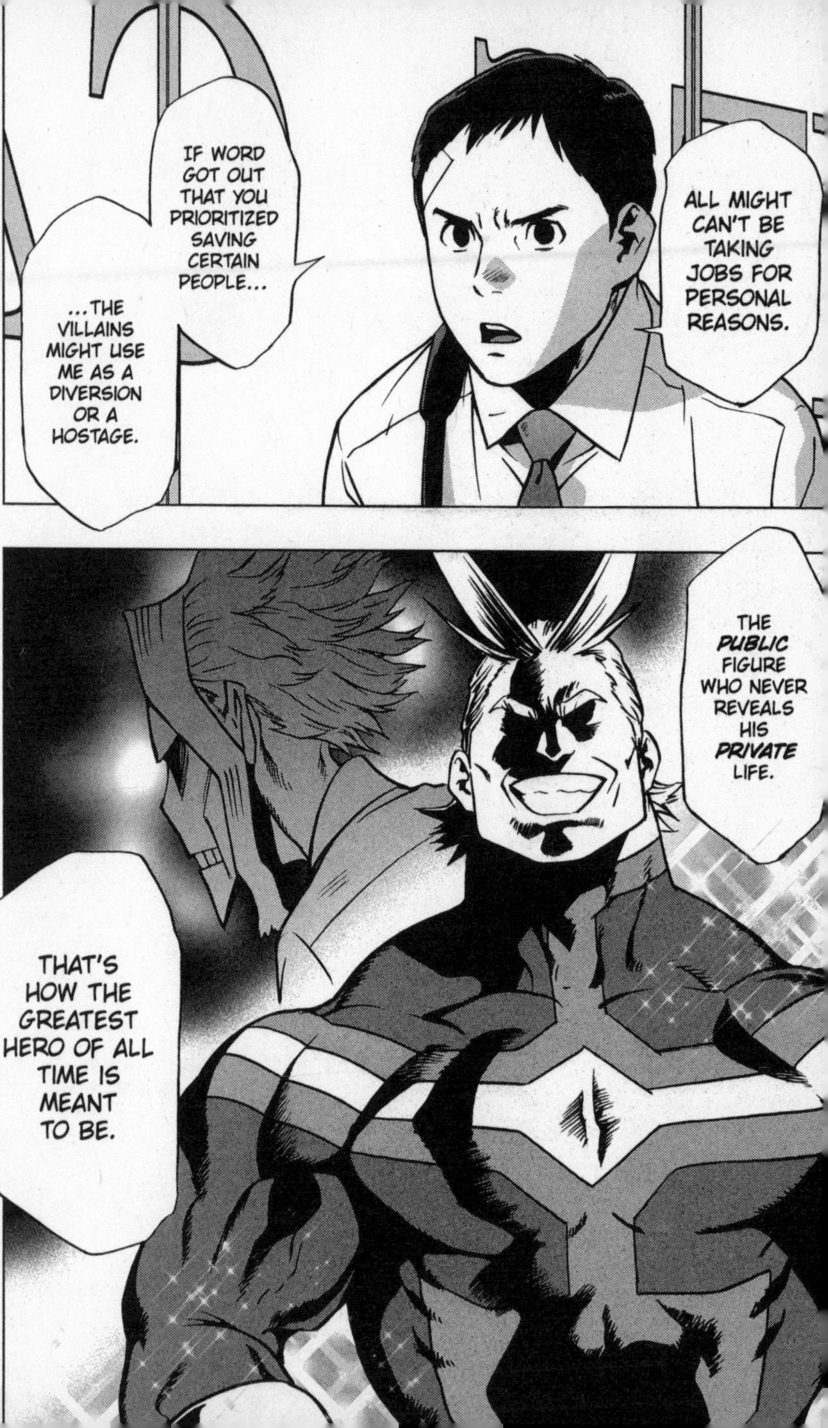
ALL MIGHT CAN'T BE TAKING JOBS FOR PERSONAL REASONS.
IF WORD GOT OUT THAT YOU PRIORITIZED SAVING CERTAIN PEOPLE...
...THE VILLAINS MIGHT USE ME AS A DIVERSION OR A HOSTAGE.
THE *PUBLIC* FIGURE WHO NEVER REVEALS HIS *PRIVATE* LIFE.
THAT'S HOW THE GREATEST HERO OF ALL TIME IS MEANT TO BE.

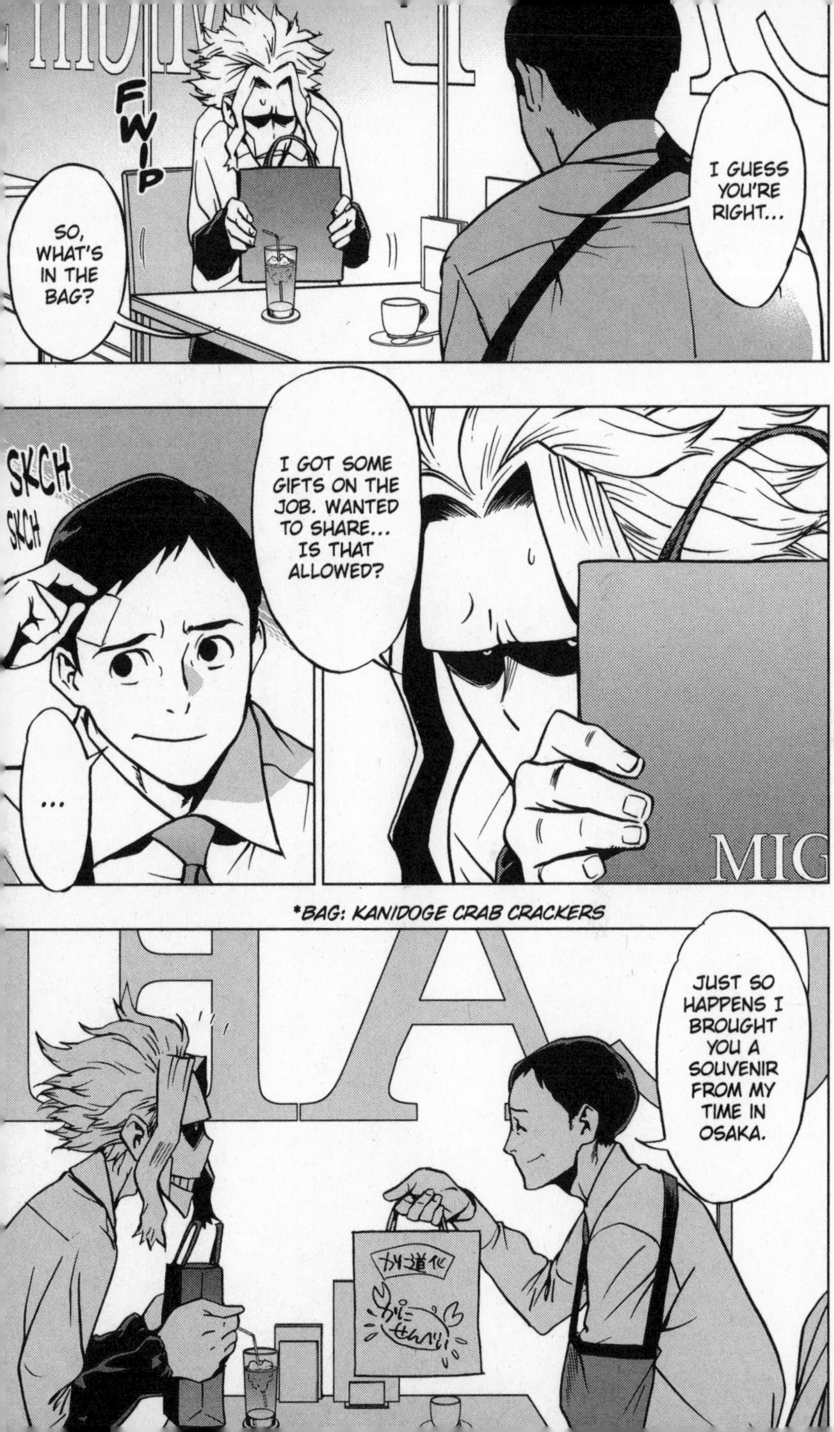
I GUESS YOU'RE RIGHT...
FWIP
SO, WHAT'S IN THE BAG?
I GOT SOME GIFTS ON THE JOB. WANTED TO SHARE... IS THAT ALLOWED?
MIG
SKCH
SKCH
...
*BAG: KANIDOGE CRAB CRACKERS
JUST SO HAPPENS I BROUGHT YOU A SOUVENIR FROM MY TIME IN OSAKA.
カニ道化
かにせんべい

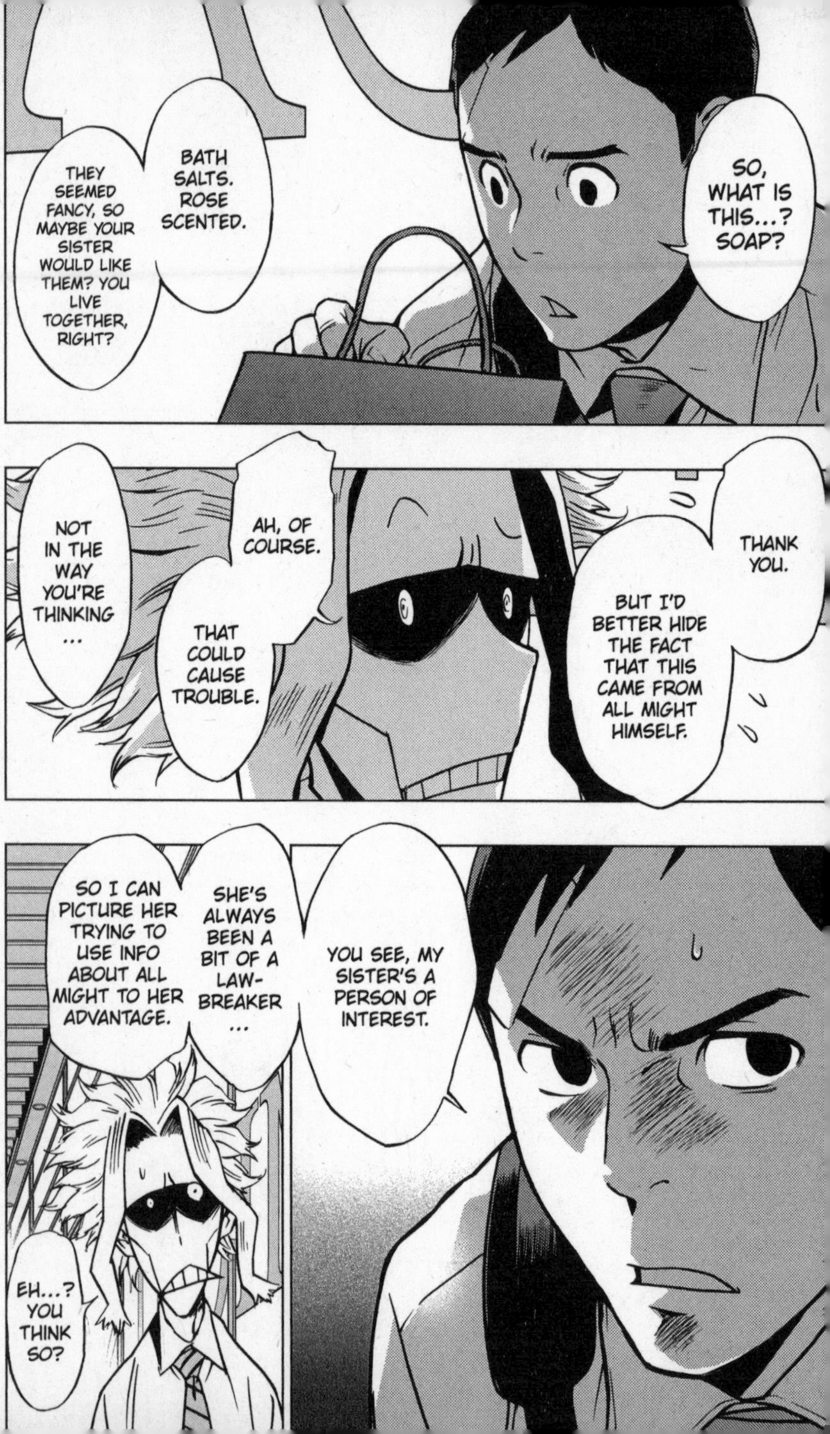
SO, WHAT IS THIS...? SOAP?
BATH SALTS. ROSE SCENTED.
THEY SEEMED FANCY, SO MAYBE YOUR SISTER WOULD LIKE THEM? YOU LIVE TOGETHER, RIGHT?
THANK YOU.
BUT I'D BETTER HIDE THE FACT THAT THIS CAME FROM ALL MIGHT HIMSELF.
AH, OF COURSE.
THAT COULD CAUSE TROUBLE.
NOT IN THE WAY YOU'RE THINKING...
YOU SEE, MY SISTER'S A PERSON OF INTEREST.
SHE'S ALWAYS BEEN A BIT OF A LAW-BREAKER...
SO I CAN PICTURE HER TRYING TO USE INFO ABOUT ALL MIGHT TO HER ADVANTAGE.
EH...? YOU THINK SO?

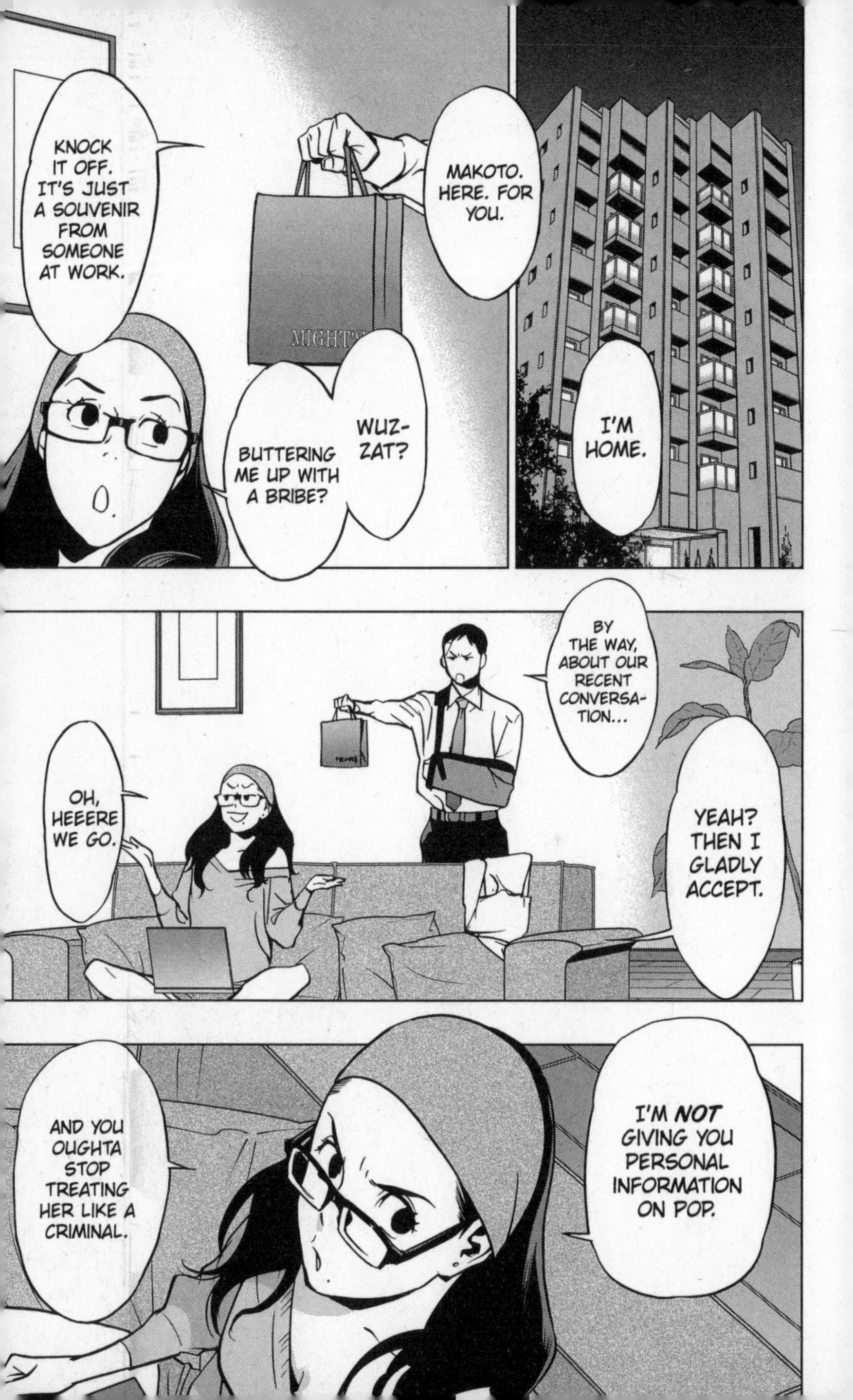
I'M HOME.
MAKOTO. HERE. FOR YOU.
MIGHT'S
WUZ-ZAT?
BUTTERING ME UP WITH A BRIBE?
KNOCK IT OFF. IT'S JUST A SOUVENIR FROM SOMEONE AT WORK.
YEAH? THEN I GLADLY ACCEPT.
BY THE WAY, ABOUT OUR RECENT CONVERSA-TION...
OH, HEEERE WE GO.
I'M **NOT** GIVING YOU PERSONAL INFORMATION ON POP.
AND YOU OUGHTA STOP TREATING HER LIKE A CRIMINAL.

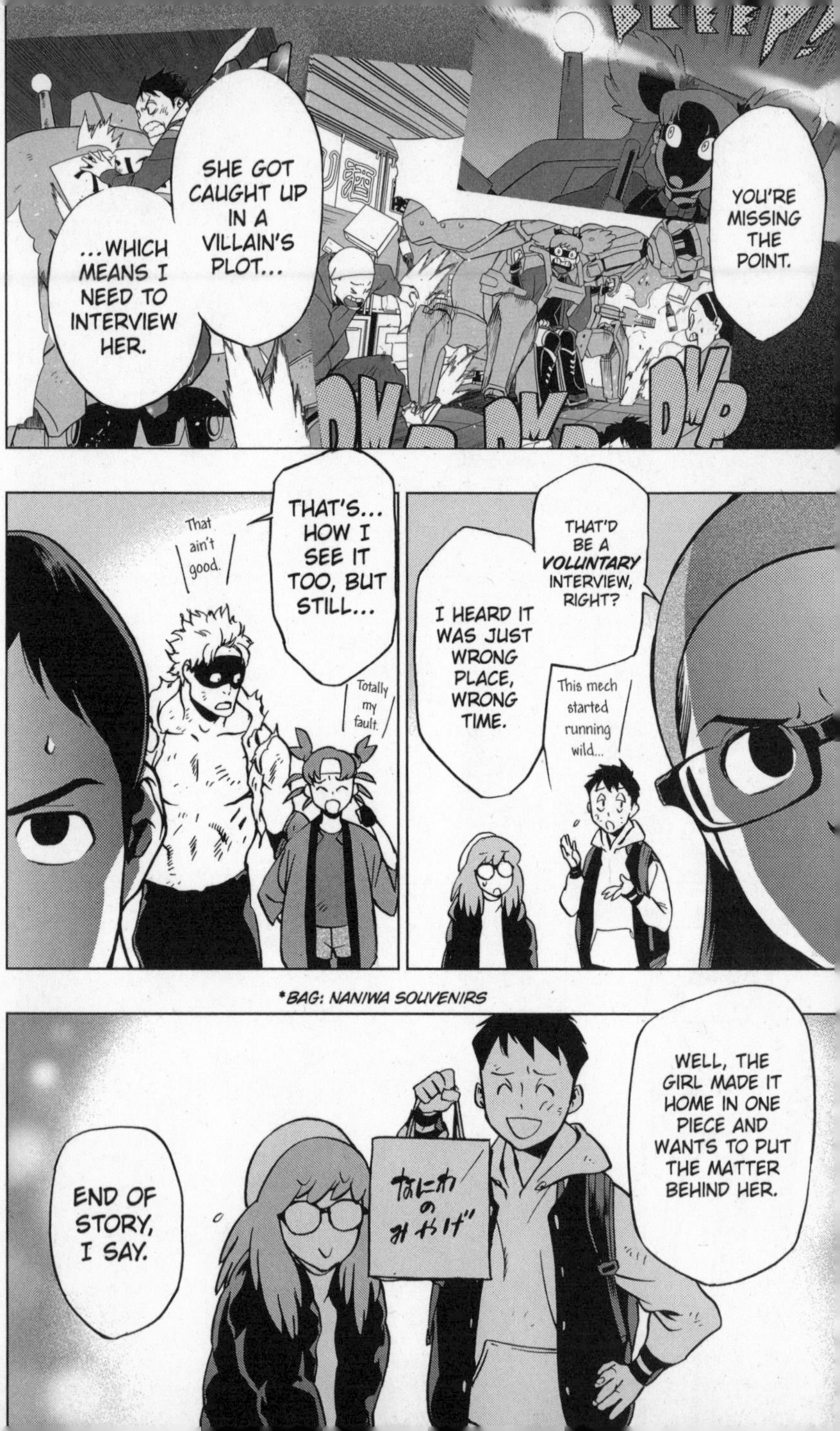
YOU'RE MISSING THE POINT.
SHE GOT CAUGHT UP IN A VILLAIN'S PLOT...
...WHICH MEANS I NEED TO INTERVIEW HER.
THAT'D BE A *VOLUNTARY* INTERVIEW, RIGHT?
I HEARD IT WAS JUST WRONG PLACE, WRONG TIME.
This mech started running wild...
THAT'S... HOW I SEE IT TOO, BUT STILL...
That ain't good.
Totally my fault.
WELL, THE GIRL MADE IT HOME IN ONE PIECE AND WANTS TO PUT THE MATTER BEHIND HER.
なにわのおみやげ
END OF STORY, I SAY.

**BAG: NANIWA SOUVENIRS*

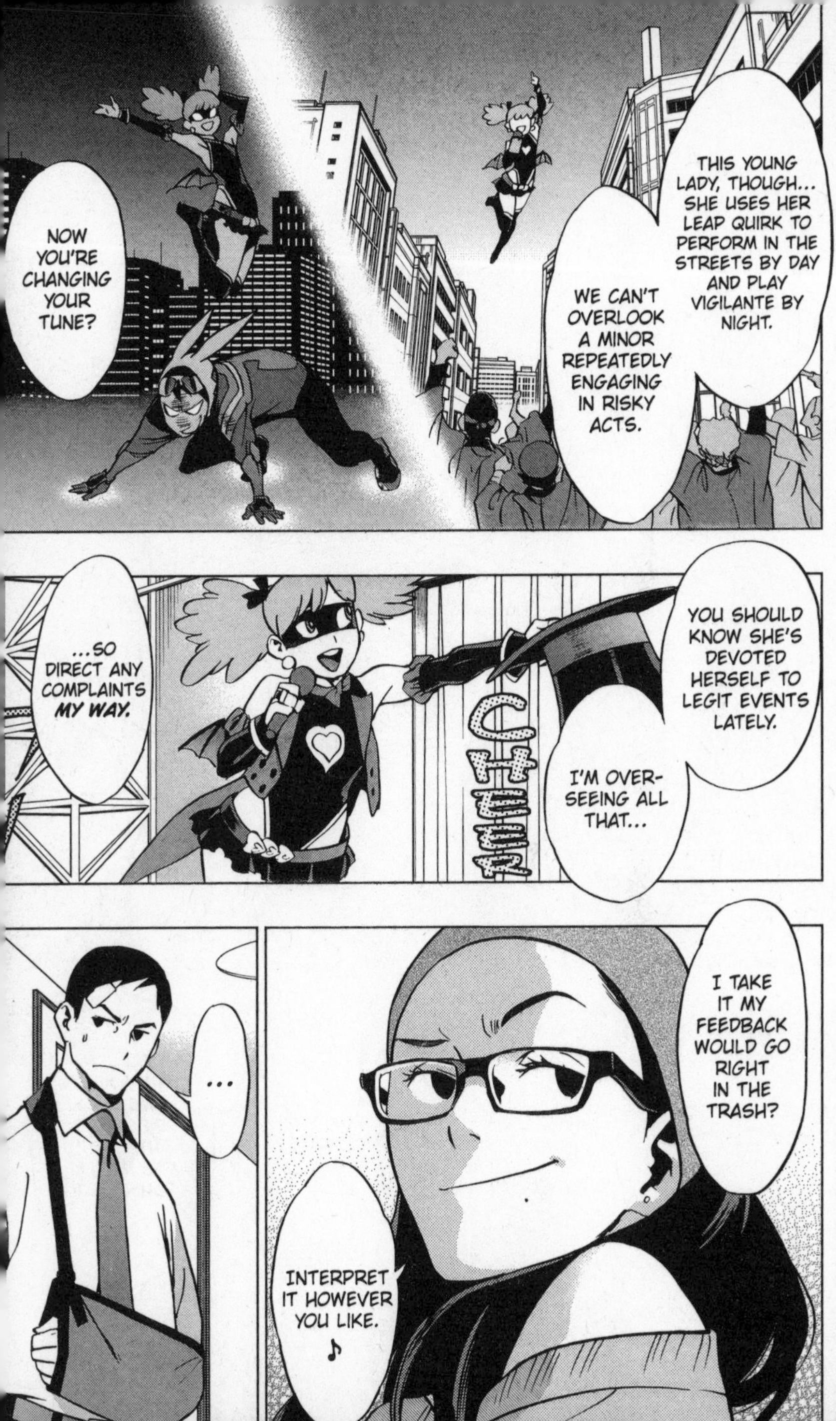
THIS YOUNG LADY, THOUGH... SHE USES HER LEAP QUIRK TO PERFORM IN THE STREETS BY DAY AND PLAY VIGILANTE BY NIGHT.
WE CAN'T OVERLOOK A MINOR REPEATEDLY ENGAGING IN RISKY ACTS.
NOW YOU'RE CHANGING YOUR TUNE?
YOU SHOULD KNOW SHE'S DEVOTED HERSELF TO LEGIT EVENTS LATELY.
I'M OVER-SEEING ALL THAT...
CHEER
...SO DIRECT ANY COMPLAINTS *MY WAY.*
I TAKE IT MY FEEDBACK WOULD GO RIGHT IN THE TRASH?
INTERPRET IT HOWEVER YOU LIKE. ♪
...

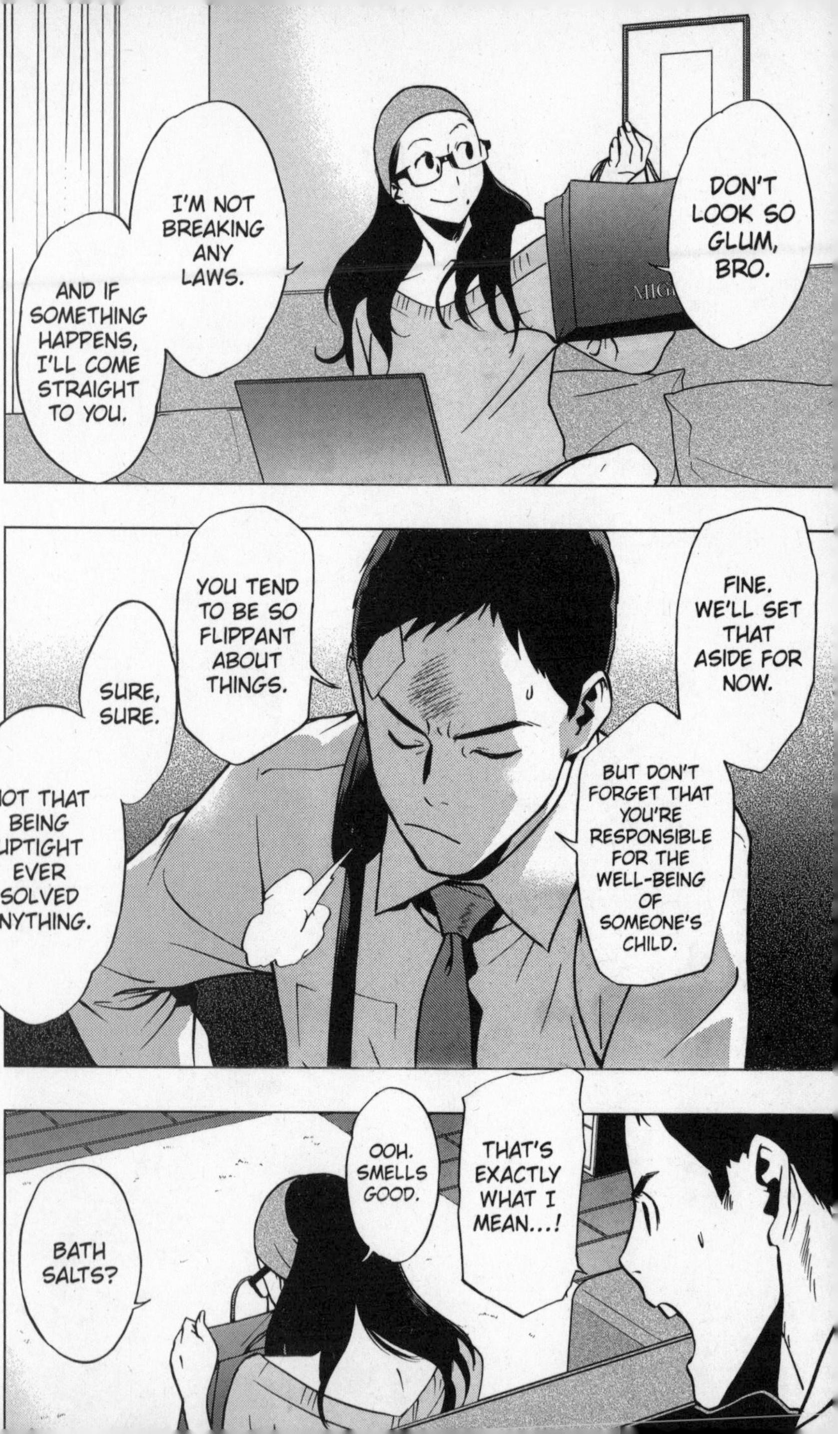
DON'T LOOK SO GLUM, BRO.
I'M NOT BREAKING ANY LAWS.
AND IF SOMETHING HAPPENS, I'LL COME STRAIGHT TO YOU.
FINE. WE'LL SET THAT ASIDE FOR NOW.
BUT DON'T FORGET THAT YOU'RE RESPONSIBLE FOR THE WELL-BEING OF SOMEONE'S CHILD.
YOU TEND TO BE SO FLIPPANT ABOUT THINGS.
SURE, SURE.
NOT THAT BEING UPTIGHT EVER SOLVED ANYTHING.
THAT'S EXACTLY WHAT I MEAN...!
OOH. SMELLS GOOD.
BATH SALTS?

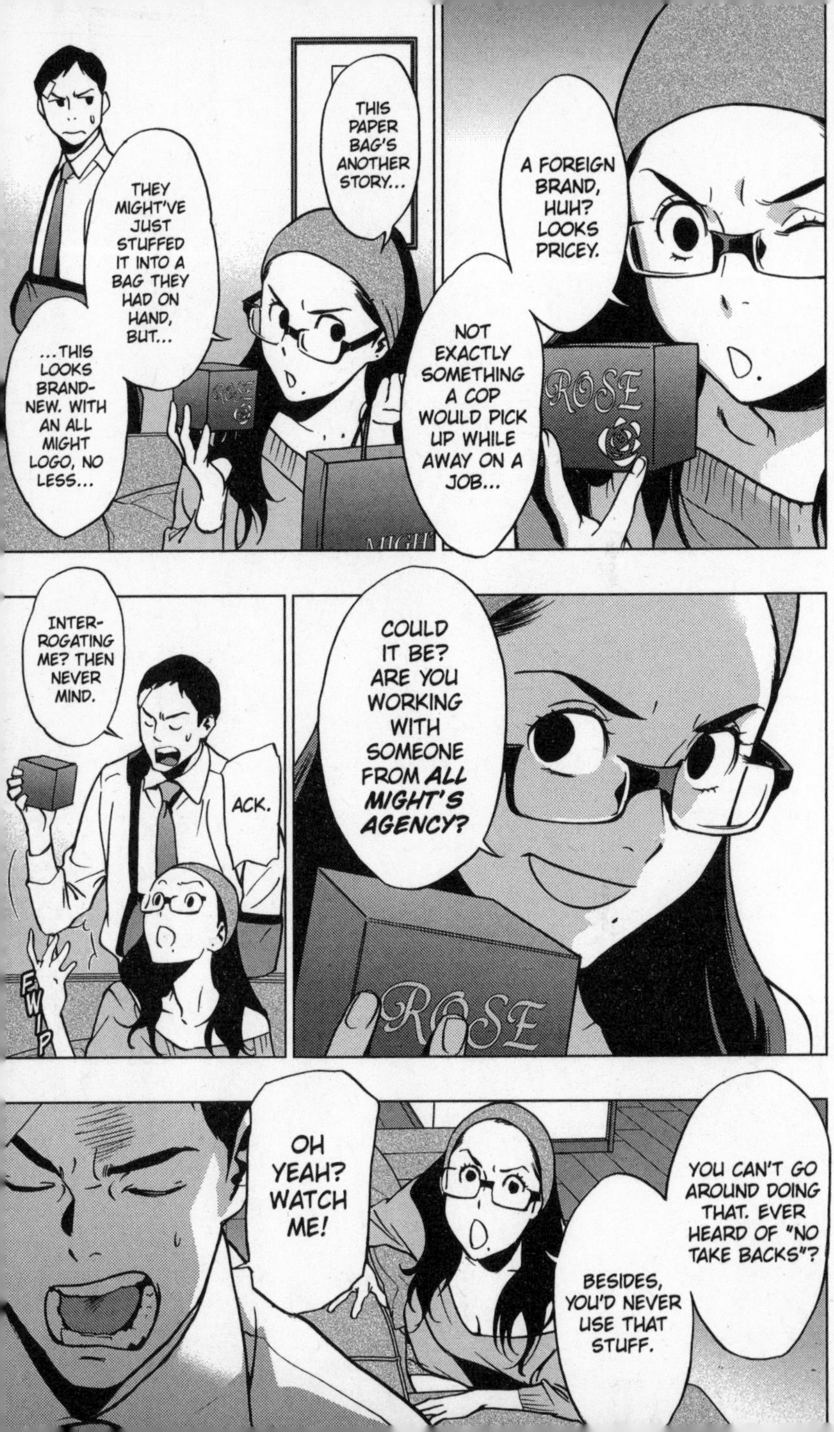
A FOREIGN BRAND, HUH? LOOKS PRICEY.
ROSE
NOT EXACTLY SOMETHING A COP WOULD PICK UP WHILE AWAY ON A JOB...
THIS PAPER BAG'S ANOTHER STORY...
THEY MIGHT'VE JUST STUFFED IT INTO A BAG THEY HAD ON HAND, BUT...
...THIS LOOKS BRAND-NEW. WITH AN ALL MIGHT LOGO, NO LESS...
COULD IT BE? ARE YOU WORKING WITH SOMEONE FROM ***ALL MIGHT'S AGENCY?***
ROSE
ACK.
INTER-ROGATING ME? THEN NEVER MIND.
FWIP
YOU CAN'T GO AROUND DOING THAT. EVER HEARD OF "NO TAKE BACKS"?
BESIDES, YOU'D NEVER USE THAT STUFF.
OH YEAH? WATCH ME!

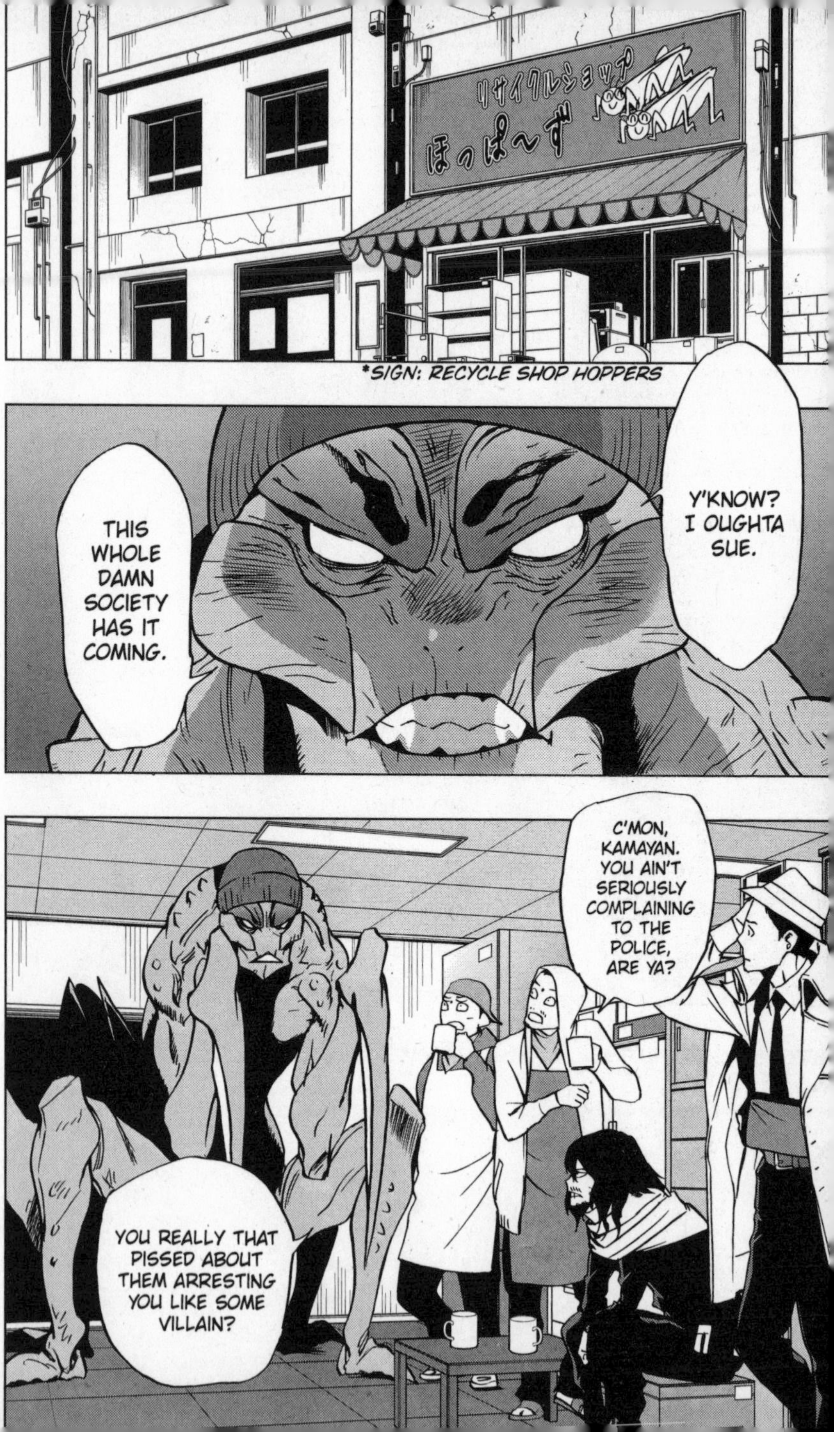
リサイクルショップ
ほっぱ〜ず
*SIGN: RECYCLE SHOP HOPPERS
Y'KNOW? I OUGHTA SUE.
THIS WHOLE DAMN SOCIETY HAS IT COMING.
C'MON, KAMAYAN. YOU AIN'T SERIOUSLY COMPLAINING TO THE POLICE, ARE YA?
YOU REALLY THAT PISSED ABOUT THEM ARRESTING YOU LIKE SOME VILLAIN?

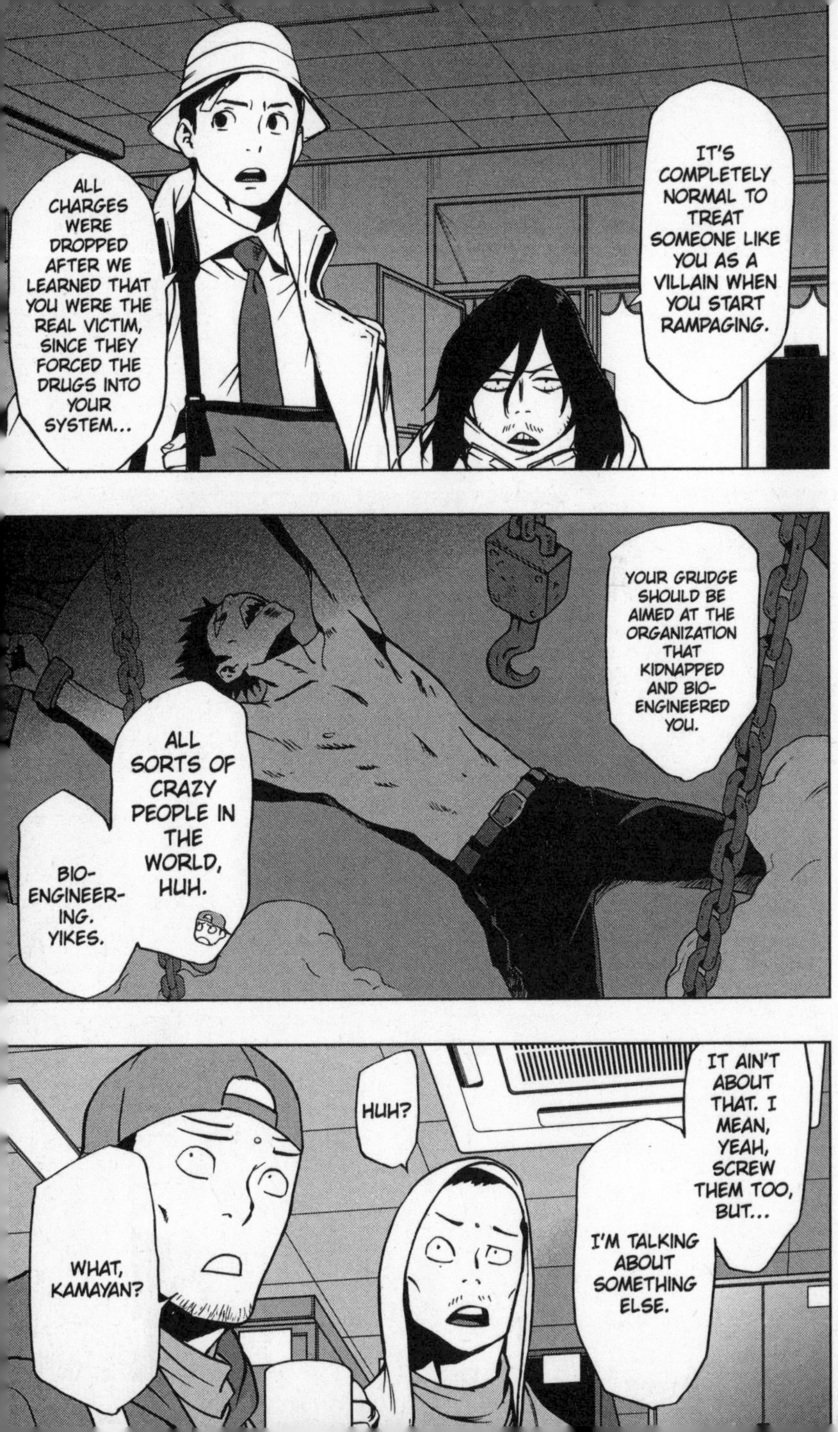
IT'S COMPLETELY NORMAL TO TREAT SOMEONE LIKE YOU AS A VILLAIN WHEN YOU START RAMPAGING.
ALL CHARGES WERE DROPPED AFTER WE LEARNED THAT YOU WERE THE REAL VICTIM, SINCE THEY FORCED THE DRUGS INTO YOUR SYSTEM...
YOUR GRUDGE SHOULD BE AIMED AT THE ORGANIZATION THAT KIDNAPPED AND BIO-ENGINEERED YOU.
ALL SORTS OF CRAZY PEOPLE IN THE WORLD, HUH.
BIO-ENGINEER-ING. YIKES.
IT AIN'T ABOUT THAT. I MEAN, YEAH, SCREW THEM TOO, BUT...
HUH?
I'M TALKING ABOUT SOMETHING ELSE.
WHAT, KAMAYAN?

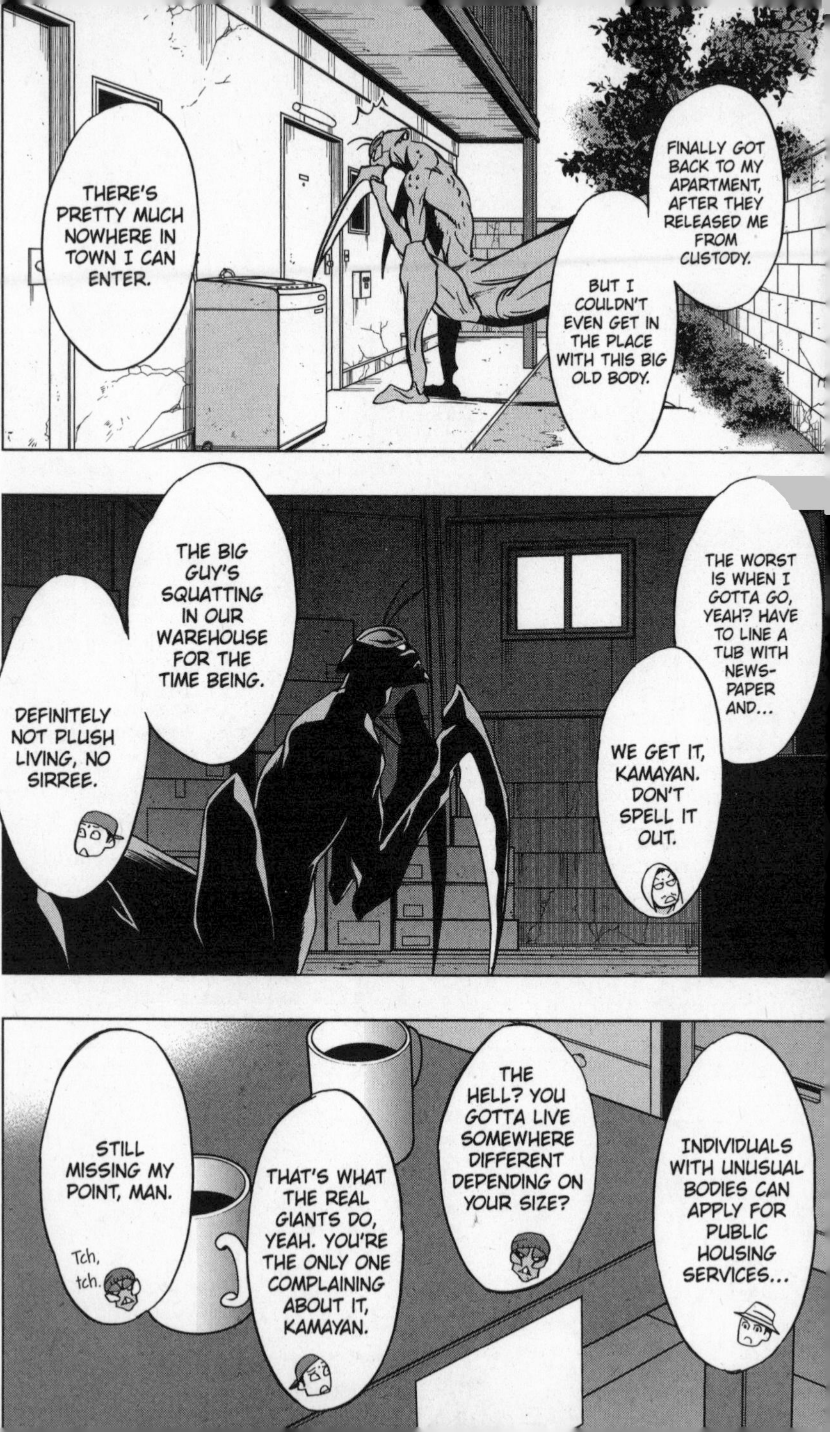
FINALLY GOT BACK TO MY APARTMENT, AFTER THEY RELEASED ME FROM CUSTODY.
BUT I COULDN'T EVEN GET IN THE PLACE WITH THIS BIG OLD BODY.
THERE'S PRETTY MUCH NOWHERE IN TOWN I CAN ENTER.
THE WORST IS WHEN I GOTTA GO, YEAH? HAVE TO LINE A TUB WITH NEWS-PAPER AND...
WE GET IT, KAMAYAN. DON'T SPELL IT OUT.
THE BIG GUY'S SQUATTING IN OUR WAREHOUSE FOR THE TIME BEING.
DEFINITELY NOT PLUSH LIVING, NO SIRREE.
INDIVIDUALS WITH UNUSUAL BODIES CAN APPLY FOR PUBLIC HOUSING SERVICES...
THE HELL? YOU GOTTA LIVE SOMEWHERE DIFFERENT DEPENDING ON YOUR SIZE?
THAT'S WHAT THE REAL GIANTS DO, YEAH. YOU'RE THE ONLY ONE COMPLAINING ABOUT IT, KAMAYAN.
STILL MISSING MY POINT, MAN.
Tch, tch.

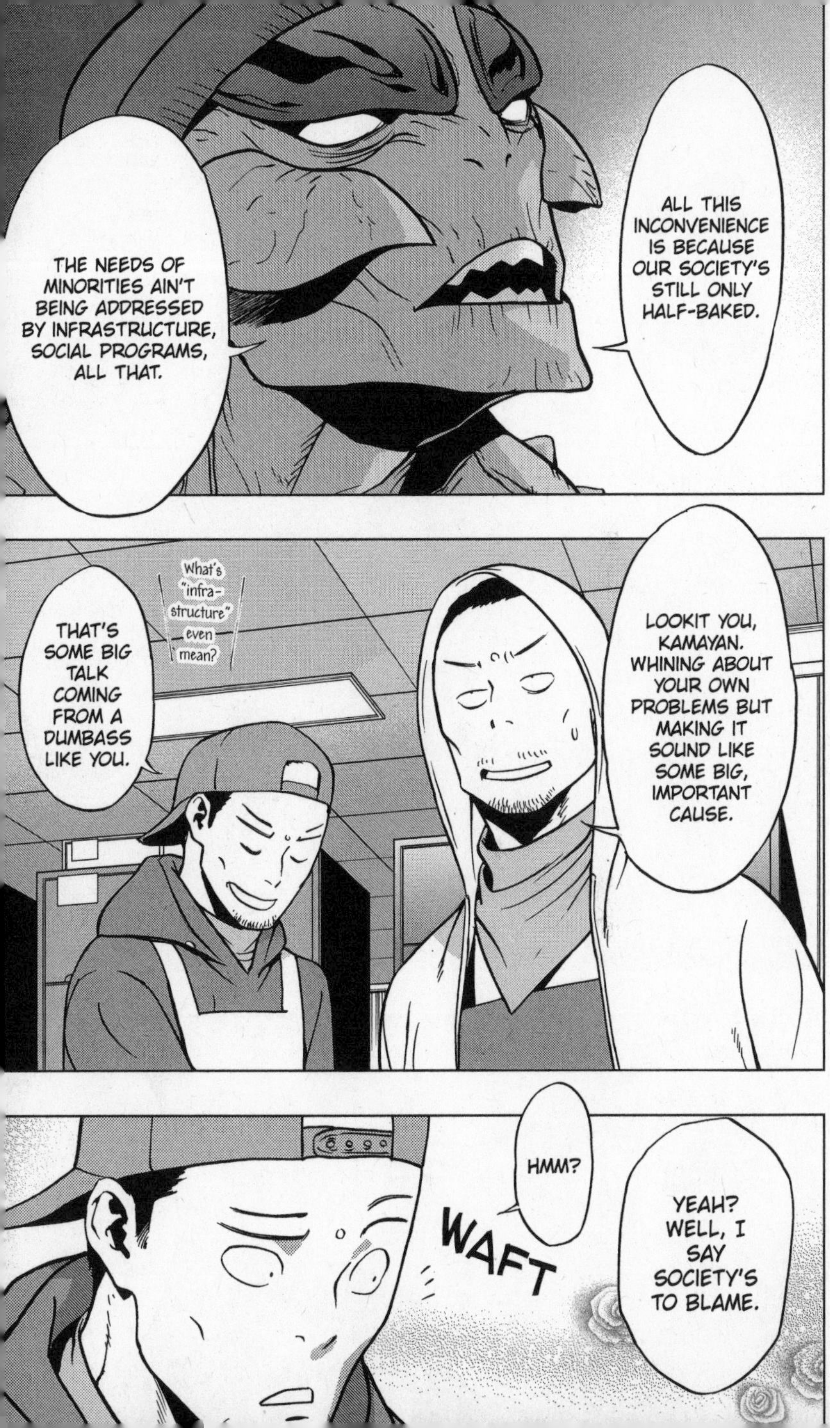
ALL THIS INCONVENIENCE IS BECAUSE OUR SOCIETY'S STILL ONLY HALF-BAKED.
THE NEEDS OF MINORITIES AIN'T BEING ADDRESSED BY INFRASTRUCTURE, SOCIAL PROGRAMS, ALL THAT.
LOOKIT YOU, KAMAYAN. WHINING ABOUT YOUR OWN PROBLEMS BUT MAKING IT SOUND LIKE SOME BIG, IMPORTANT CAUSE.
What's "infra-structure" even mean?
THAT'S SOME BIG TALK COMING FROM A DUMBASS LIKE YOU.
YEAH? WELL, I SAY SOCIETY'S TO BLAME.
HMM?
WAFT

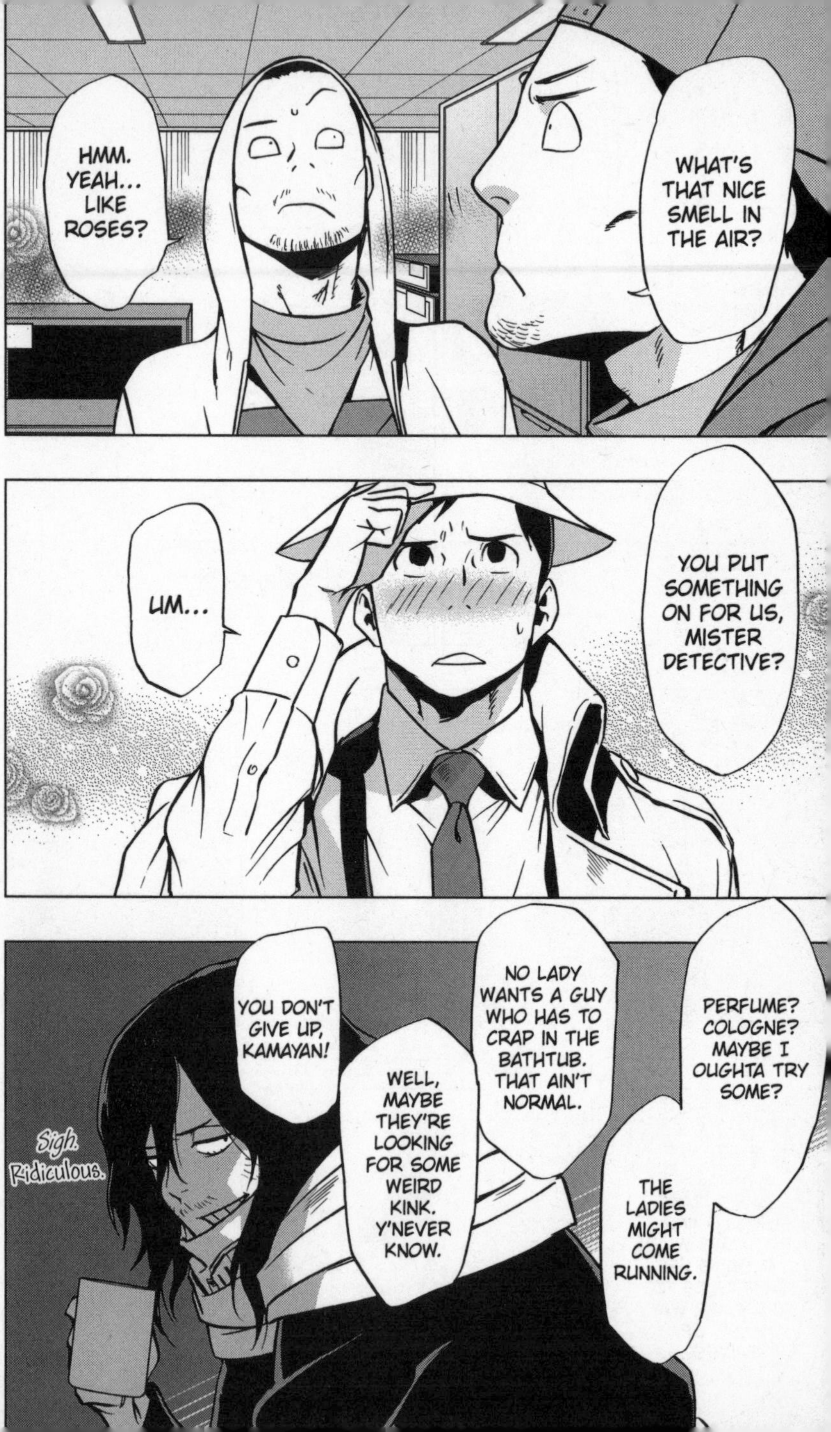
WHAT'S THAT NICE SMELL IN THE AIR?
HMM. YEAH... LIKE ROSES?
YOU PUT SOMETHING ON FOR US, MISTER DETECTIVE?
UM...
PERFUME? COLOGNE? MAYBE I OUGHTA TRY SOME?
THE LADIES MIGHT COME RUNNING.
NO LADY WANTS A GUY WHO HAS TO CRAP IN THE BATHTUB. THAT AIN'T NORMAL.
WELL, MAYBE THEY'RE LOOKING FOR SOME WEIRD KINK. Y'NEVER KNOW.
YOU DON'T GIVE UP, KAMAYAN!
Sigh. Ridiculous.

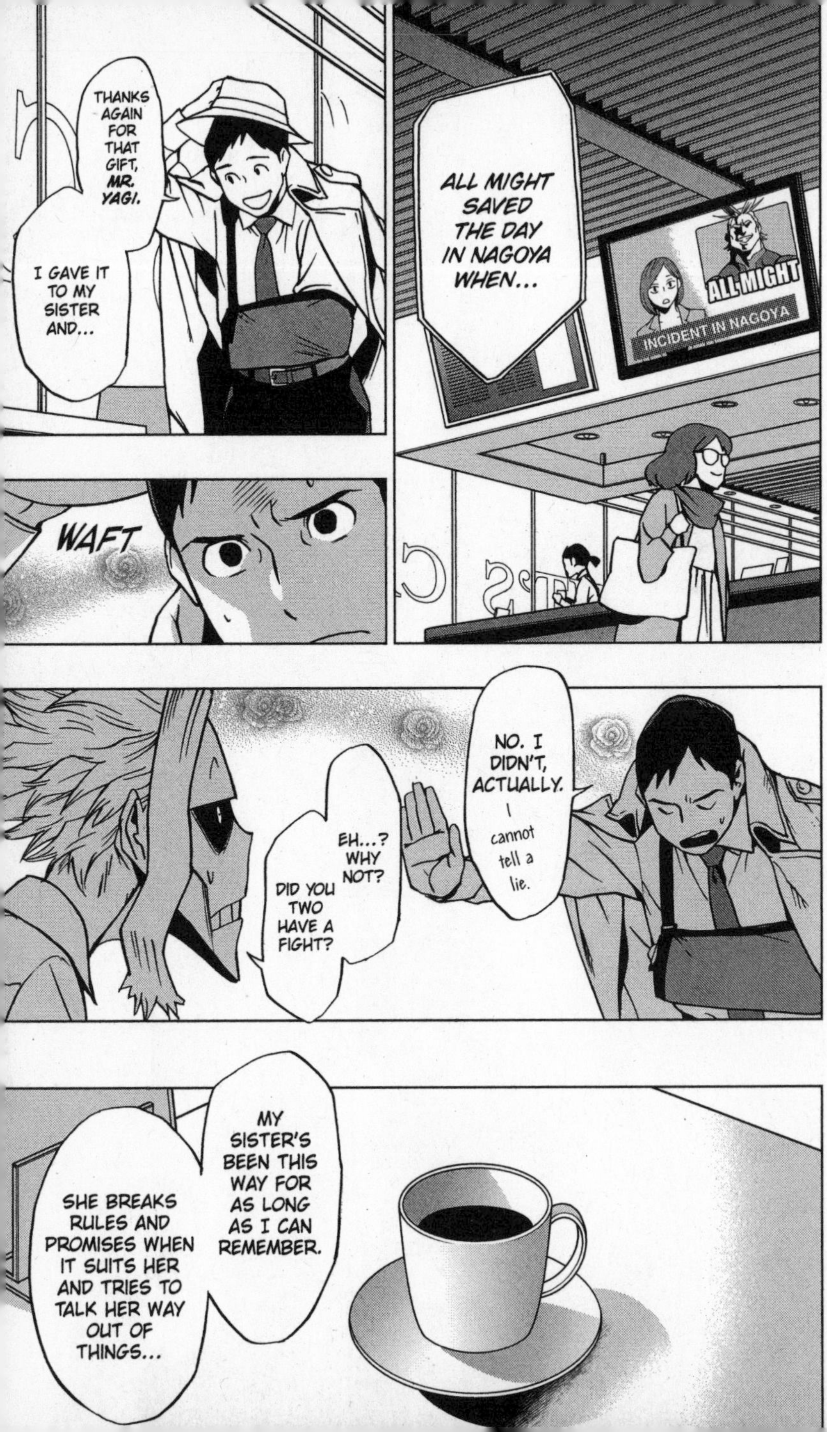
ALL MIGHT SAVED THE DAY IN NAGOYA WHEN...
ALL MIGHT
INCIDENT IN NAGOYA
THANKS AGAIN FOR THAT GIFT, MR. YAGI.
I GAVE IT TO MY SISTER AND...
WAFT
NO. I DIDN'T, ACTUALLY.
I cannot tell a lie.
EH...? WHY NOT?
DID YOU TWO HAVE A FIGHT?
MY SISTER'S BEEN THIS WAY FOR AS LONG AS I CAN REMEMBER.
SHE BREAKS RULES AND PROMISES WHEN IT SUITS HER AND TRIES TO TALK HER WAY OUT OF THINGS...

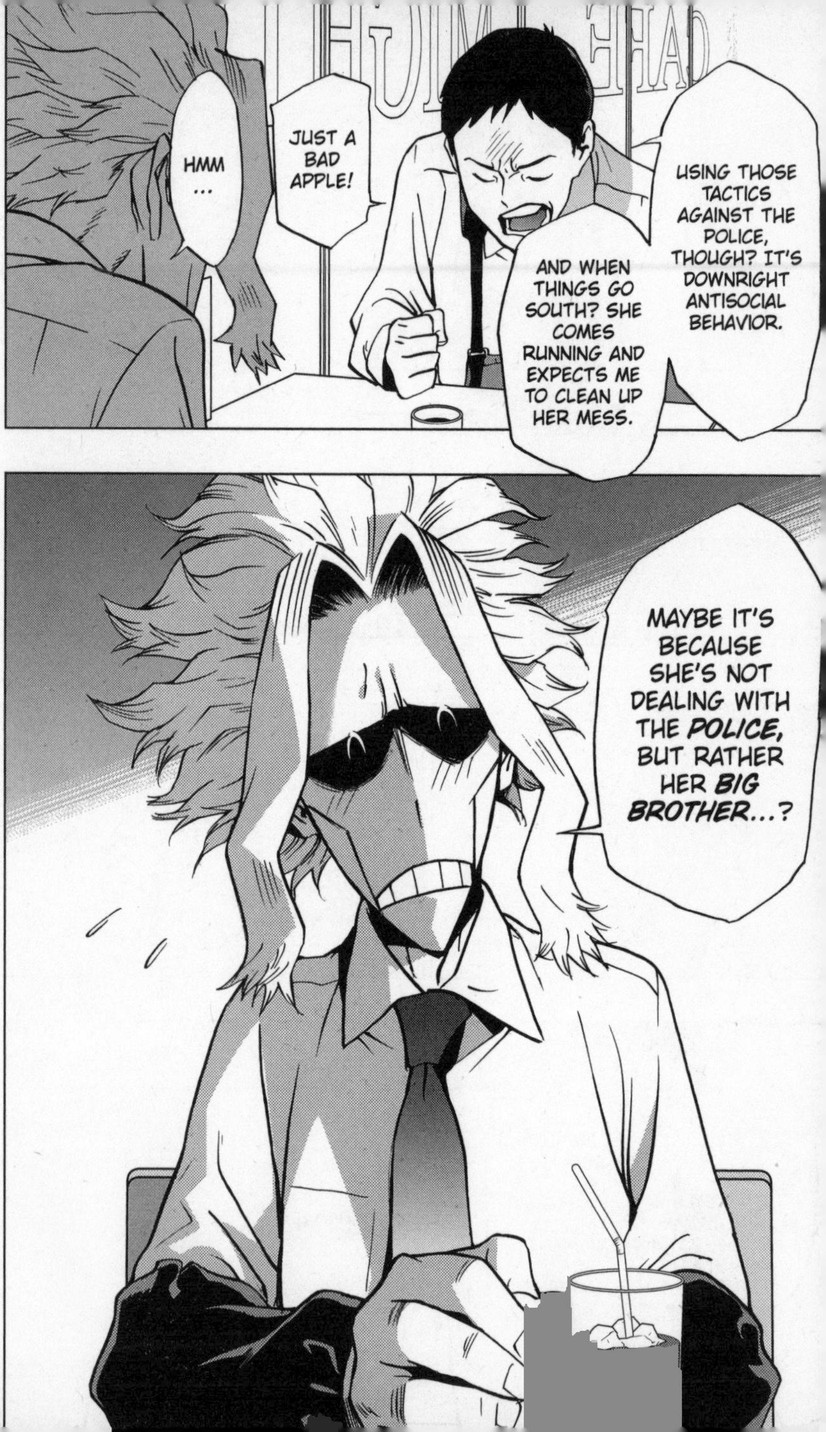
USING THOSE TACTICS AGAINST THE POLICE, THOUGH? IT'S DOWNRIGHT ANTISOCIAL BEHAVIOR.
AND WHEN THINGS GO SOUTH? SHE COMES RUNNING AND EXPECTS ME TO CLEAN UP HER MESS.
JUST A BAD APPLE!
HMM ...
MAYBE IT'S BECAUSE SHE'S NOT DEALING WITH THE *POLICE,* BUT RATHER HER *BIG BROTHER*...?

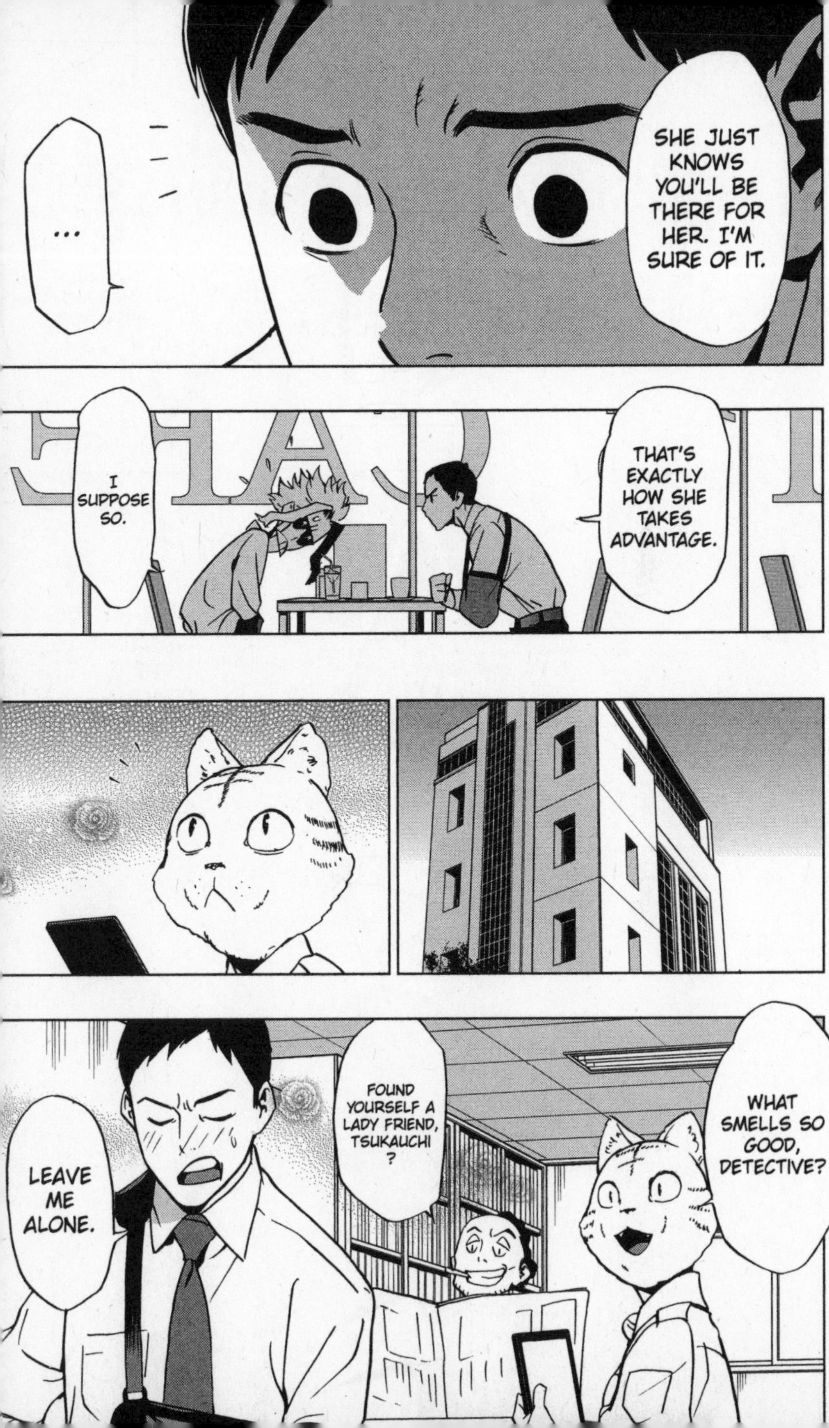
SHE JUST KNOWS YOU'LL BE THERE FOR HER. I'M SURE OF IT.
...
THAT'S EXACTLY HOW SHE TAKES ADVANTAGE.
I SUPPOSE SO.
WHAT SMELLS SO GOOD, DETECTIVE?
FOUND YOURSELF A LADY FRIEND, TSUKAUCHI?
LEAVE ME ALONE.

THE COLUMN

THE TSUKAUCHI SIBLINGS

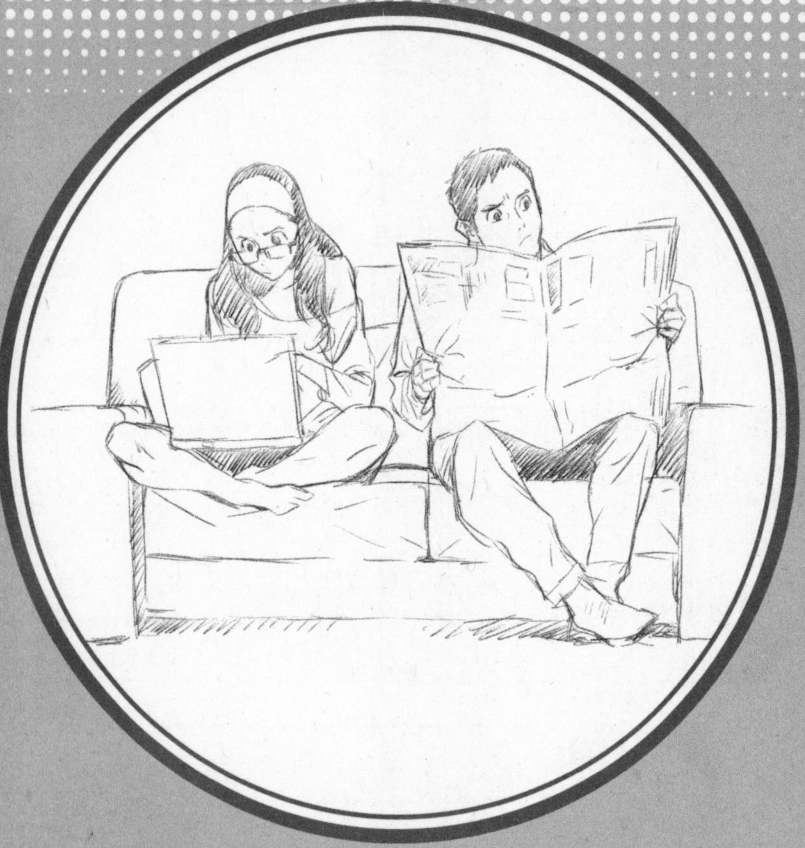

In *Vigilantes*, Detective Tsukauchi sort of serves as Mr. Common Sense who's always getting the short end of it, so I wanted to be sure to portray him as...highly competent. His younger sister Makoto has been good at coaxing favors out of him ever since she was a kid. She's 12 whole years younger than him, so she tends to come out on top in arguments.

—Furuhashi

There's something about their interactions that I love and always look forward to. Maybe it's the juxtaposition of Mr. Analog and Ms. Digital? (LOL)

—Betten

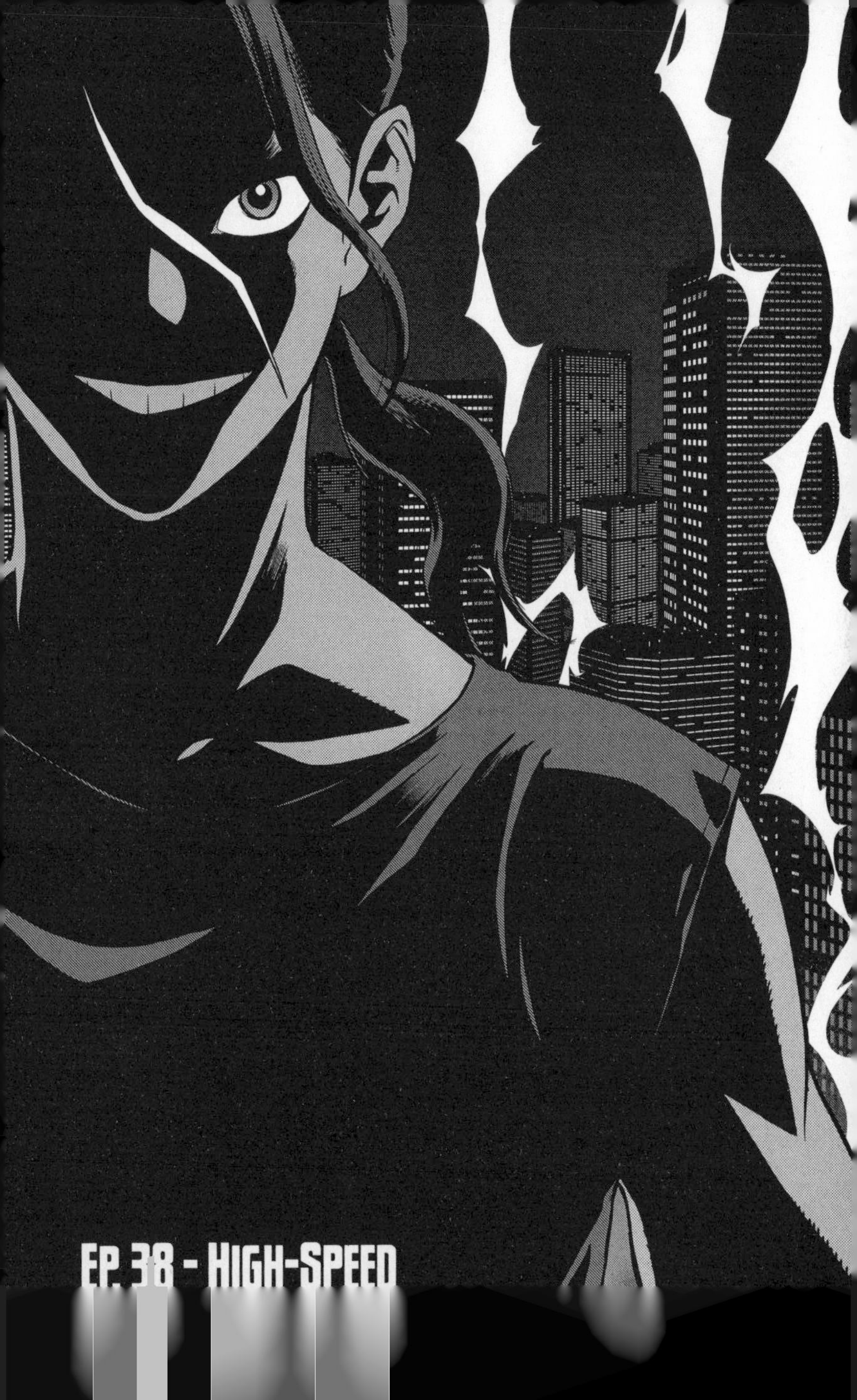
Ep. 38 - High-Speed

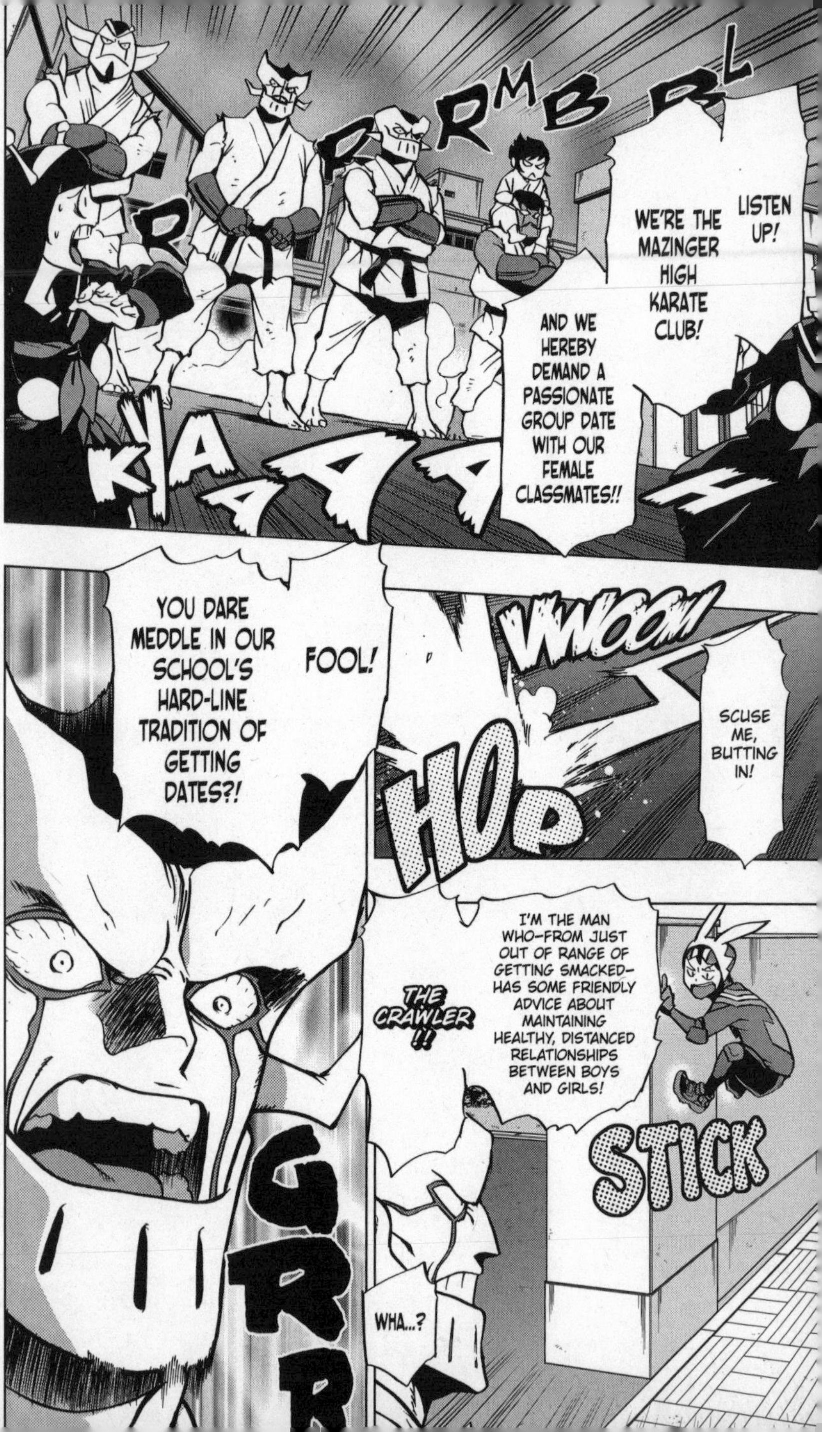
LISTEN UP!
WE'RE THE MAZINGER HIGH KARATE CLUB!
AND WE HEREBY DEMAND A PASSIONATE GROUP DATE WITH OUR FEMALE CLASSMATES!!
KIAAAAH
SCUSE ME, BUTTING IN!
WOOOM
HOP
FOOL!
YOU DARE MEDDLE IN OUR SCHOOL'S HARD-LINE TRADITION OF GETTING DATES?!
I'M THE MAN WHO—FROM JUST OUT OF RANGE OF GETTING SMACKED—HAS SOME FRIENDLY ADVICE ABOUT MAINTAINING HEALTHY, DISTANCED RELATIONSHIPS BETWEEN BOYS AND GIRLS!
STICK
THE CRAWLER!!
WHA...?
GRRR

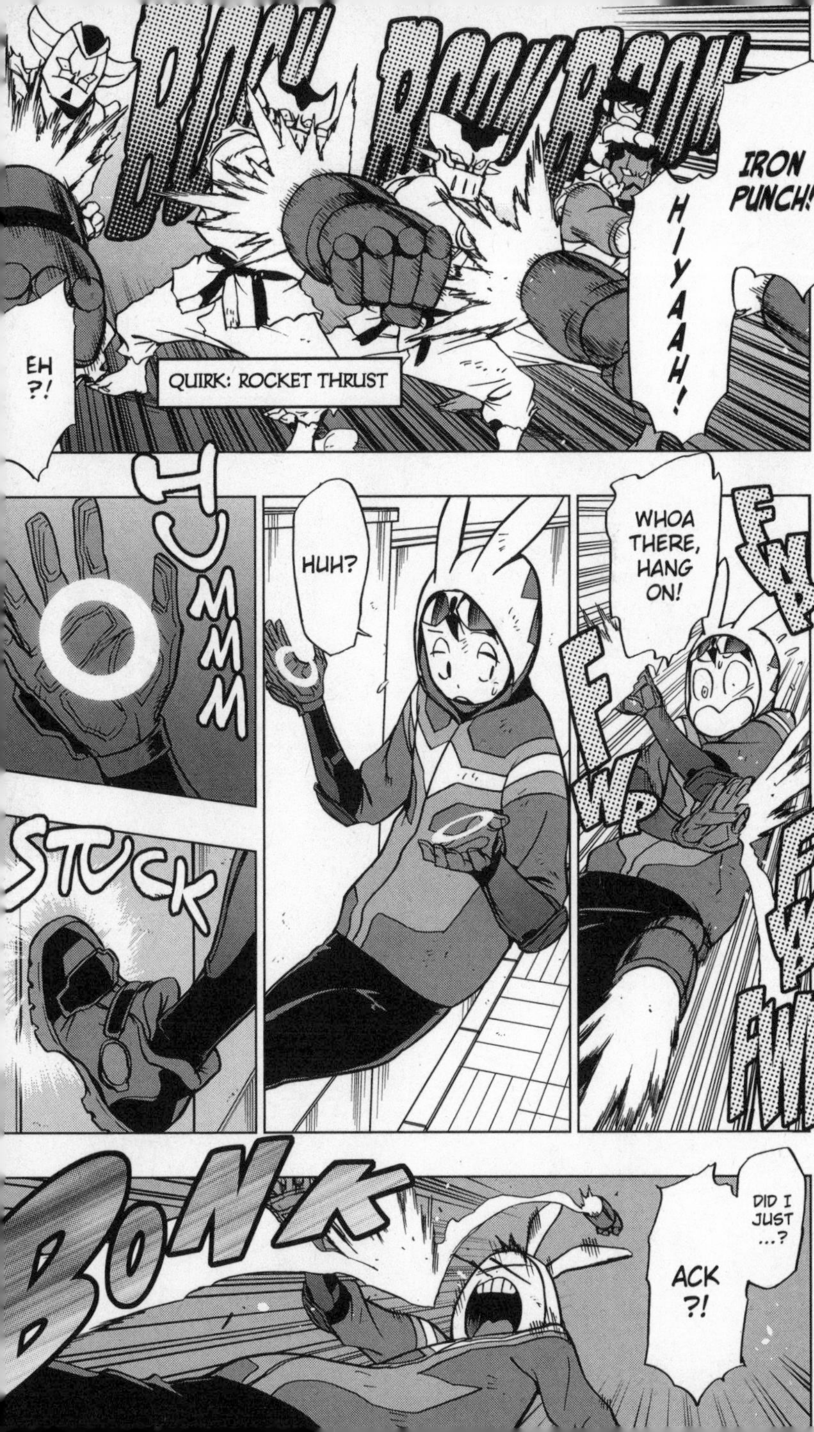
IRON PUNCH!
HIYAAAH!
QUIRK: ROCKET THRUST
EH?!
WHOA THERE, HANG ON!
HUH?
STUCK
DID I JUST ...?
ACK ?!
BONK

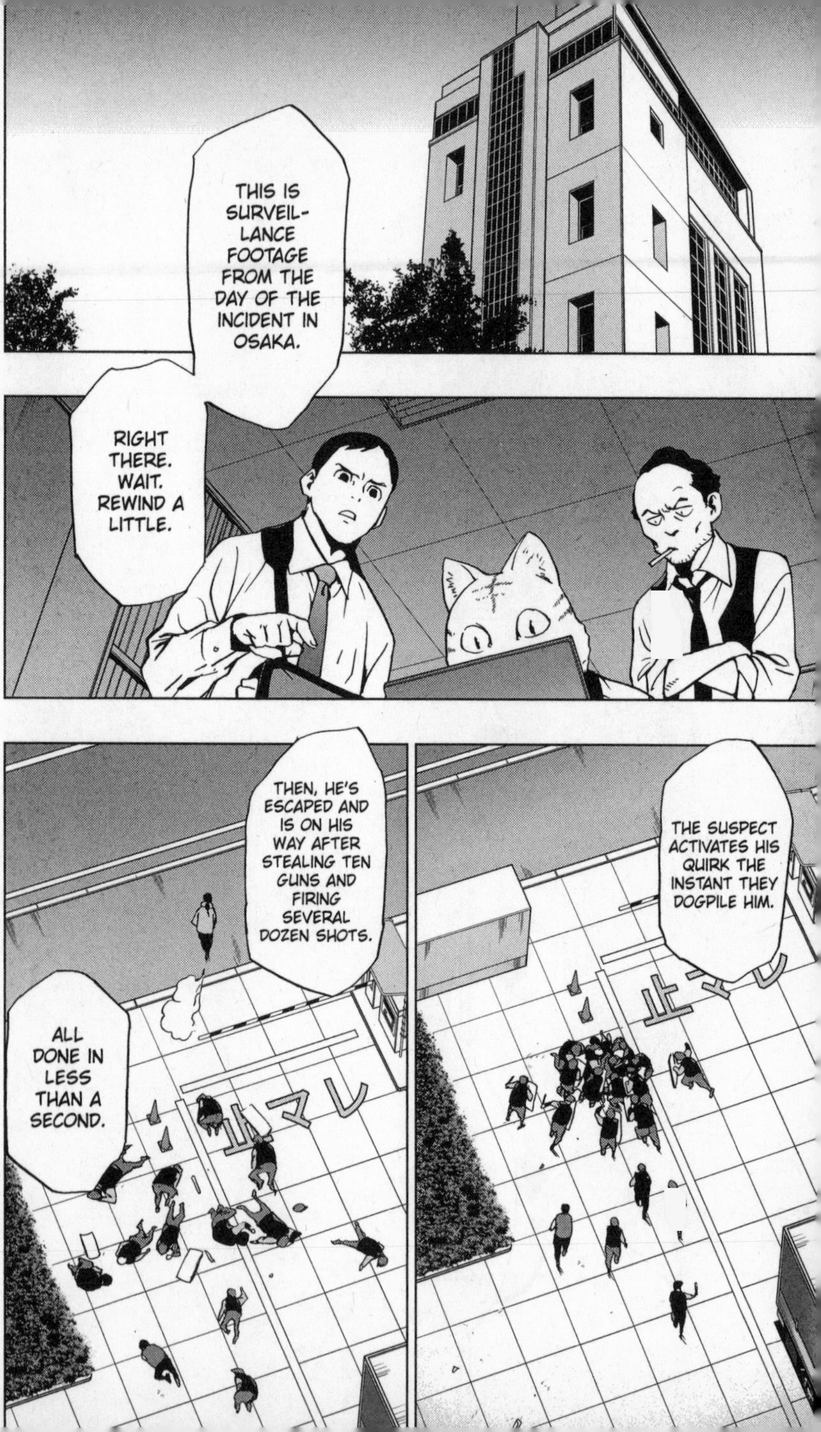
THIS IS SURVEILLANCE FOOTAGE FROM THE DAY OF THE INCIDENT IN OSAKA.
RIGHT THERE. WAIT. REWIND A LITTLE.
THE SUSPECT ACTIVATES HIS QUIRK THE INSTANT THEY DOGPILE HIM.
THEN, HE'S ESCAPED AND IS ON HIS WAY AFTER STEALING TEN GUNS AND FIRING SEVERAL DOZEN SHOTS.
ALL DONE IN LESS THAN A SECOND.

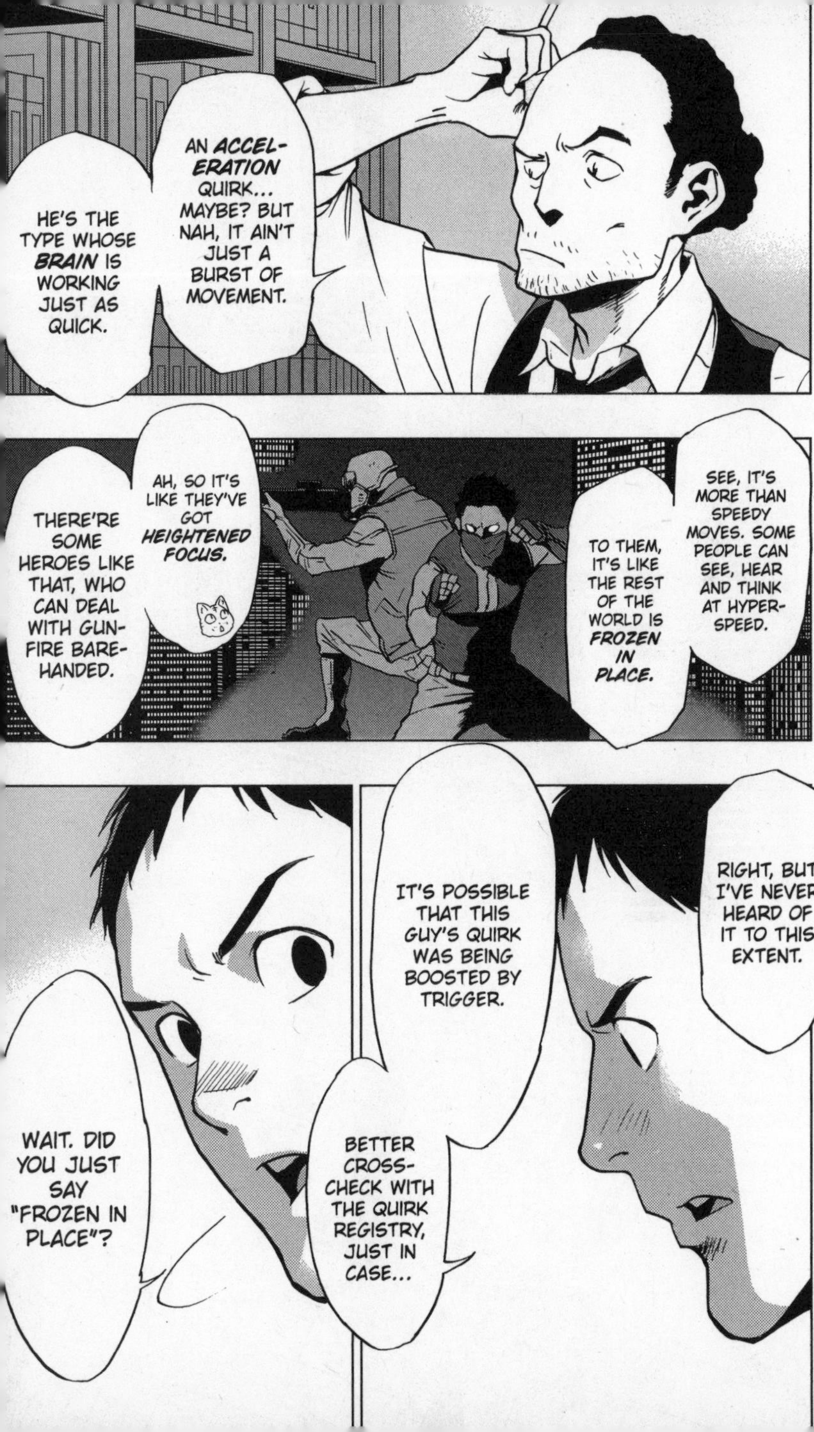
AN ACCEL-ERATION QUIRK... MAYBE? BUT NAH, IT AIN'T JUST A BURST OF MOVEMENT.
HE'S THE TYPE WHOSE BRAIN IS WORKING JUST AS QUICK.
SEE, IT'S MORE THAN SPEEDY MOVES. SOME PEOPLE CAN SEE, HEAR AND THINK AT HYPER-SPEED.
TO THEM, IT'S LIKE THE REST OF THE WORLD IS FROZEN IN PLACE.
AH, SO IT'S LIKE THEY'VE GOT HEIGHTENED FOCUS.
THERE'RE SOME HEROES LIKE THAT, WHO CAN DEAL WITH GUN-FIRE BARE-HANDED.
RIGHT, BUT I'VE NEVER HEARD OF IT TO THIS EXTENT.
IT'S POSSIBLE THAT THIS GUY'S QUIRK WAS BEING BOOSTED BY TRIGGER.
BETTER CROSS-CHECK WITH THE QUIRK REGISTRY, JUST IN CASE...
WAIT. DID YOU JUST SAY "FROZEN IN PLACE"?

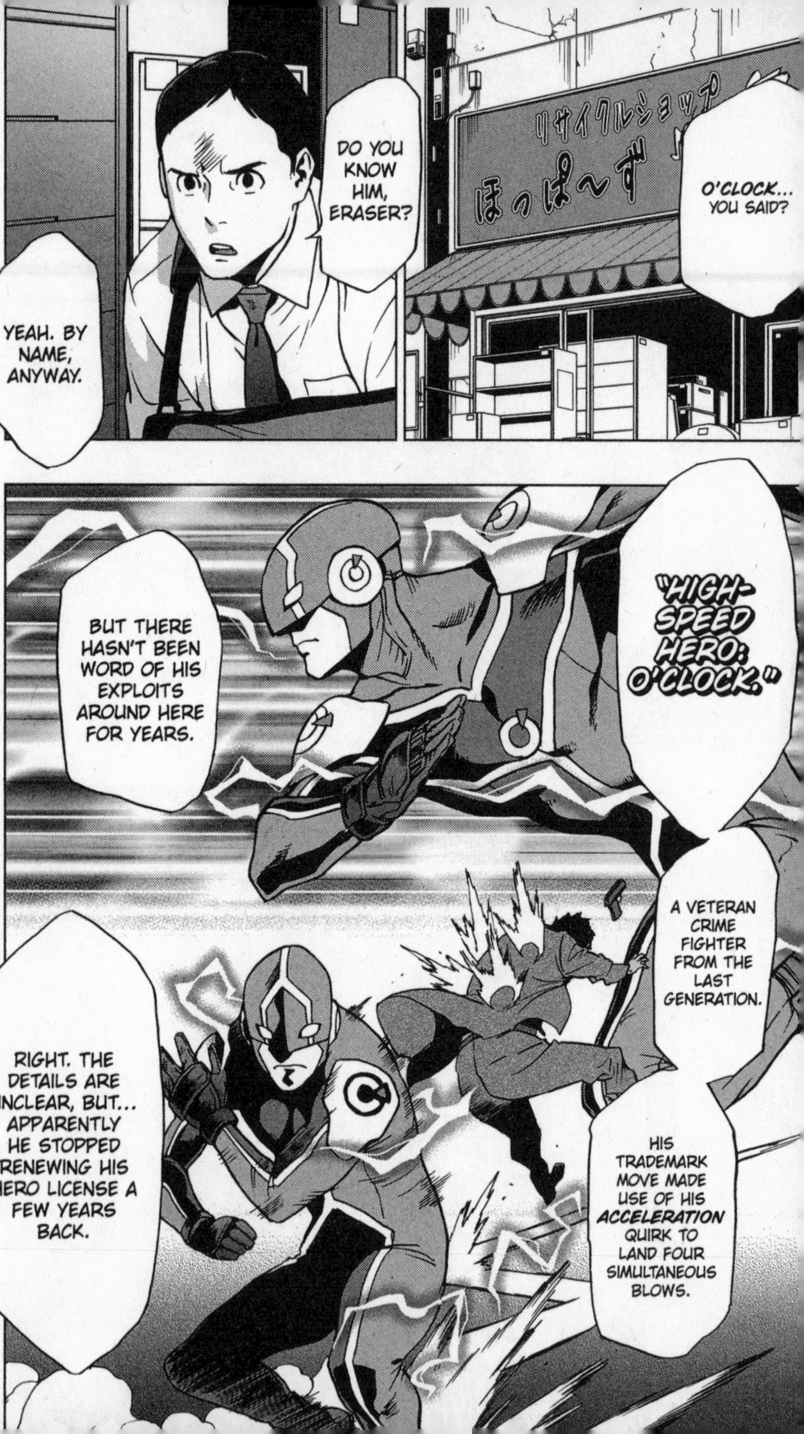
リサイクルショップ
ほっぱ〜ず
O'CLOCK... YOU SAID?
DO YOU KNOW HIM, ERASER?
YEAH. BY NAME, ANYWAY.
"HIGH-SPEED HERO: O'CLOCK."
A VETERAN CRIME FIGHTER FROM THE LAST GENERATION.
HIS TRADEMARK MOVE MADE USE OF HIS ***ACCELERATION*** QUIRK TO LAND FOUR SIMULTANEOUS BLOWS.
BUT THERE HASN'T BEEN WORD OF HIS EXPLOITS AROUND HERE FOR YEARS.
RIGHT. THE DETAILS ARE UNCLEAR, BUT... APPARENTLY HE STOPPED RENEWING HIS HERO LICENSE A FEW YEARS BACK.

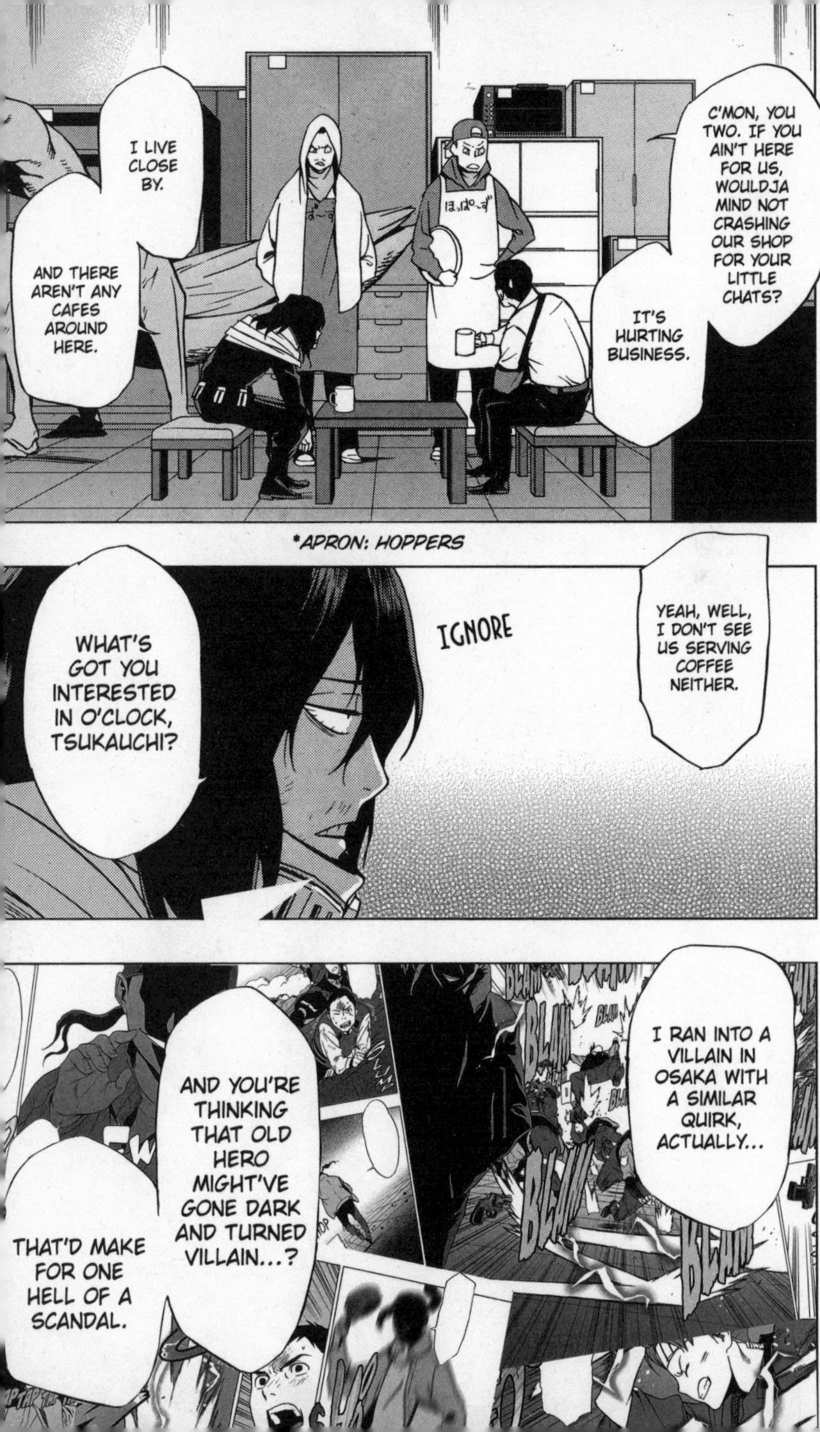
C'MON, YOU TWO. IF YOU AIN'T HERE FOR US, WOULDJA MIND NOT CRASHING OUR SHOP FOR YOUR LITTLE CHATS?
IT'S HURTING BUSINESS.
ほっぱーず
I LIVE CLOSE BY.
AND THERE AREN'T ANY CAFES AROUND HERE.
*APRON: HOPPERS
YEAH, WELL, I DON'T SEE US SERVING COFFEE NEITHER.
IGNORE
WHAT'S GOT YOU INTERESTED IN O'CLOCK, TSUKAUCHI?
I RAN INTO A VILLAIN IN OSAKA WITH A SIMILAR QUIRK, ACTUALLY...
AND YOU'RE THINKING THAT OLD HERO MIGHT'VE GONE DARK AND TURNED VILLAIN...?
THAT'D MAKE FOR ONE HELL OF A SCANDAL.

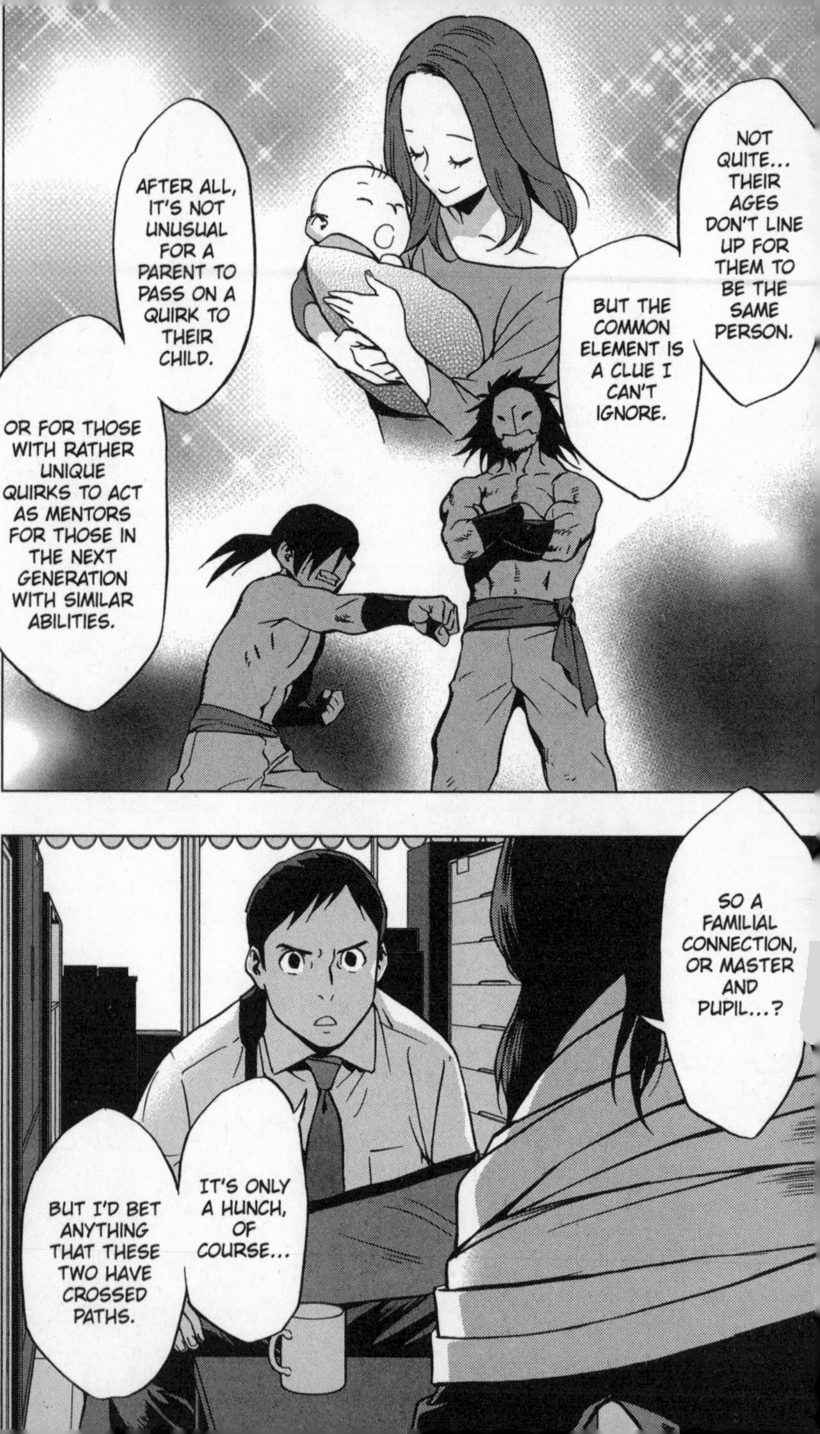
NOT QUITE... THEIR AGES DON'T LINE UP FOR THEM TO BE THE SAME PERSON.
BUT THE COMMON ELEMENT IS A CLUE I CAN'T IGNORE.
AFTER ALL, IT'S NOT UNUSUAL FOR A PARENT TO PASS ON A QUIRK TO THEIR CHILD.
OR FOR THOSE WITH RATHER UNIQUE QUIRKS TO ACT AS MENTORS FOR THOSE IN THE NEXT GENERATION WITH SIMILAR ABILITIES.
SO A FAMILIAL CONNECTION, OR MASTER AND PUPIL...?
IT'S ONLY A HUNCH, OF COURSE...
BUT I'D BET ANYTHING THAT THESE TWO HAVE CROSSED PATHS.

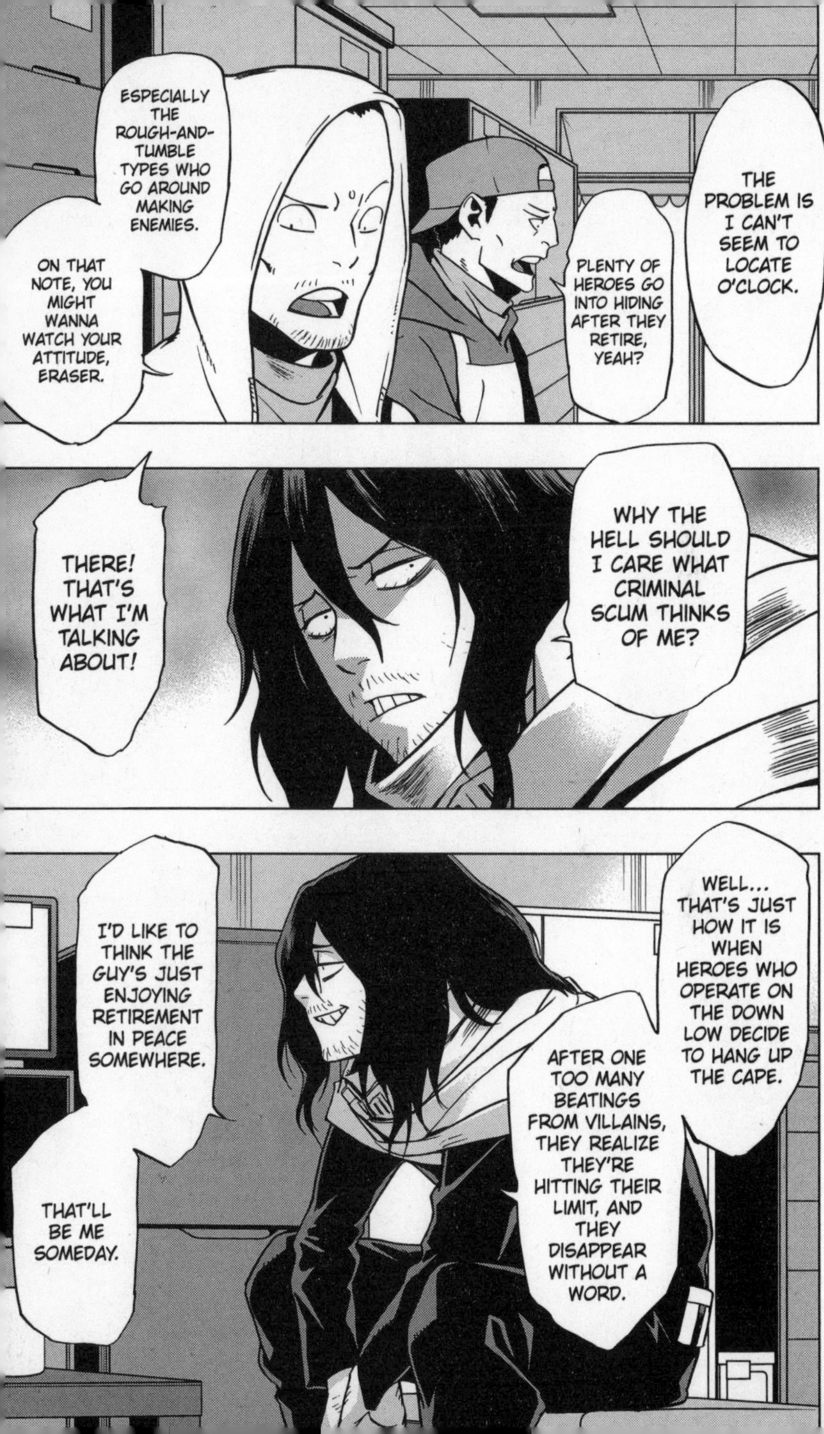
THE PROBLEM IS I CAN'T SEEM TO LOCATE O'CLOCK.
PLENTY OF HEROES GO INTO HIDING AFTER THEY RETIRE, YEAH?
ESPECIALLY THE ROUGH-AND-TUMBLE TYPES WHO GO AROUND MAKING ENEMIES.
ON THAT NOTE, YOU MIGHT WANNA WATCH YOUR ATTITUDE, ERASER.
WHY THE HELL SHOULD I CARE WHAT CRIMINAL SCUM THINKS OF ME?
THERE! THAT'S WHAT I'M TALKING ABOUT!
WELL... THAT'S JUST HOW IT IS WHEN HEROES WHO OPERATE ON THE DOWN LOW DECIDE TO HANG UP THE CAPE.
AFTER ONE TOO MANY BEATINGS FROM VILLAINS, THEY REALIZE THEY'RE HITTING THEIR LIMIT, AND THEY DISAPPEAR WITHOUT A WORD.
I'D LIKE TO THINK THE GUY'S JUST ENJOYING RETIREMENT IN PEACE SOMEWHERE.
THAT'LL BE ME SOMEDAY.

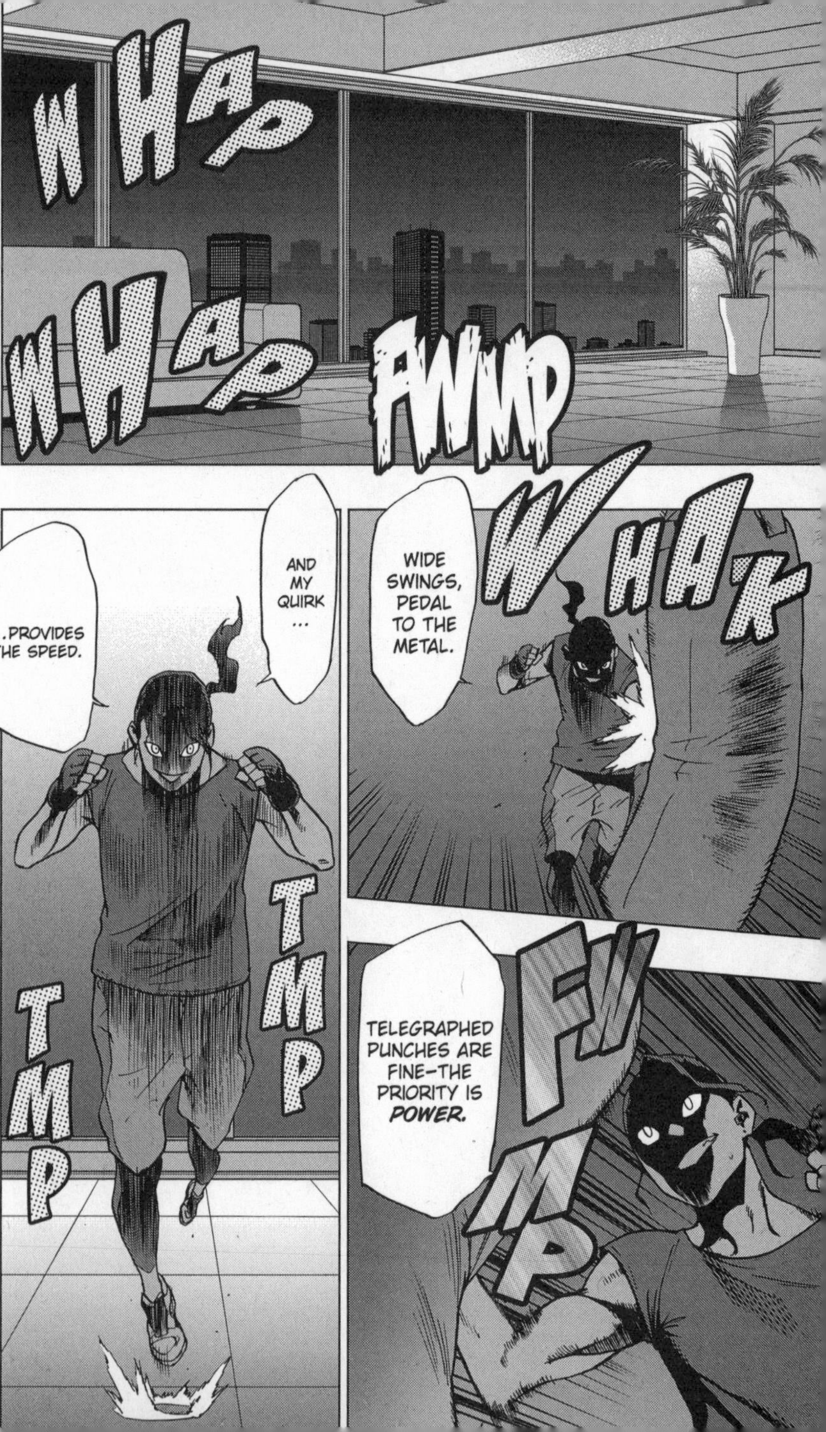
WHAP
WHAP
FWMP
WHAK
WIDE SWINGS, PEDAL TO THE METAL.
TELEGRAPHED PUNCHES ARE FINE—THE PRIORITY IS *POWER.*
FWMP
AND MY QUIRK...
...PROVIDES THE SPEED.
TMP
TMP

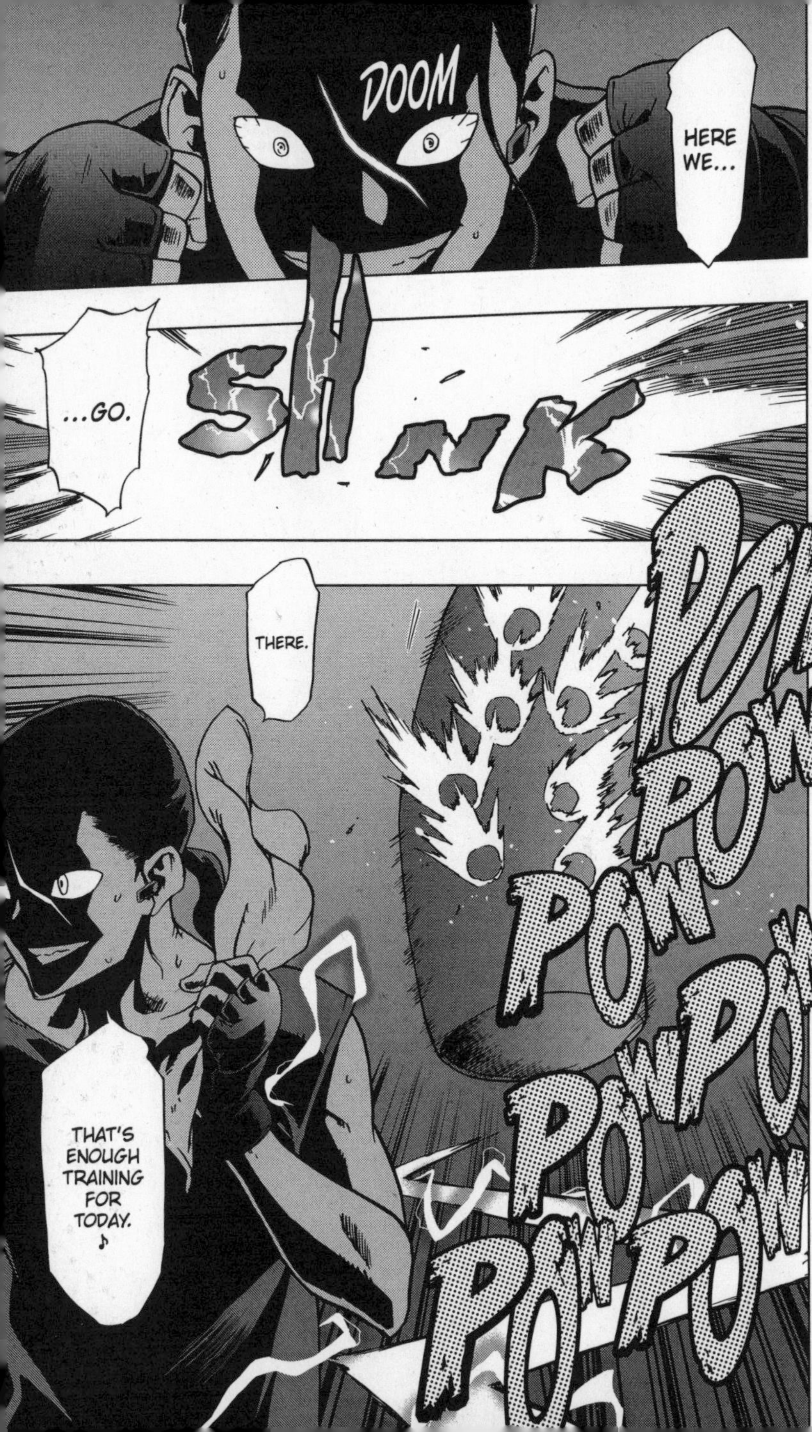
HERE WE...
DOOM
SHINK
...GO.
POW POW
POW POW
POW POW
POW POW
THERE.
THAT'S ENOUGH TRAINING FOR TODAY. ♪

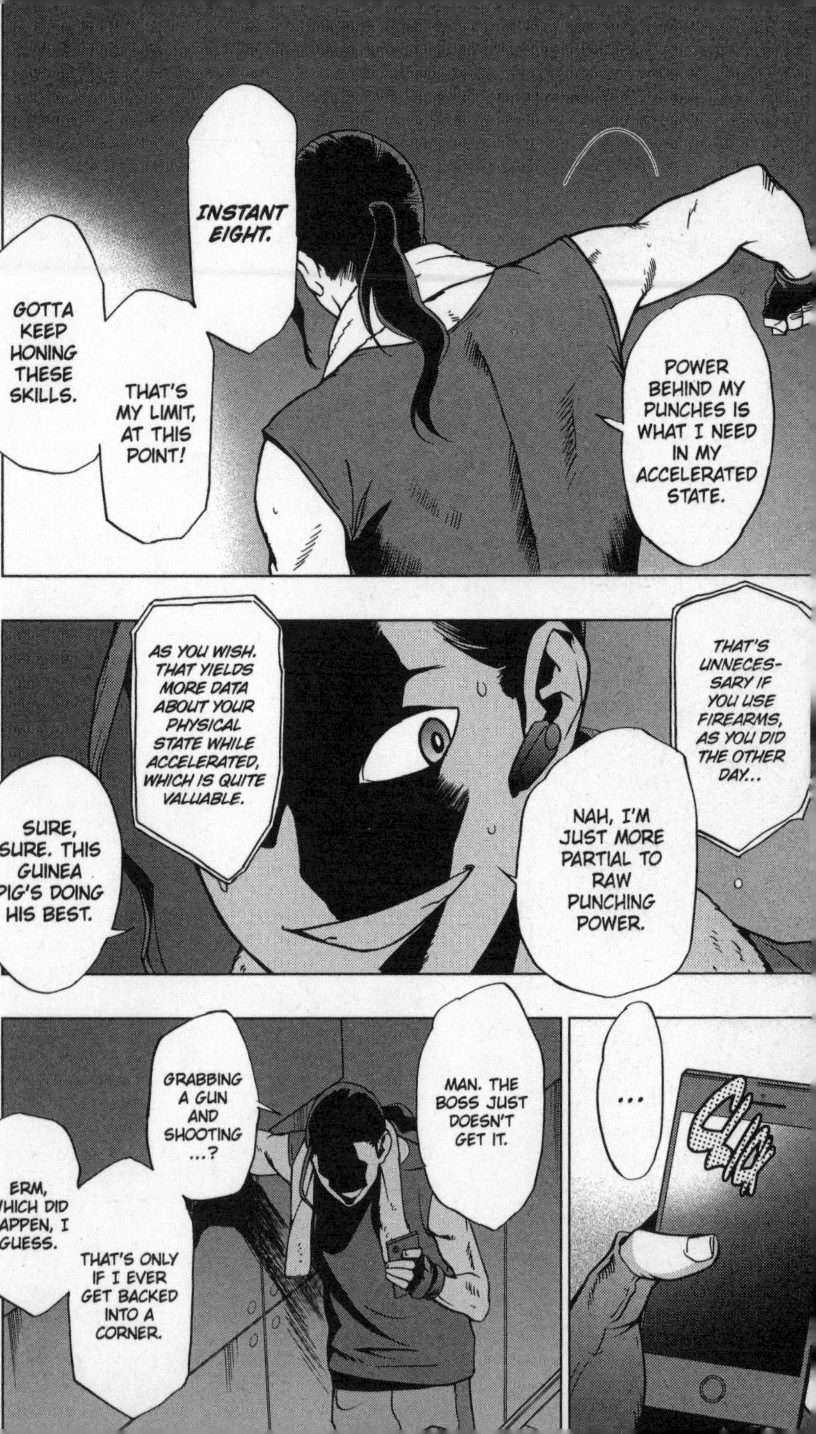
INSTANT EIGHT.
THAT'S MY LIMIT, AT THIS POINT!
GOTTA KEEP HONING THESE SKILLS.
POWER BEHIND MY PUNCHES IS WHAT I NEED IN MY ACCELERATED STATE.
THAT'S UNNECES-SARY IF YOU USE FIREARMS, AS YOU DID THE OTHER DAY...
NAH, I'M JUST MORE PARTIAL TO RAW PUNCHING POWER.
AS YOU WISH. THAT YIELDS MORE DATA ABOUT YOUR PHYSICAL STATE WHILE ACCELERATED, WHICH IS QUITE VALUABLE.
SURE, SURE. THIS GUINEA PIG'S DOING HIS BEST.
...
MAN. THE BOSS JUST DOESN'T GET IT.
GRABBING A GUN AND SHOOTING ...?
THAT'S ONLY IF I EVER GET BACKED INTO A CORNER.
ERM, WHICH DID HAPPEN, I GUESS.

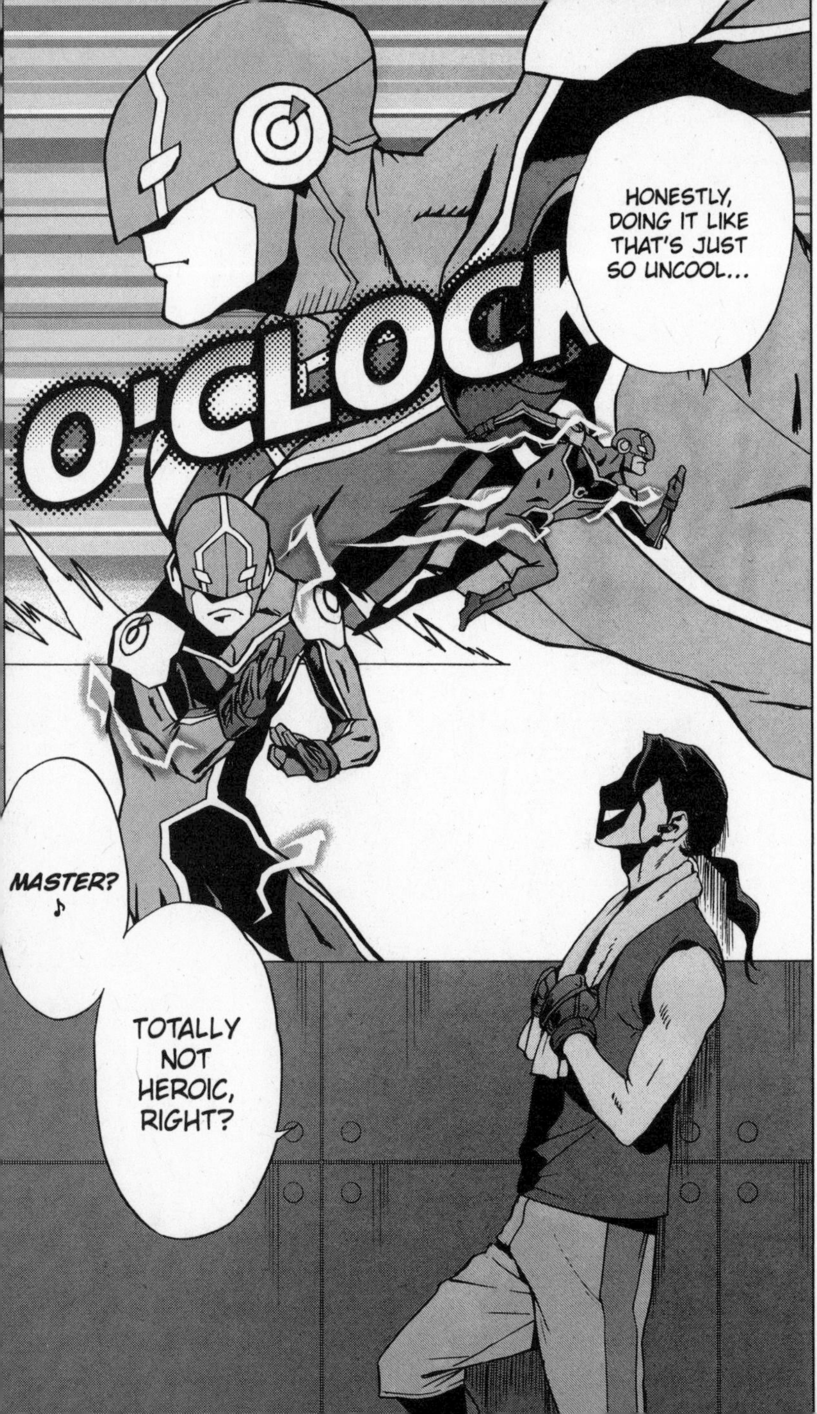
HONESTLY, DOING IT LIKE THAT'S JUST SO UNCOOL...
O'CLOCK
MASTER? ♪
TOTALLY NOT HEROIC, RIGHT?

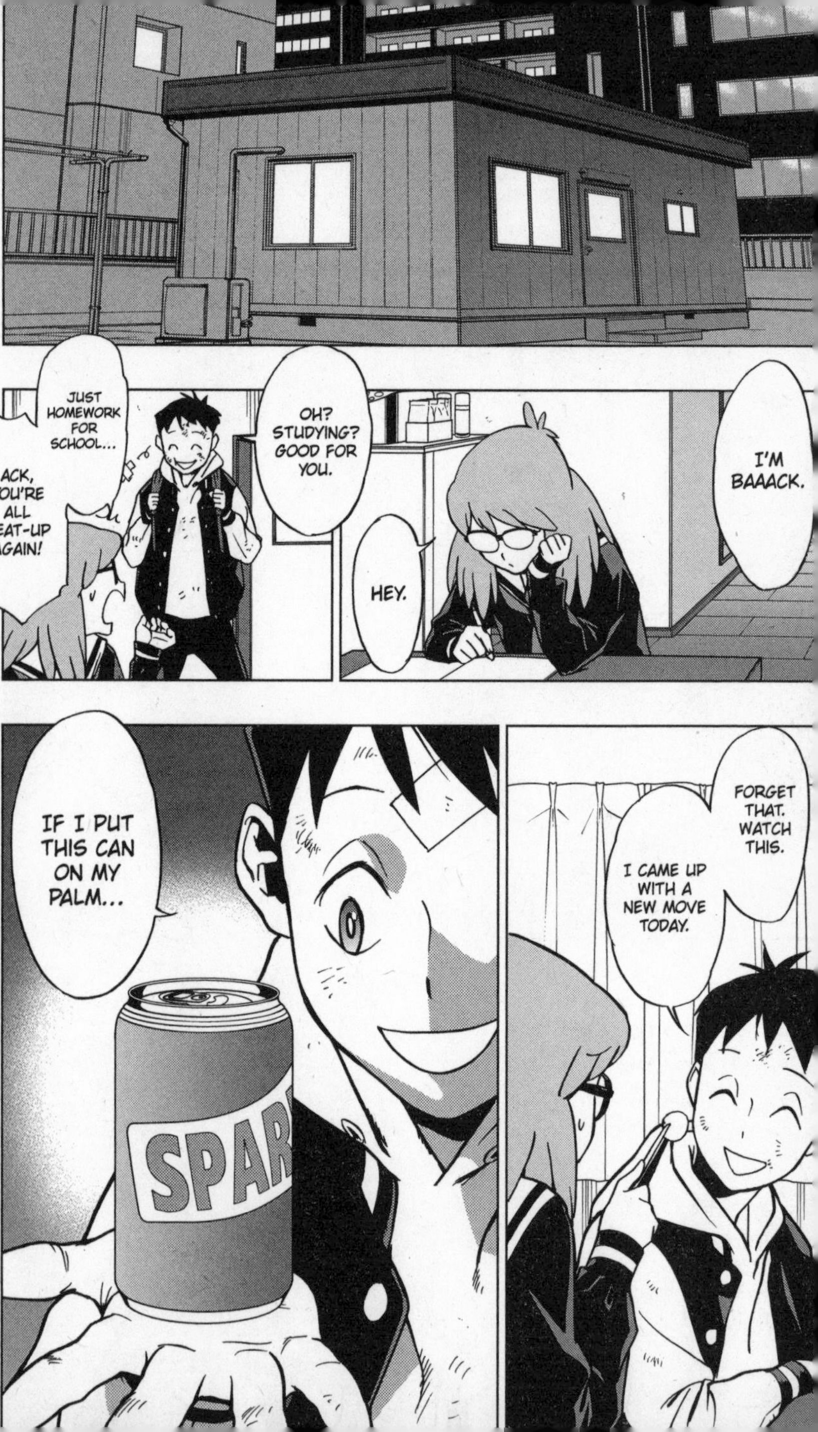
I'M BAAACK.
HEY.
OH? STUDYING? GOOD FOR YOU.
JUST HOMEWORK FOR SCHOOL...
ACK, YOU'RE ALL BEAT-UP AGAIN!
FORGET THAT. WATCH THIS.
I CAME UP WITH A NEW MOVE TODAY.
IF I PUT THIS CAN ON MY PALM...
SPAR

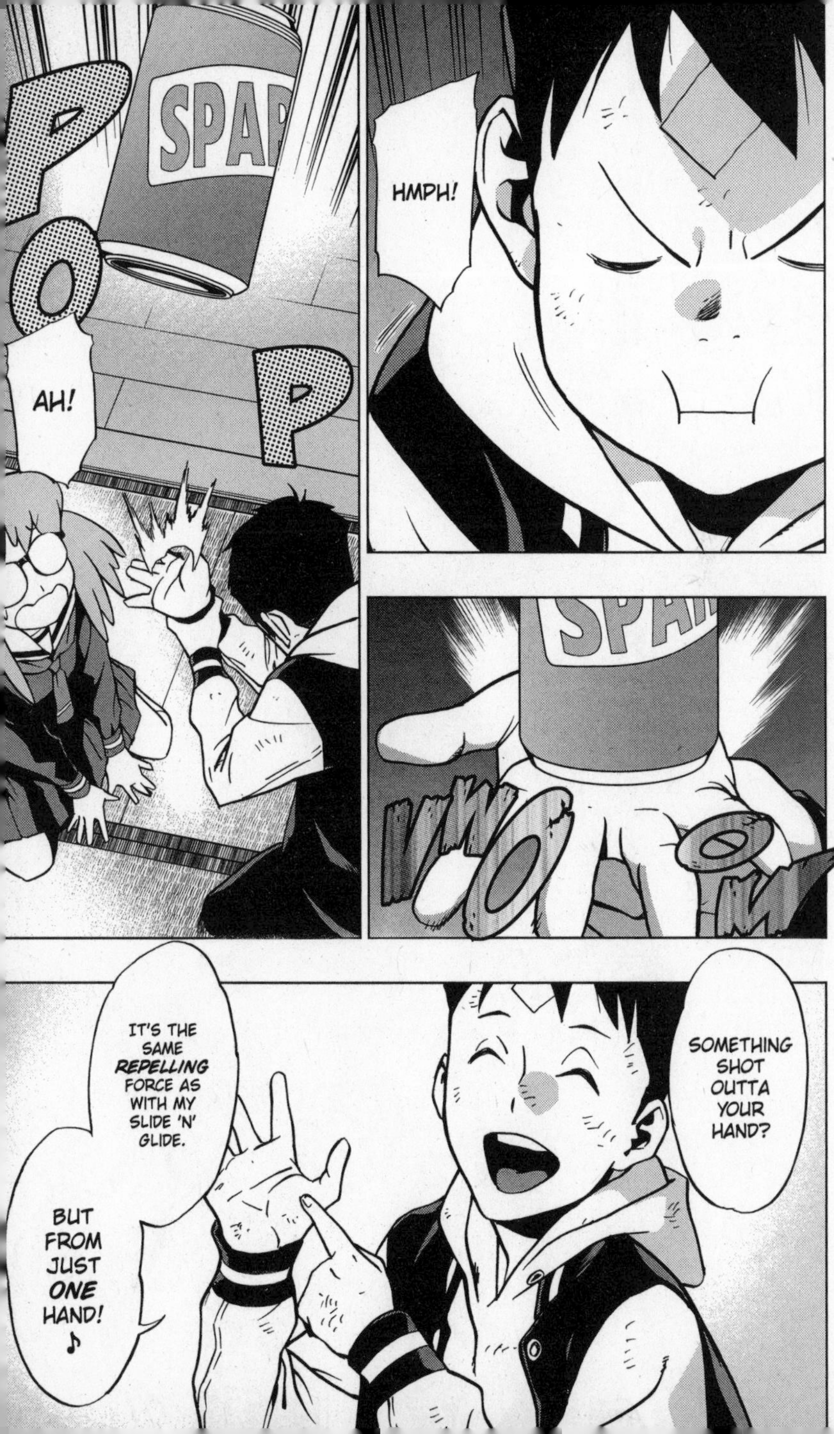
HMPH!
POP
AH!
SOMETHING SHOT OUTTA YOUR HAND?
IT'S THE SAME ***REPELLING*** FORCE AS WITH MY SLIDE 'N' GLIDE.
BUT FROM JUST ***ONE*** HAND! ♪

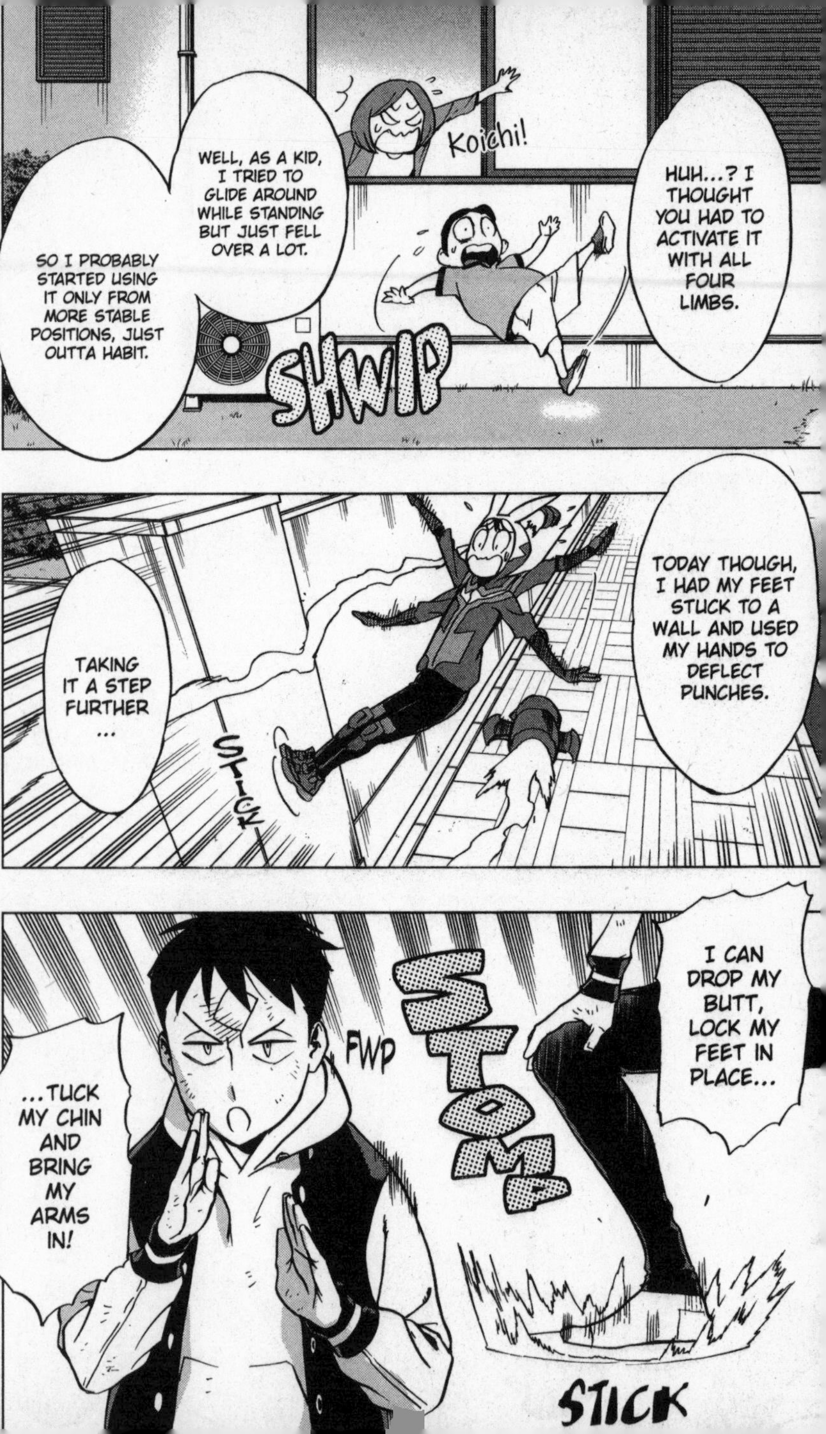
HUH...? I THOUGHT YOU HAD TO ACTIVATE IT WITH ALL FOUR LIMBS.
Koichi!
WELL, AS A KID, I TRIED TO GLIDE AROUND WHILE STANDING BUT JUST FELL OVER A LOT.
SO I PROBABLY STARTED USING IT ONLY FROM MORE STABLE POSITIONS, JUST OUTTA HABIT.
SHWIP
TODAY THOUGH, I HAD MY FEET STUCK TO A WALL AND USED MY HANDS TO DEFLECT PUNCHES.
TAKING IT A STEP FURTHER ...
STICK
I CAN DROP MY BUTT, LOCK MY FEET IN PLACE...
STOMP
FWP
...TUCK MY CHIN AND BRING MY ARMS IN!
STICK

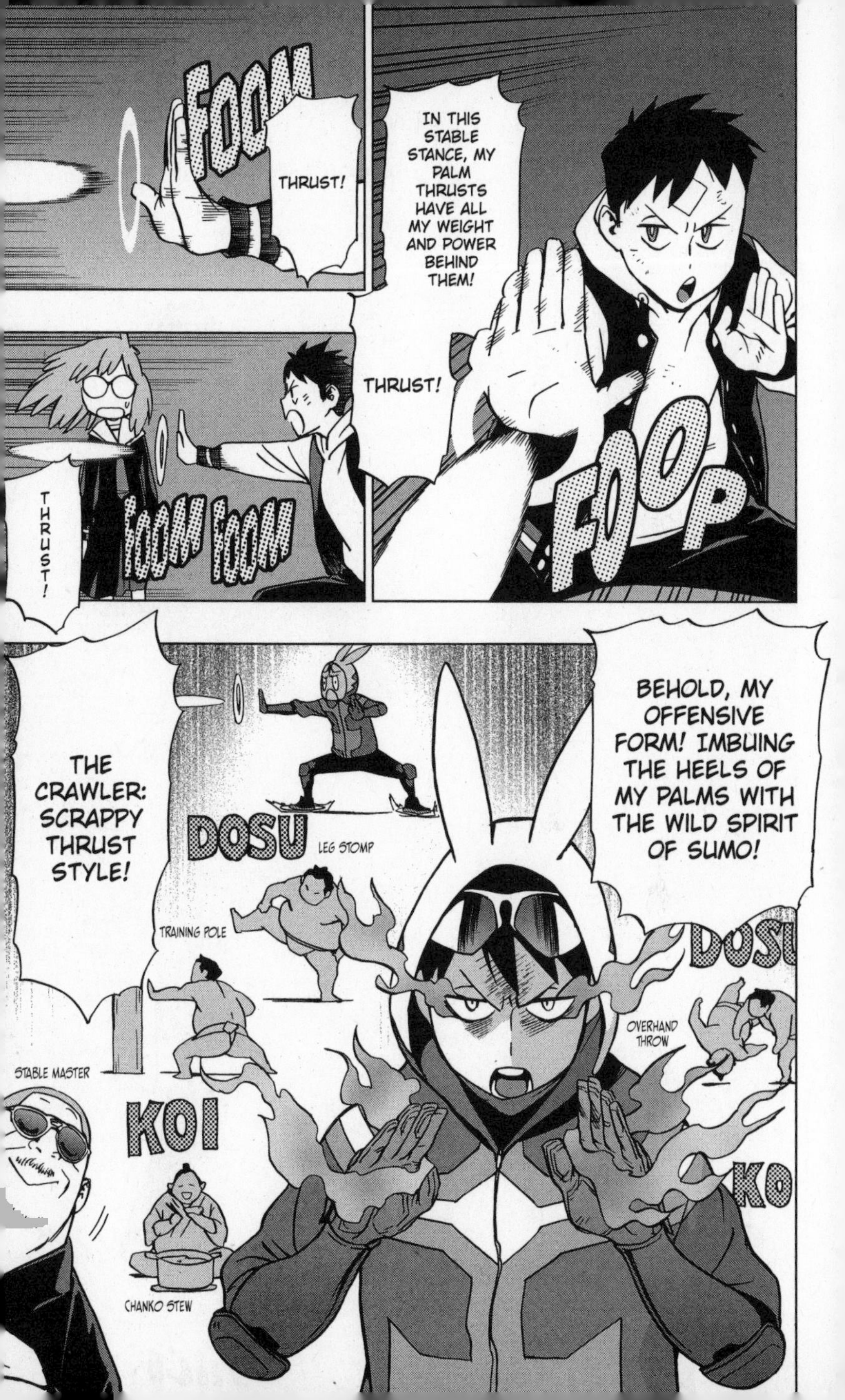
IN THIS STABLE STANCE, MY PALM THRUSTS HAVE ALL MY WEIGHT AND POWER BEHIND THEM!
THRUST!
FOOP
FOOM
THRUST!
FOOM FOOM
THRUST!
BEHOLD, MY OFFENSIVE FORM! IMBUING THE HEELS OF MY PALMS WITH THE WILD SPIRIT OF SUMO!
DOSU
OVERHAND THROW
KO
THE CRAWLER: SCRAPPY THRUST STYLE!
DOSU
LEG STOMP
TRAINING POLE
STABLE MASTER
KOI
CHANKO STEW

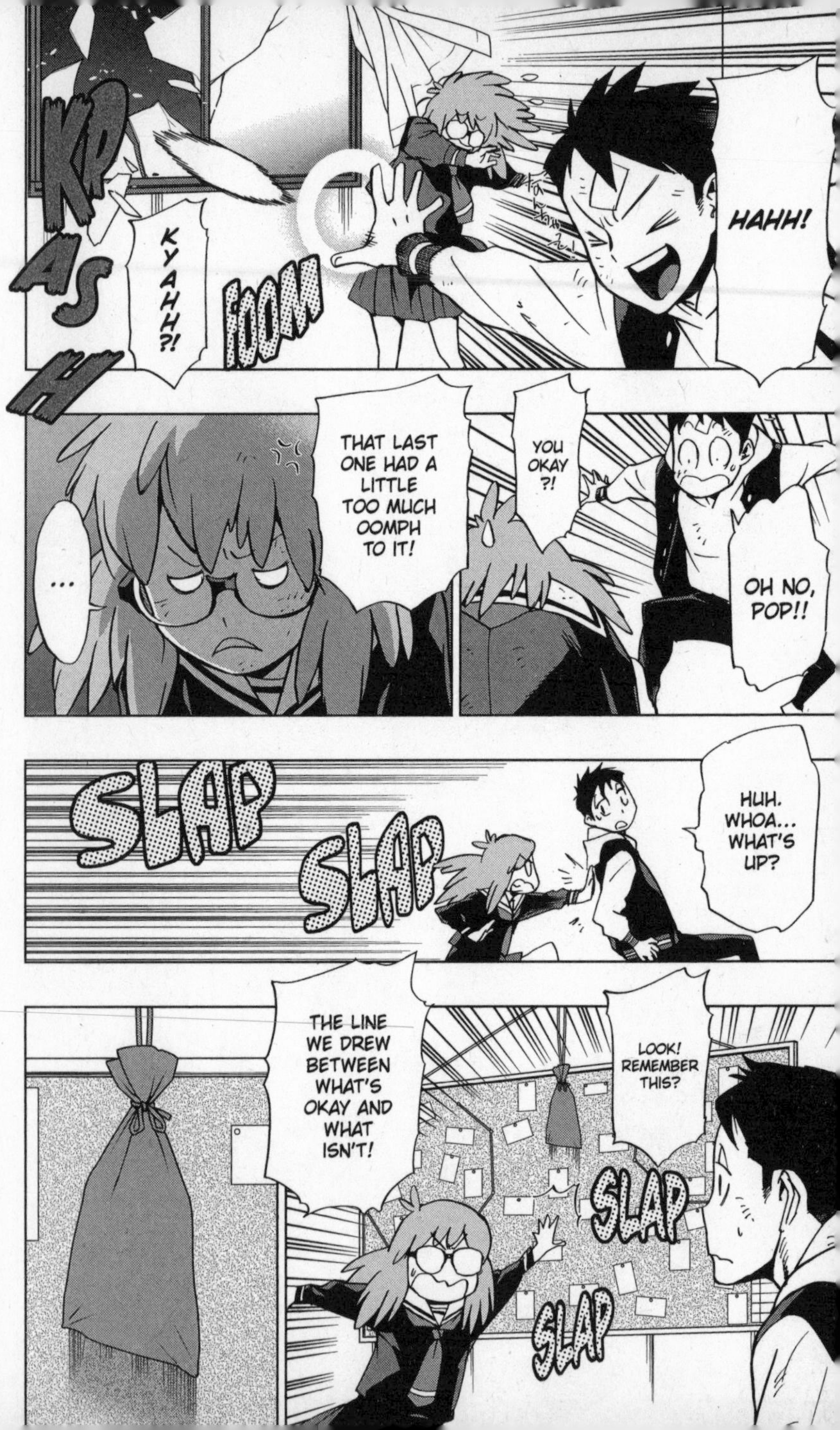
HAHH!
FOOM
KYAHH?!
KRASH
OH NO, POP!!
YOU OKAY?!
THAT LAST ONE HAD A LITTLE TOO MUCH OOMPH TO IT!
...
HUH. WHOA... WHAT'S UP?
SLAP
SLAP
LOOK! REMEMBER THIS?
SLAP
SLAP
THE LINE WE DREW BETWEEN WHAT'S OKAY AND WHAT ISN'T!

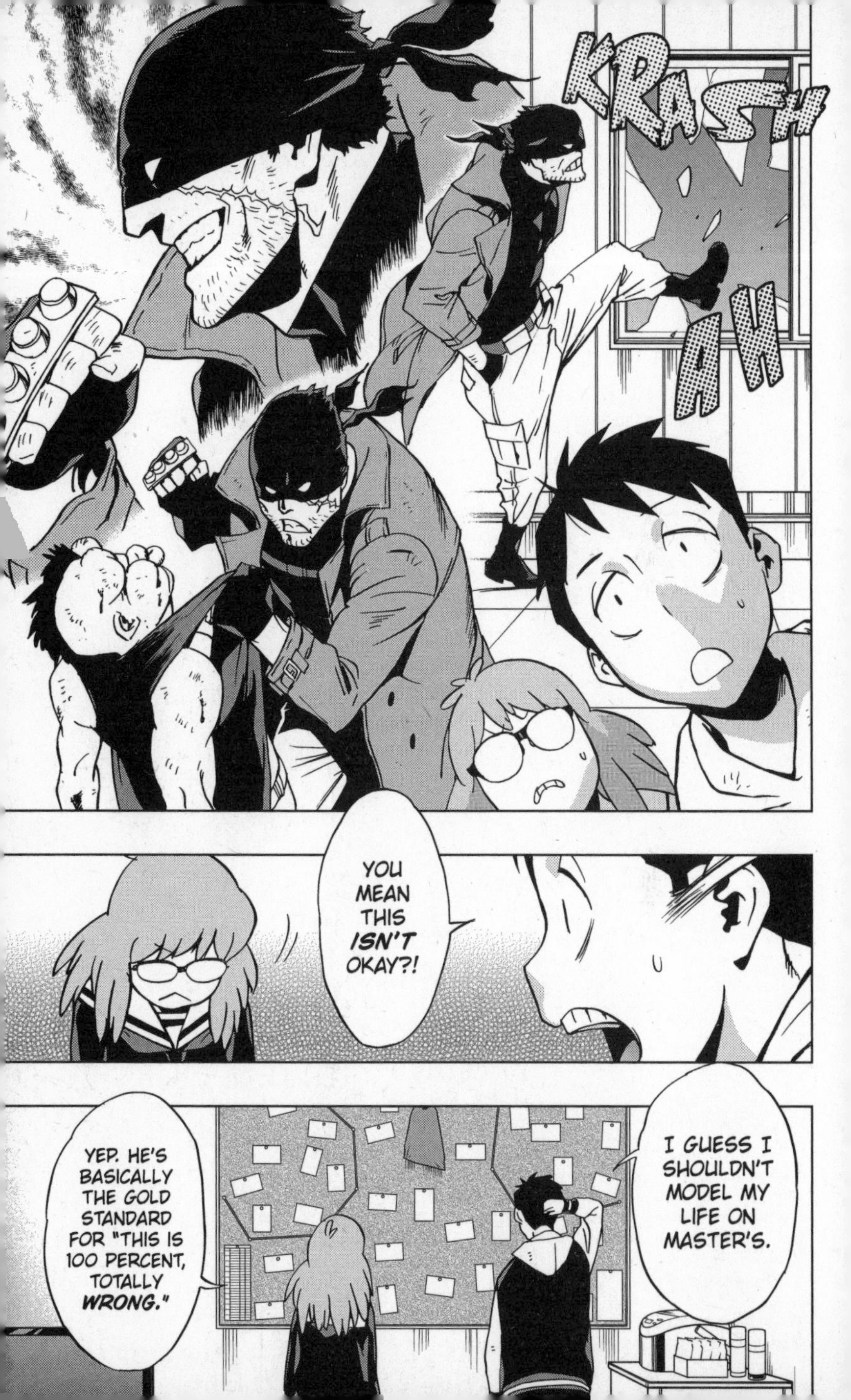
KRASH
AH
YOU MEAN THIS ISN'T OKAY?!
I GUESS I SHOULDN'T MODEL MY LIFE ON MASTER'S.
YEP. HE'S BASICALLY THE GOLD STANDARD FOR "THIS IS 100 PERCENT, TOTALLY WRONG."

O'CLOCK

THE ROUGH DESIGN

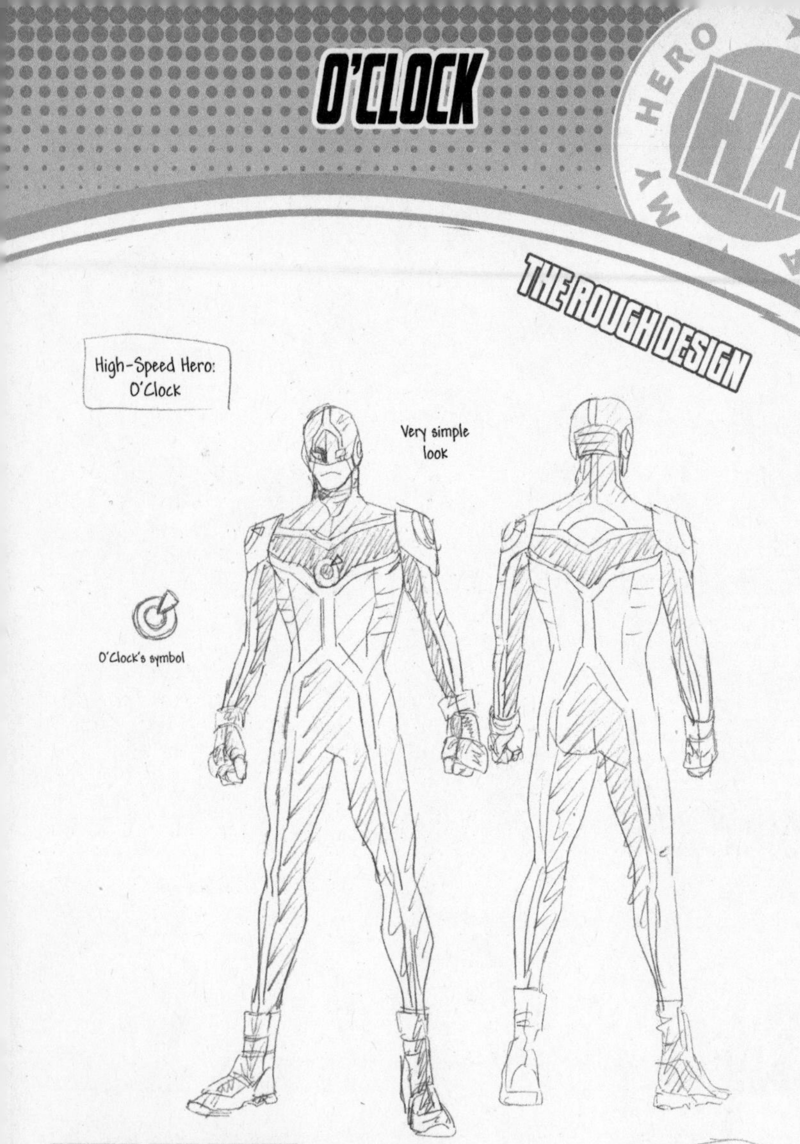

High-Speed Hero: O'Clock
Very simple look
O'Clock's symbol

BEHIND THE SCENES

I wanted an upright hero in a mask and full bodysuit, modeled off DC Comics' the Flash. Just you wait, because we'll be learning more and more about this guy as the story progresses.

—Furuhashi

Since he is such an orthodox-looking hero, I tried to work in elements of the Nebula M78 beings…

—Betten

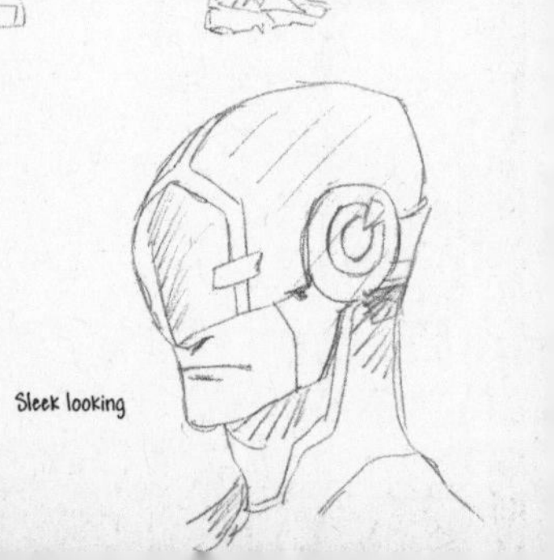

Sleek looking

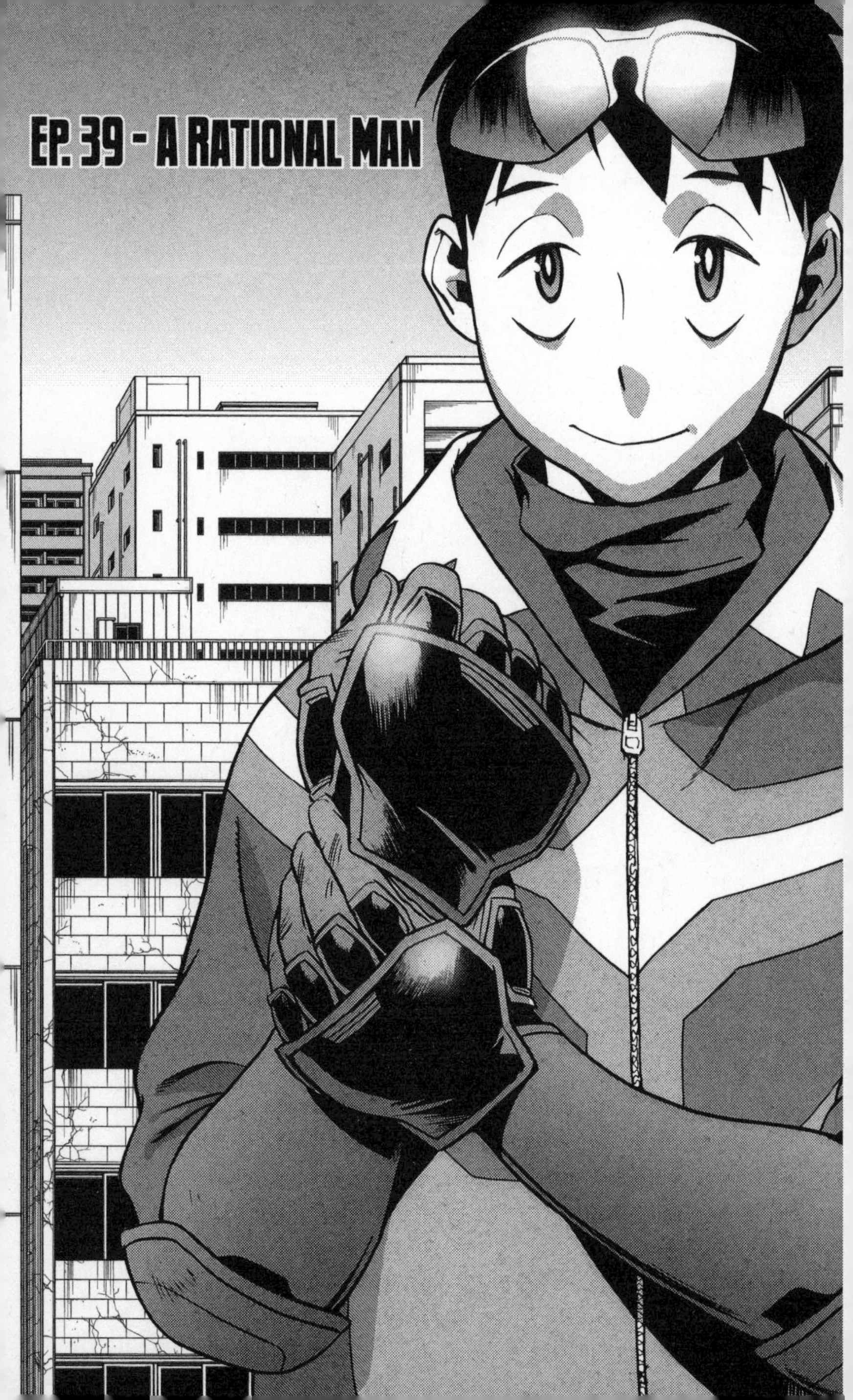
EP. 39 - A RATIONAL MAN

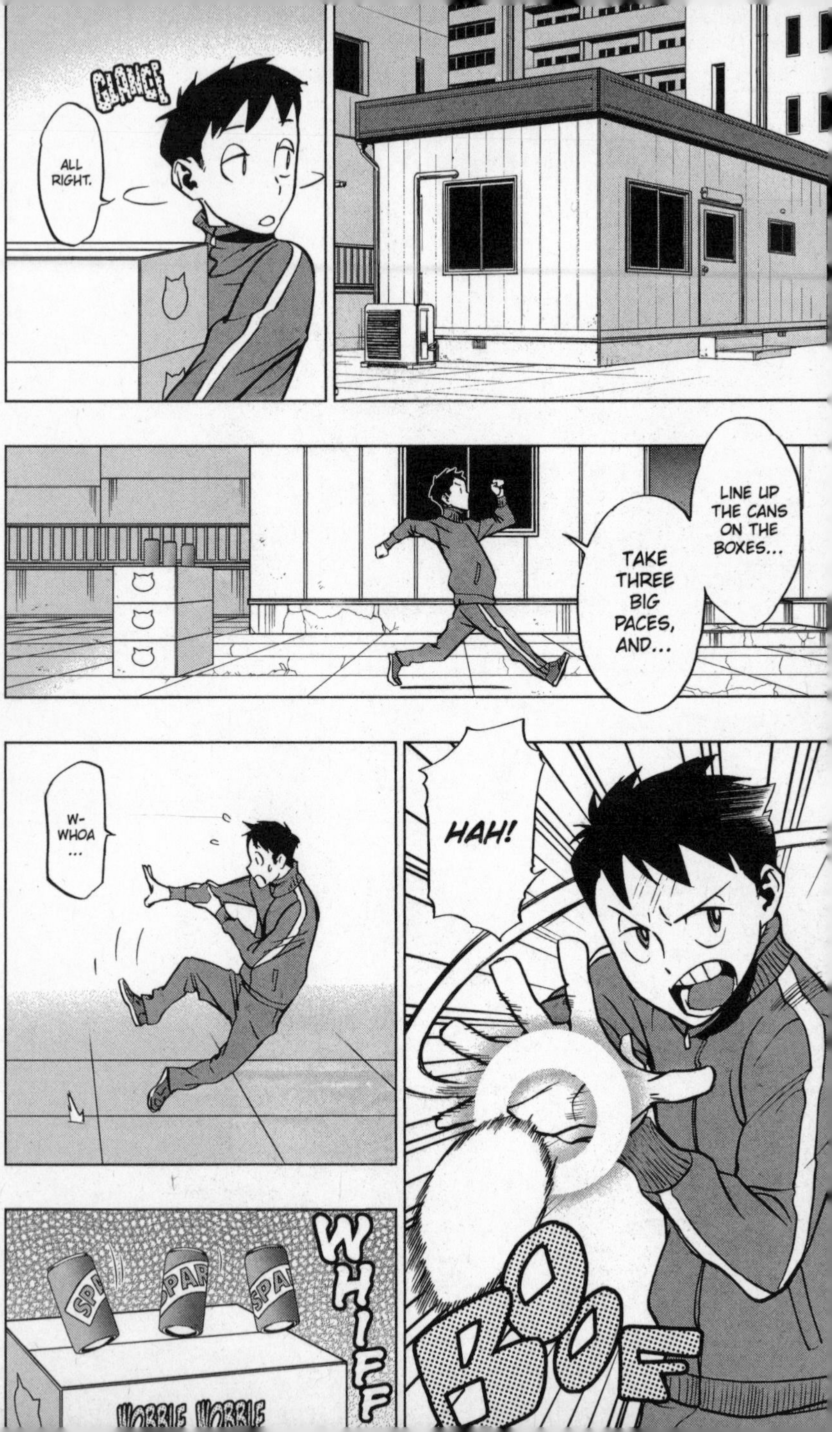
GLANCE
ALL RIGHT.
LINE UP THE CANS ON THE BOXES...
TAKE THREE BIG PACES, AND...
HAH!
BOOF
W-WHOA...
WHIFF
WOBBLE WOBBLE

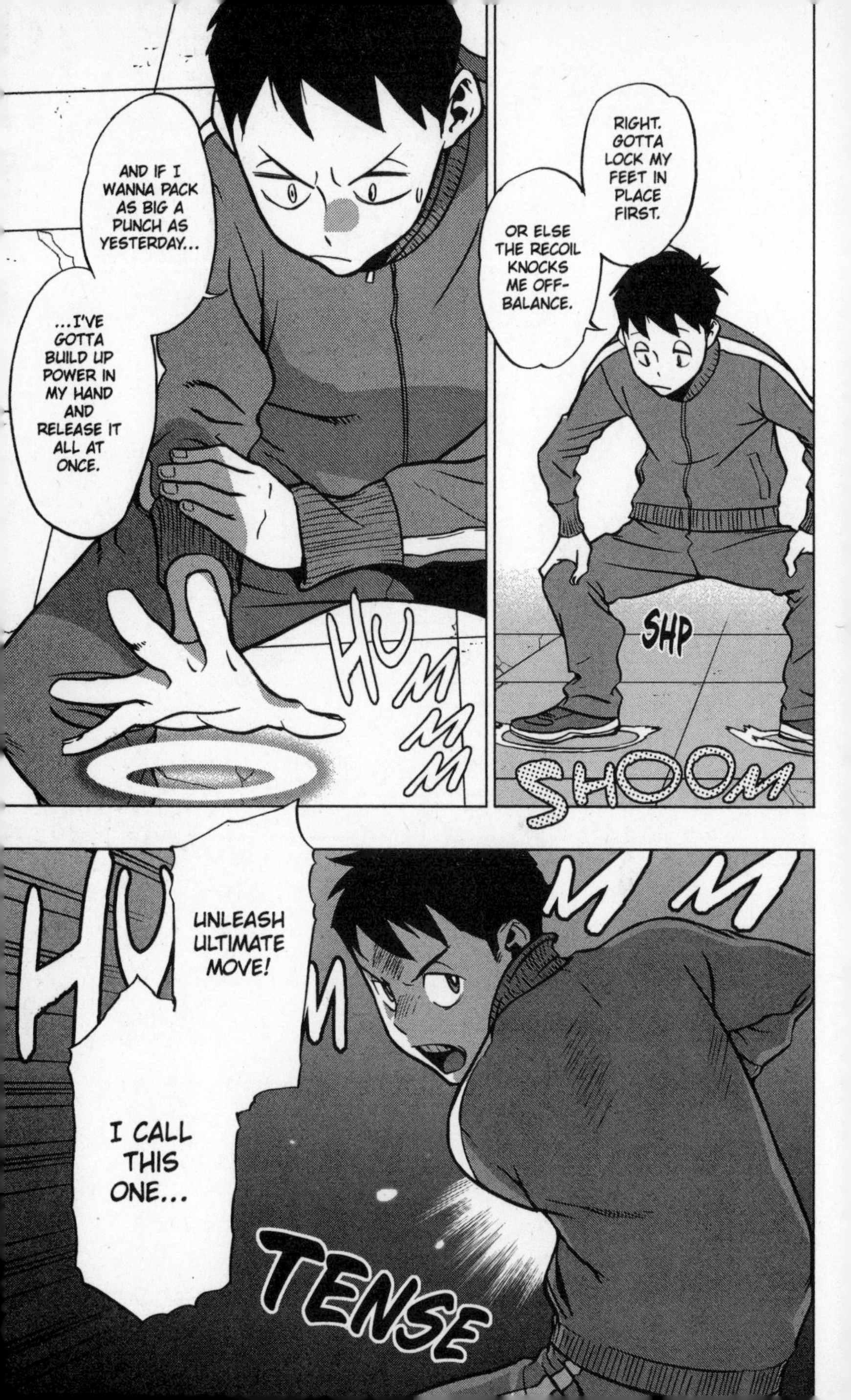
RIGHT. GOTTA LOCK MY FEET IN PLACE FIRST.
OR ELSE THE RECOIL KNOCKS ME OFF-BALANCE.
SHP
SHOOM
AND IF I WANNA PACK AS BIG A PUNCH AS YESTERDAY...
...I'VE GOTTA BUILD UP POWER IN MY HAND AND RELEASE IT ALL AT ONCE.
HUMMM
UNLEASH ULTIMATE MOVE!
I CALL THIS ONE...
HUMMMM
TENSE

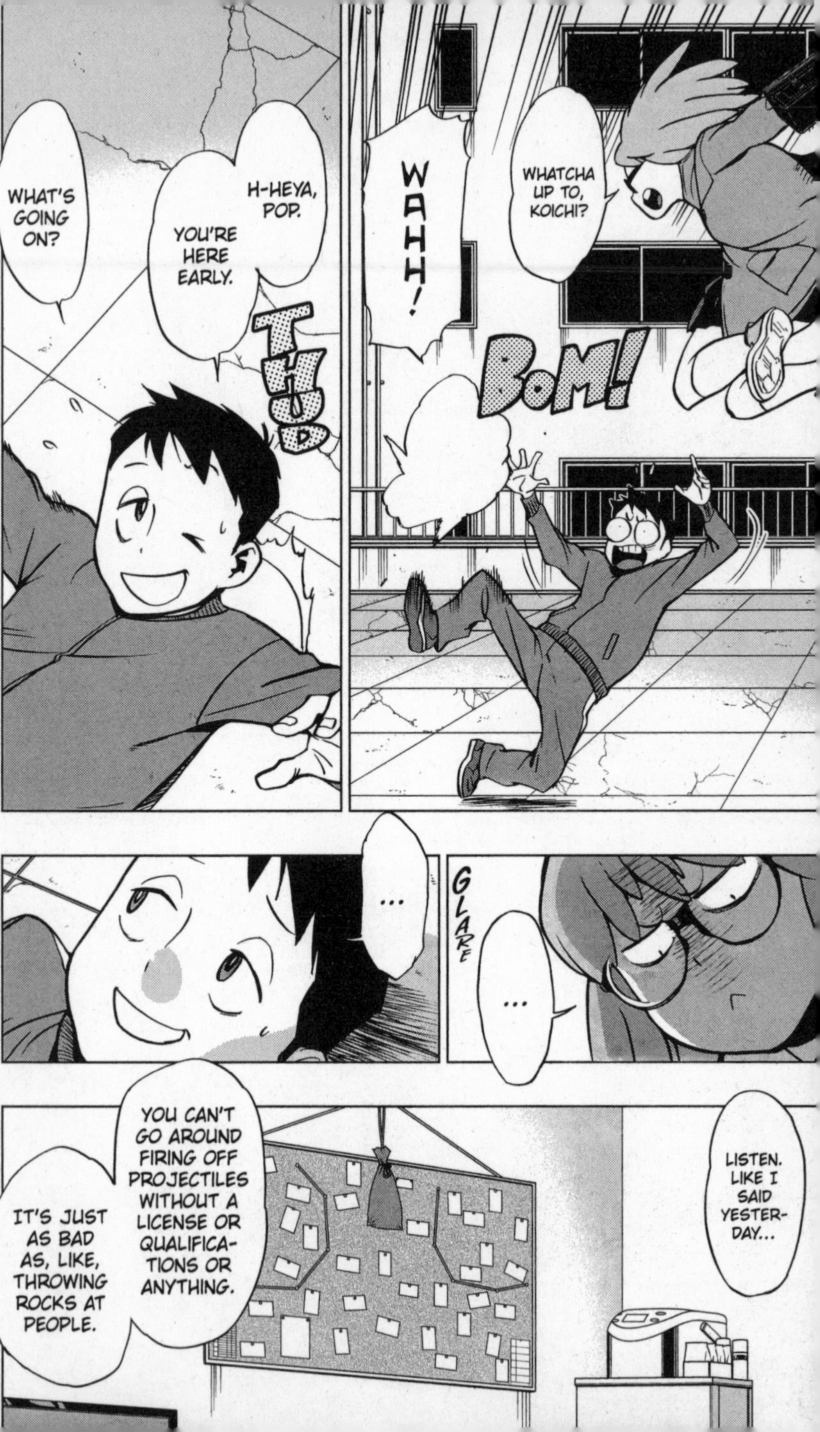
WHATCHA UP TO, KOICHI?
WAHH!
BOM!
H-HEYA, POP.
YOU'RE HERE EARLY.
THUD
WHAT'S GOING ON?
GLARE
...
...
LISTEN. LIKE I SAID YESTER-DAY...
YOU CAN'T GO AROUND FIRING OFF PROJECTILES WITHOUT A LICENSE OR QUALIFICA-TIONS OR ANYTHING.
IT'S JUST AS BAD AS, LIKE, THROWING ROCKS AT PEOPLE.

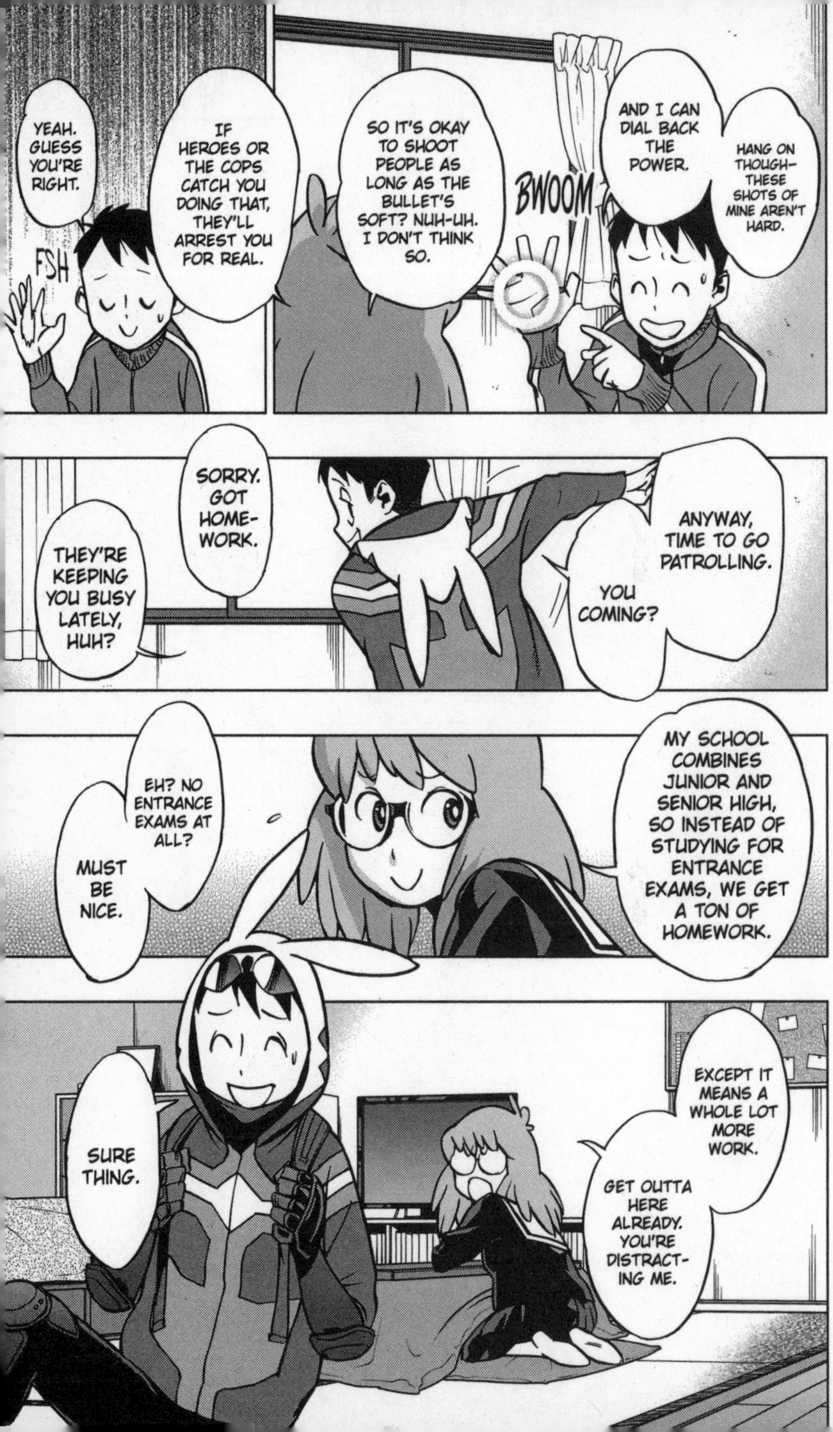
HANG ON THOUGH— THESE SHOTS OF MINE AREN'T HARD.
AND I CAN DIAL BACK THE POWER.
BWOOM
SO IT'S OKAY TO SHOOT PEOPLE AS LONG AS THE BULLET'S SOFT? NUH-UH. I DON'T THINK SO.
IF HEROES OR THE COPS CATCH YOU DOING THAT, THEY'LL ARREST YOU FOR REAL.
YEAH. GUESS YOU'RE RIGHT.
FSH
ANYWAY, TIME TO GO PATROLLING.
YOU COMING?
SORRY. GOT HOME-WORK.
THEY'RE KEEPING YOU BUSY LATELY, HUH?
MY SCHOOL COMBINES JUNIOR AND SENIOR HIGH, SO INSTEAD OF STUDYING FOR ENTRANCE EXAMS, WE GET A TON OF HOMEWORK.
EH? NO ENTRANCE EXAMS AT ALL?
MUST BE NICE.
EXCEPT IT MEANS A WHOLE LOT MORE WORK.
GET OUTTA HERE ALREADY. YOU'RE DISTRACT-ING ME.
SURE THING.

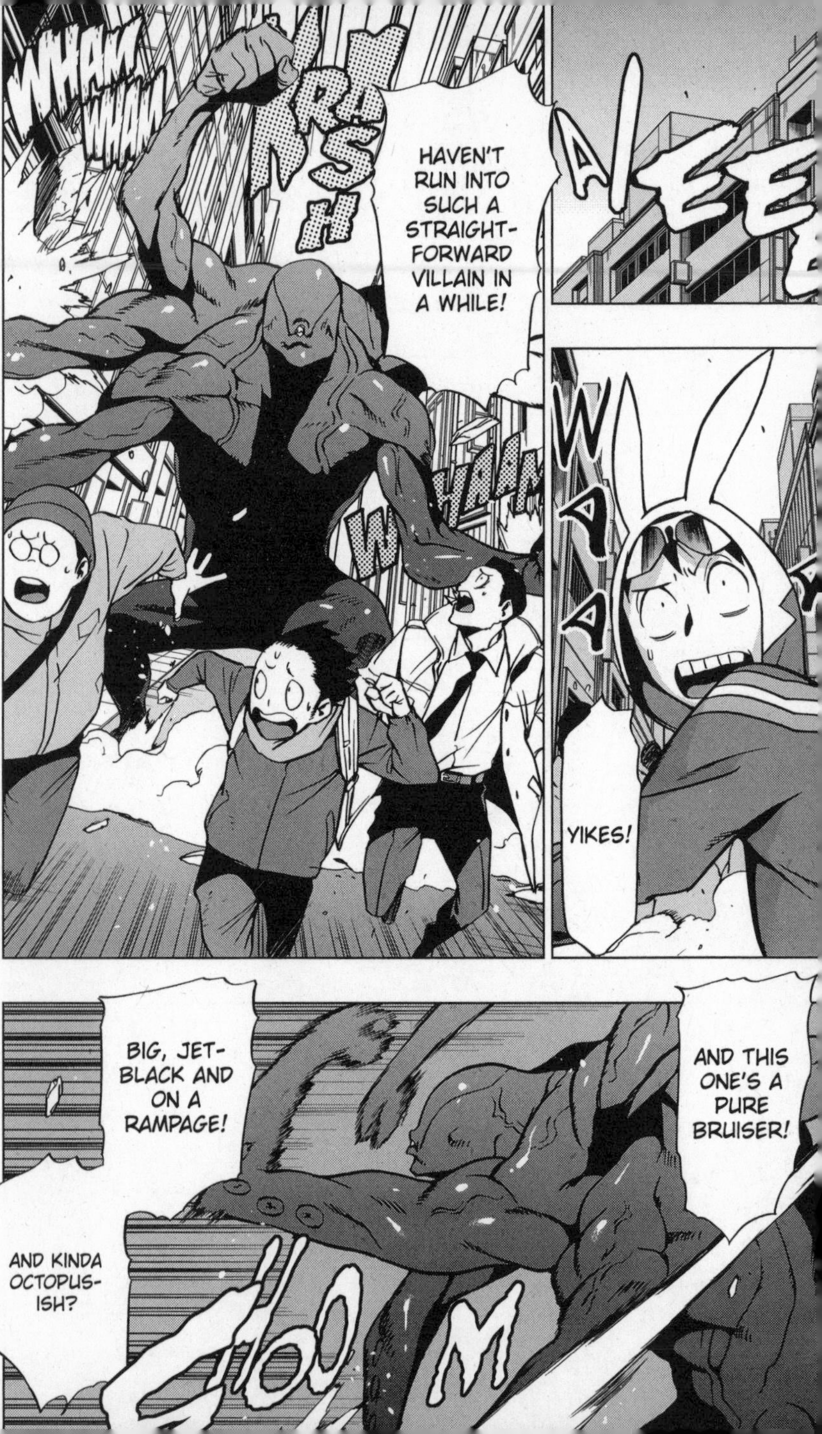
AIEE
WAAA
YIKES!
WHAM WHAM
KRASH
HAVEN'T RUN INTO SUCH A STRAIGHT-FORWARD VILLAIN IN A WHILE!
WHAM
AND THIS ONE'S A PURE BRUISER!
BIG, JET-BLACK AND ON A RAMPAGE!
AND KINDA OCTOPUS-ISH?
DOOM

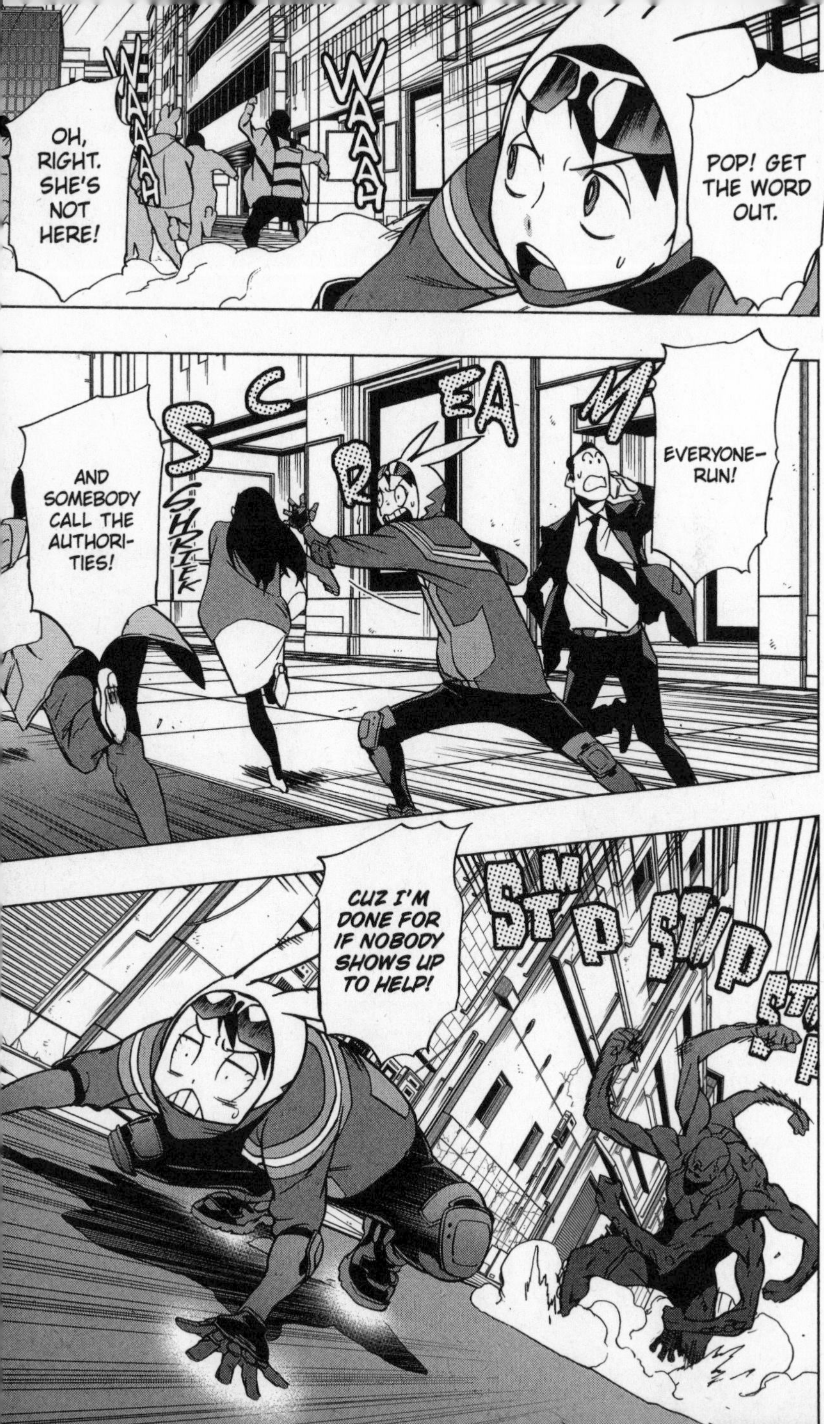
POP! GET THE WORD OUT.
WAAAH
WAAAH
OH, RIGHT. SHE'S NOT HERE!
EVERYONE–RUN!
SCREAM
SHRIEK
AND SOMEBODY CALL THE AUTHORITIES!
STMP STMP
CUZ I'M DONE FOR IF NOBODY SHOWS UP TO HELP!

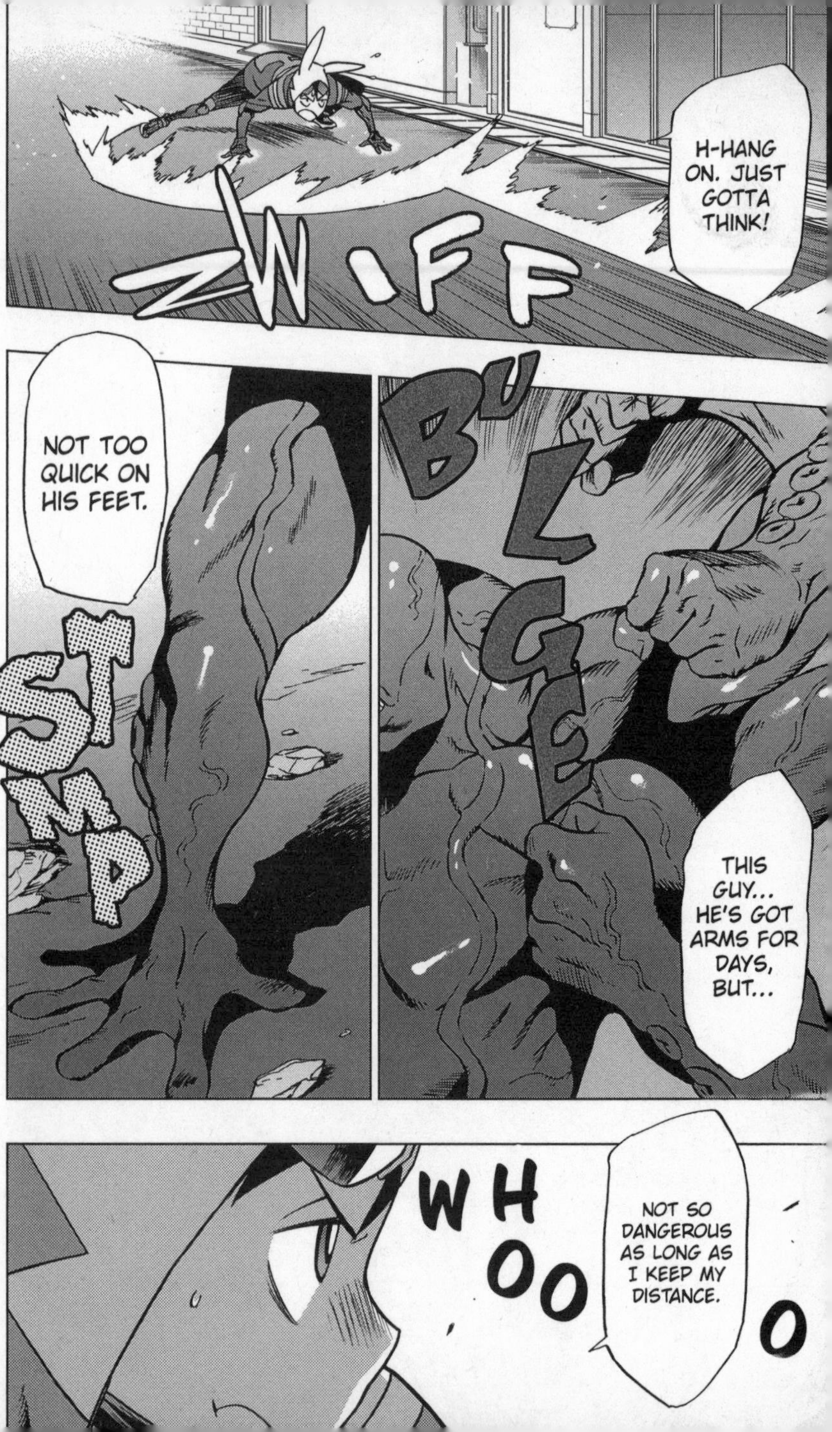
H-HANG ON. JUST GOTTA THINK!
ZWIFF
BULGE
THIS GUY... HE'S GOT ARMS FOR DAYS, BUT...
NOT TOO QUICK ON HIS FEET.
STMP
NOT SO DANGEROUS AS LONG AS I KEEP MY DISTANCE.
WHOOO

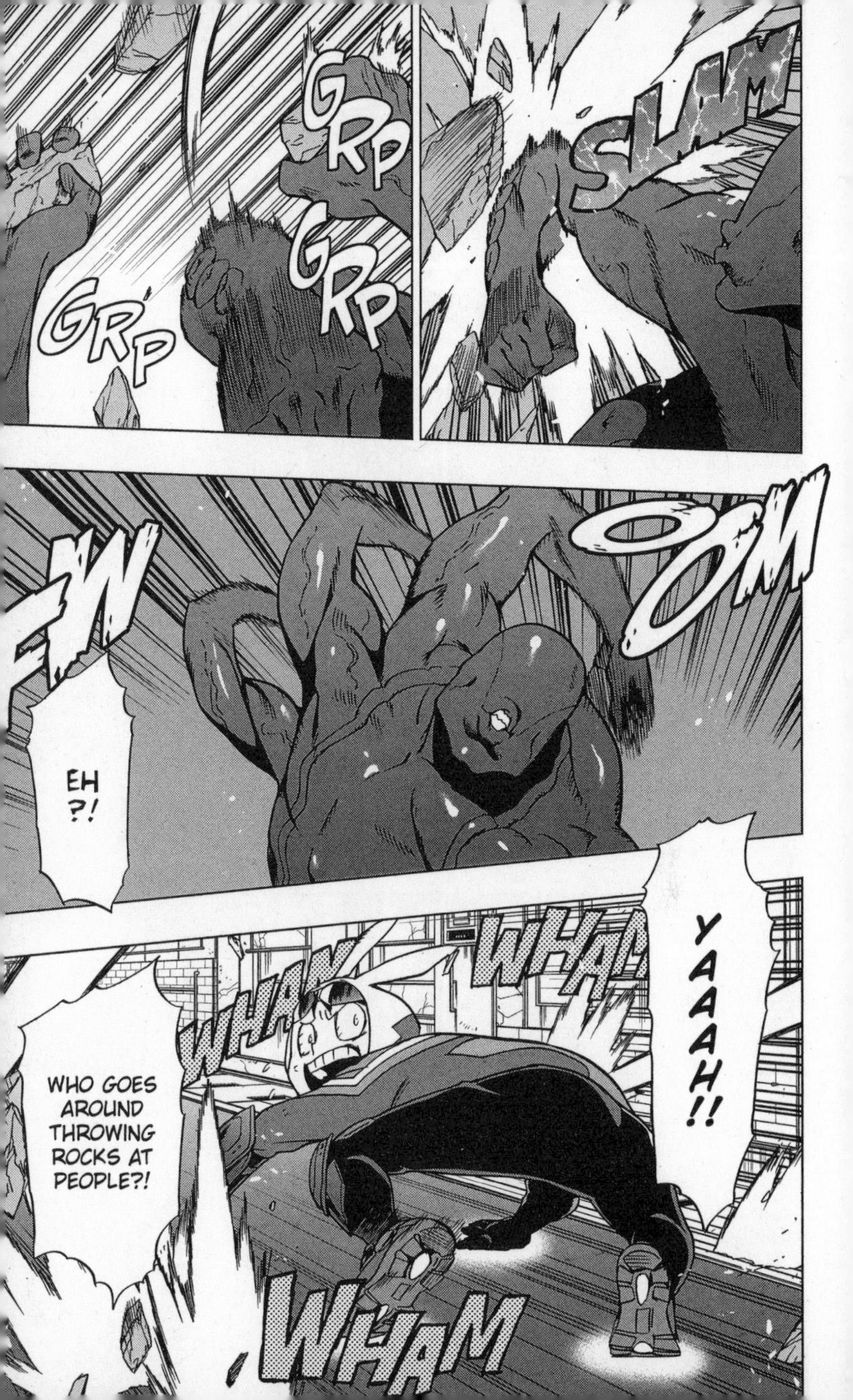
SLAM
GRP
GRP
GRP
FWOOM
EH?!
YAAAAH!!
WHAM
WHAK
WHO GOES AROUND THROWING ROCKS AT PEOPLE?!
WHAM

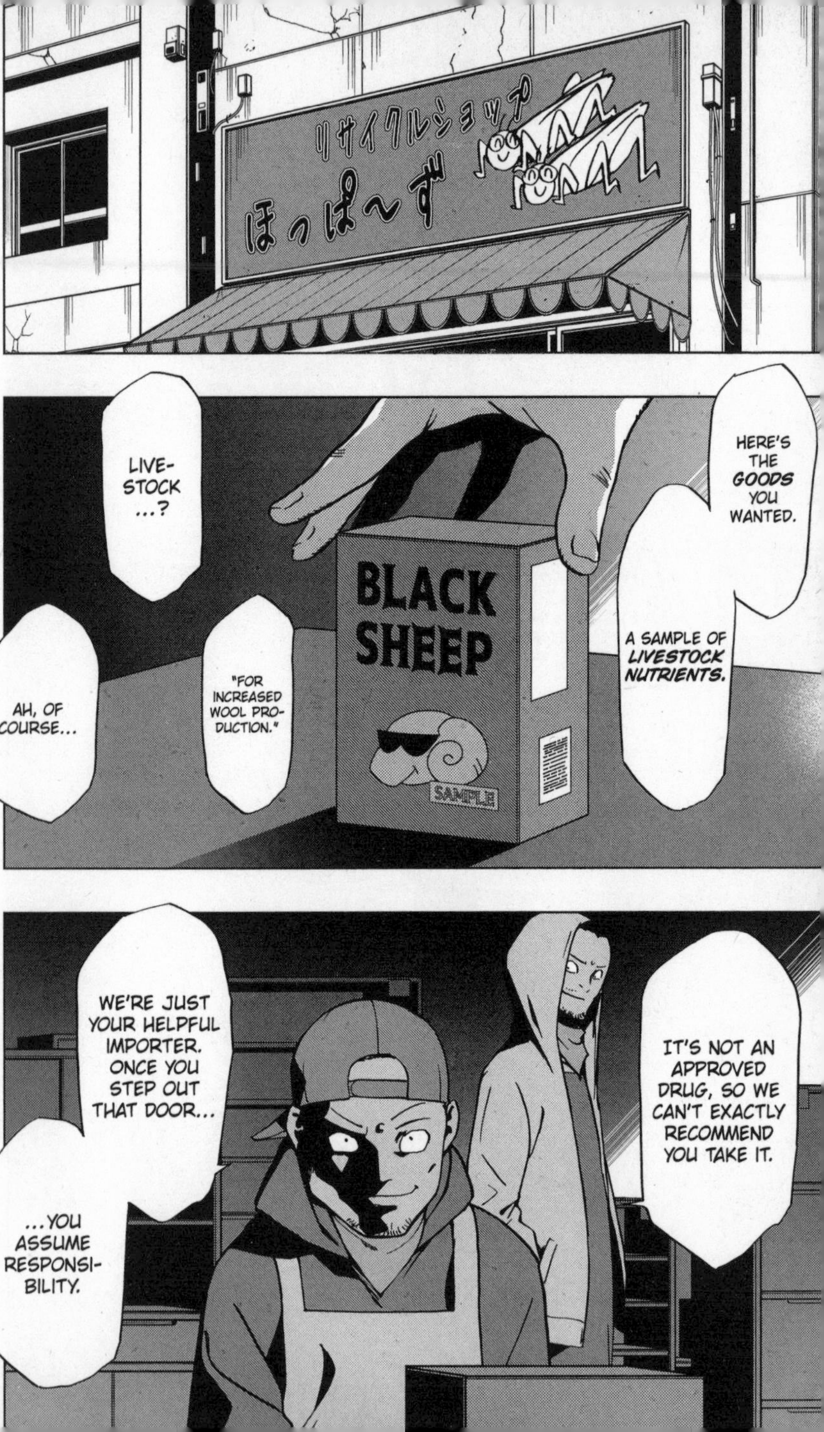
リサイクルショップ
ほっぱ〜ず
HERE'S THE GOODS YOU WANTED.
A SAMPLE OF LIVESTOCK NUTRIENTS.
BLACK SHEEP
SAMPLE
LIVE-STOCK ...?
"FOR INCREASED WOOL PRO-DUCTION."
AH, OF COURSE...
IT'S NOT AN APPROVED DRUG, SO WE CAN'T EXACTLY RECOMMEND YOU TAKE IT.
WE'RE JUST YOUR HELPFUL IMPORTER. ONCE YOU STEP OUT THAT DOOR...
...YOU ASSUME RESPONSI-BILITY.

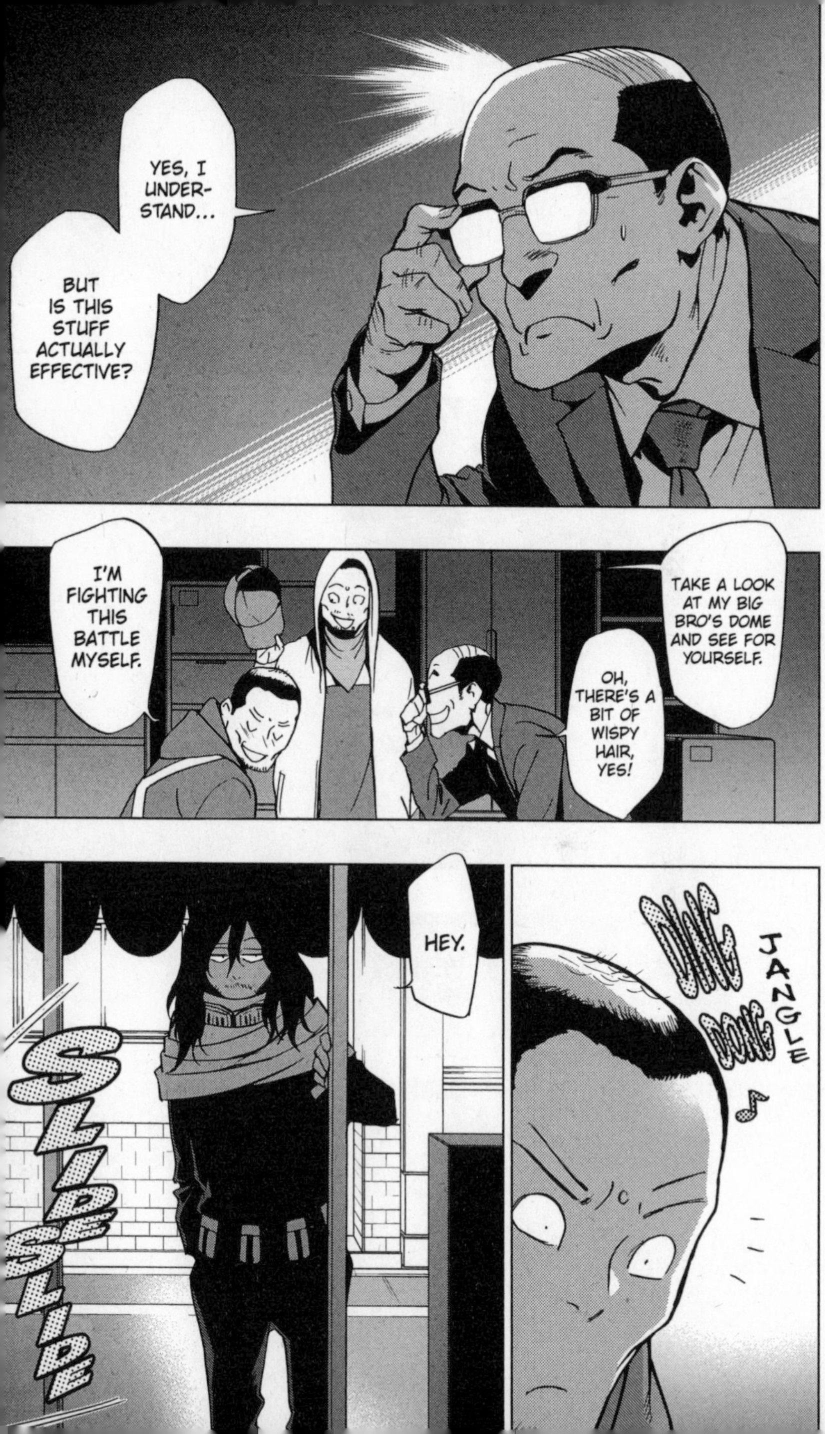
YES, I UNDERSTAND...
BUT IS THIS STUFF ACTUALLY EFFECTIVE?
TAKE A LOOK AT MY BIG BRO'S DOME AND SEE FOR YOURSELF.
OH, THERE'S A BIT OF WISPY HAIR, YES!
I'M FIGHTING THIS BATTLE MYSELF.
DING
DONG
JANGLE
HEY.
SLIDE SLIDE

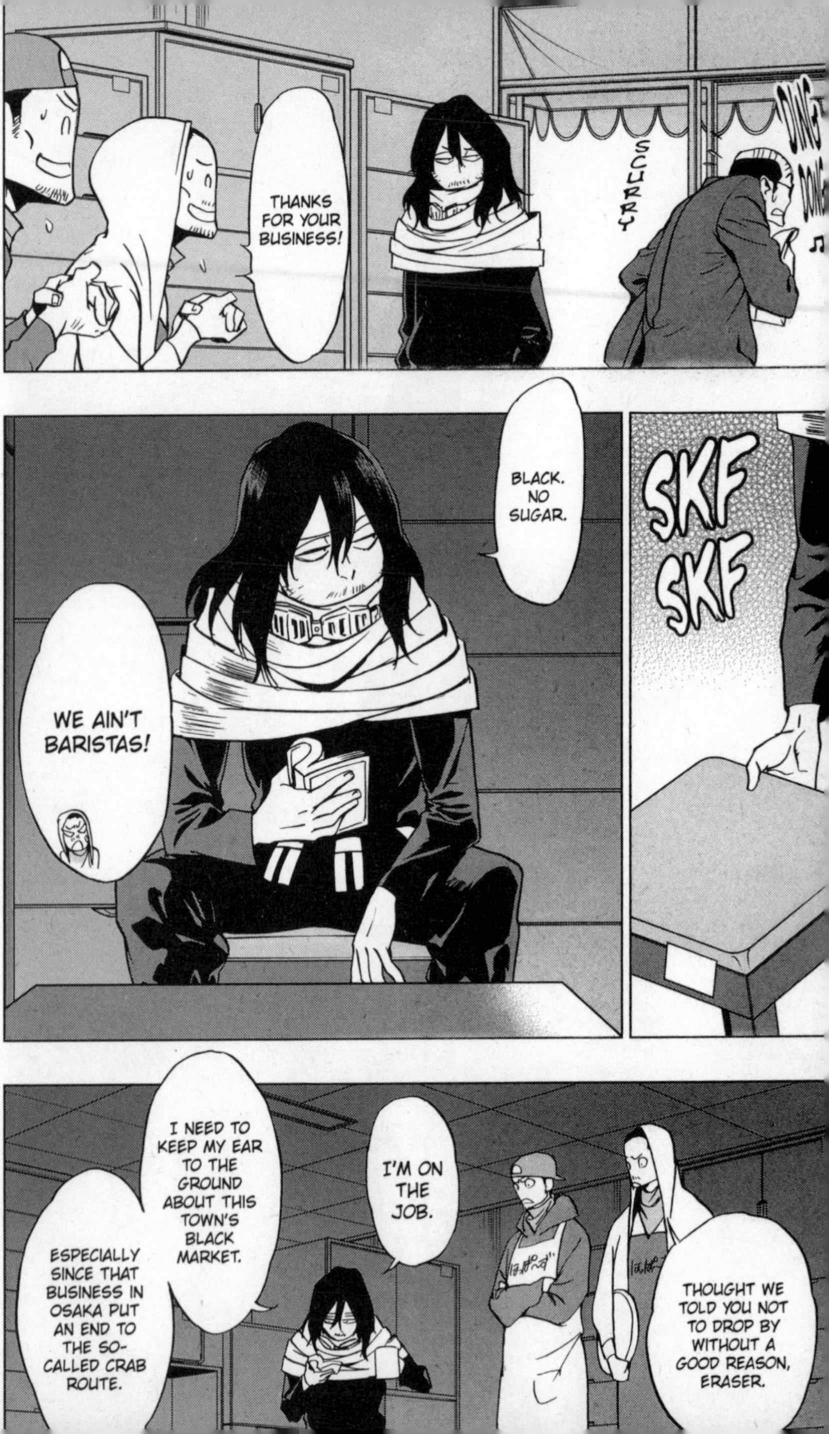
DING DONG
SCURRY
THANKS FOR YOUR BUSINESS!
SKF SKF
BLACK. NO SUGAR.
WE AIN'T BARISTAS!
THOUGHT WE TOLD YOU NOT TO DROP BY WITHOUT A GOOD REASON, ERASER.
I'M ON THE JOB.
I NEED TO KEEP MY EAR TO THE GROUND ABOUT THIS TOWN'S BLACK MARKET.
ESPECIALLY SINCE THAT BUSINESS IN OSAKA PUT AN END TO THE SO-CALLED CRAB ROUTE.

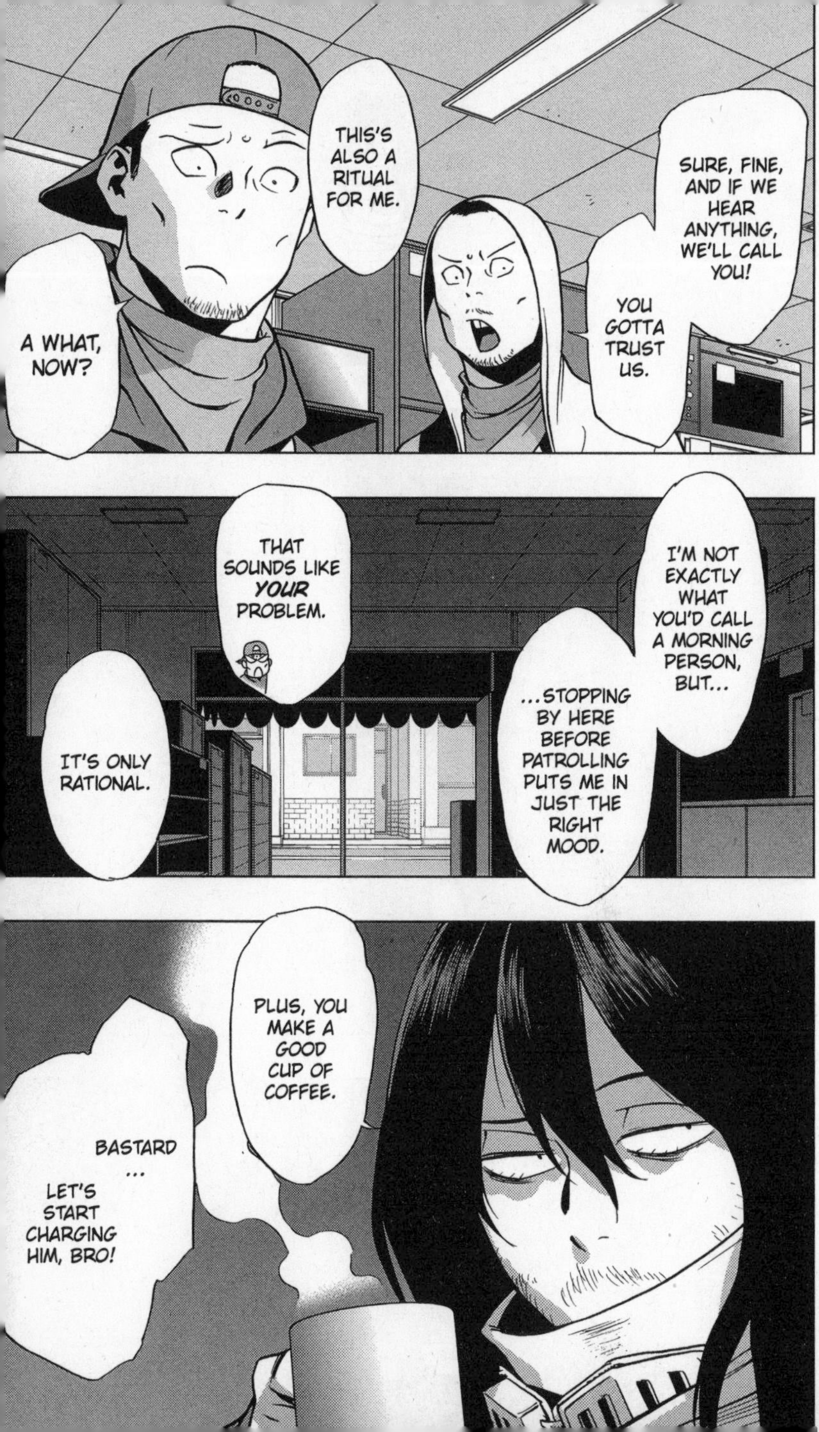
SURE, FINE, AND IF WE HEAR ANYTHING, WE'LL CALL YOU!
YOU GOTTA TRUST US.
THIS'S ALSO A RITUAL FOR ME.
A WHAT, NOW?
I'M NOT EXACTLY WHAT YOU'D CALL A MORNING PERSON, BUT...
...STOPPING BY HERE BEFORE PATROLLING PUTS ME IN JUST THE RIGHT MOOD.
THAT SOUNDS LIKE *YOUR* PROBLEM.
IT'S ONLY RATIONAL.
PLUS, YOU MAKE A GOOD CUP OF COFFEE.
BASTARD...
LET'S START CHARGING HIM, BRO!

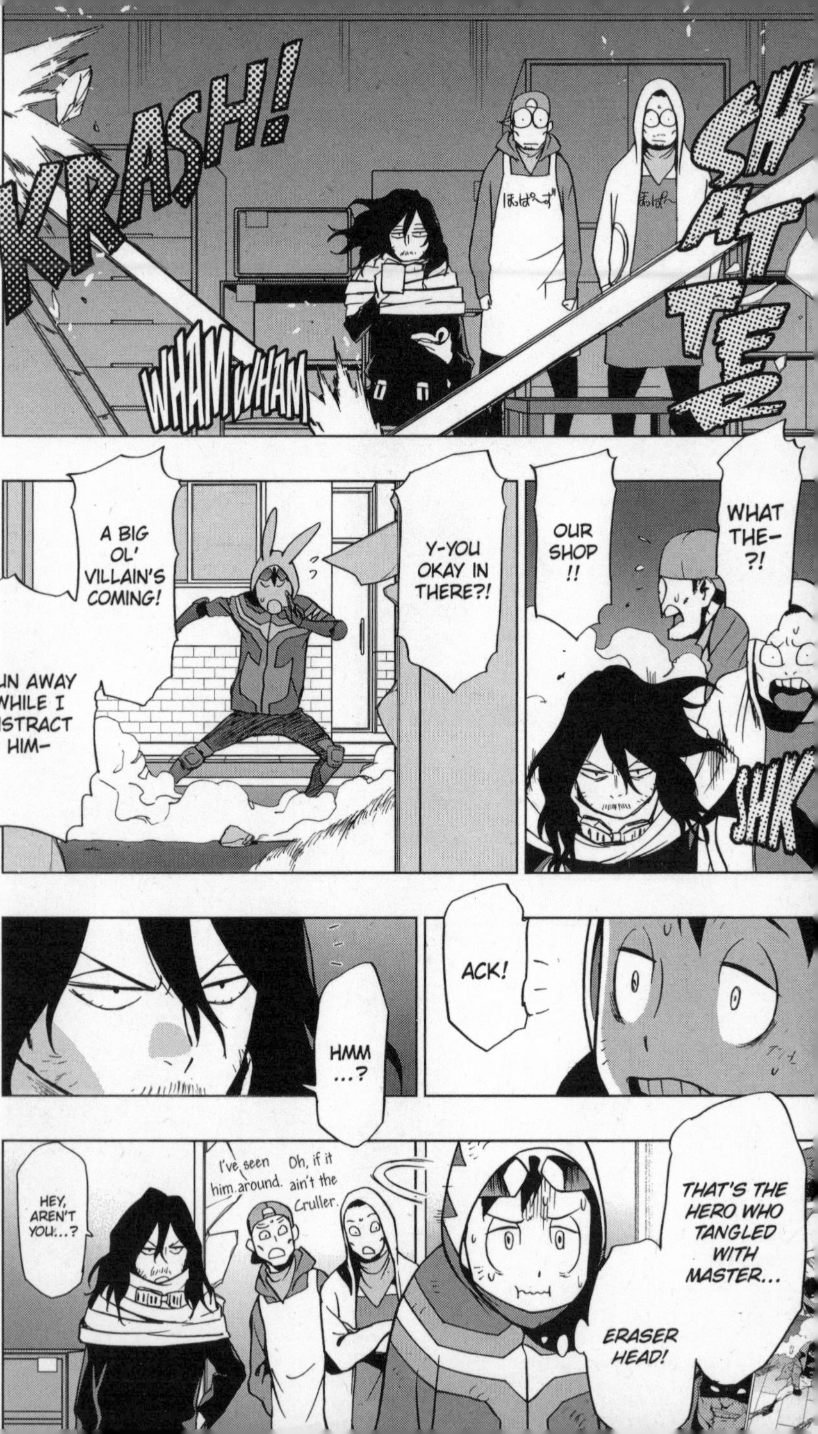
SHATTER
KRASH!
WHAM WHAM
WHAT THE-?!
OUR SHOP!!
SHK
Y-YOU OKAY IN THERE?!
A BIG OL' VILLAIN'S COMING!
RUN AWAY WHILE I DISTRACT HIM-
ACK!
HMM...?
THAT'S THE HERO WHO TANGLED WITH MASTER...
ERASER HEAD!
Oh, if it ain't the Cruller.
I've seen him around.
HEY, AREN'T YOU...?

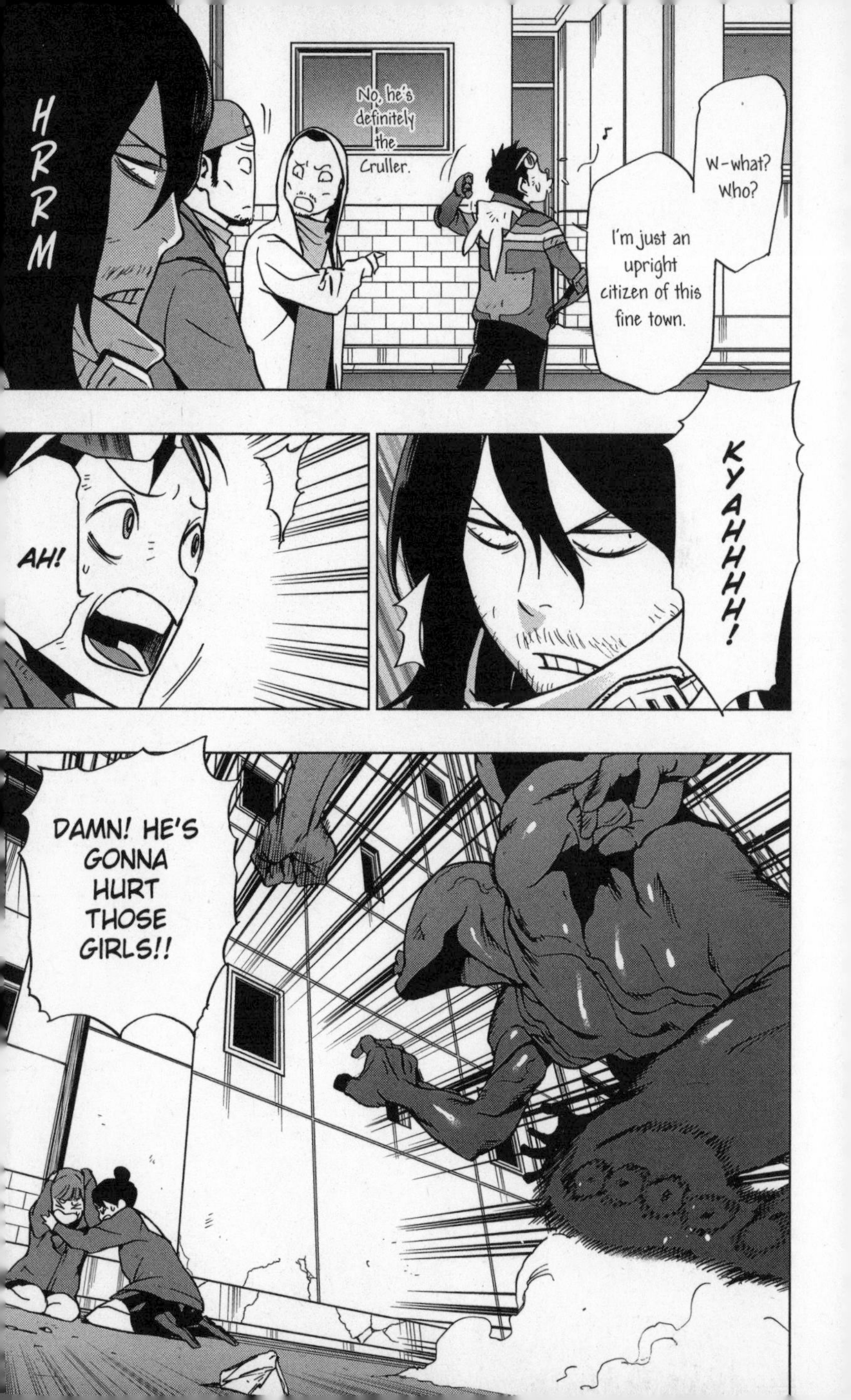
W-what? Who?
I'm just an upright citizen of this fine town.
No, he's definitely the Cruller.
HRRM
KYAHHHHH!
AH!
DAMN! HE'S GONNA HURT THOSE GIRLS!!

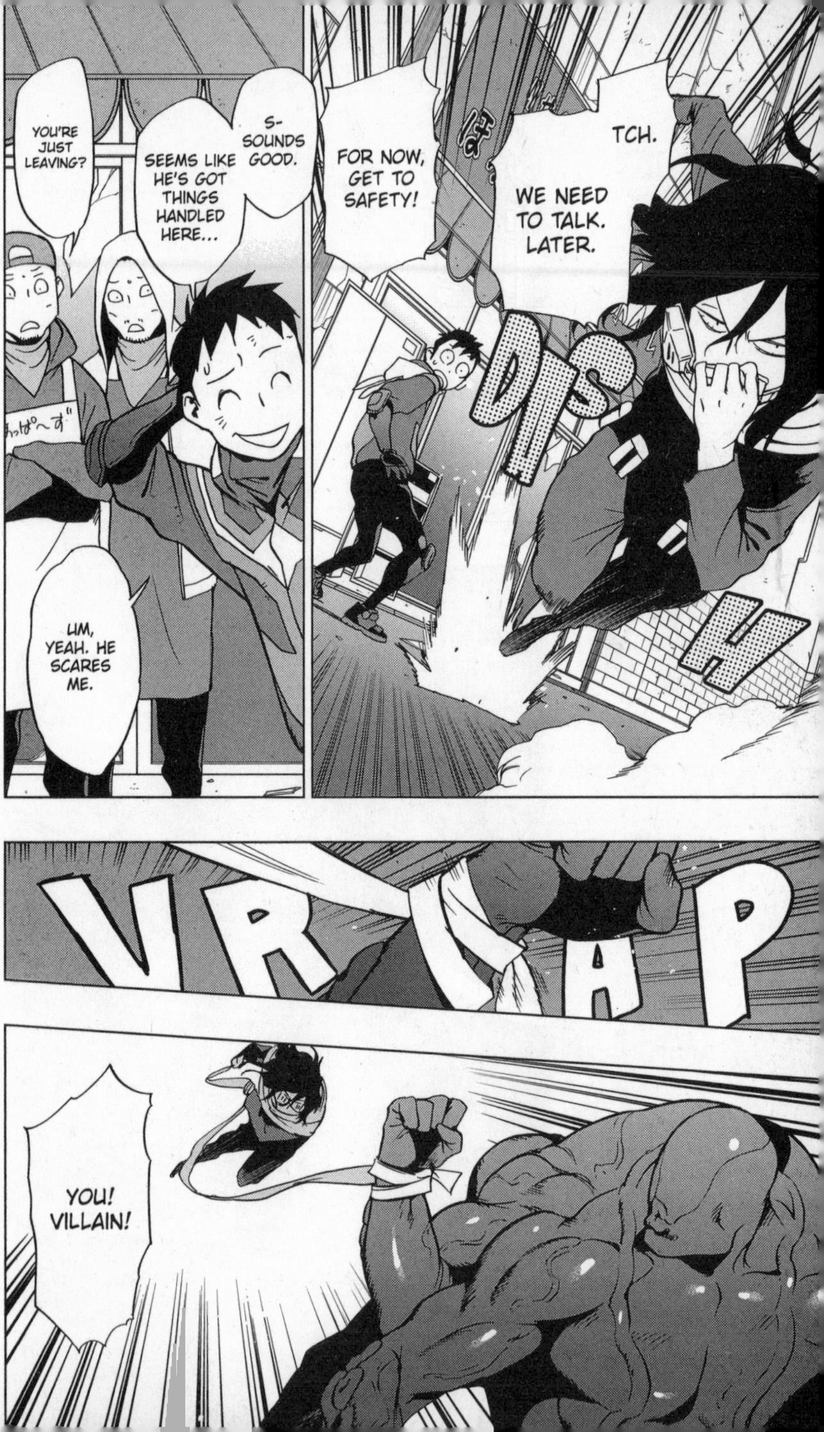
TCH.
WE NEED TO TALK. LATER.
FOR NOW, GET TO SAFETY!
DTSH
S-SOUNDS GOOD.
SEEMS LIKE HE'S GOT THINGS HANDLED HERE...
YOU'RE JUST LEAVING?
UM, YEAH. HE SCARES ME.
VRAP
YOU! VILLAIN!

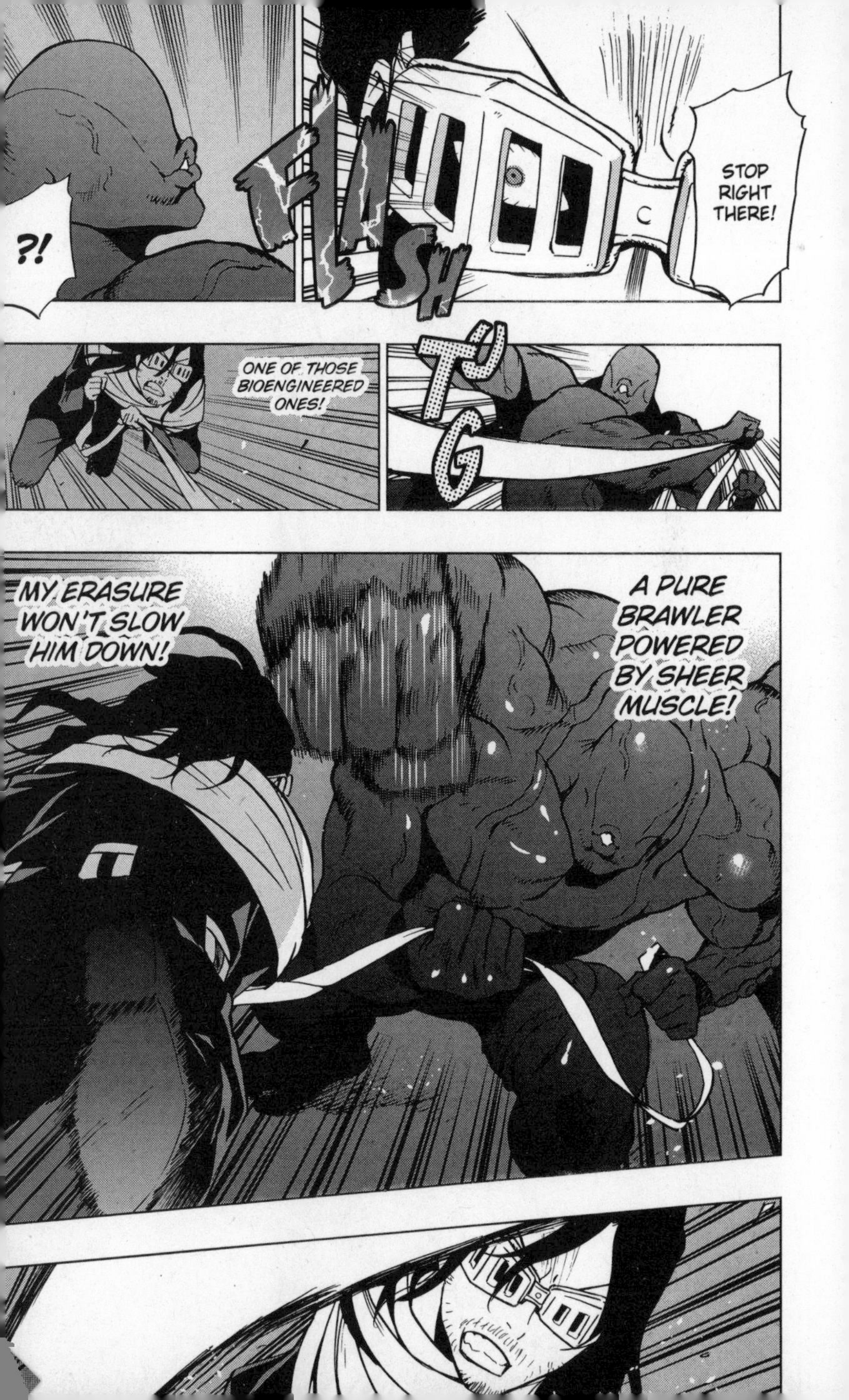
FLASH
STOP RIGHT THERE!
?!
TUG
ONE OF THOSE BIOENGINEERED ONES!
A PURE BRAWLER POWERED BY SHEER MUSCLE!
MY ERASURE WON'T SLOW HIM DOWN!

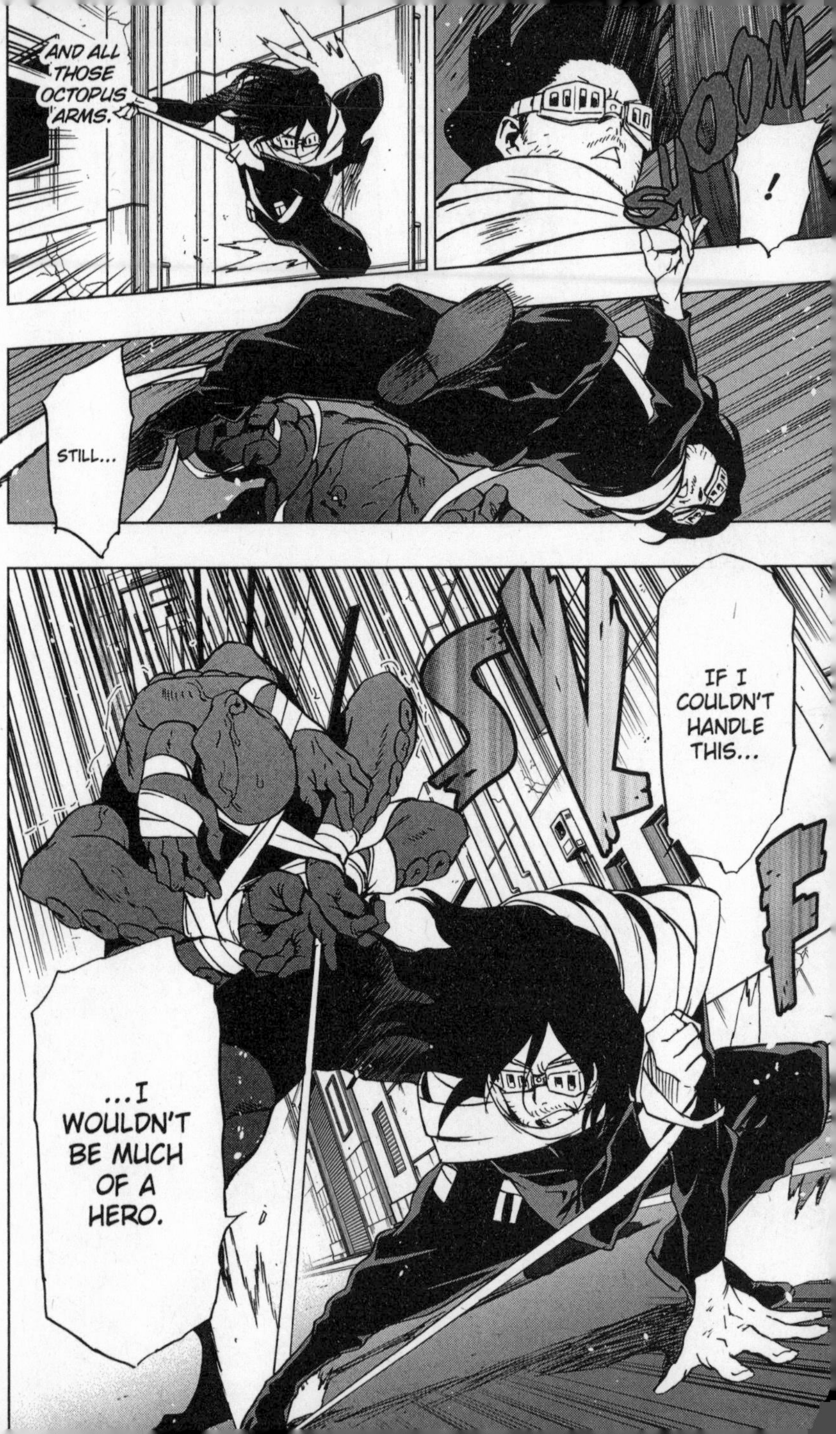
SHOOM
!
AND ALL THOSE OCTOPUS ARMS.
STILL...
IF I COULDN'T HANDLE THIS...
...I WOULDN'T BE MUCH OF A HERO.

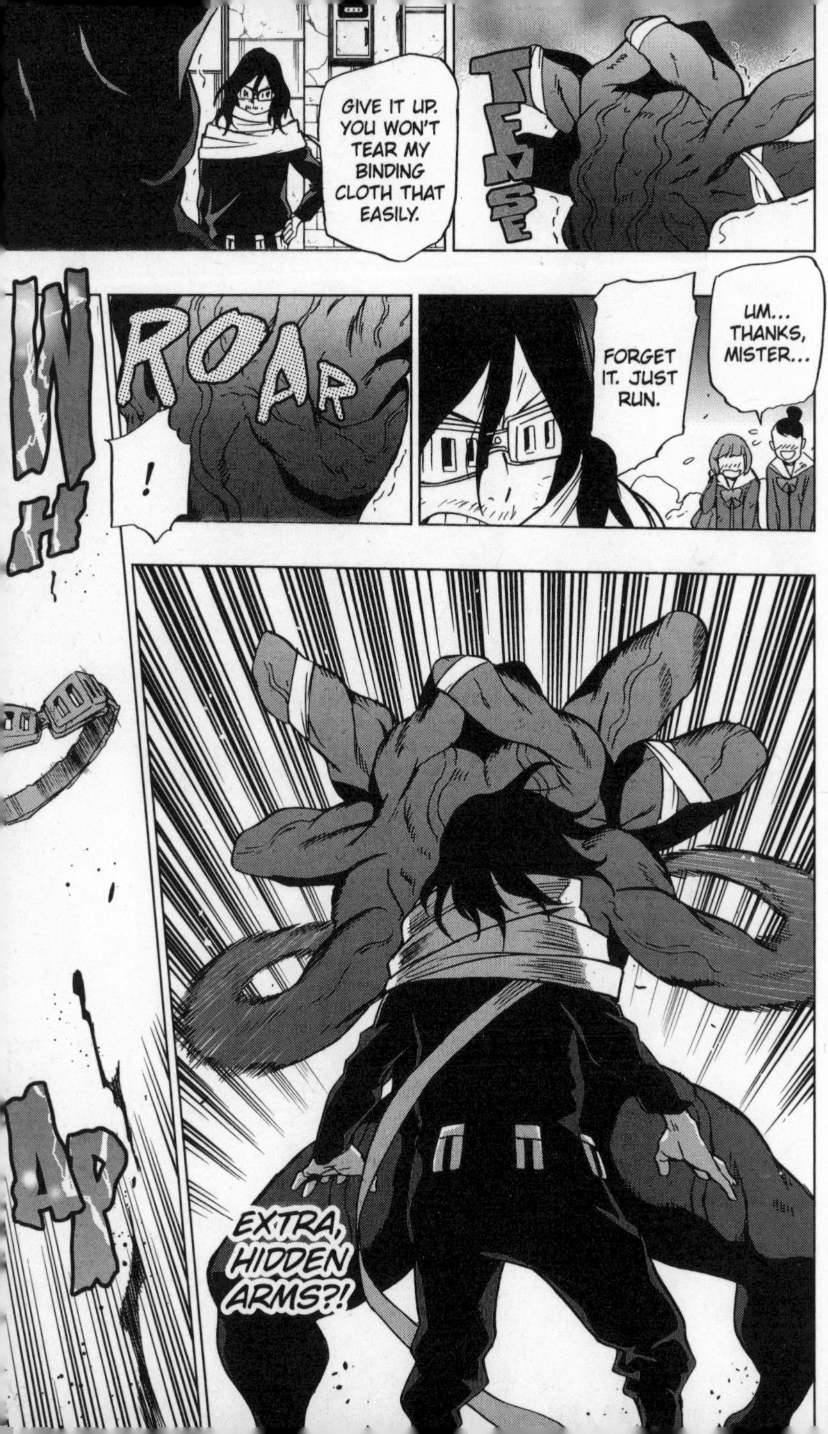
TENSE
GIVE IT UP. YOU WON'T TEAR MY BINDING CLOTH THAT EASILY.
UM... THANKS, MISTER...
FORGET IT. JUST RUN.
ROAR
!
WH
AP
EXTRA, HIDDEN ARMS?!

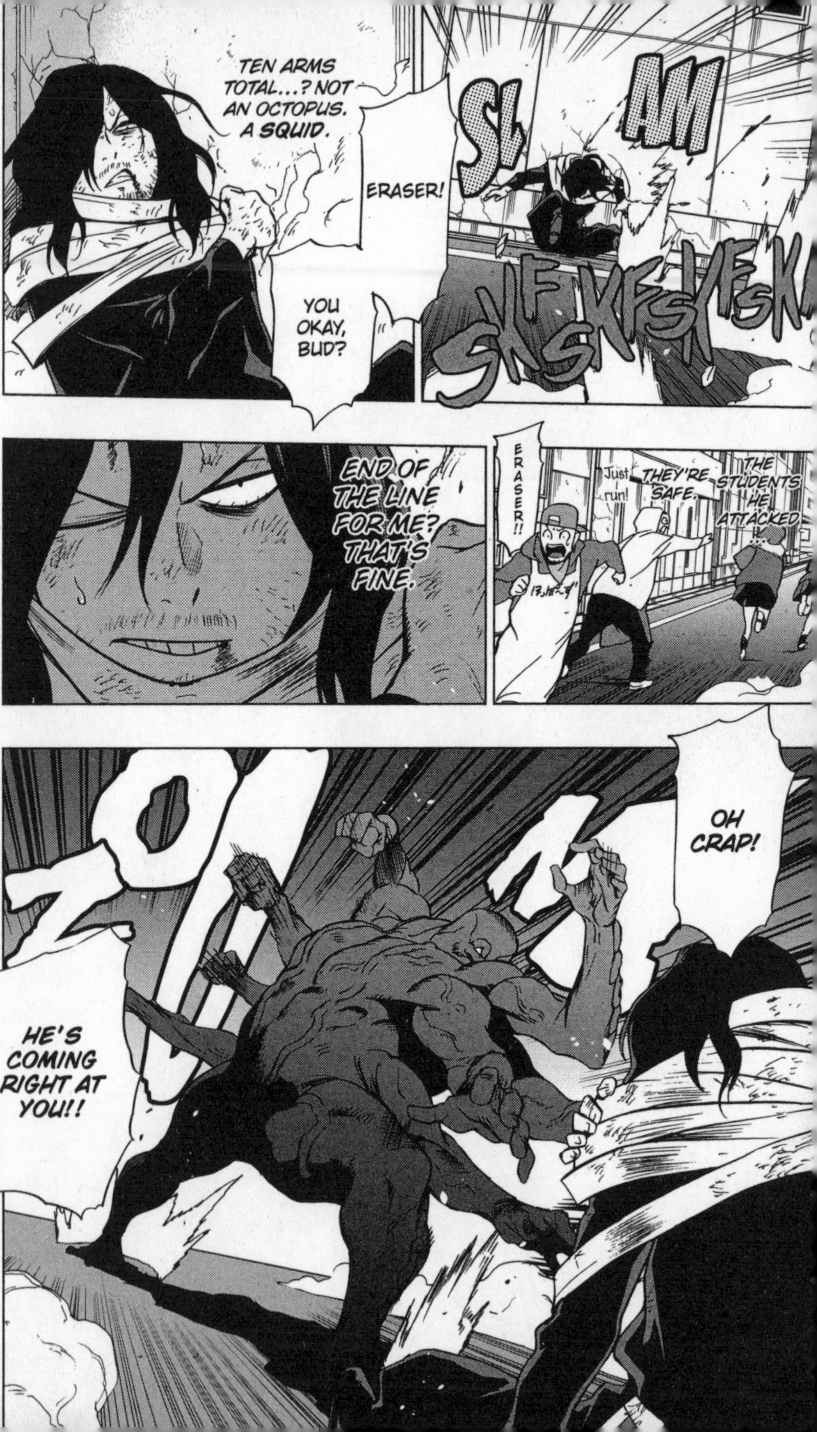
SLAM
ERASER!
YOU OKAY, BUD?
TEN ARMS TOTAL...? NOT AN OCTOPUS. A SQUID.
ERASER!!
THE STUDENTS HE ATTACKED...
THEY'RE SAFE.
Just run!
END OF THE LINE FOR ME? THAT'S FINE.
OH CRAP!
HE'S COMING RIGHT AT YOU!!

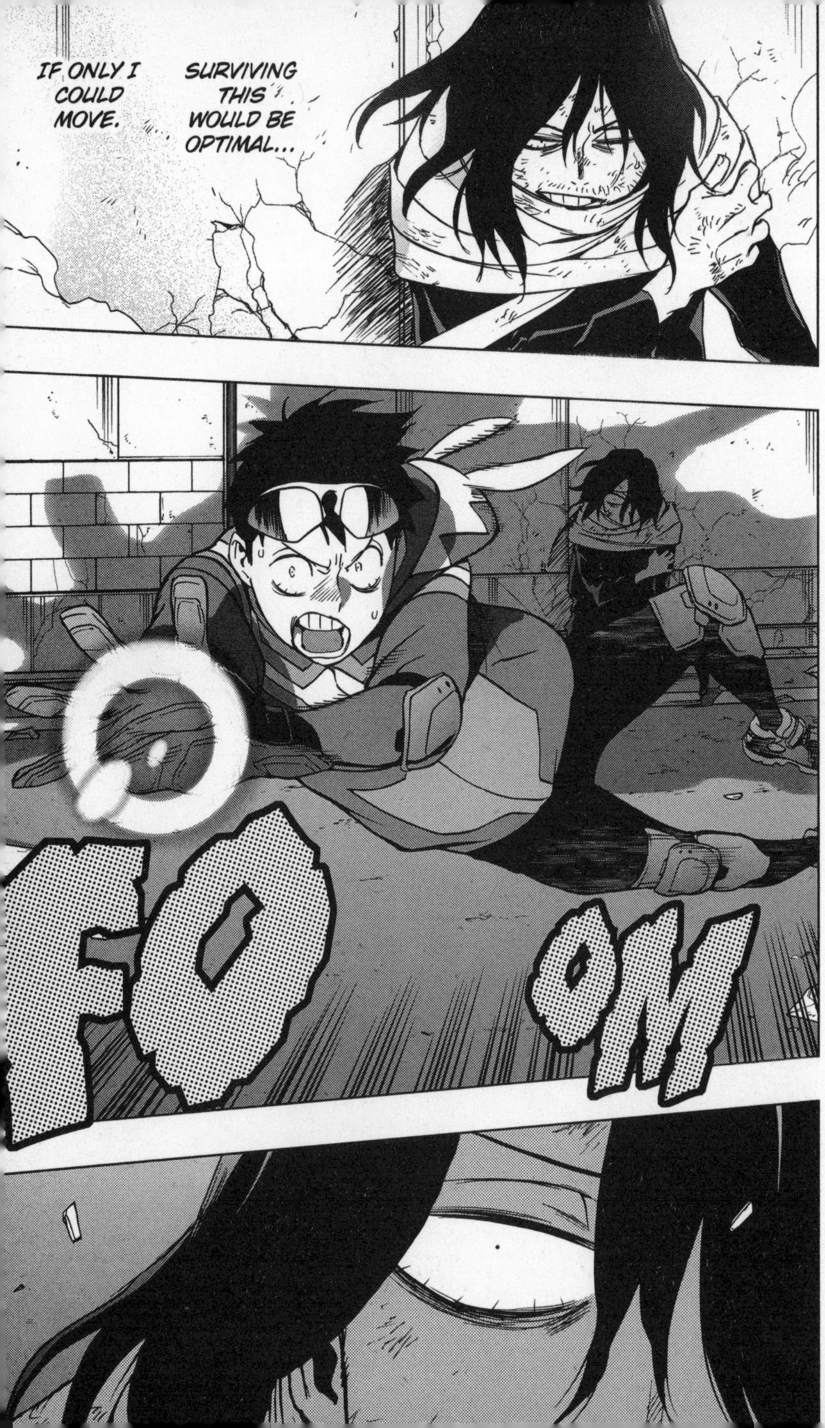
SURVIVING THIS WOULD BE OPTIMAL...
IF ONLY I COULD MOVE.
FOOM

OCTOPUS VILLAIN

THE ROUGH DESIGN

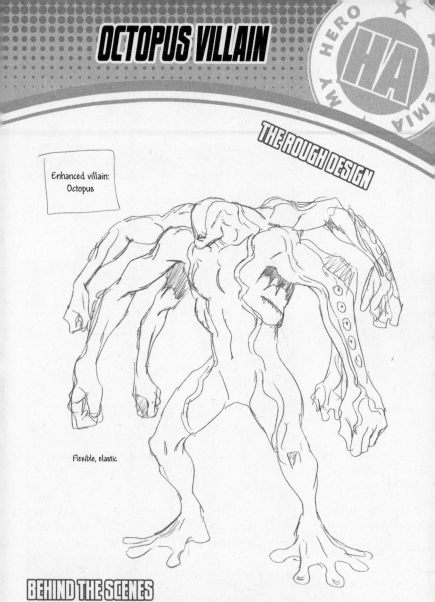

Enhanced villain:
Octopus

Flexible, elastic

BEHIND THE SCENES

Speed and power! I like how this guy feels like a simple, overwhelmingly powerful villain.
Every time I received art of him in action, I'd think, "Nice octopus! Octo!" Betten-san came up
with the idea to give him two hidden arms (meaning eight total, besides the legs), which meant
he'd be well matched against the scarred man's eight-hit combo.

   —Furuhashi

I know the whole "He's not an octopus—he's a squid!" gimmick is sort of corny, but it's
something I've been wanting to do, and I'm glad I got to do it.

   —Betten

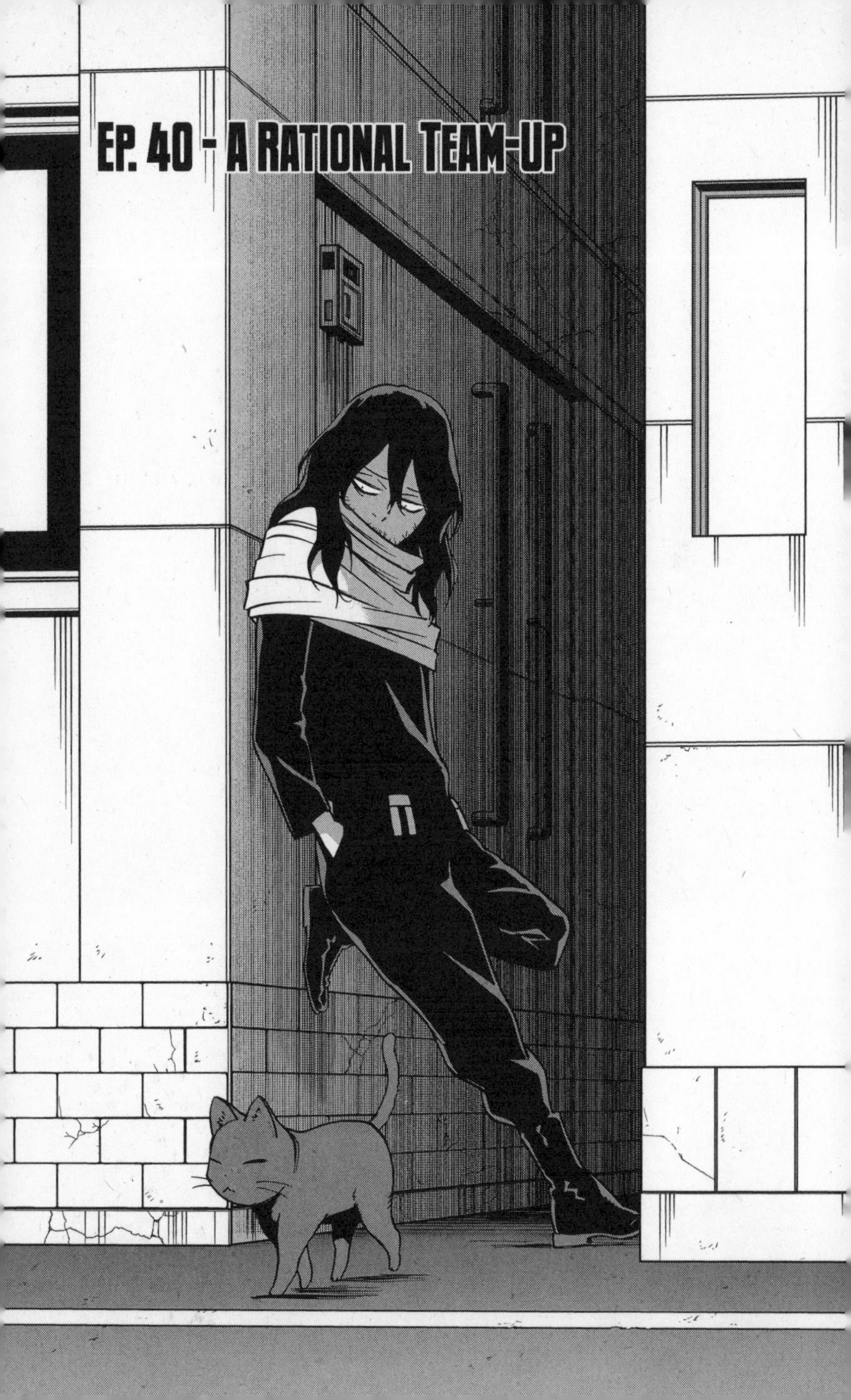
Ep. 40 - A Rational Team-Up

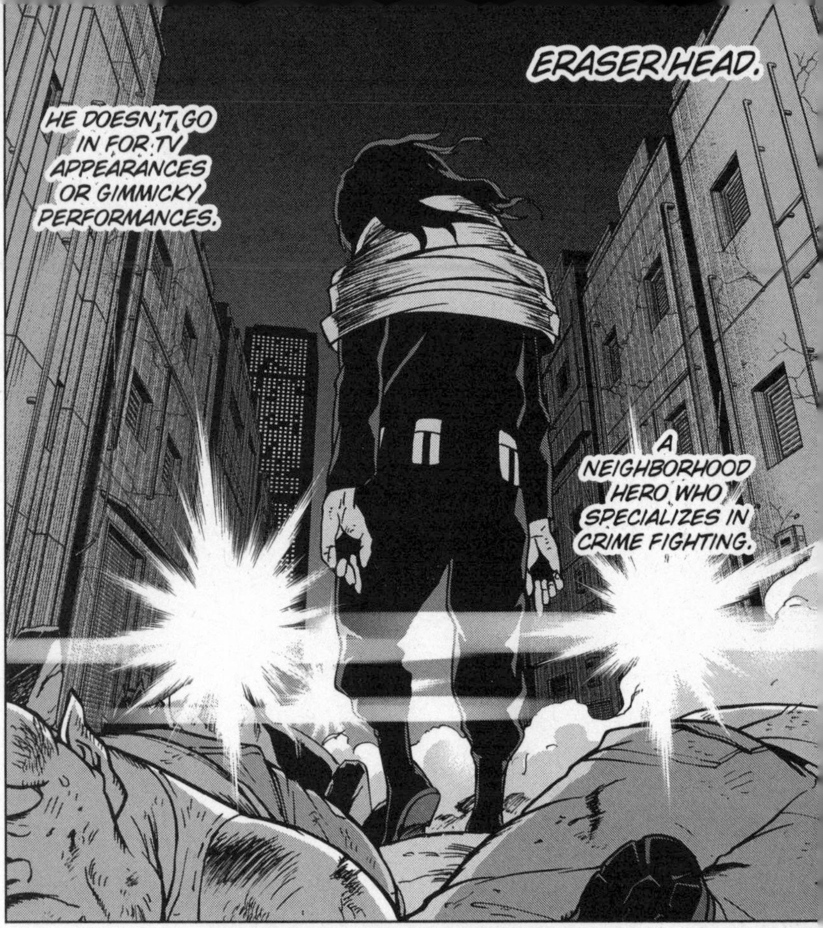
ERASER HEAD.
HE DOESN'T GO IN FOR TV APPEARANCES OR GIMMICKY PERFORMANCES.
A NEIGHBORHOOD HERO WHO SPECIALIZES IN CRIME FIGHTING.

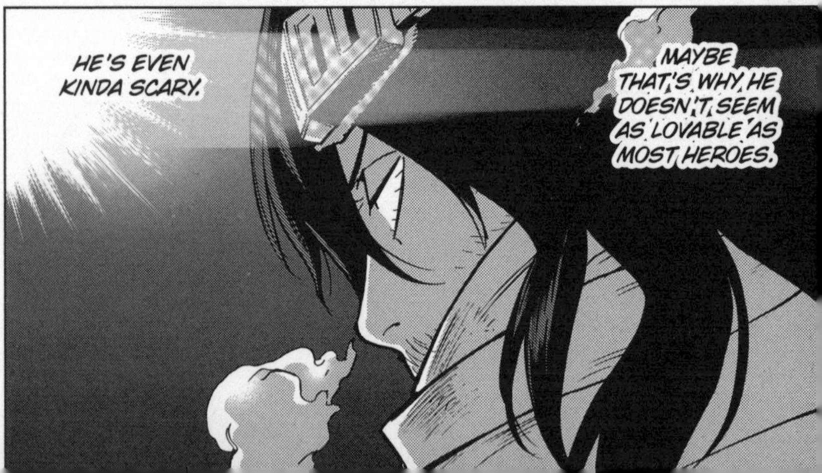
MAYBE THAT'S WHY HE DOESN'T SEEM AS LOVABLE AS MOST HEROES.
HE'S EVEN KINDA SCARY.

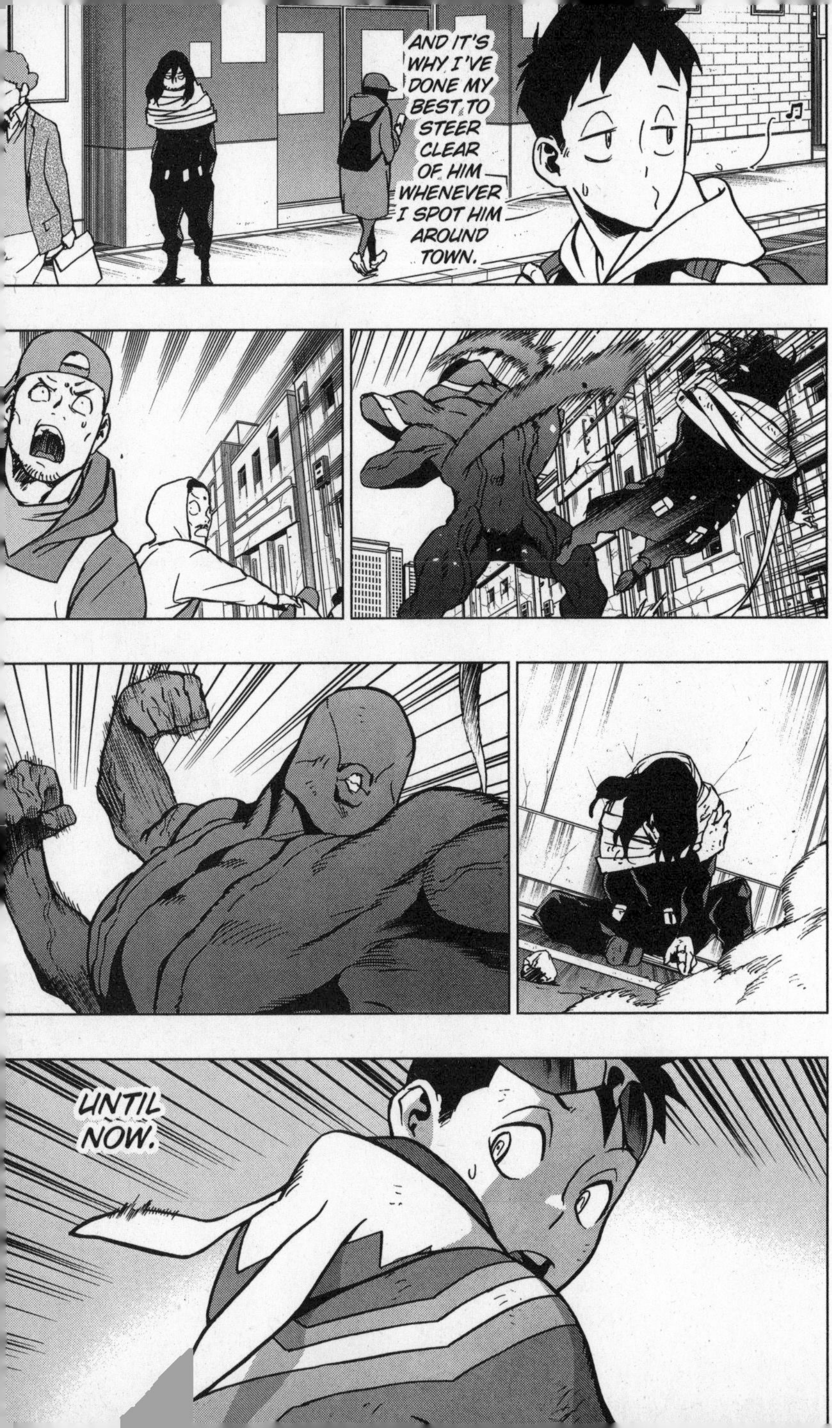
AND IT'S WHY I'VE DONE MY BEST TO STEER CLEAR OF HIM WHENEVER I SPOT HIM AROUND TOWN.
UNTIL NOW.

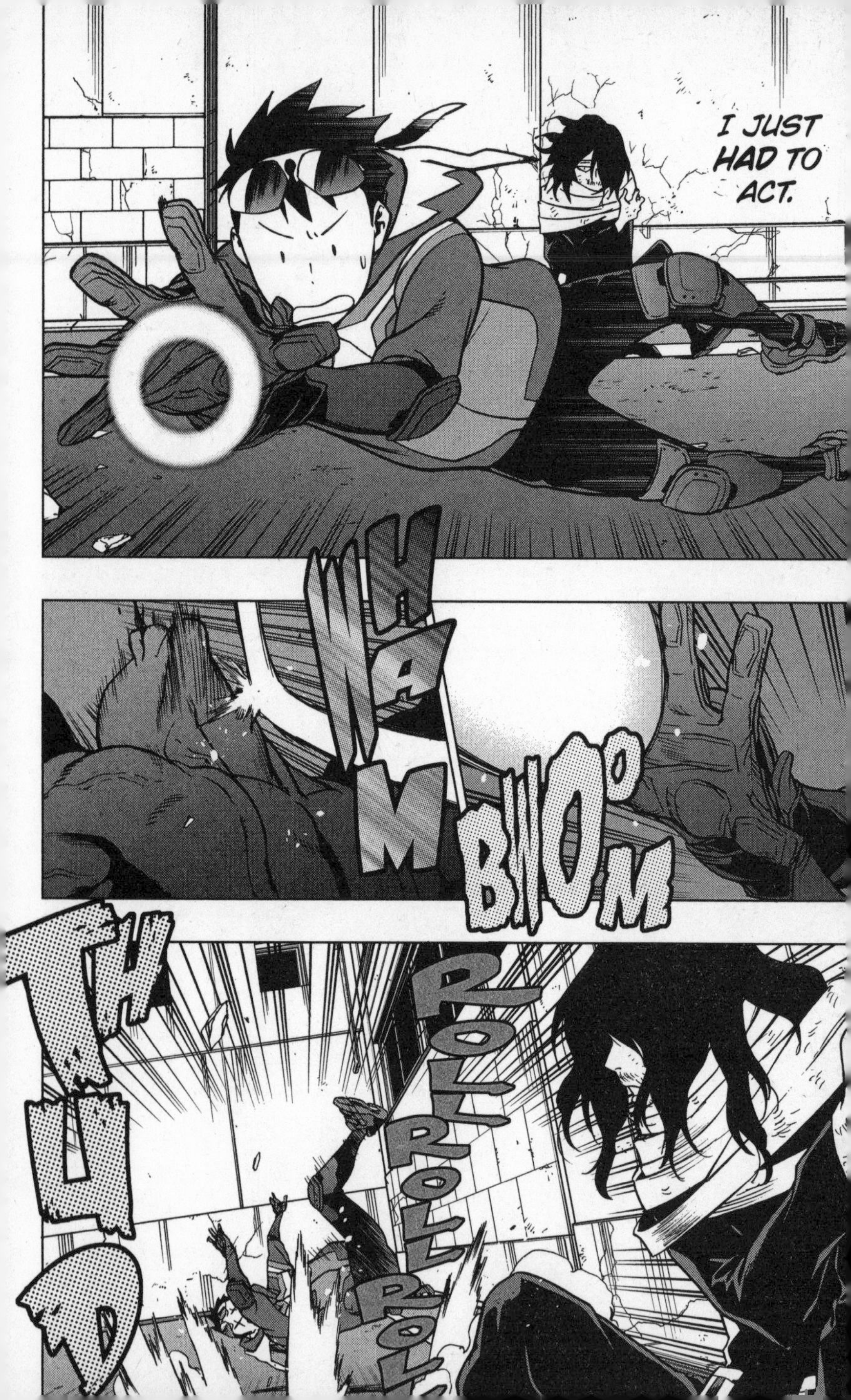
I JUST HAD TO ACT.
WHAM
BOOM
ROLL ROLL ROL
THUD

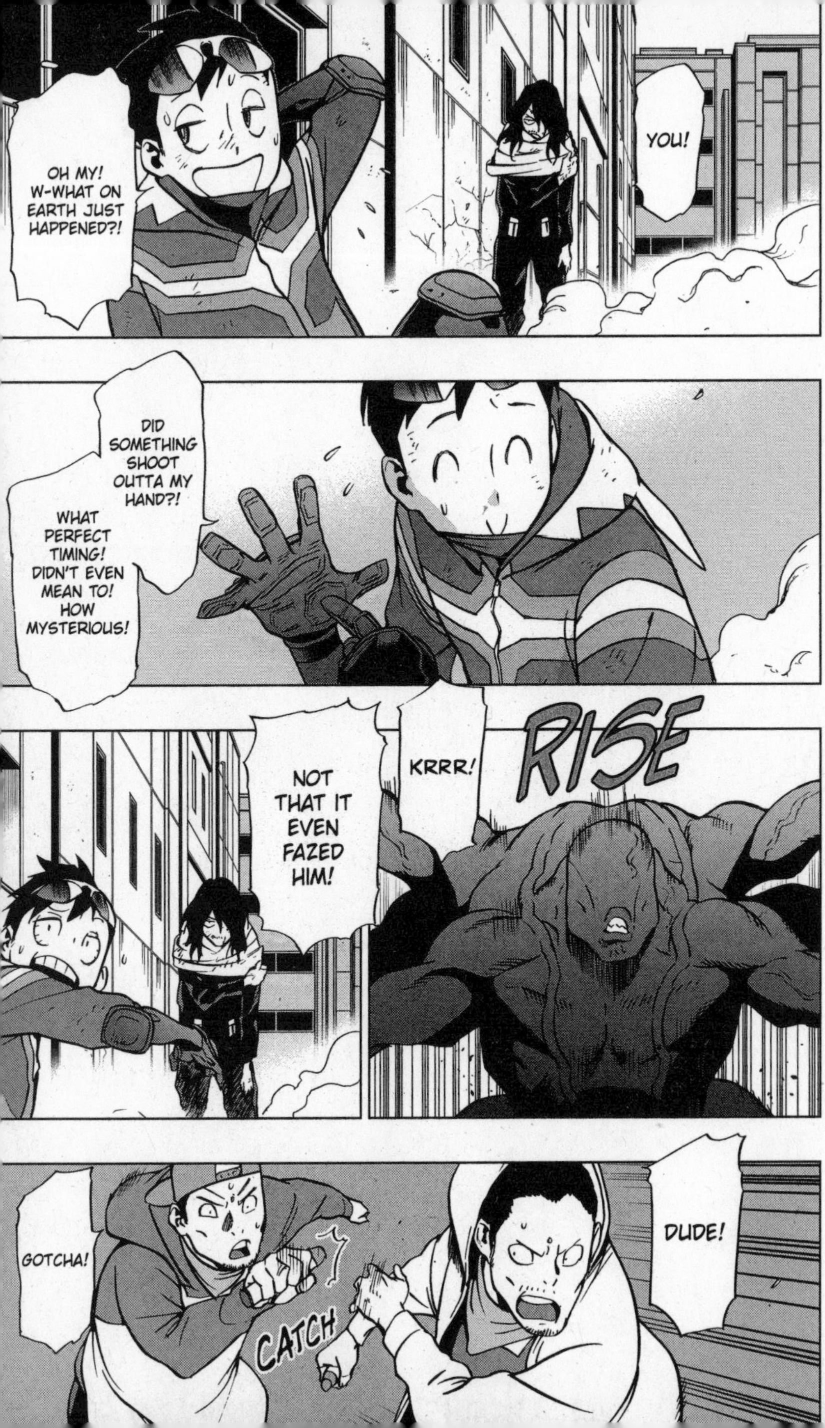
YOU!
OH MY! W-WHAT ON EARTH JUST HAPPENED?!
DID SOMETHING SHOOT OUTTA MY HAND?!
WHAT PERFECT TIMING! DIDN'T EVEN MEAN TO! HOW MYSTERIOUS!
RISE
KRRR!
NOT THAT IT EVEN FAZED HIM!
DUDE!
CATCH
GOTCHA!

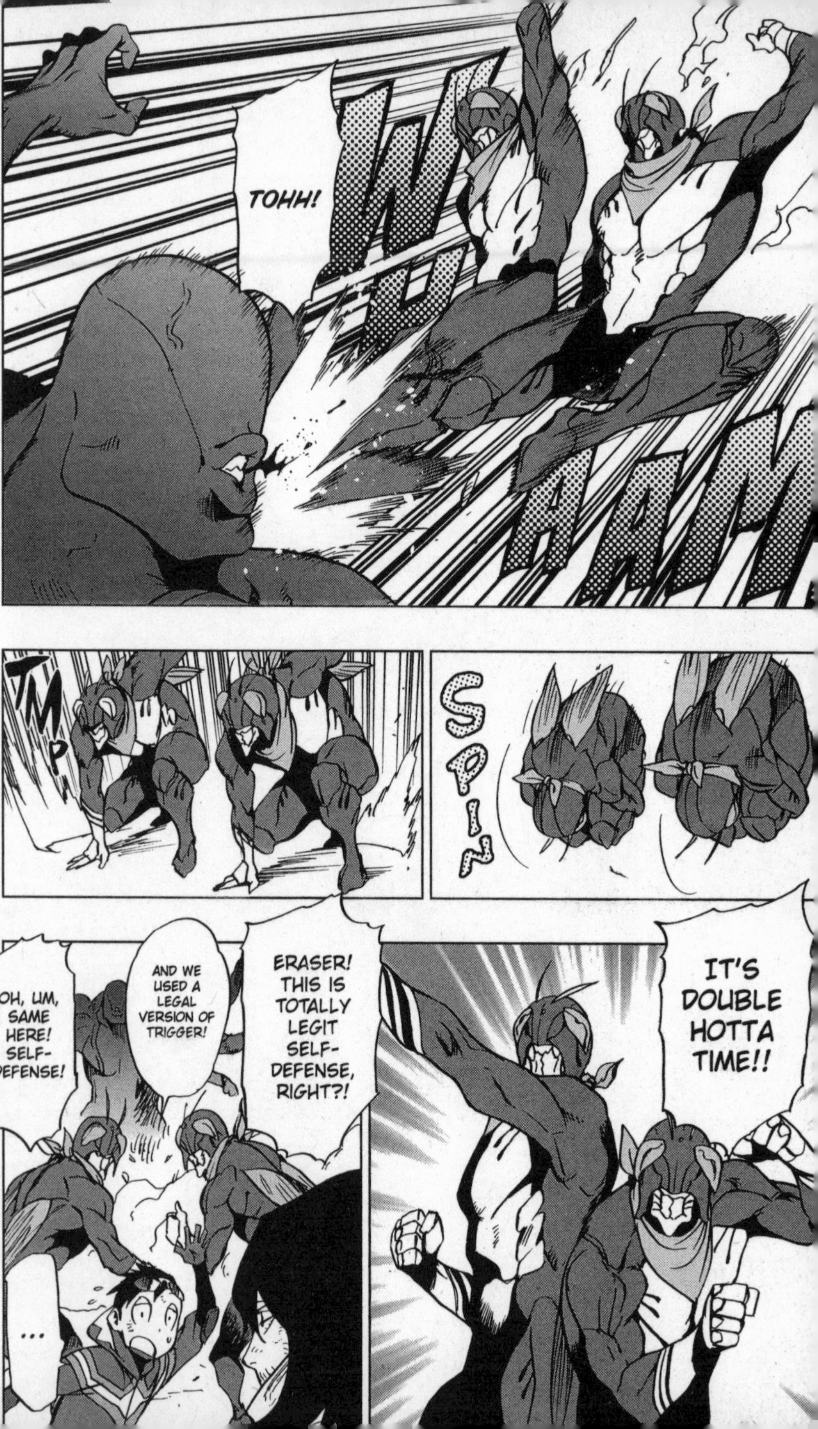
TOHH!
SPIN
TMP
IT'S DOUBLE HOTTA TIME!!
ERASER! THIS IS TOTALLY LEGIT SELF-DEFENSE, RIGHT?!
AND WE USED A LEGAL VERSION OF TRIGGER!
OH, UM, SAME HERE! SELF-DEFENSE!
...

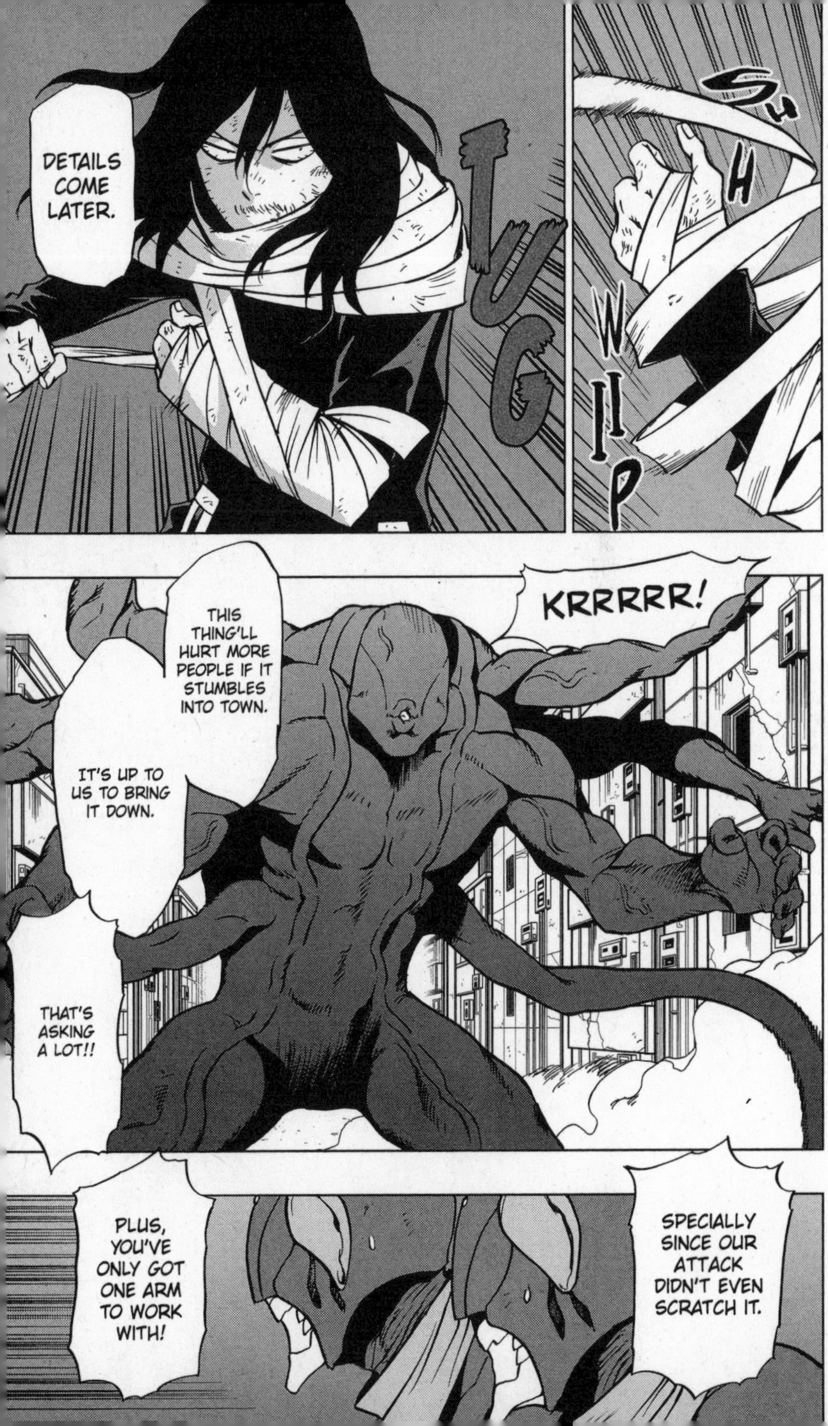
SHWIP
DETAILS COME LATER.
TUG
KRRRRR!
THIS THING'LL HURT MORE PEOPLE IF IT STUMBLES INTO TOWN.
IT'S UP TO US TO BRING IT DOWN.
THAT'S ASKING A LOT!!
SPECIALLY SINCE OUR ATTACK DIDN'T EVEN SCRATCH IT.
PLUS, YOU'VE ONLY GOT ONE ARM TO WORK WITH!

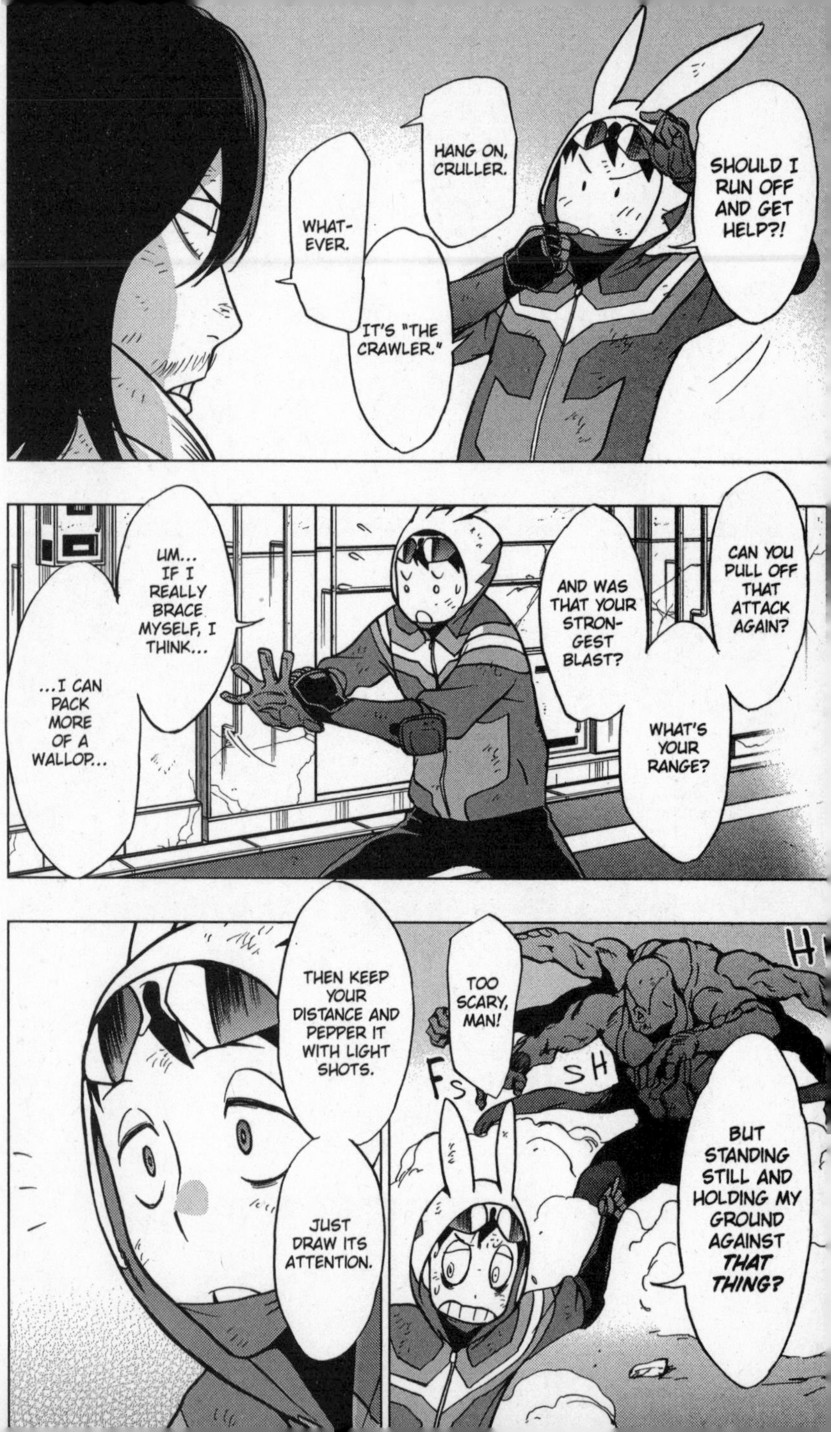
SHOULD I RUN OFF AND GET HELP?!
HANG ON, CRULLER.
IT'S "THE CRAWLER."
WHAT-EVER.
CAN YOU PULL OFF THAT ATTACK AGAIN?
AND WAS THAT YOUR STRON-GEST BLAST?
WHAT'S YOUR RANGE?
UM... IF I REALLY BRACE MYSELF, I THINK...
...I CAN PACK MORE OF A WALLOP...
H
BUT STANDING STILL AND HOLDING MY GROUND AGAINST *THAT THING?*
SH
FS
TOO SCARY, MAN!
THEN KEEP YOUR DISTANCE AND PEPPER IT WITH LIGHT SHOTS.
JUST DRAW ITS ATTENTION.

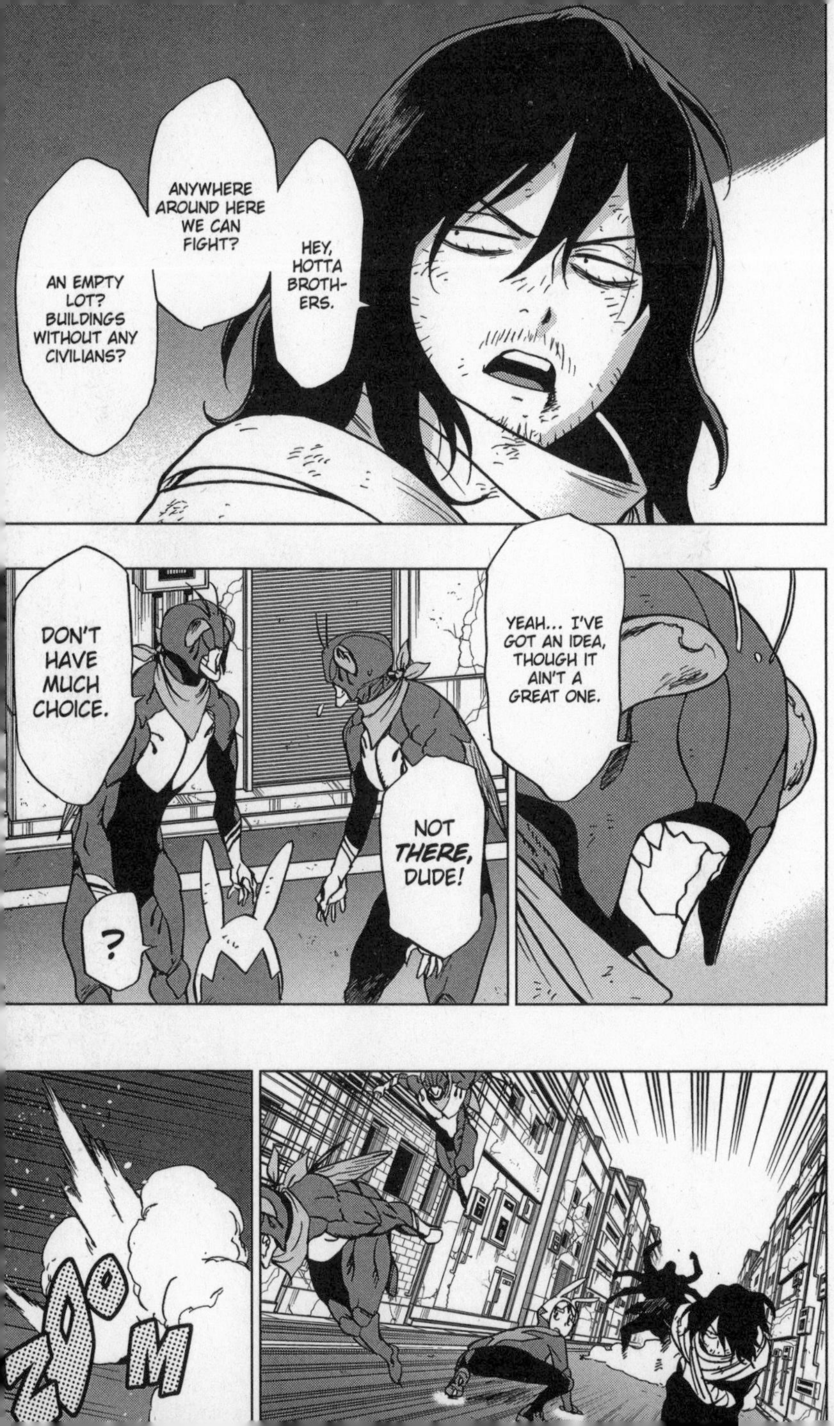
HEY, HOTTA BROTHERS.
ANYWHERE AROUND HERE WE CAN FIGHT?
AN EMPTY LOT? BUILDINGS WITHOUT ANY CIVILIANS?
YEAH... I'VE GOT AN IDEA, THOUGH IT AIN'T A GREAT ONE.
DON'T HAVE MUCH CHOICE.
NOT *THERE*, DUDE!
?
ZOOM

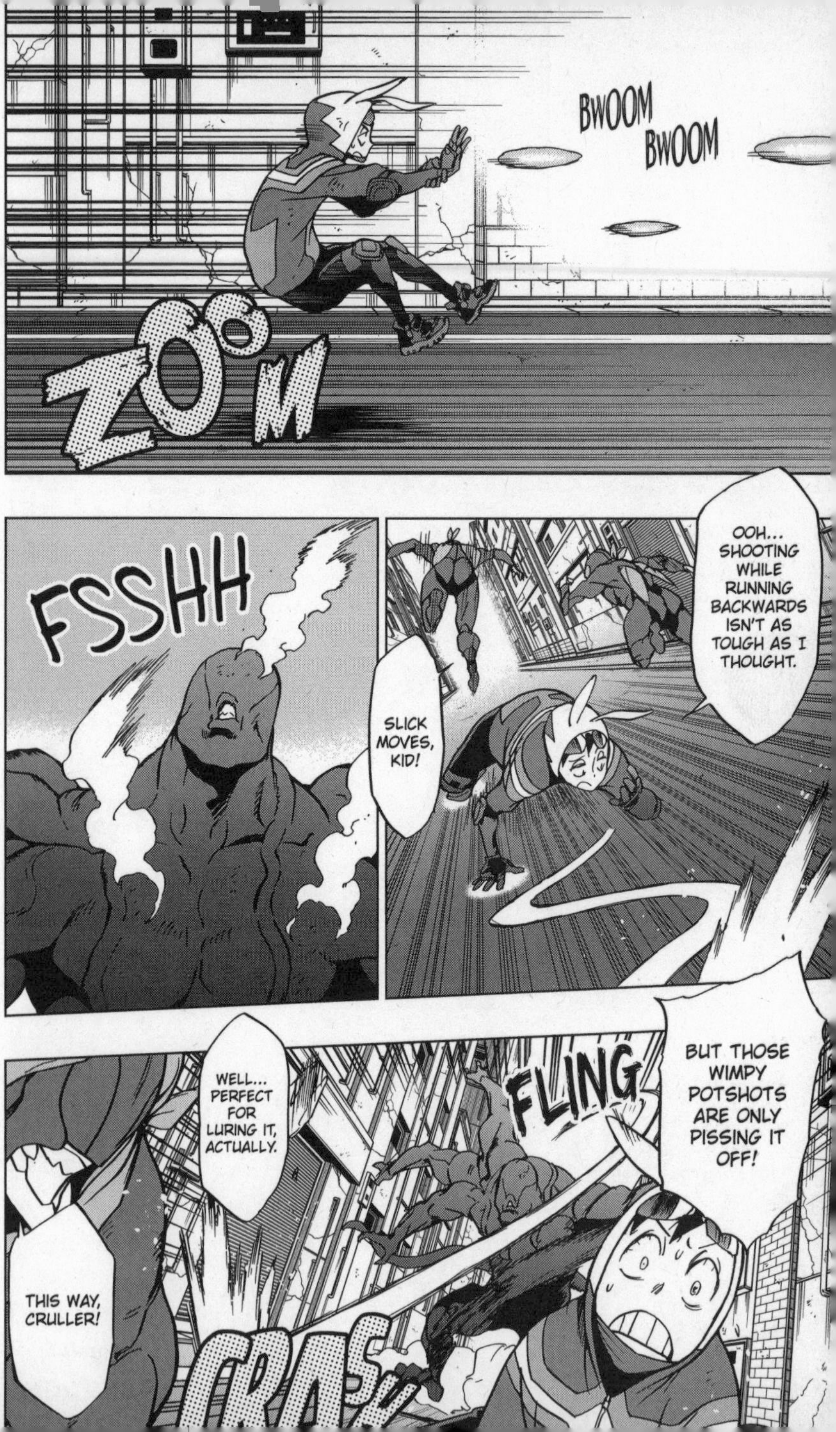
BWOOM
BWOOM
ZOOOM
OOH... SHOOTING WHILE RUNNING BACKWARDS ISN'T AS TOUGH AS I THOUGHT.
SLICK MOVES, KID!
FSSHH
BUT THOSE WIMPY POTSHOTS ARE ONLY PISSING IT OFF!
FLING
WELL... PERFECT FOR LURING IT, ACTUALLY.
THIS WAY, CRULLER!

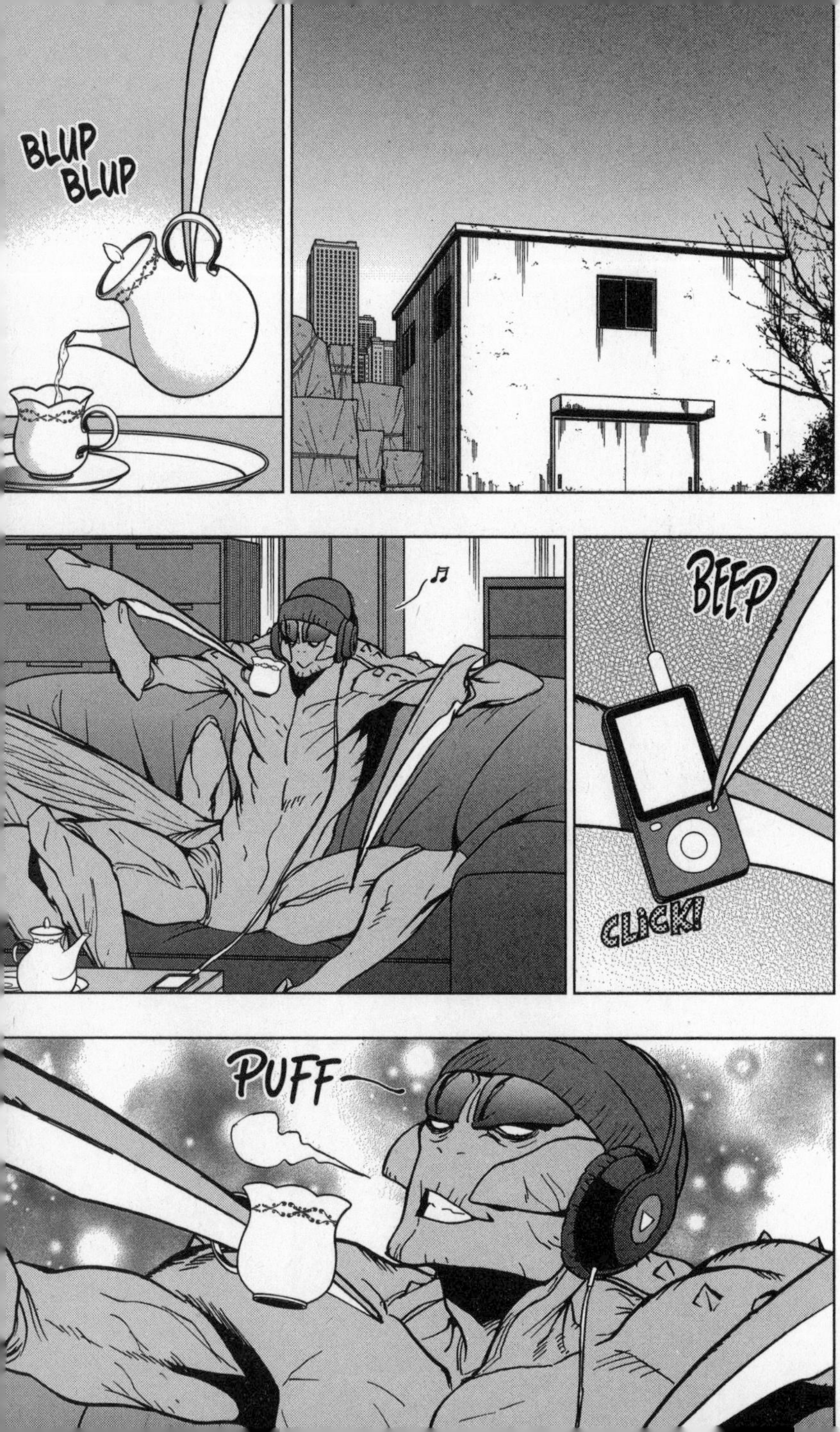
BLUP
BLUP
BEEP
CLICK!
PUFF

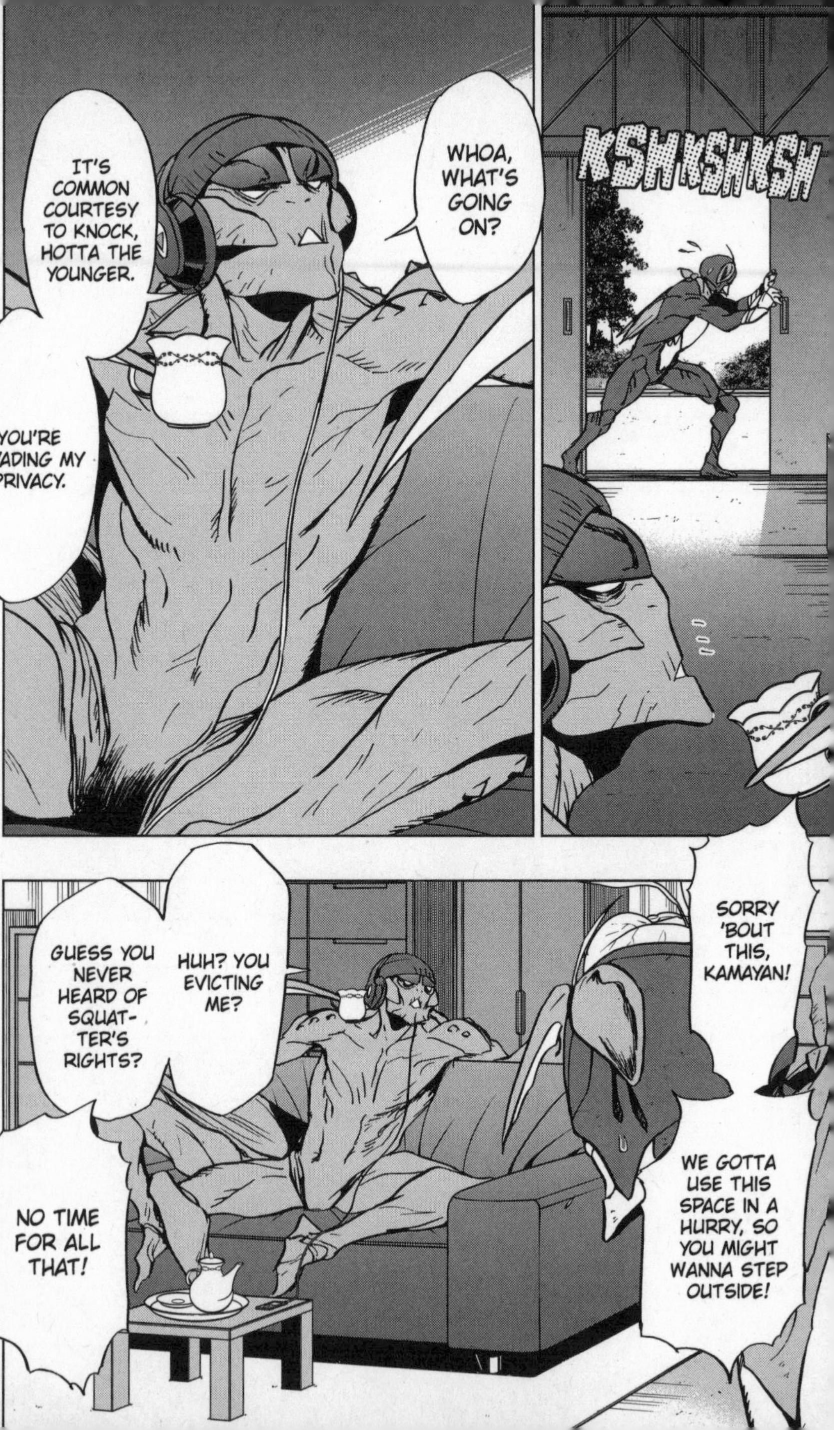
KSHKSHKSH
WHOA, WHAT'S GOING ON?
IT'S COMMON COURTESY TO KNOCK, HOTTA THE YOUNGER.
YOU'RE INVADING MY PRIVACY.
SORRY 'BOUT THIS, KAMAYAN!
HUH? YOU EVICTING ME?
GUESS YOU NEVER HEARD OF SQUAT-TER'S RIGHTS?
WE GOTTA USE THIS SPACE IN A HURRY, SO YOU MIGHT WANNA STEP OUTSIDE!
NO TIME FOR ALL THAT!

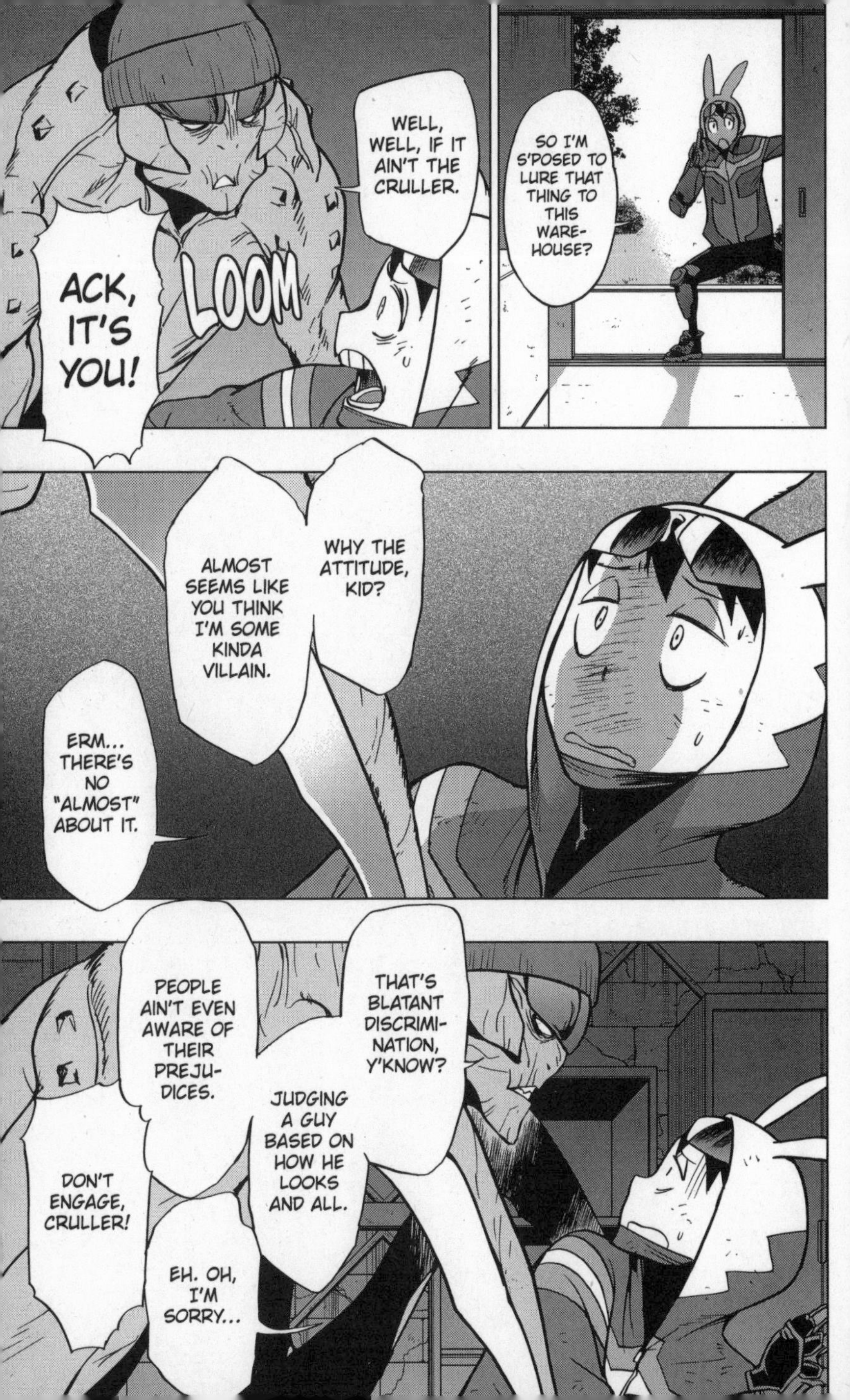
SO I'M S'POSED TO LURE THAT THING TO THIS WARE-HOUSE?
WELL, WELL, IF IT AIN'T THE CRULLER.
LOOM
ACK, IT'S YOU!
WHY THE ATTITUDE, KID?
ALMOST SEEMS LIKE YOU THINK I'M SOME KINDA VILLAIN.
ERM... THERE'S NO "ALMOST" ABOUT IT.
THAT'S BLATANT DISCRIMI-NATION, Y'KNOW?
PEOPLE AIN'T EVEN AWARE OF THEIR PREJU-DICES.
JUDGING A GUY BASED ON HOW HE LOOKS AND ALL.
DON'T ENGAGE, CRULLER!
EH. OH, I'M SORRY...

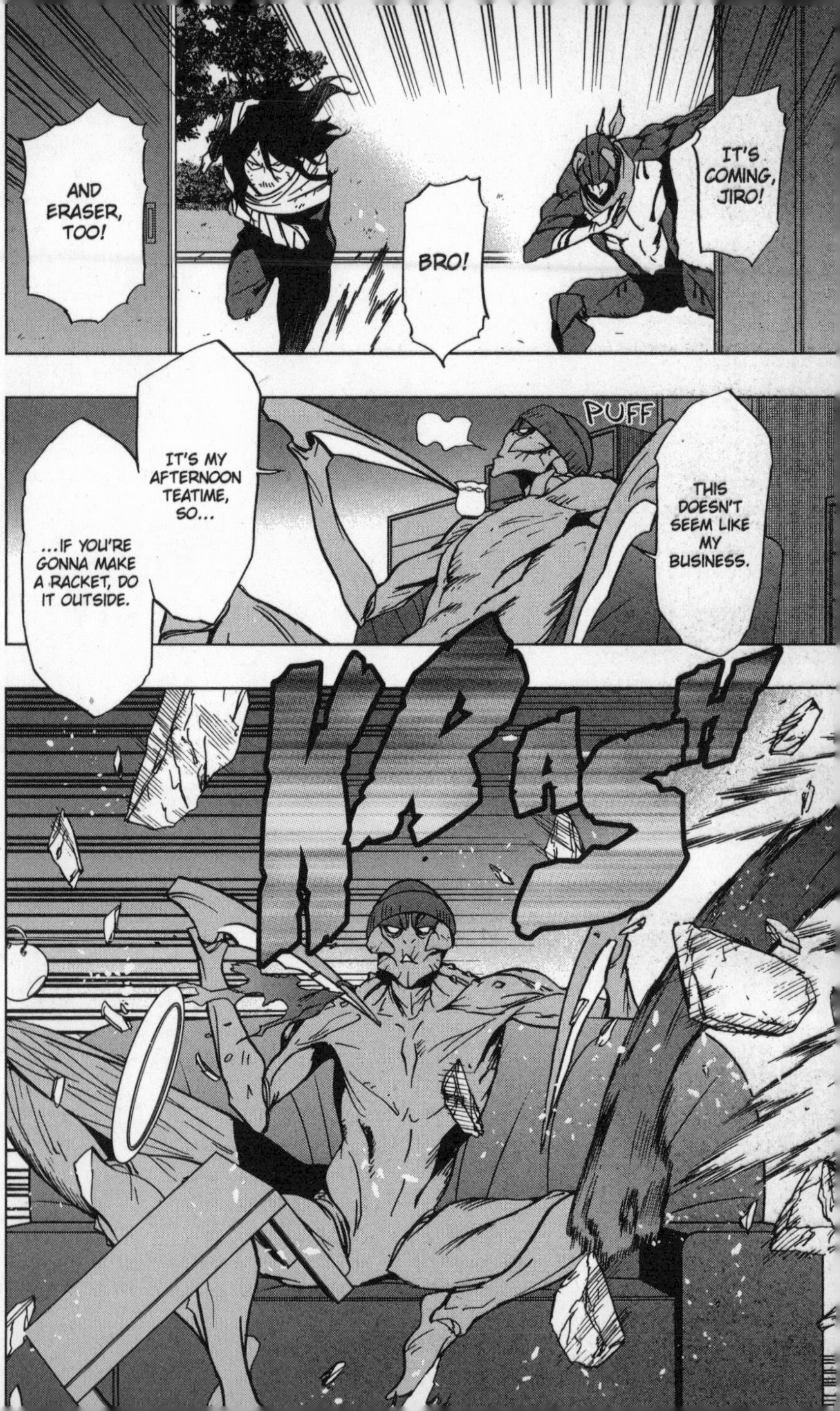
IT'S COMING, JIRO!
BRO!
AND ERASER, TOO!
PUFF
THIS DOESN'T SEEM LIKE MY BUSINESS.
IT'S MY AFTERNOON TEATIME, SO...
...IF YOU'RE GONNA MAKE A RACKET, DO IT OUTSIDE.
KRASH

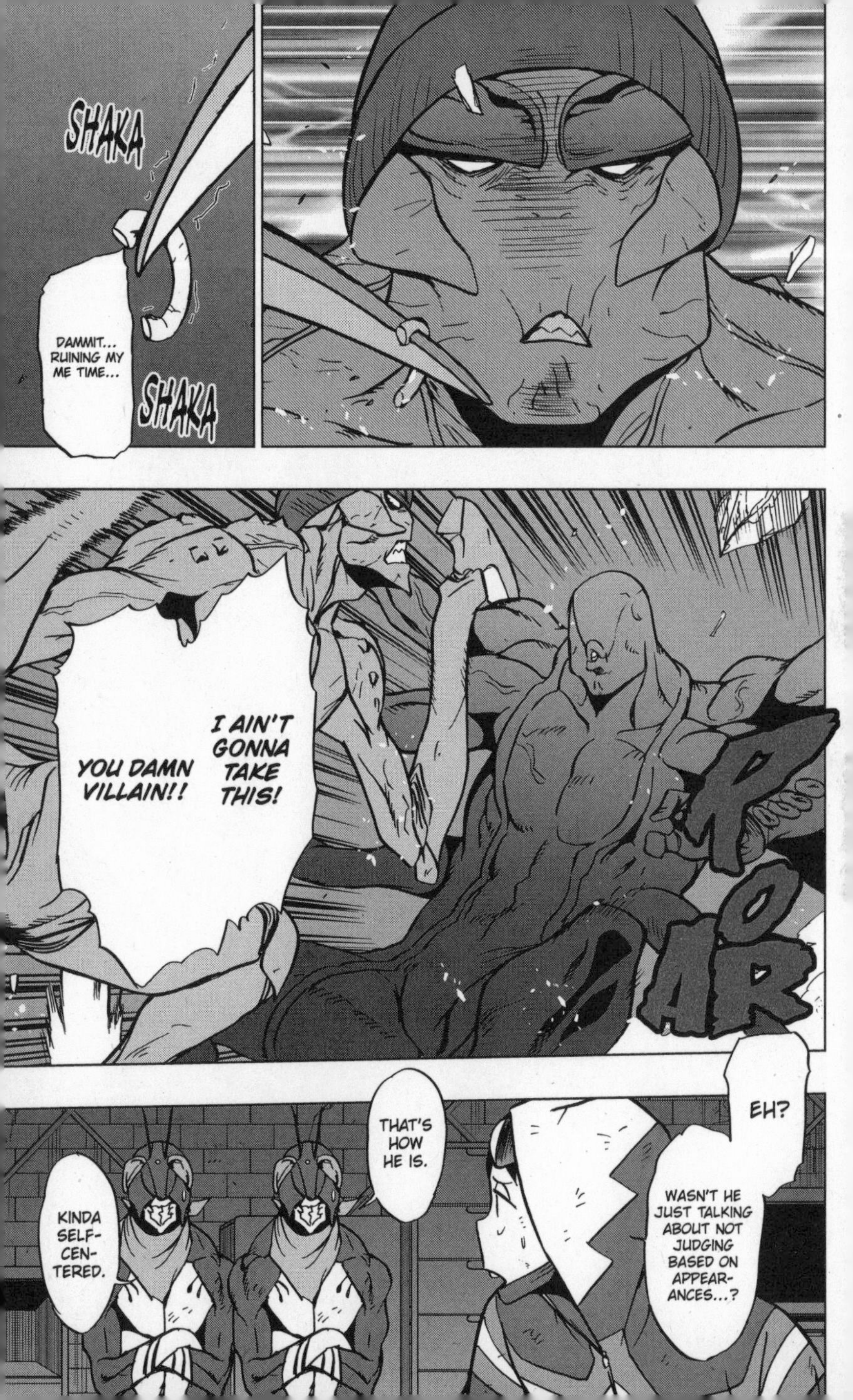
SHAKA
DAMMIT... RUINING MY ME TIME...
SHAKA
I AIN'T GONNA TAKE THIS!
YOU DAMN VILLAIN!!
ROAR
EH?
WASN'T HE JUST TALKING ABOUT NOT JUDGING BASED ON APPEAR-ANCES...?
THAT'S HOW HE IS.
KINDA SELF-CEN-TERED.

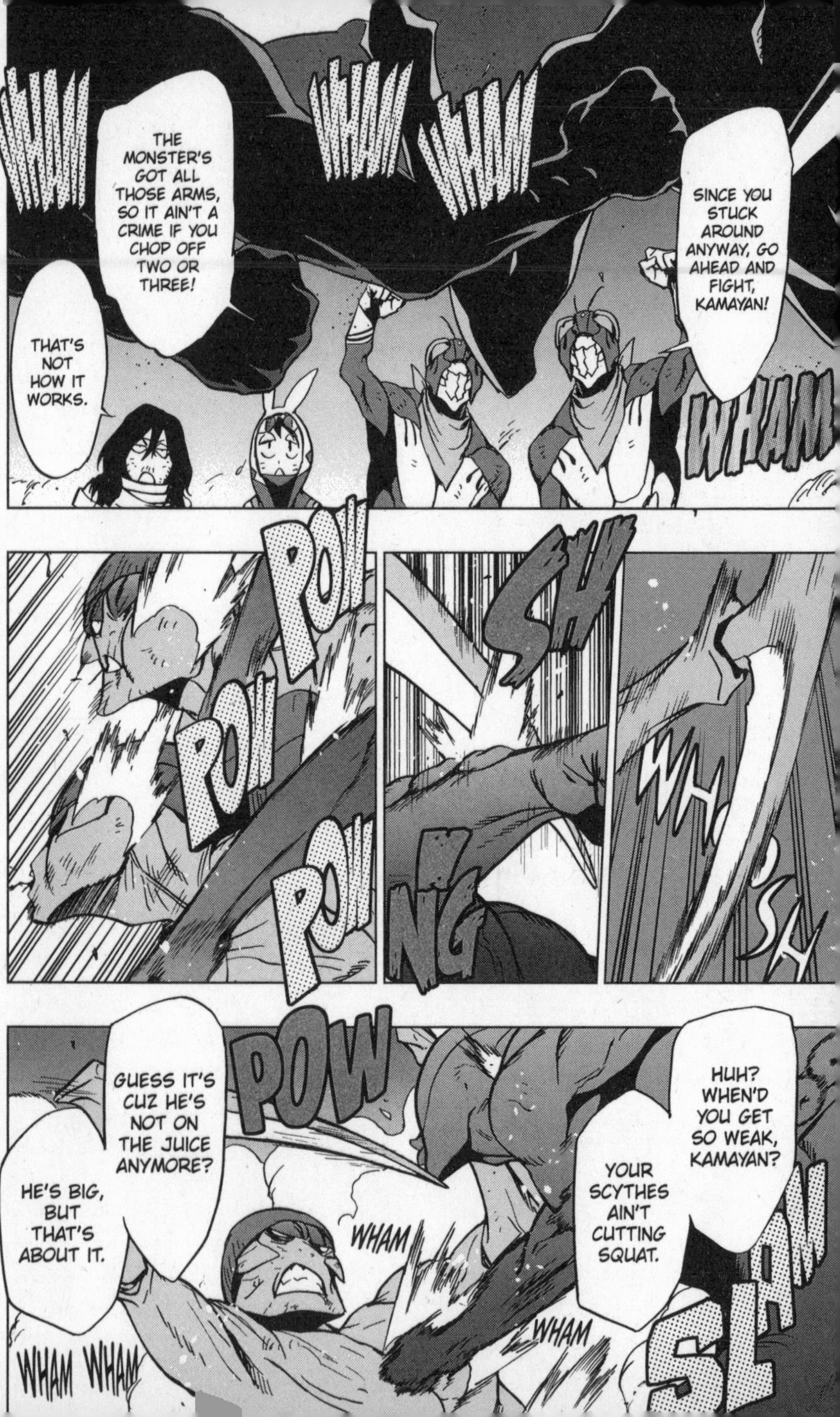
WHAM
SINCE YOU STUCK AROUND ANYWAY, GO AHEAD AND FIGHT, KAMAYAN!
THE MONSTER'S GOT ALL THOSE ARMS, SO IT AIN'T A CRIME IF YOU CHOP OFF TWO OR THREE!
THAT'S NOT HOW IT WORKS.
POW
POW
POW
POW
SLAM
HUH? WHEN'D YOU GET SO WEAK, KAMAYAN?
YOUR SCYTHES AIN'T CUTTING SQUAT.
WHAM
POW
GUESS IT'S CUZ HE'S NOT ON THE JUICE ANYMORE?
HE'S BIG, BUT THAT'S ABOUT IT.
WHAM
WHAM WHAM

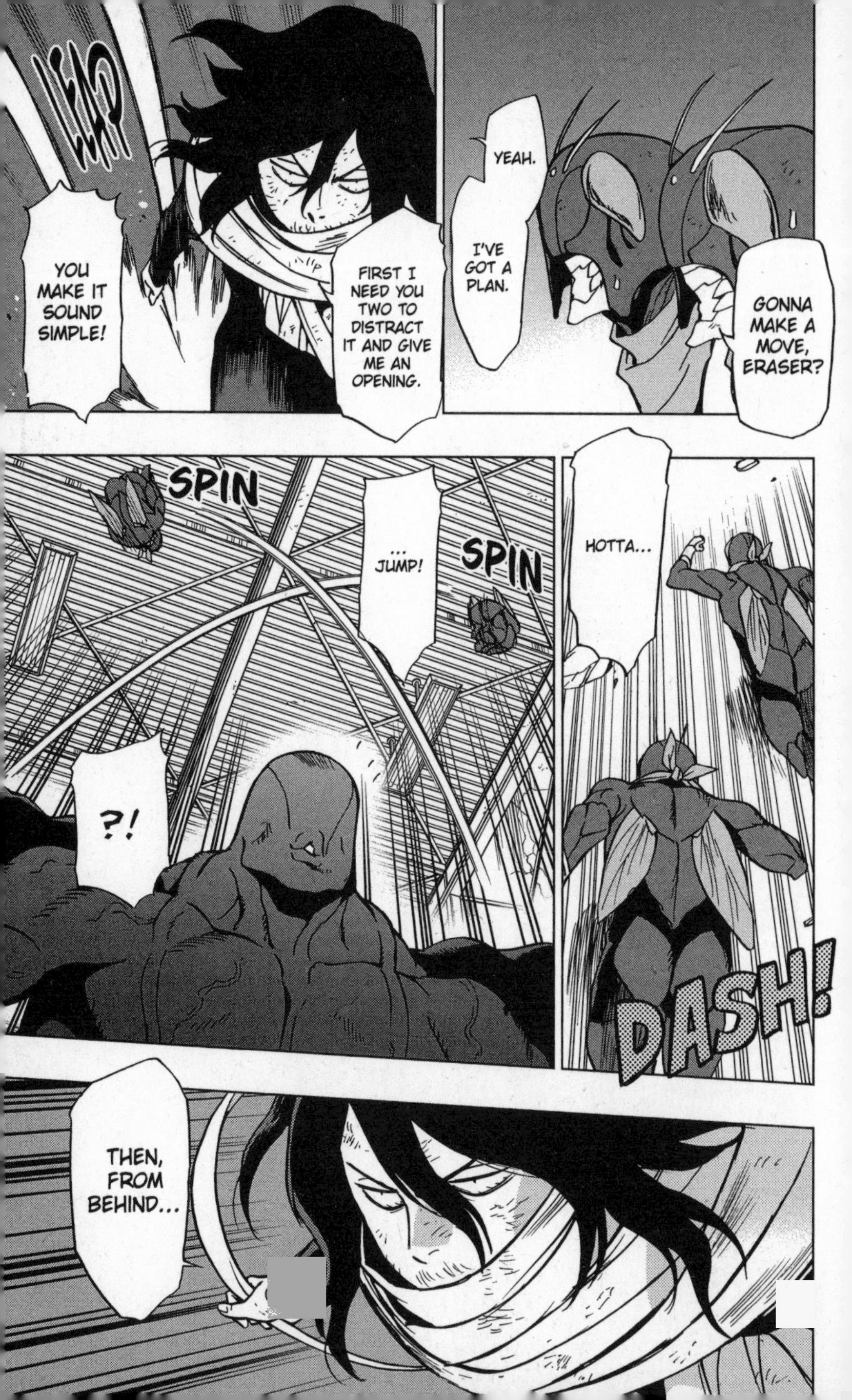
GONNA MAKE A MOVE, ERASER?
YEAH.
I'VE GOT A PLAN.
LEAP!
FIRST I NEED YOU TWO TO DISTRACT IT AND GIVE ME AN OPENING.
YOU MAKE IT SOUND SIMPLE!
HOTTA...
DASH!
...JUMP!
SPIN
SPIN
?!
THEN, FROM BEHIND...

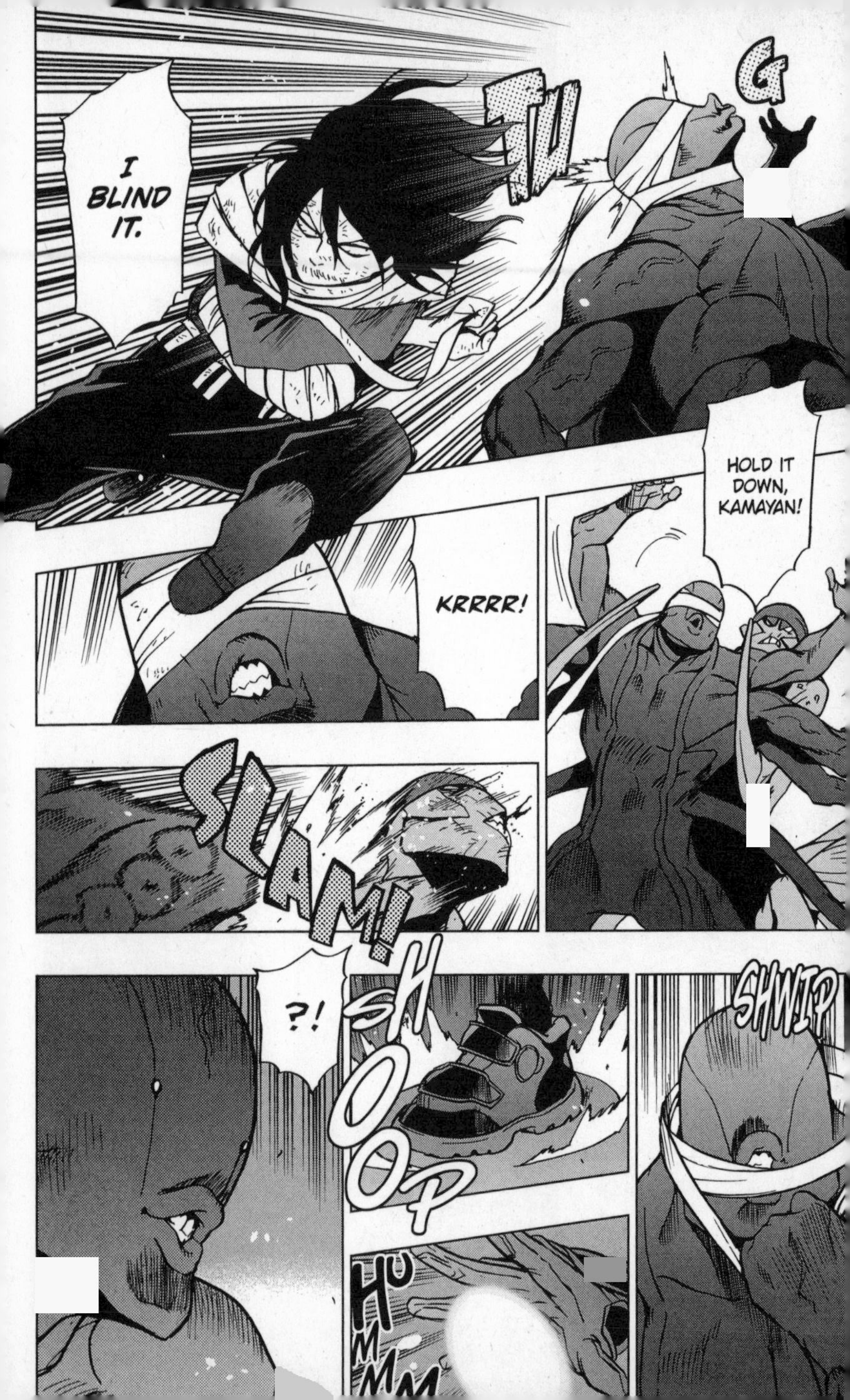

TUG
I BLIND IT.
HOLD IT DOWN, KAMAYAN!
KRRRR!
SLAM!
SHWIP
SHOOOP
HUMMM
?!

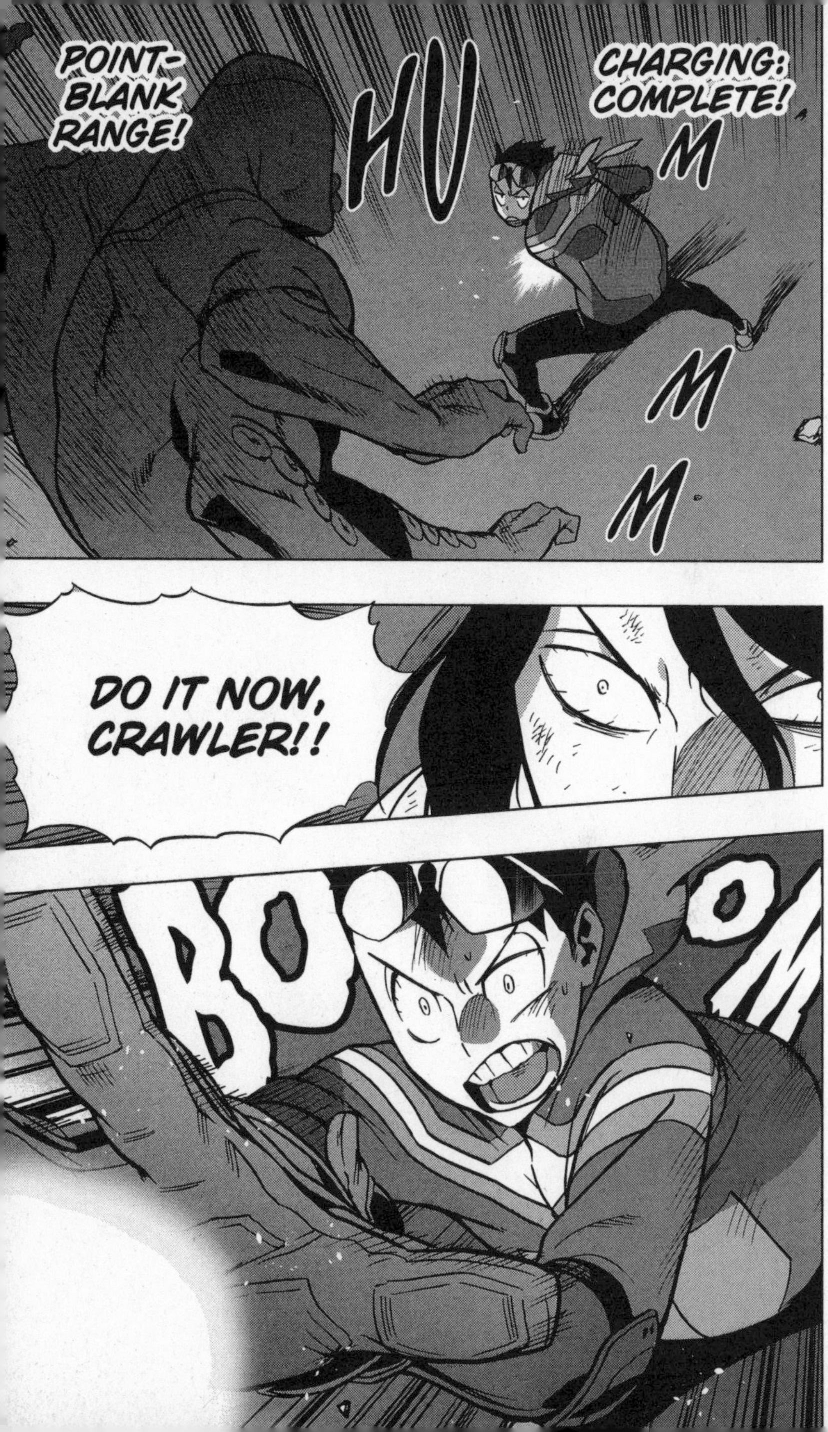
CHARGING: COMPLETE!
POINT-BLANK RANGE!
HUMMMM
DO IT NOW, CRAWLER!!
BOOM

THE COLUMN

POP☆STEP

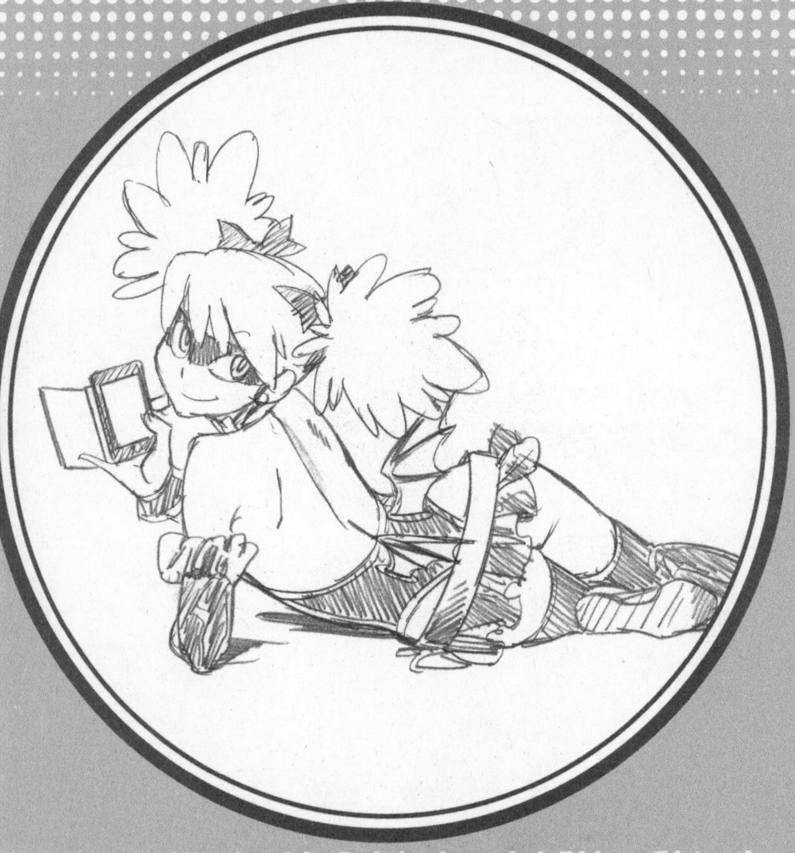

This sketch was done fairly early on. At first, Pop had much more of a devilish-imp motif, but once her friendship with Koichi solidified, she settled into more of a stabilizing role. When guys and gals hang out together, the gals tend to grow more mature while the guys remain blockheads forever... That's the idea I was going for here.

—Furuhashi

I put this sketch up on Twitter way back when. At first we were planning to have her be a lot sharper tongued, but as we went on, there were fewer and fewer chances to show that, so that idea kind of fell apart. (hah)

—Betten

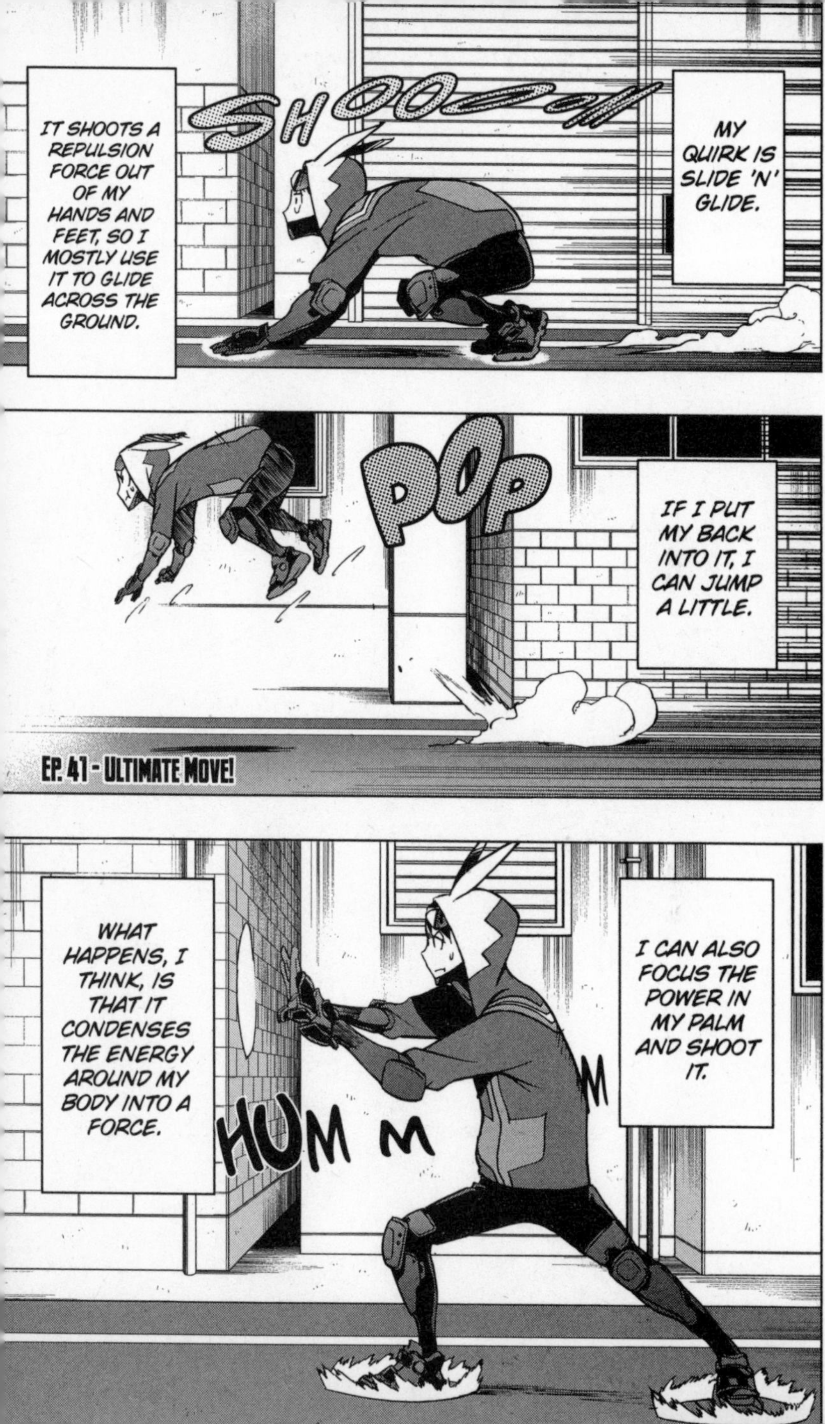
MY QUIRK IS SLIDE 'N' GLIDE.
SHOOOOOH
IT SHOOTS A REPULSION FORCE OUT OF MY HANDS AND FEET, SO I MOSTLY USE IT TO GLIDE ACROSS THE GROUND.
IF I PUT MY BACK INTO IT, I CAN JUMP A LITTLE.
POP
EP. 41 - ULTIMATE MOVE!
I CAN ALSO FOCUS THE POWER IN MY PALM AND SHOOT IT.
HUM M M M
WHAT HAPPENS, I THINK, IS THAT IT CONDENSES THE ENERGY AROUND MY BODY INTO A FORCE.

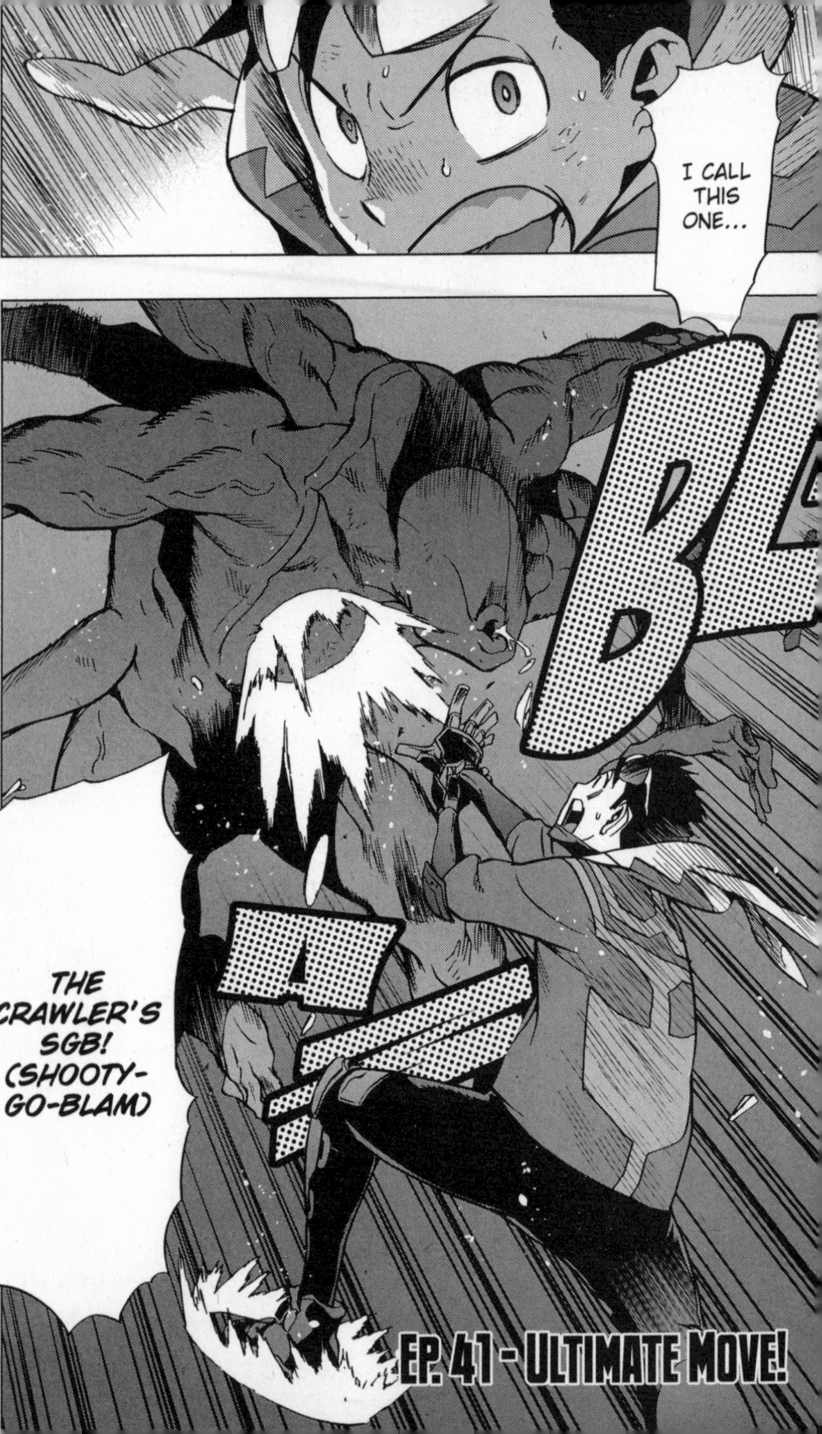
I CALL THIS ONE...
BLAM
THE CRAWLER'S SGB! (SHOOTY-GO-BLAM)
EP. 41 - ULTIMATE MOVE!

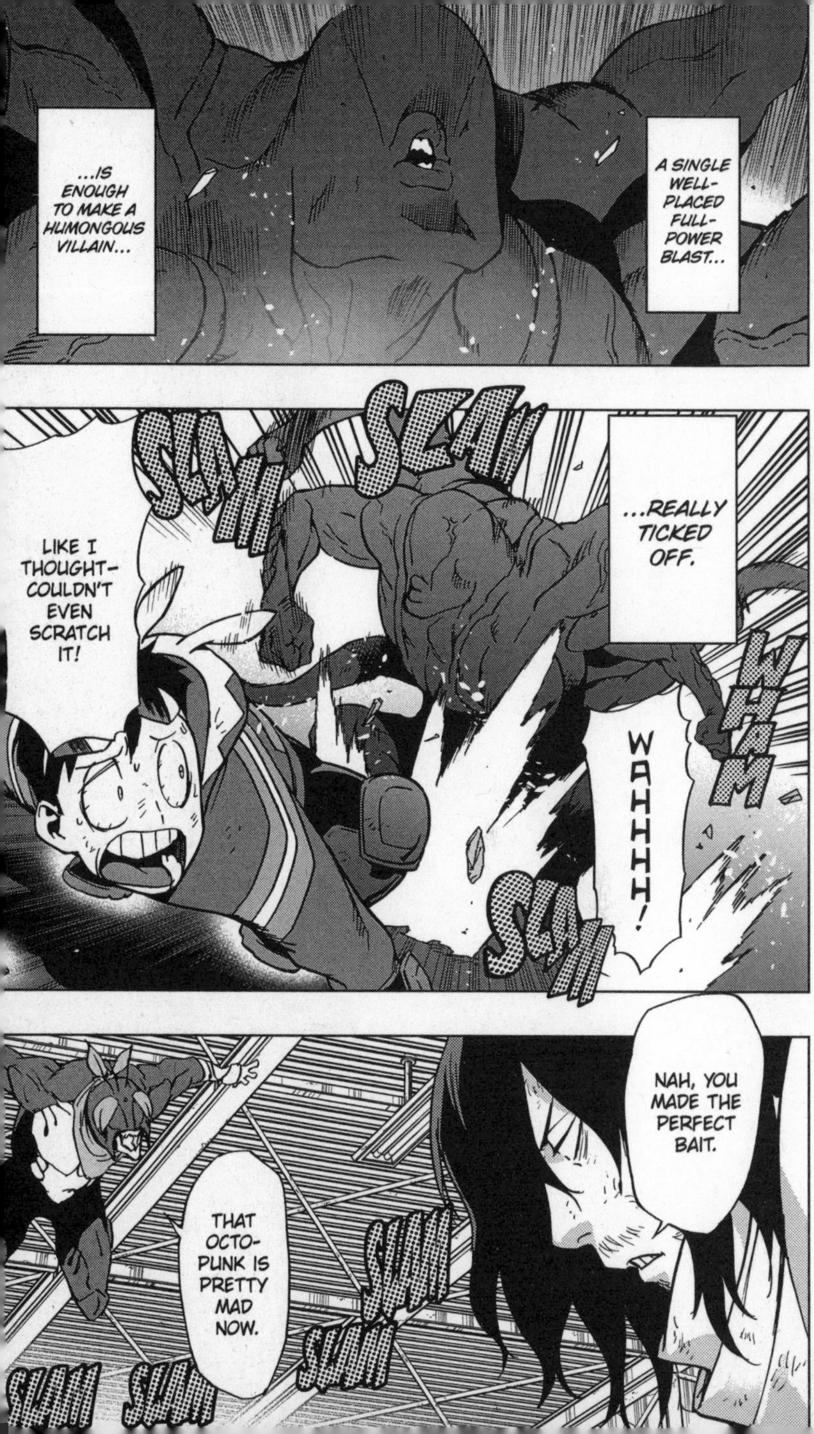
A SINGLE WELL-PLACED FULL-POWER BLAST...
...IS ENOUGH TO MAKE A HUMONGOUS VILLAIN...
...REALLY TICKED OFF.
WHAM
SLAM
SLAM
WAHHHH!
SLAM
LIKE I THOUGHT-COULDN'T EVEN SCRATCH IT!
NAH, YOU MADE THE PERFECT BAIT.
THAT OCTO-PUNK IS PRETTY MAD NOW.

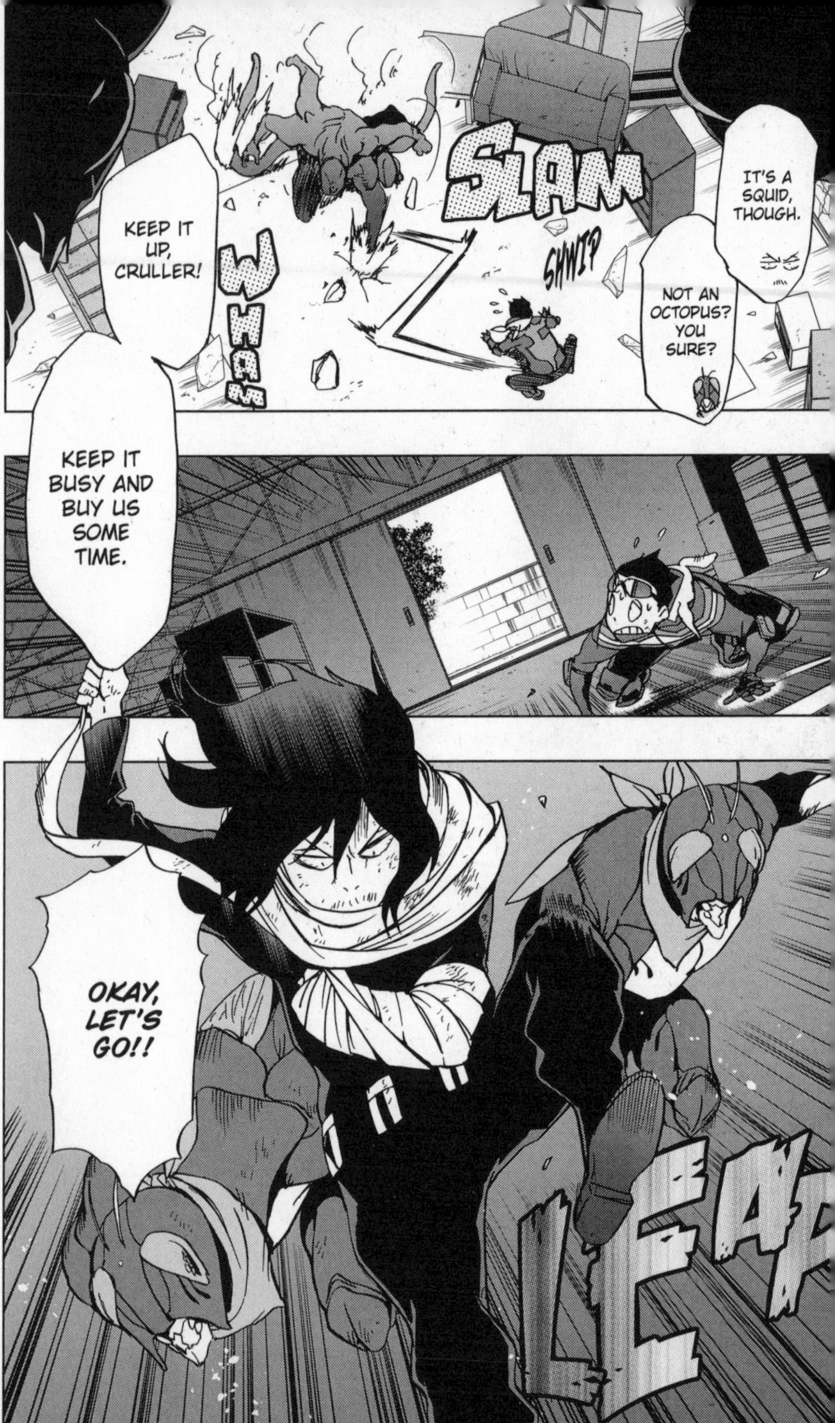
IT'S A SQUID, THOUGH.
NOT AN OCTOPUS? YOU SURE?
SLAM
SHWIP
KEEP IT UP, CRULLER!
KEEP IT BUSY AND BUY US SOME TIME.
OKAY, LET'S GO!!

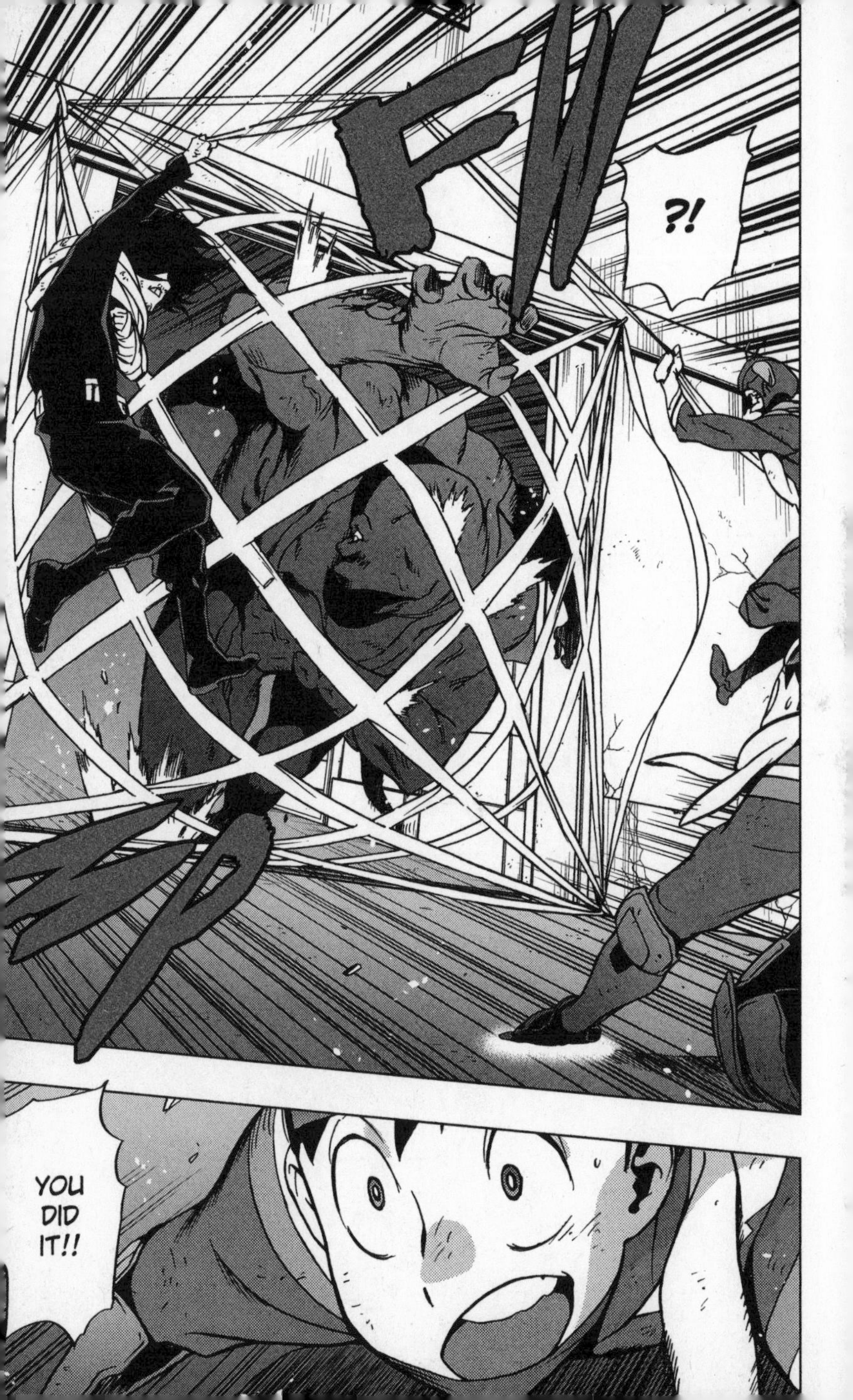
?!
FWIP
YOU DID IT!!

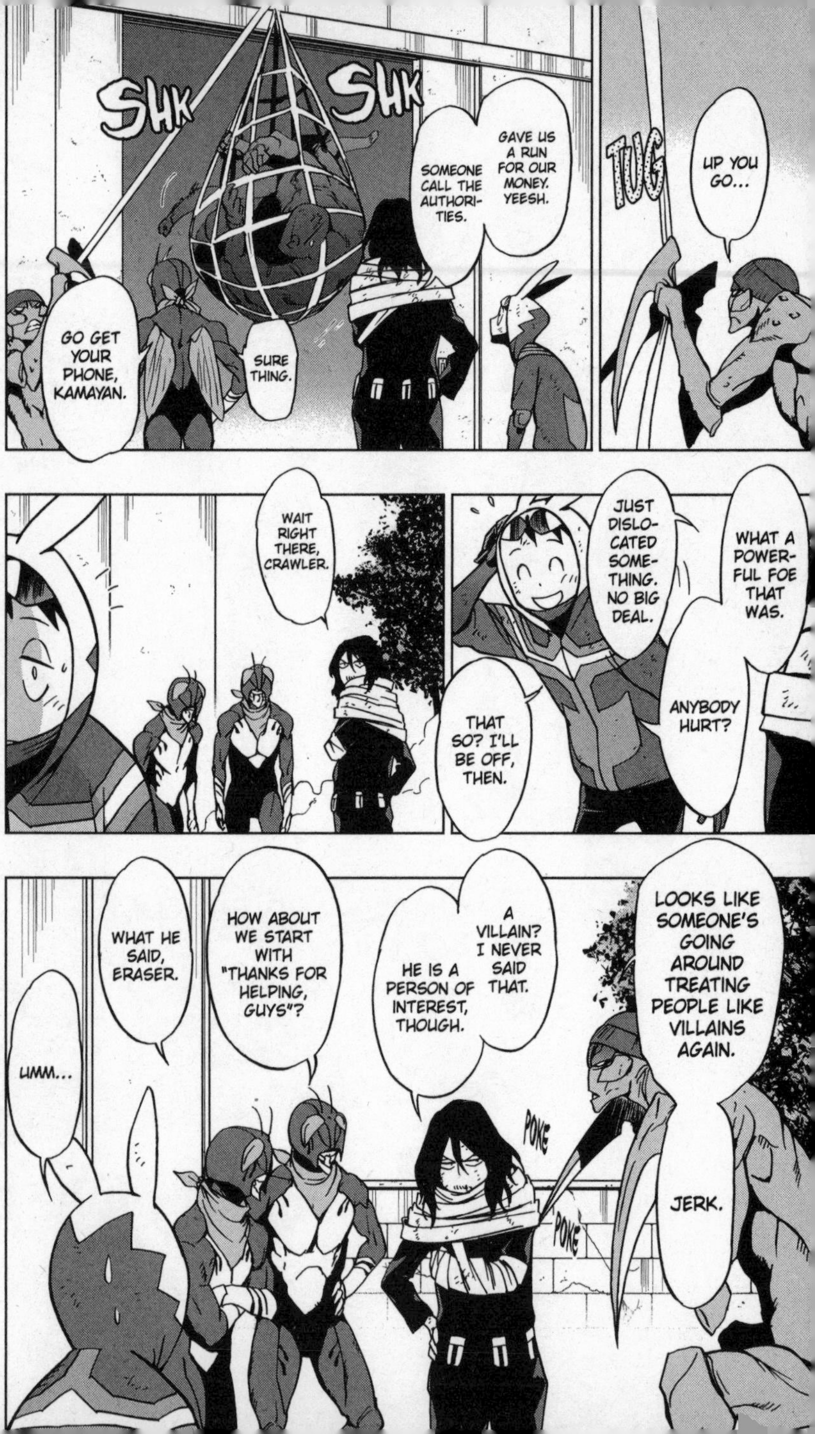
TUG
UP YOU GO...
GAVE US A RUN FOR OUR MONEY. YEESH.
SOMEONE CALL THE AUTHORITIES.
SHK
SHK
GO GET YOUR PHONE, KAMAYAN.
SURE THING.
WHAT A POWERFUL FOE THAT WAS.
ANYBODY HURT?
JUST DISLOCATED SOMETHING. NO BIG DEAL.
THAT SO? I'LL BE OFF, THEN.
WAIT RIGHT THERE, CRAWLER.
LOOKS LIKE SOMEONE'S GOING AROUND TREATING PEOPLE LIKE VILLAINS AGAIN.
A VILLAIN? I NEVER SAID THAT.
HE IS A PERSON OF INTEREST, THOUGH.
HOW ABOUT WE START WITH "THANKS FOR HELPING, GUYS"?
WHAT HE SAID, ERASER.
JERK.
POKE
POKE
UMM...

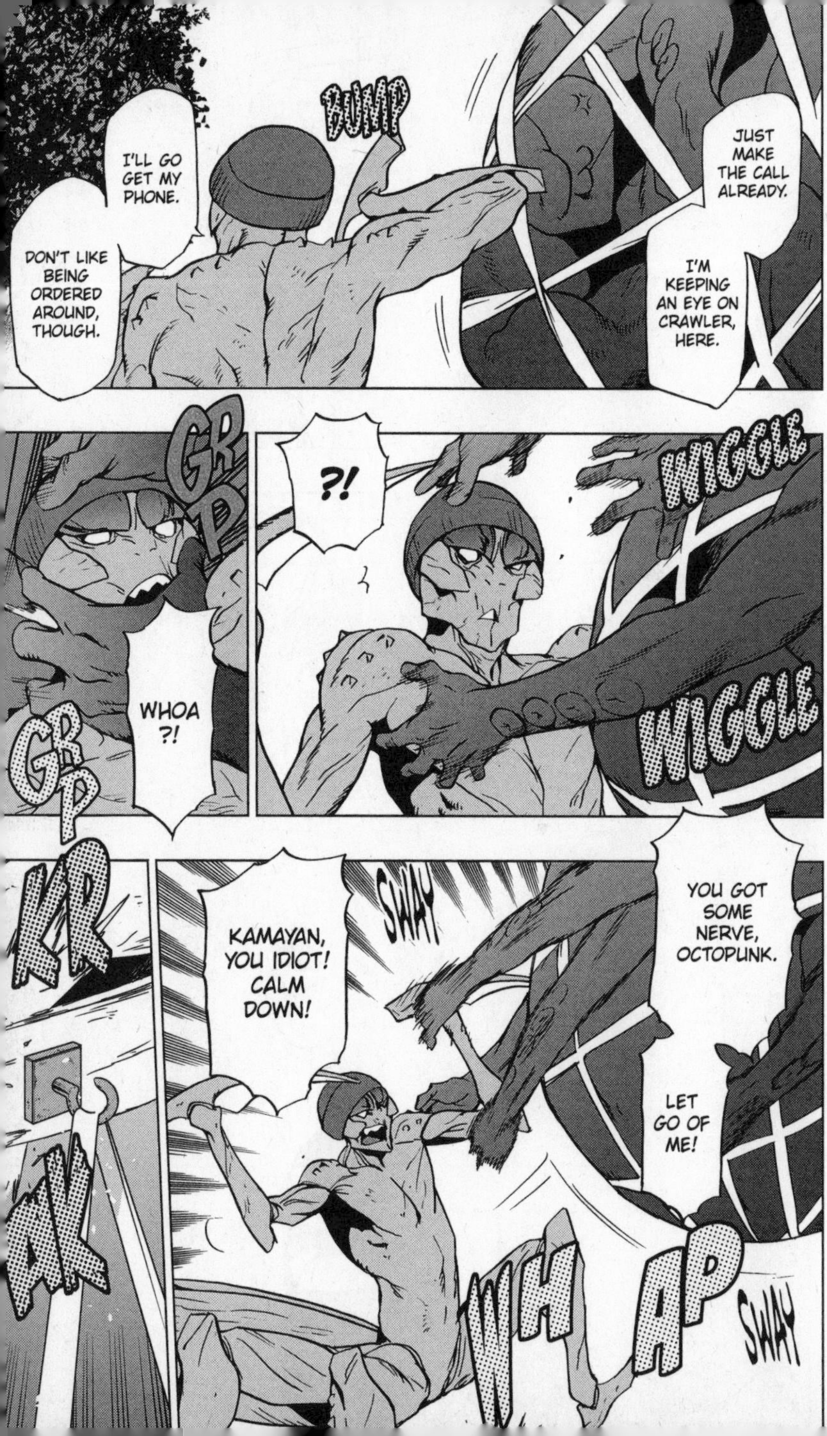
JUST MAKE THE CALL ALREADY.
I'M KEEPING AN EYE ON CRAWLER, HERE.
BUMP
I'LL GO GET MY PHONE.
DON'T LIKE BEING ORDERED AROUND, THOUGH.
?!
WIGGLE
WIGGLE
GRP
WHOA ?!
GRP
YOU GOT SOME NERVE, OCTOPUNK.
LET GO OF ME!
SWAY
KAMAYAN, YOU IDIOT! CALM DOWN!
WHAP
SWAY
KRAK

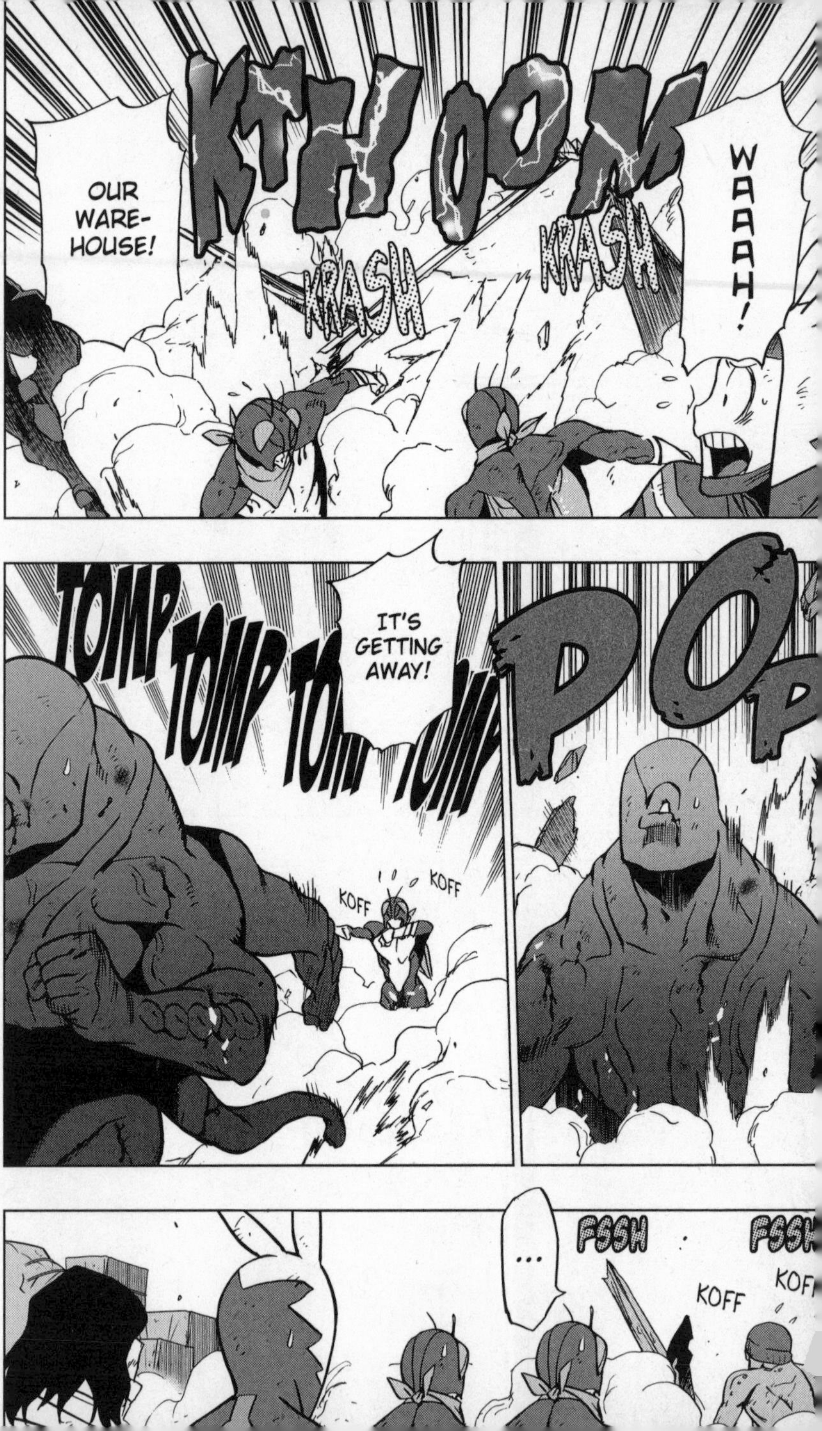
WAAAAH!
KTHOOOM
KRASH
KRASH
OUR WARE-HOUSE!
POP
TOMP TOMP TOMP TOMP
IT'S GETTING AWAY!
KOFF
KOFF
FSSH
FSSH
KOFF
KOFF
...

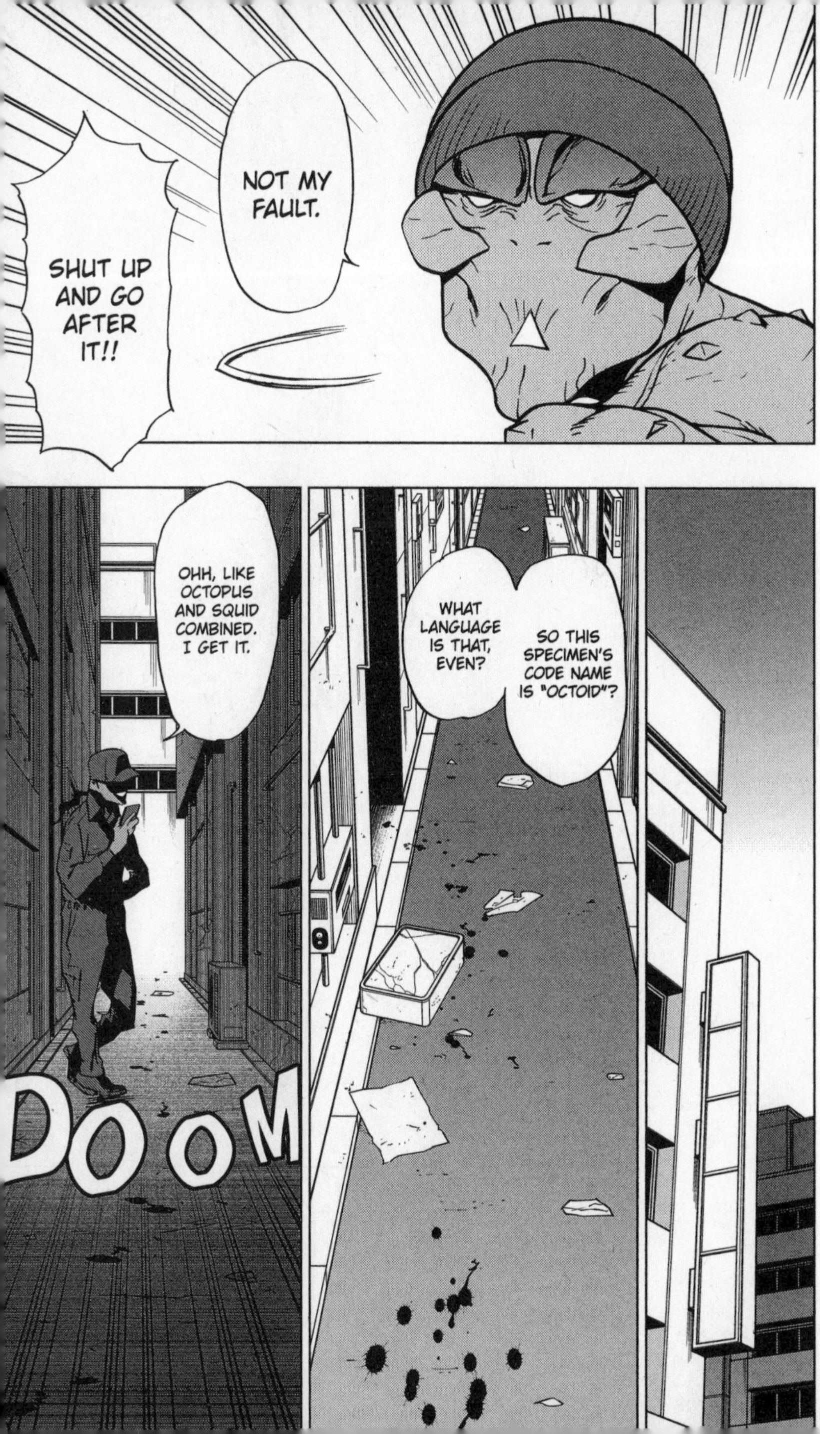
NOT MY FAULT.
SHUT UP AND GO AFTER IT!!
SO THIS SPECIMEN'S CODE NAME IS "OCTOID"?
WHAT LANGUAGE IS THAT, EVEN?
OHH, LIKE OCTOPUS AND SQUID COMBINED. I GET IT.
DOOM

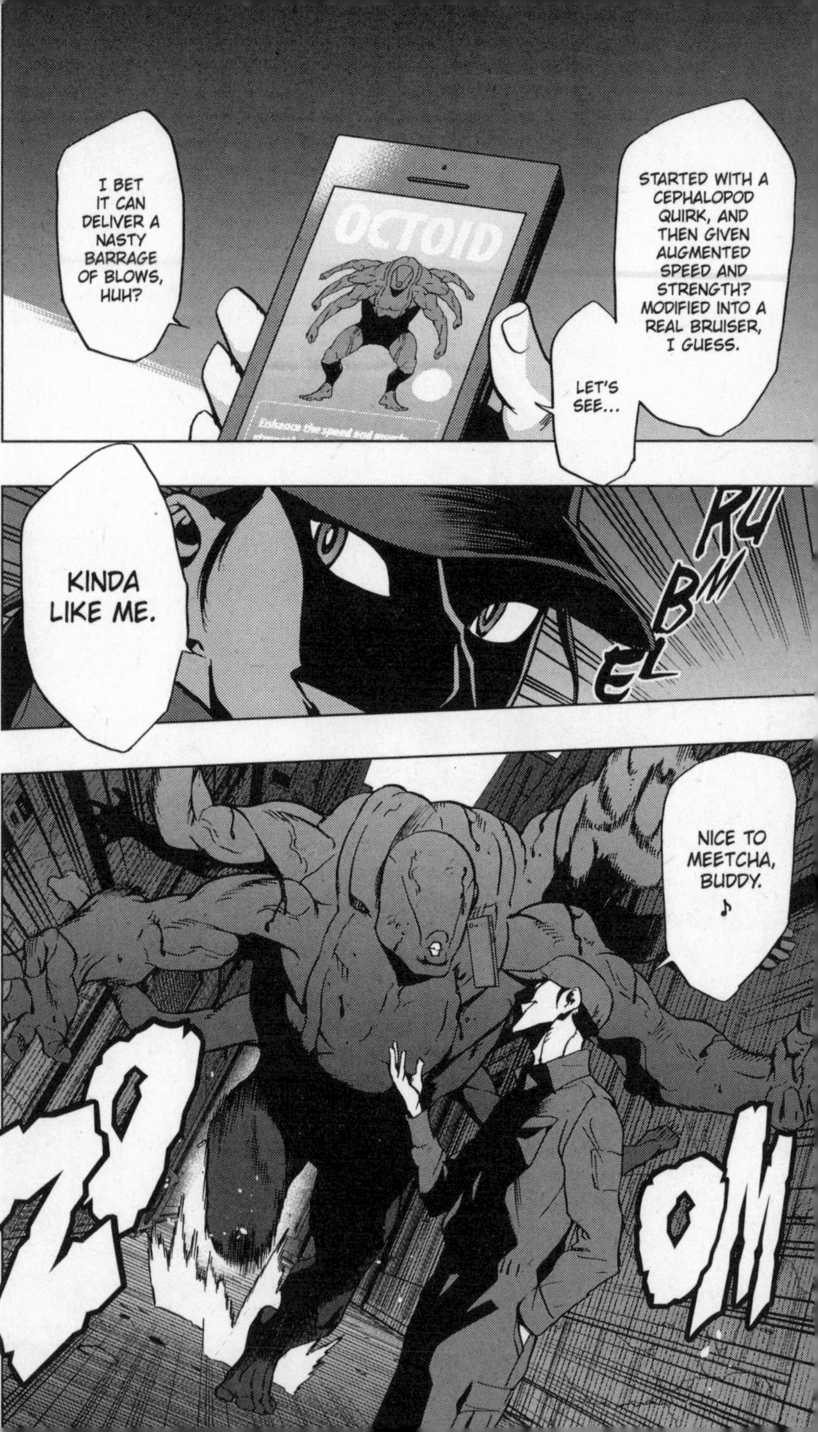
STARTED WITH A CEPHALOPOD QUIRK, AND THEN GIVEN AUGMENTED SPEED AND STRENGTH? MODIFIED INTO A REAL BRUISER, I GUESS.
LET'S SEE...
OCTOID
I BET IT CAN DELIVER A NASTY BARRAGE OF BLOWS, HUH?
RUMBLE
KINDA LIKE ME.
NICE TO MEETCHA, BUDDY. ♪
ZOOM

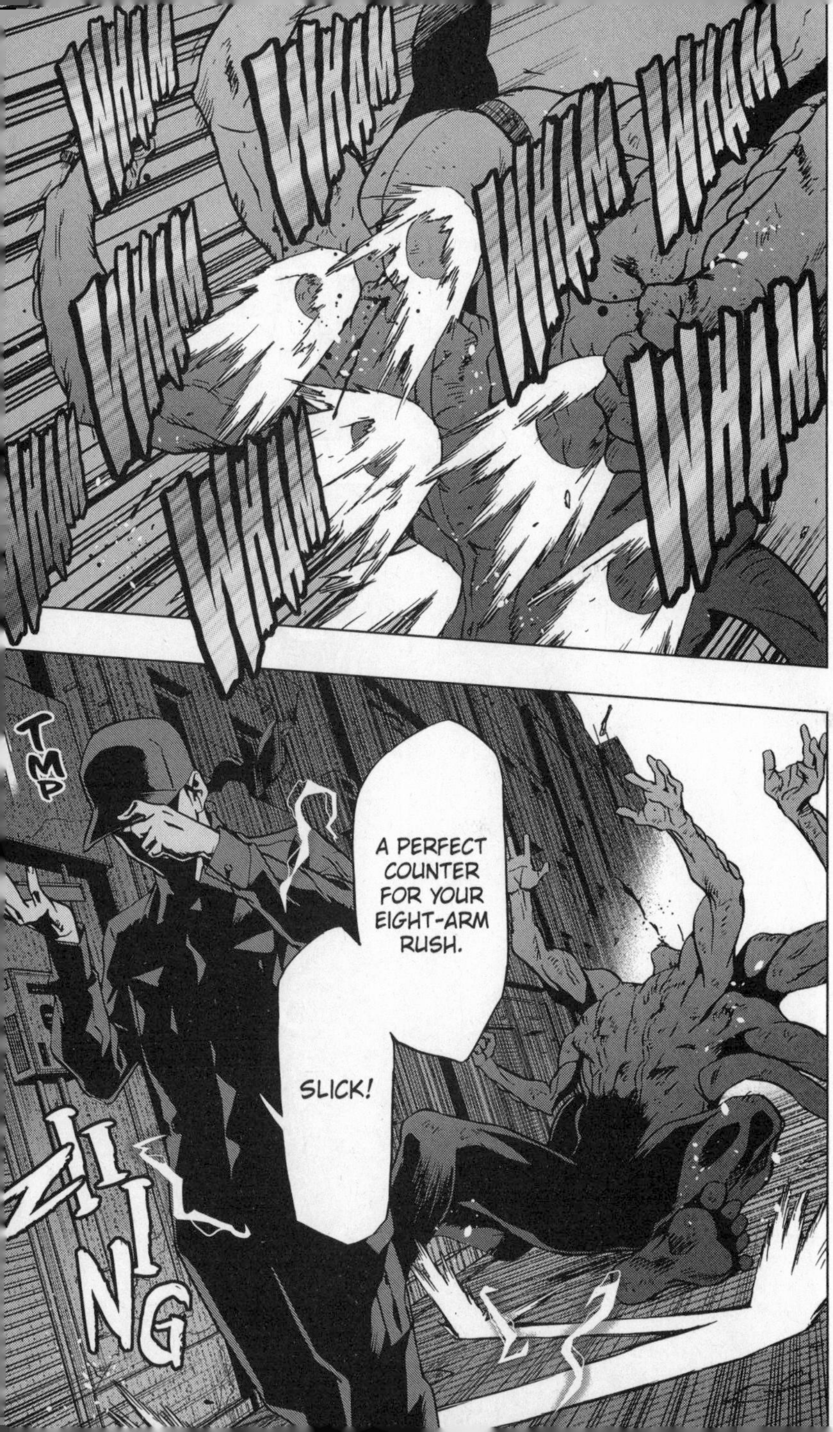
WHAM
WHAM
WHAM
WHAM
WHAM
WHAM
WHAM
WHAM
TMP
A PERFECT COUNTER FOR YOUR EIGHT-ARM RUSH.
SLICK!
ZHIING

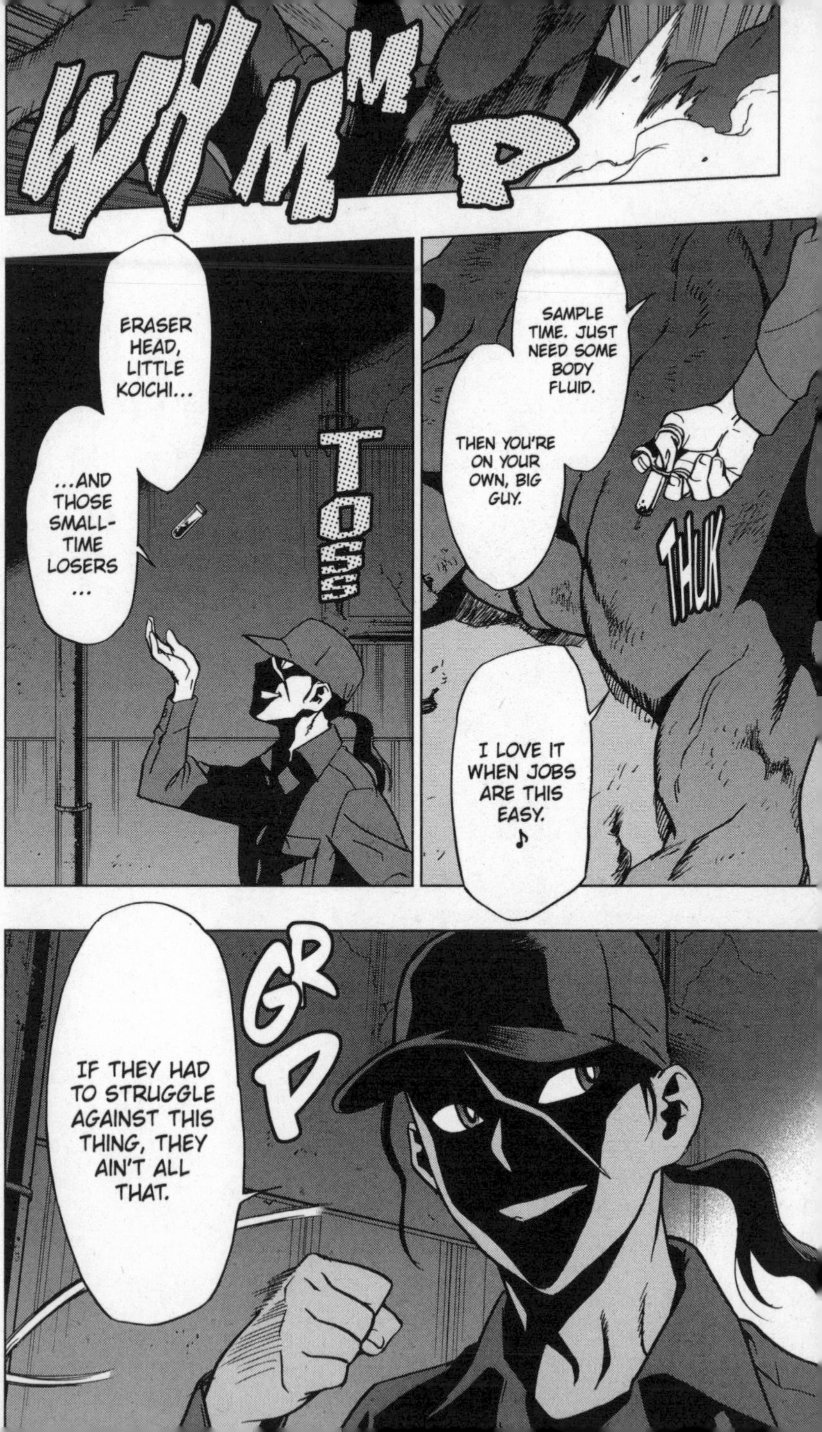
WHMMP
SAMPLE TIME. JUST NEED SOME BODY FLUID.
THEN YOU'RE ON YOUR OWN, BIG GUY.
THUK
I LOVE IT WHEN JOBS ARE THIS EASY. ♪
ERASER HEAD, LITTLE KOICHI...
...AND THOSE SMALL-TIME LOSERS...
TOSS
GRP
IF THEY HAD TO STRUGGLE AGAINST THIS THING, THEY AIN'T ALL THAT.

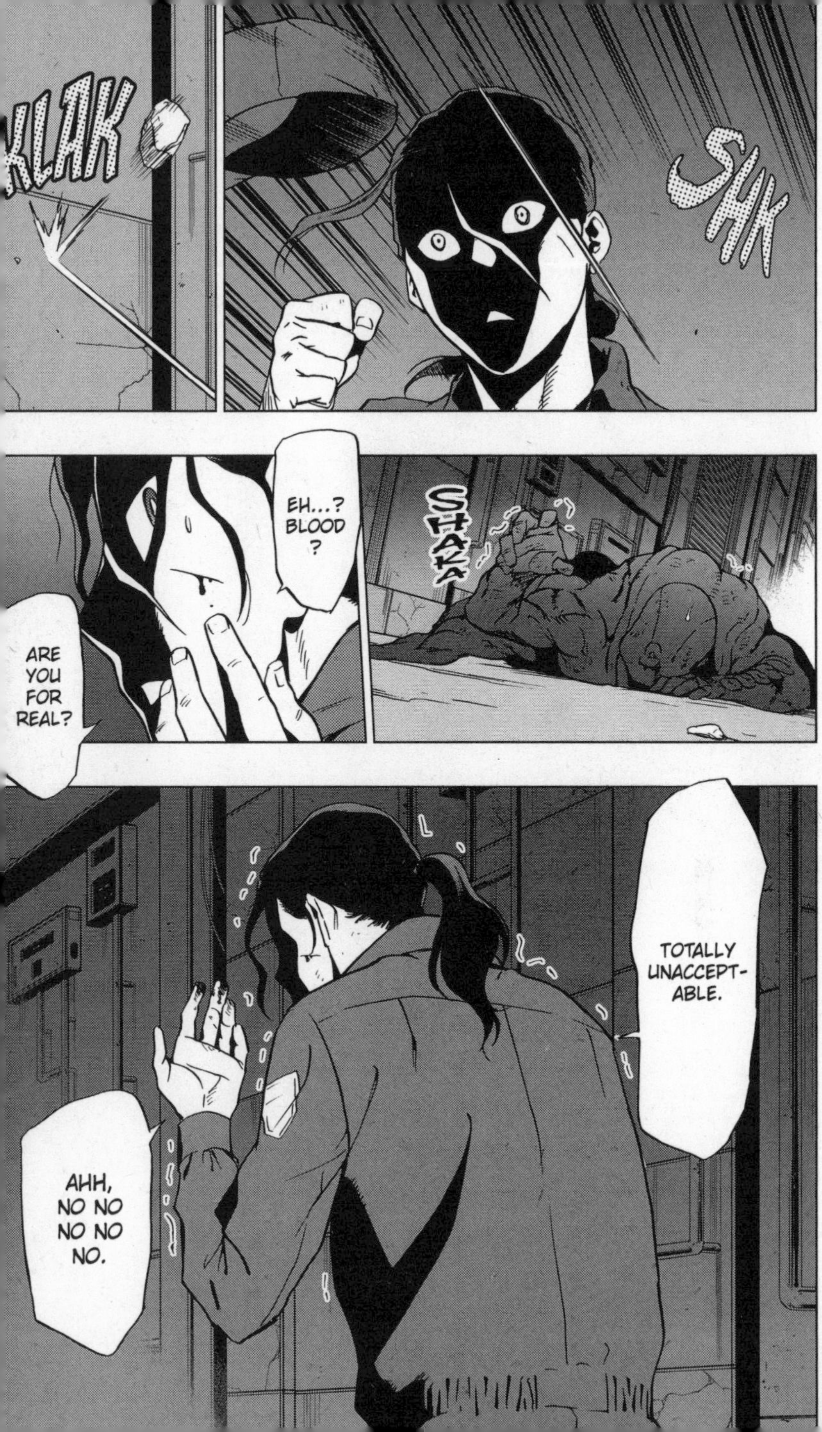
SHK
KLAK
SHAKA
EH...? BLOOD ?
ARE YOU FOR REAL?
TOTALLY UNACCEPT-ABLE.
AHH, NO NO NO NO NO.

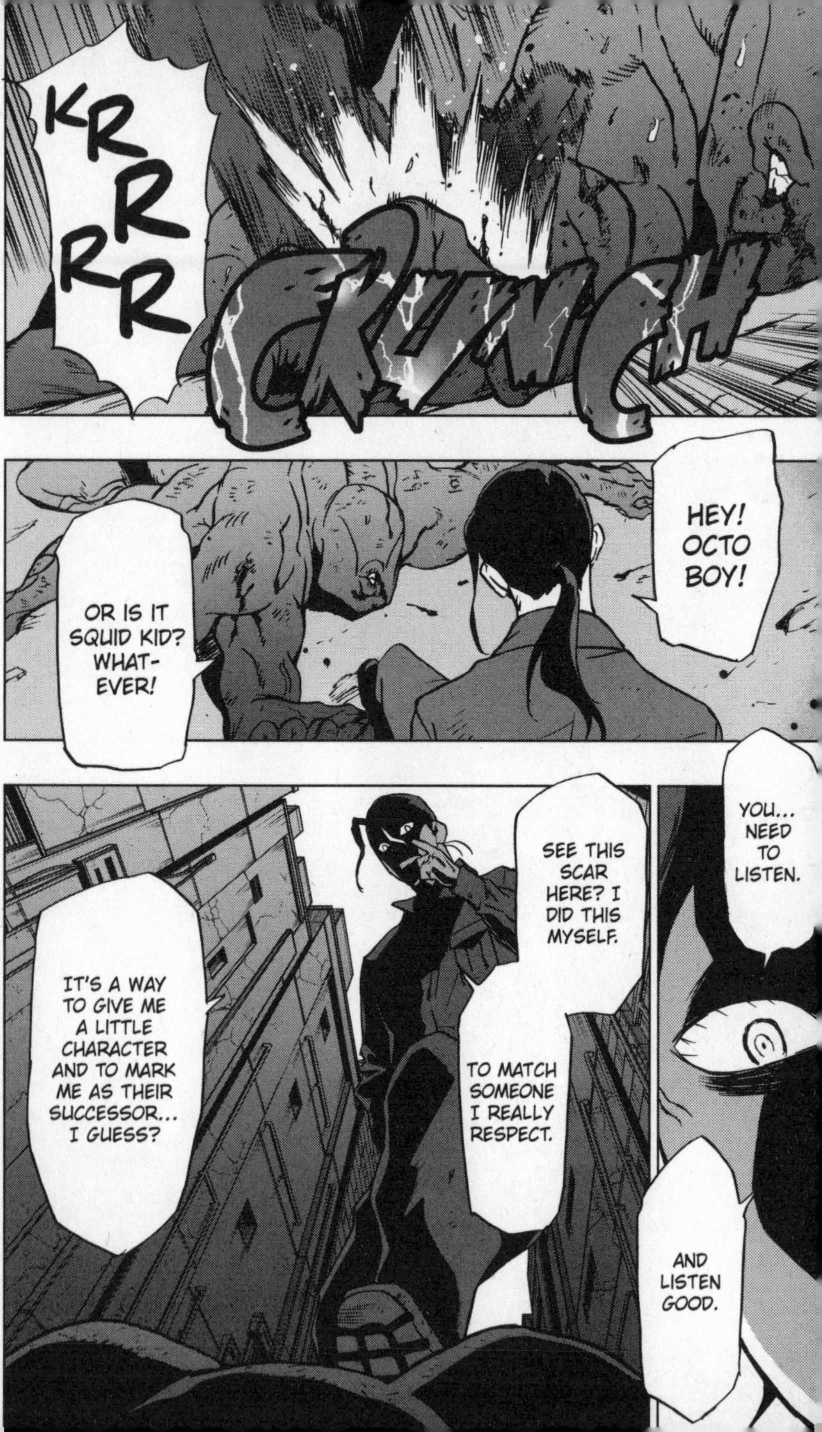
CRUNCH
KRRRR
HEY! OCTO BOY!
OR IS IT SQUID KID? WHATEVER!
YOU... NEED TO LISTEN.
AND LISTEN GOOD.
SEE THIS SCAR HERE? I DID THIS MYSELF.
TO MATCH SOMEONE I REALLY RESPECT.
IT'S A WAY TO GIVE ME A LITTLE CHARACTER AND TO MARK ME AS THEIR SUCCESSOR... I GUESS?

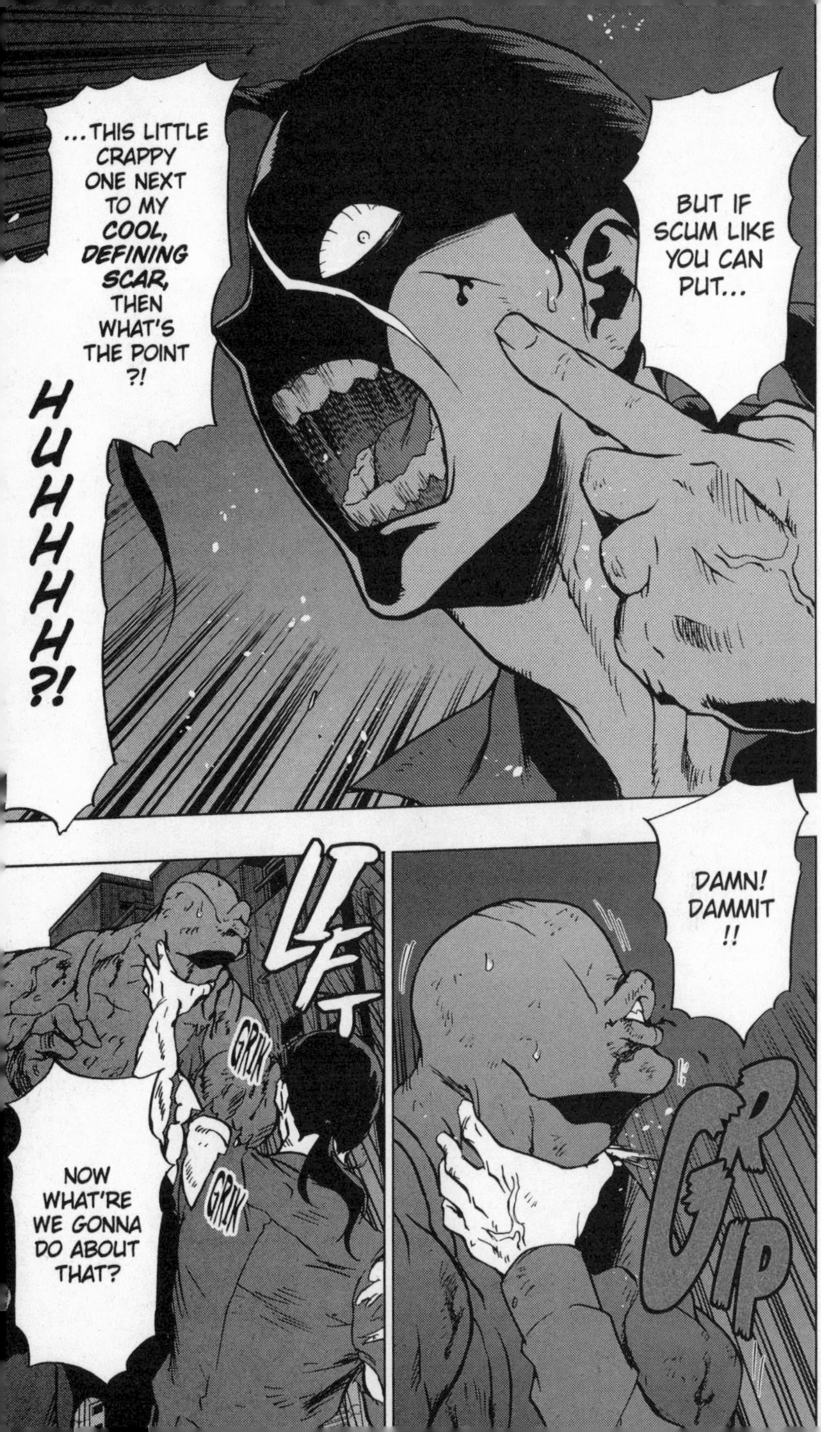
BUT IF SCUM LIKE YOU CAN PUT...
...THIS LITTLE CRAPPY ONE NEXT TO MY COOL, DEFINING SCAR, THEN WHAT'S THE POINT ?!
HUHHHHHH?!
DAMN! DAMMIT !!
GRIP
LIFT
GRIK
GRIK
NOW WHAT'RE WE GONNA DO ABOUT THAT?

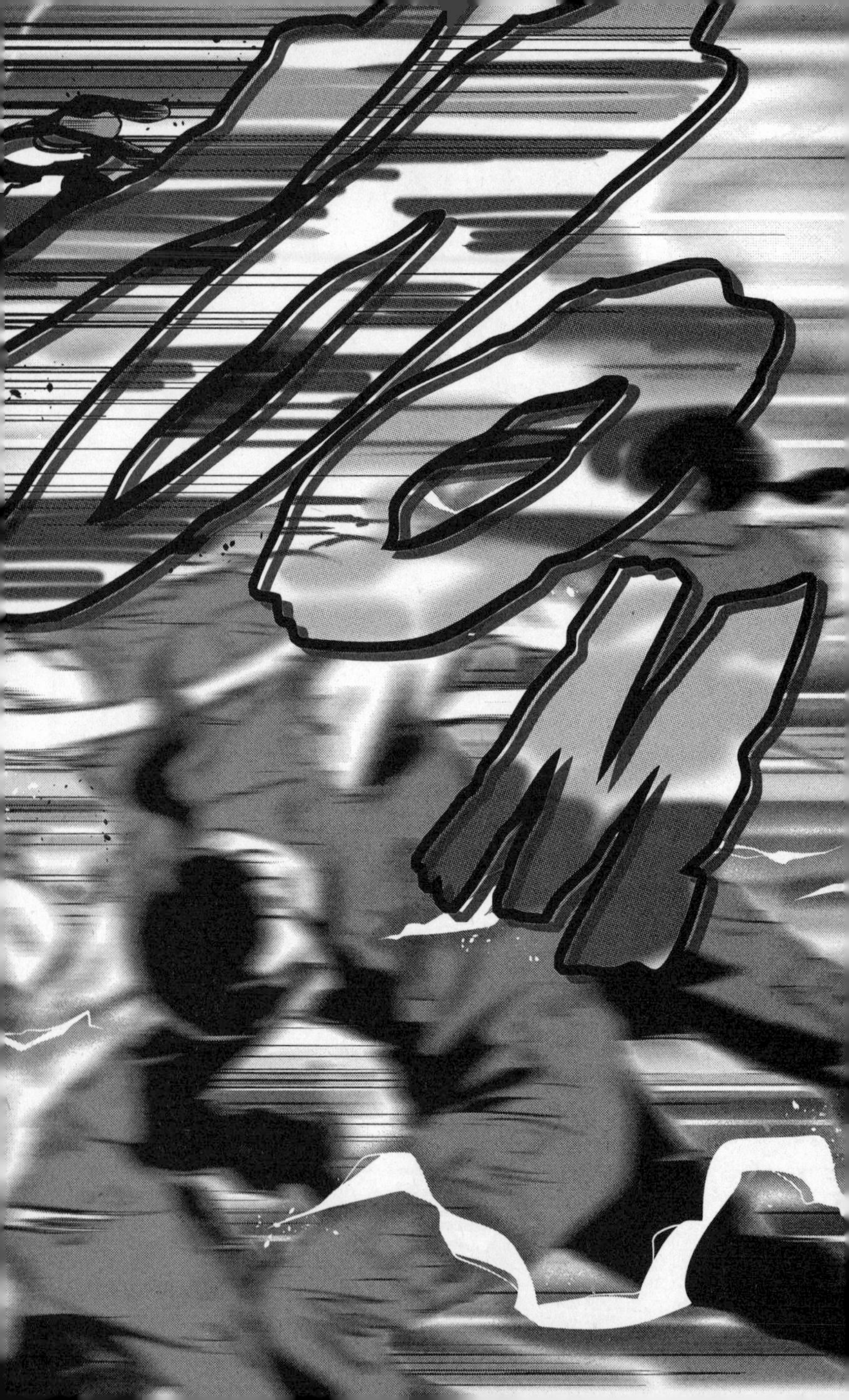

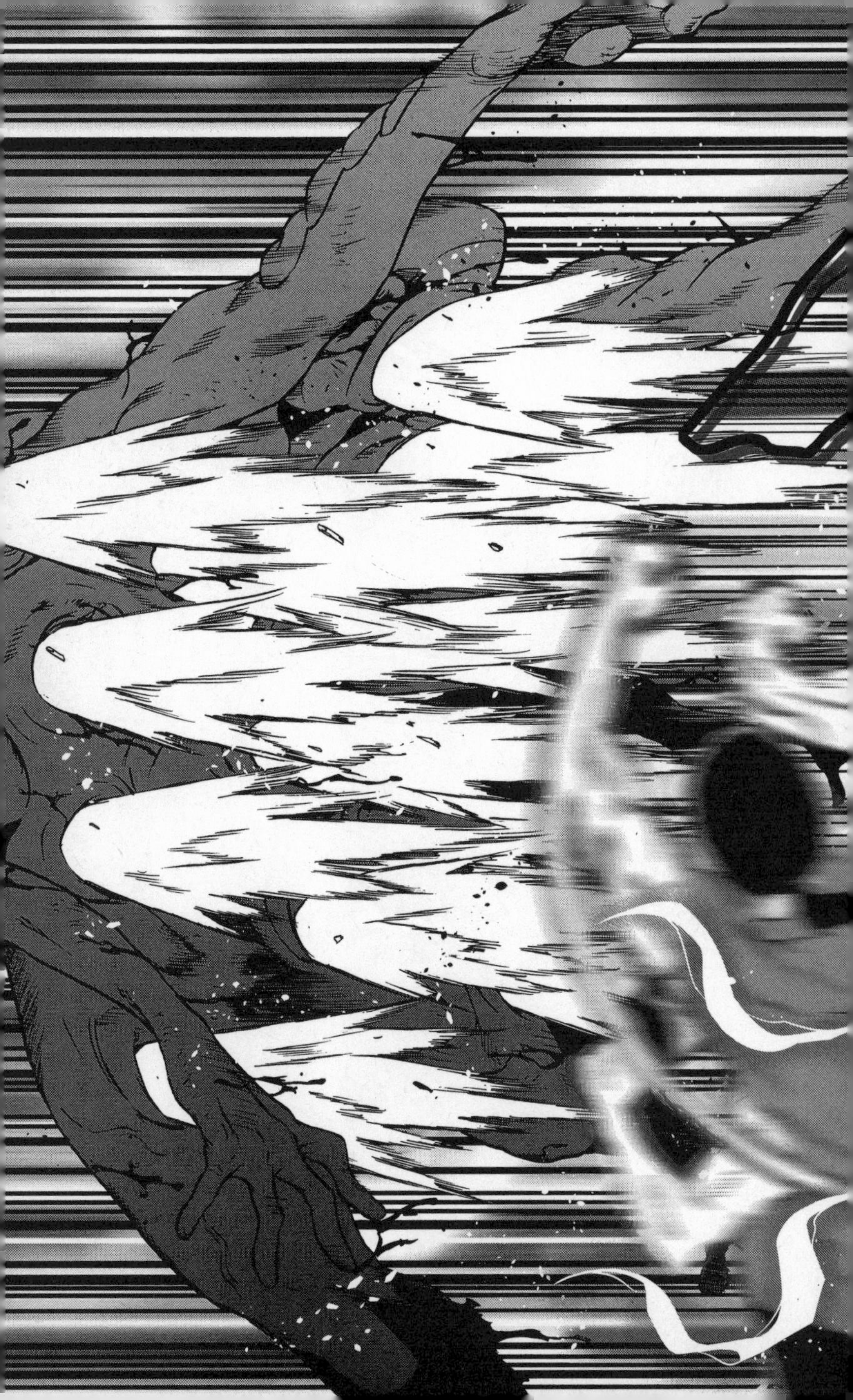

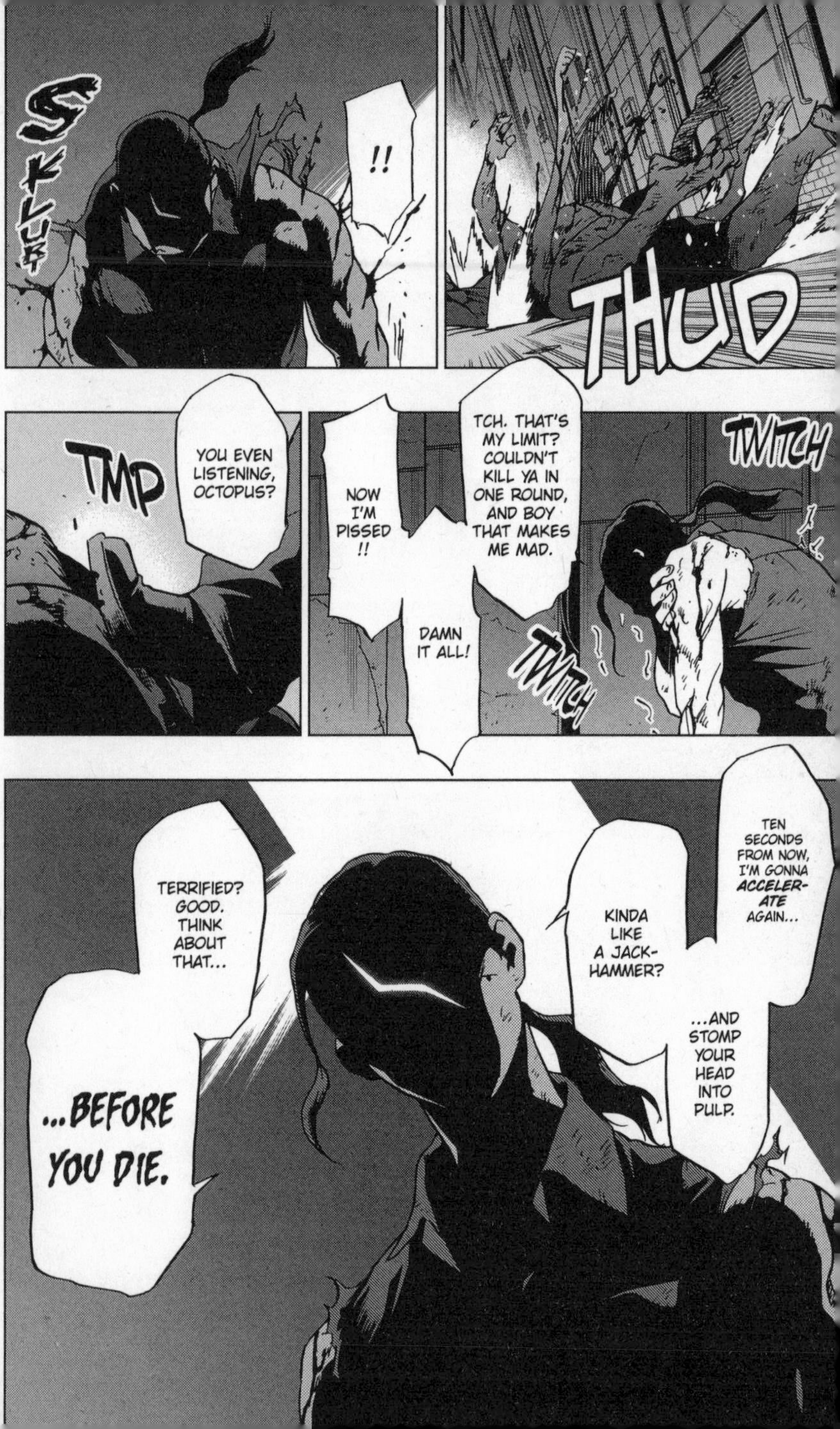
THUD
SKLURT
!!
TWITCH
TCH. THAT'S MY LIMIT? COULDN'T KILL YA IN ONE ROUND, AND BOY THAT MAKES ME MAD.
NOW I'M PISSED!!
DAMN IT ALL!
TWITCH
YOU EVEN LISTENING, OCTOPUS?
TMP
TEN SECONDS FROM NOW, I'M GONNA *ACCELERATE* AGAIN...
KINDA LIKE A JACKHAMMER?
...AND STOMP YOUR HEAD INTO PULP.
TERRIFIED? GOOD. THINK ABOUT THAT...
...BEFORE YOU DIE.

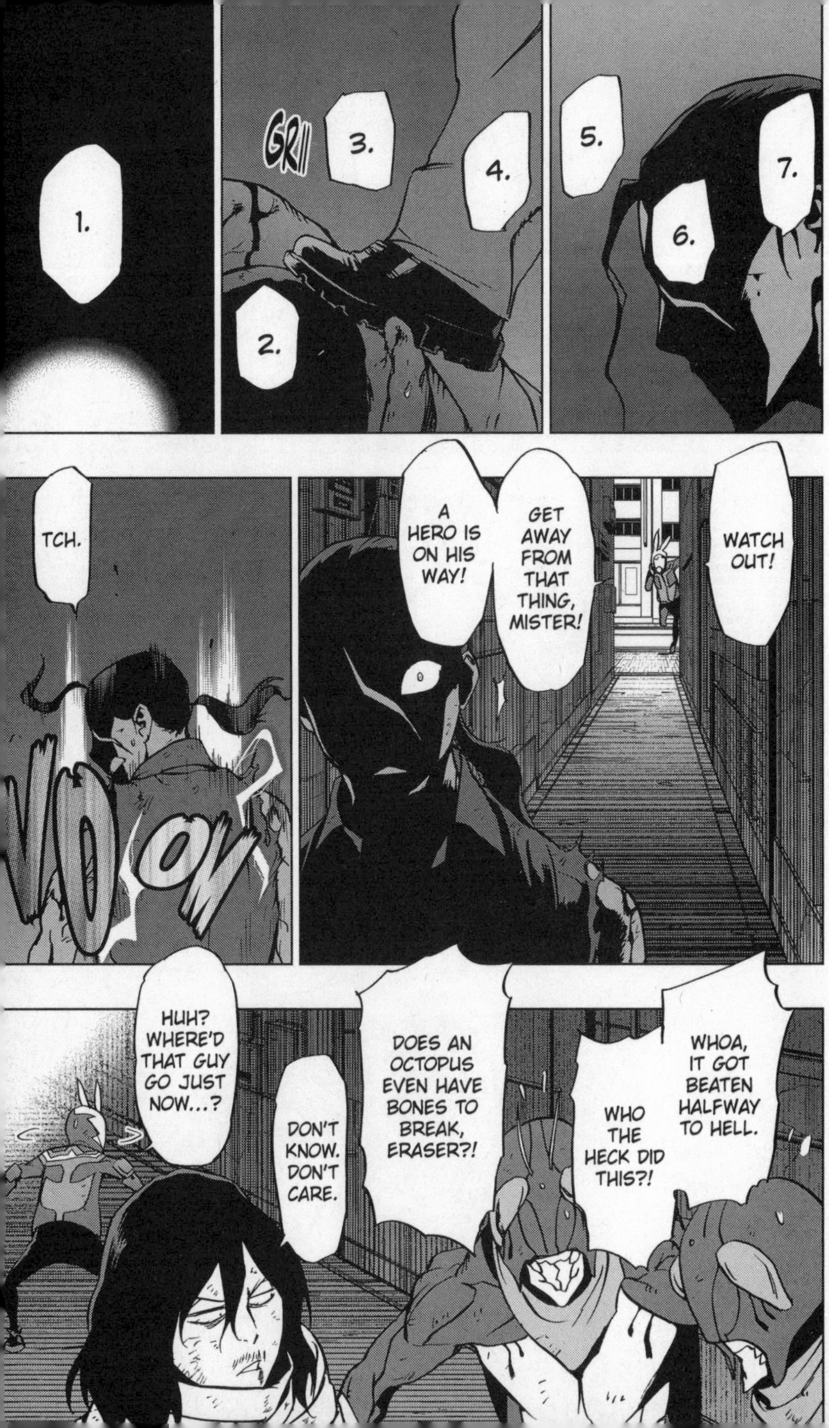
7.
6.
5.
4.
3.
GRII
2.
1.
WATCH OUT!
GET AWAY FROM THAT THING, MISTER!
A HERO IS ON HIS WAY!
TCH.
VOOV
WHOA, IT GOT BEATEN HALFWAY TO HELL.
WHO THE HECK DID THIS?!
DOES AN OCTOPUS EVEN HAVE BONES TO BREAK, ERASER?!
DON'T KNOW. DON'T CARE.
HUH? WHERE'D THAT GUY GO JUST NOW...?

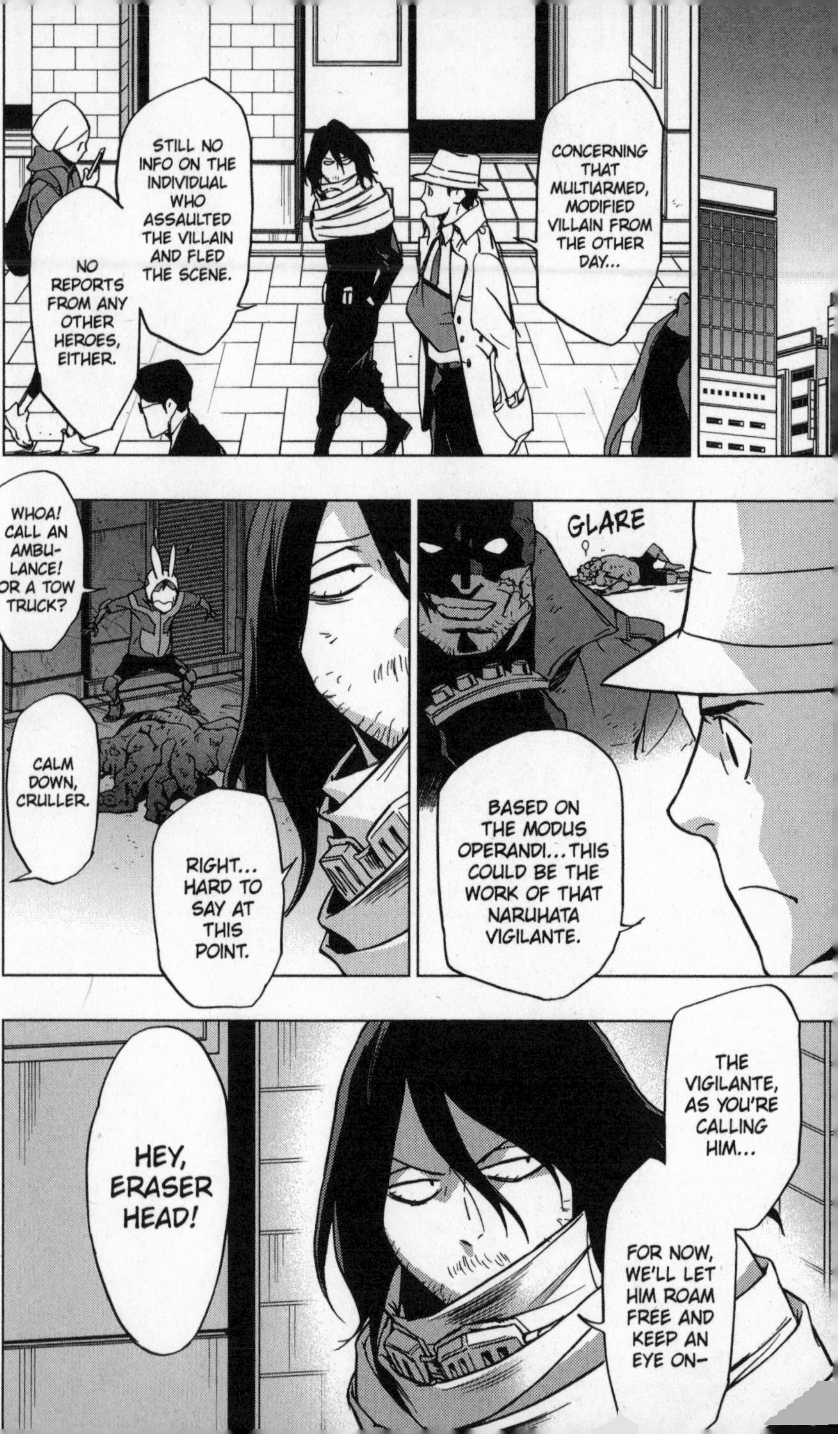
CONCERNING THAT MULTIARMED, MODIFIED VILLAIN FROM THE OTHER DAY...
STILL NO INFO ON THE INDIVIDUAL WHO ASSAULTED THE VILLAIN AND FLED THE SCENE.
NO REPORTS FROM ANY OTHER HEROES, EITHER.
GLARE
BASED ON THE MODUS OPERANDI... THIS COULD BE THE WORK OF THAT NARUHATA VIGILANTE.
RIGHT... HARD TO SAY AT THIS POINT.
WHOA! CALL AN AMBULANCE! OR A TOW TRUCK?
CALM DOWN, CRULLER.
THE VIGILANTE, AS YOU'RE CALLING HIM...
FOR NOW, WE'LL LET HIM ROAM FREE AND KEEP AN EYE ON-
HEY, ERASER HEAD!

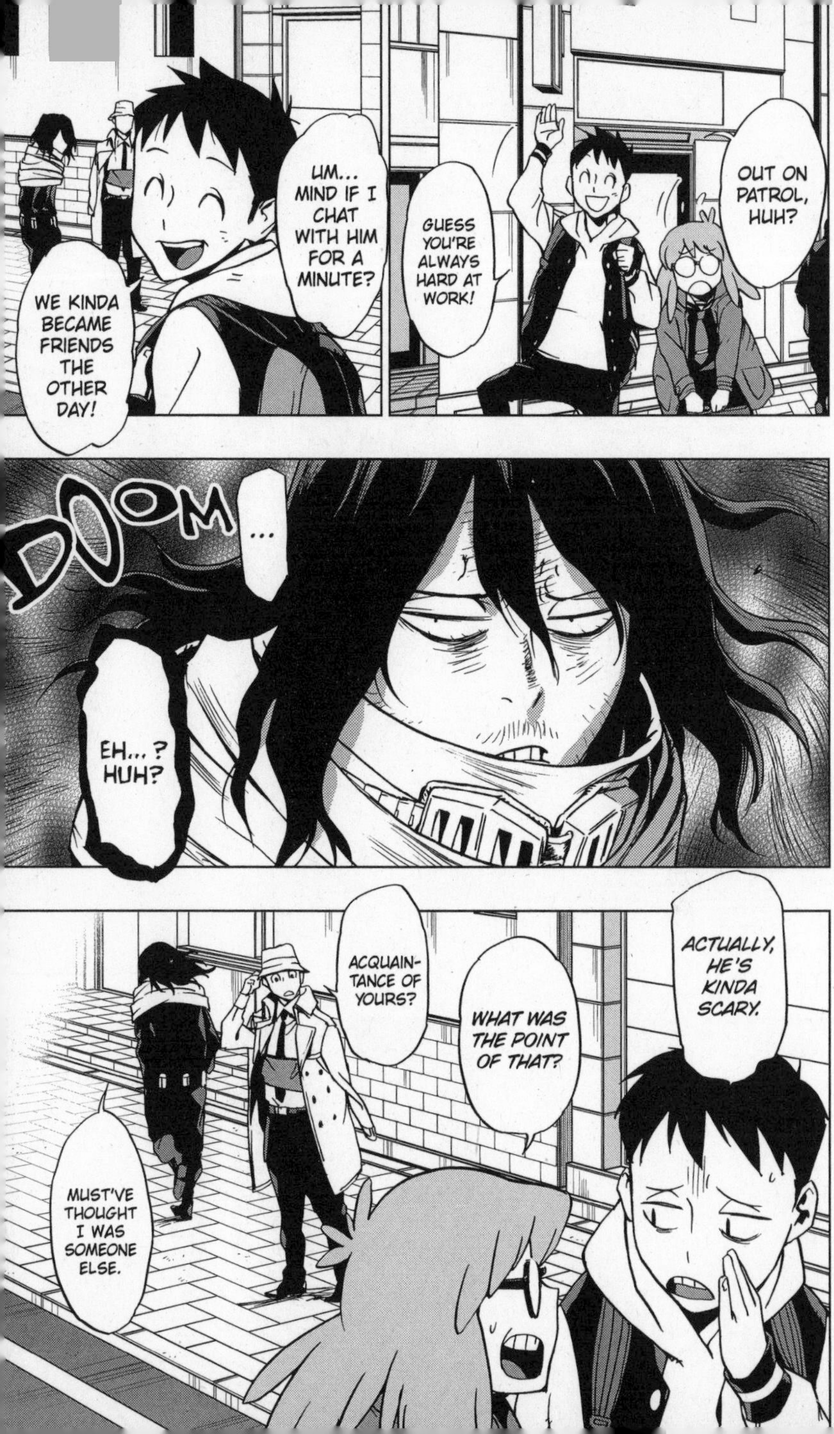
OUT ON PATROL, HUH?
GUESS YOU'RE ALWAYS HARD AT WORK!
UM... MIND IF I CHAT WITH HIM FOR A MINUTE?
WE KINDA BECAME FRIENDS THE OTHER DAY!
...
DOOM
EH...? HUH?
ACTUALLY, HE'S KINDA SCARY.
WHAT WAS THE POINT OF THAT?
ACQUAIN-TANCE OF YOURS?
MUST'VE THOUGHT I WAS SOMEONE ELSE.

THE SCARRED MAN

BEHIND THE SCENES

I was planning to flesh out his characterization very slowly over time, but having him prowl around without any real identity for so long made for a weak villain. It was a relief to finally give him some clear motivation and purpose in this last chapter.

—Furuhashi

He was dressed as a rescue worker (?) in his very first appearance, and even since then, he always looks like some kind of service worker. (LOL) I can't wait to draw him with his face *not* in shadow.

—Betten

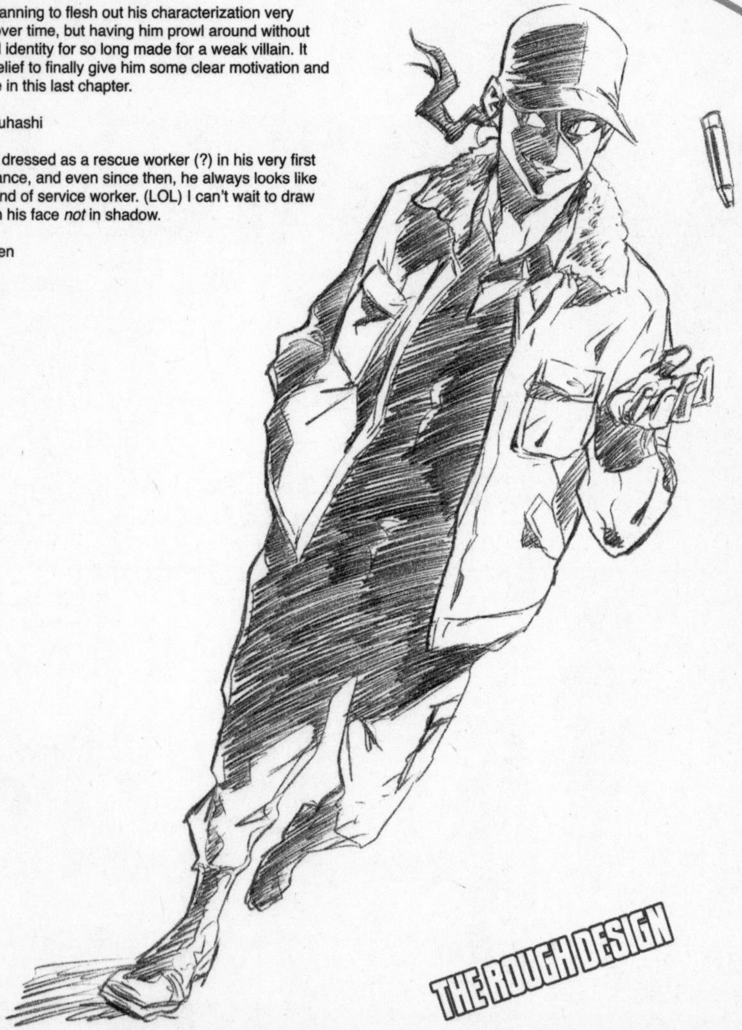

THE ROUGH DESIGN

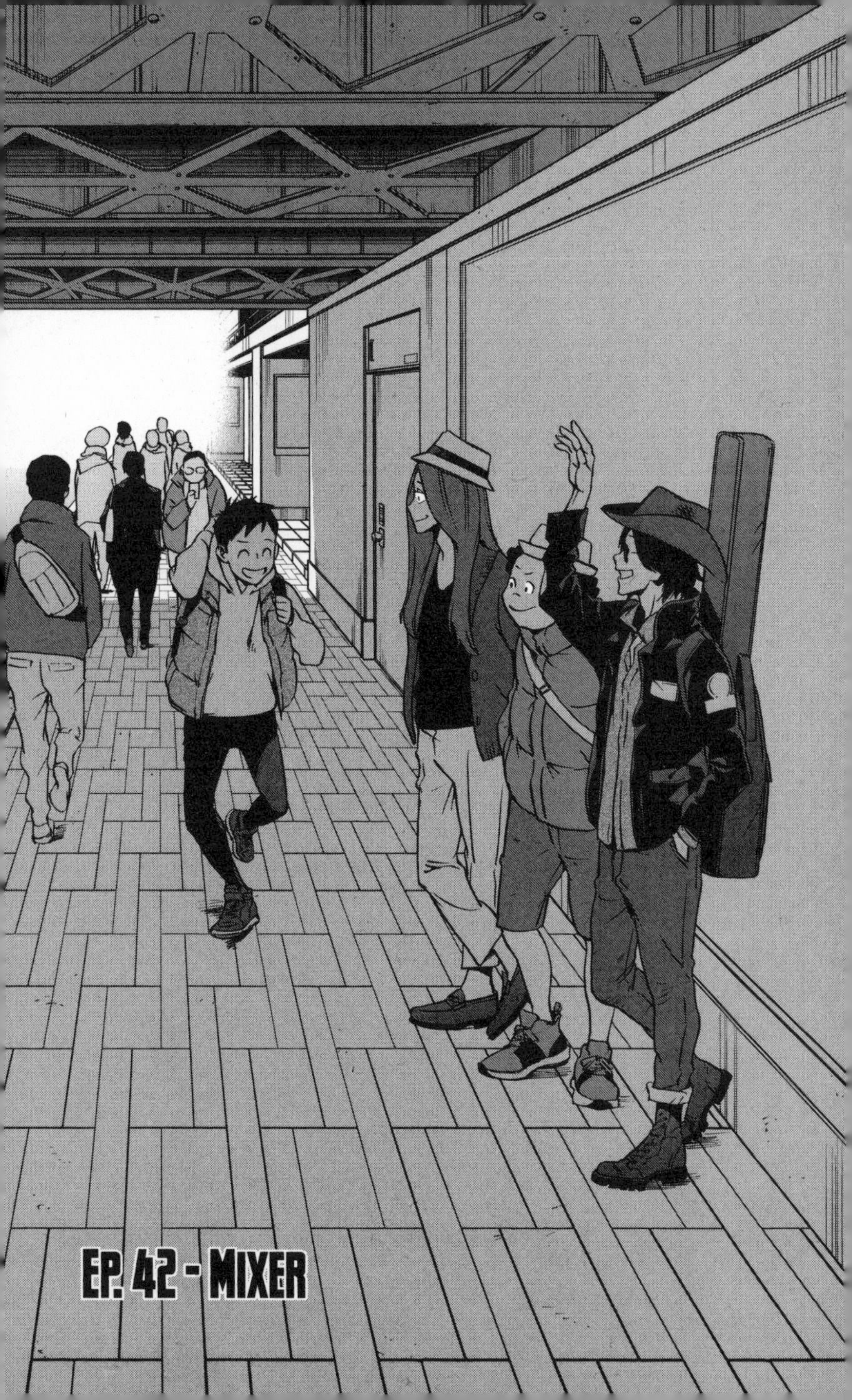
EP. 42 - MIXER

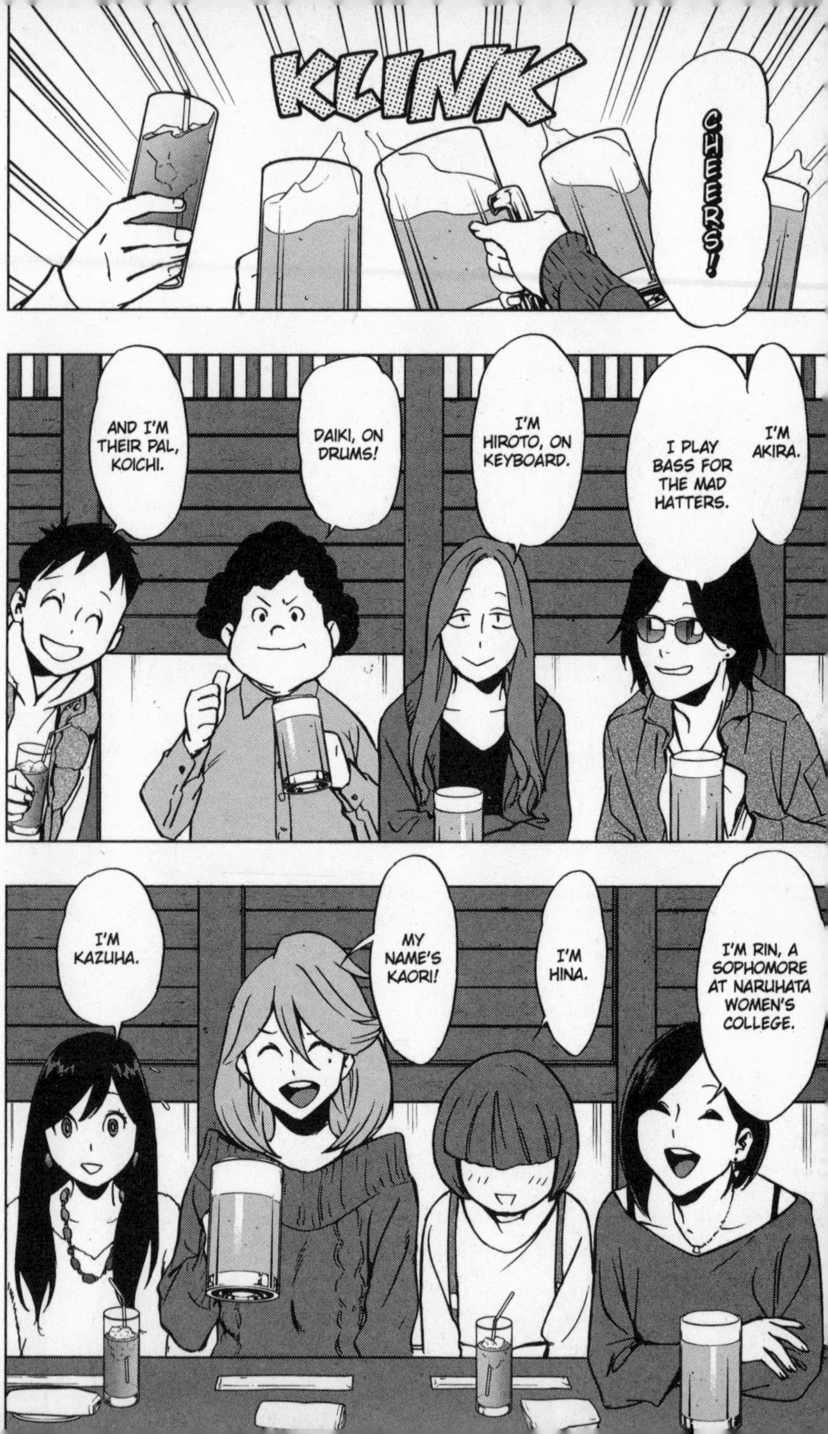
CHEERS!
KLINK
I'M AKIRA.
I PLAY BASS FOR THE MAD HATTERS.
I'M HIROTO, ON KEYBOARD.
DAIKI, ON DRUMS!
AND I'M THEIR PAL, KOICHI.
I'M RIN, A SOPHOMORE AT NARUHATA WOMEN'S COLLEGE.
I'M HINA.
MY NAME'S KAORI!
I'M KAZUHA.

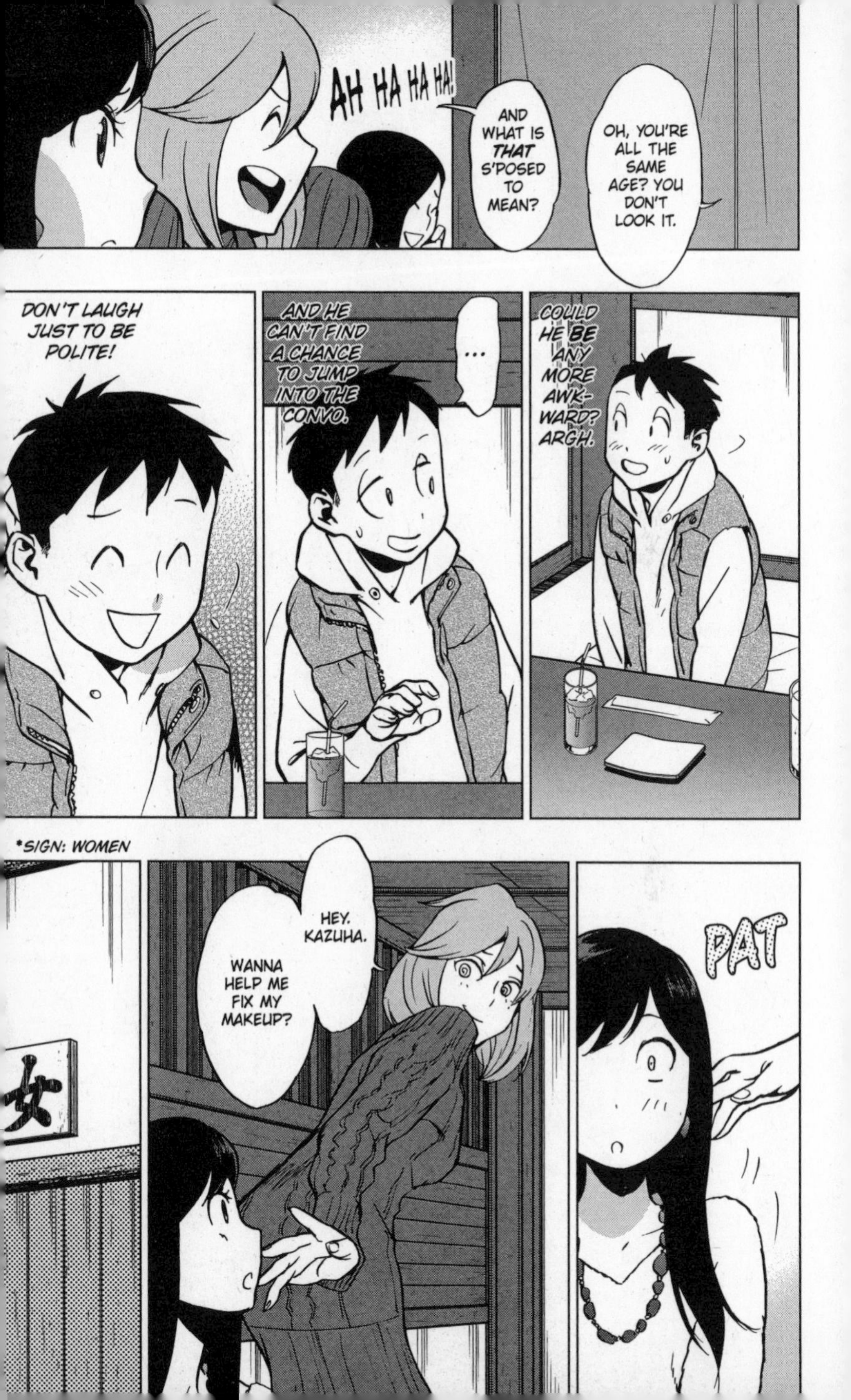
OH, YOU'RE ALL THE SAME AGE? YOU DON'T LOOK IT.
AND WHAT IS THAT S'POSED TO MEAN?
AH HA HA HA!
COULD HE BE ANY MORE AWK-WARD? ARGH.
...
AND HE CAN'T FIND A CHANCE TO JUMP INTO THE CONVO.
DON'T LAUGH JUST TO BE POLITE!
*SIGN: WOMEN
PAT
HEY. KAZUHA.
WANNA HELP ME FIX MY MAKEUP?
女

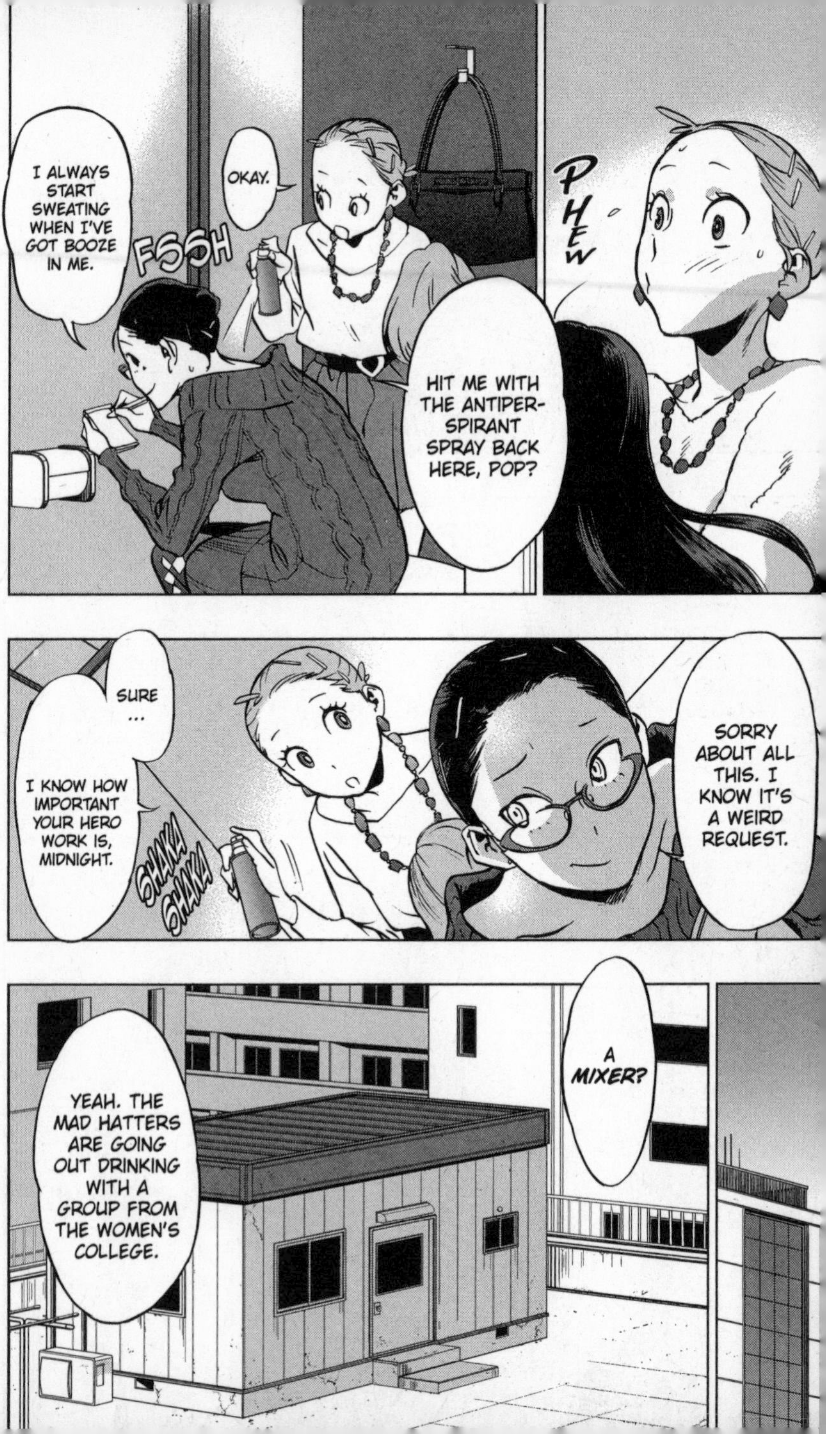
PHEW
HIT ME WITH THE ANTIPER-SPIRANT SPRAY BACK HERE, POP?
OKAY.
FSSH
I ALWAYS START SWEATING WHEN I'VE GOT BOOZE IN ME.
SORRY ABOUT ALL THIS. I KNOW IT'S A WEIRD REQUEST.
SHAKA SHAKA
SURE ...
I KNOW HOW IMPORTANT YOUR HERO WORK IS, MIDNIGHT.
A *MIXER?*
YEAH. THE MAD HATTERS ARE GOING OUT DRINKING WITH A GROUP FROM THE WOMEN'S COLLEGE.

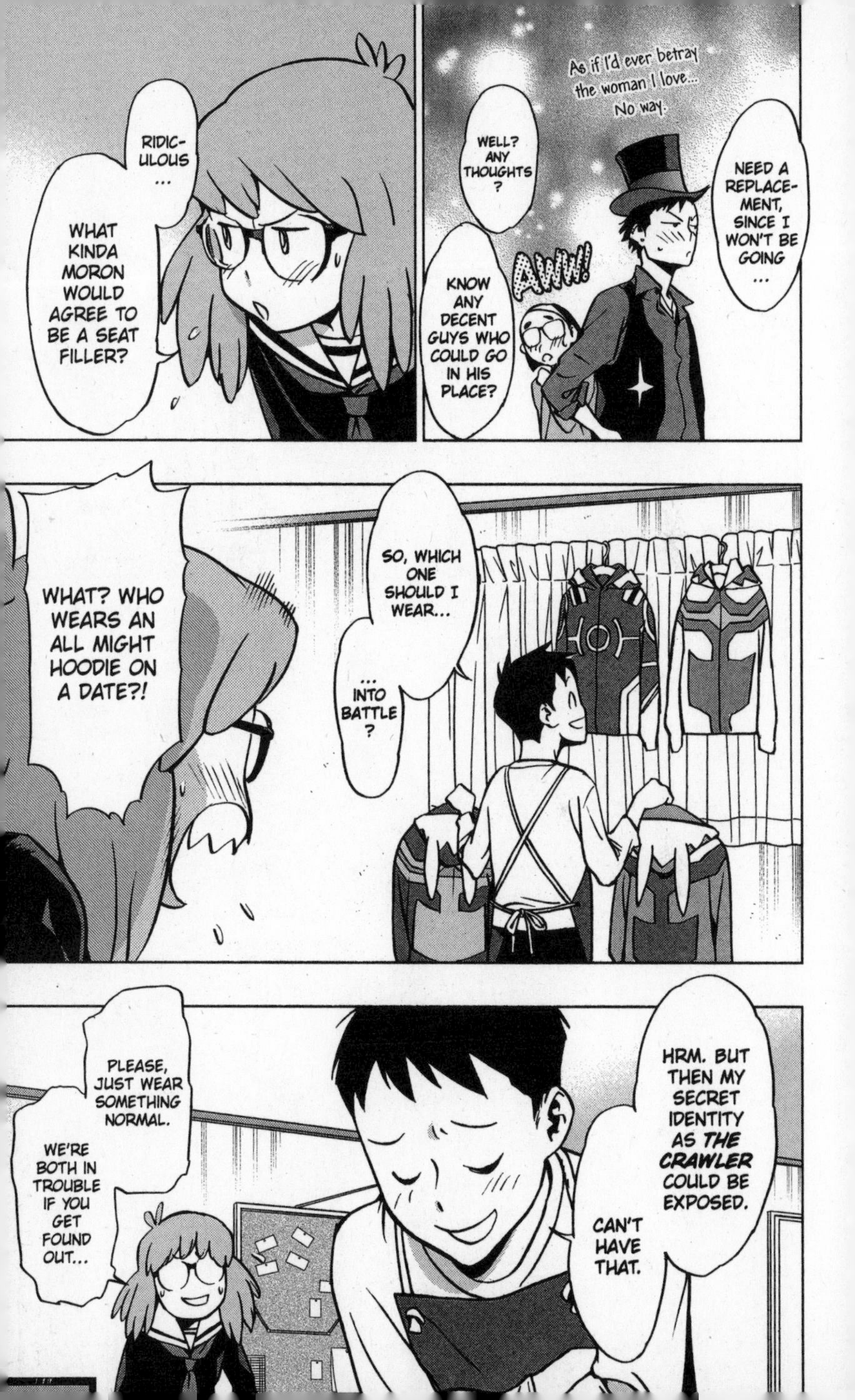
As if I'd ever betray the woman I love... No way.
NEED A REPLACEMENT, SINCE I WON'T BE GOING...
AWW!
WELL? ANY THOUGHTS?
KNOW ANY DECENT GUYS WHO COULD GO IN HIS PLACE?
RIDICULOUS...
WHAT KINDA MORON WOULD AGREE TO BE A SEAT FILLER?
SO, WHICH ONE SHOULD I WEAR...
...INTO BATTLE?
WHAT? WHO WEARS AN ALL MIGHT HOODIE ON A DATE?!
HRM. BUT THEN MY SECRET IDENTITY AS ***THE CRAWLER*** COULD BE EXPOSED.
CAN'T HAVE THAT.
PLEASE, JUST WEAR SOMETHING NORMAL.
WE'RE BOTH IN TROUBLE IF YOU GET FOUND OUT...

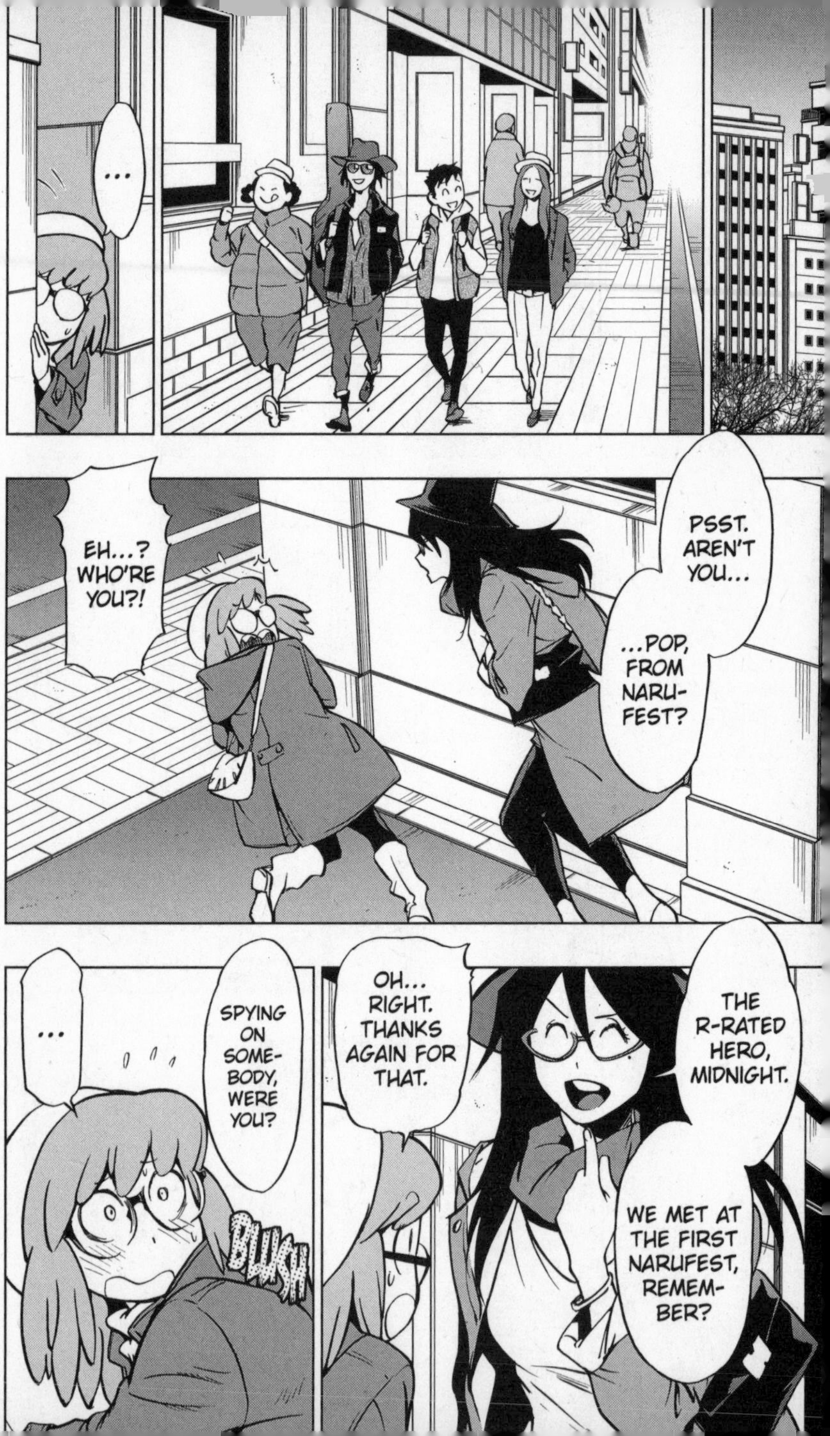
...
PSST. AREN'T YOU...
...POP, FROM NARU-FEST?
EH...? WHO'RE YOU?!
THE R-RATED HERO, MIDNIGHT.
WE MET AT THE FIRST NARUFEST, REMEMBER?
OH... RIGHT. THANKS AGAIN FOR THAT.
SPYING ON SOME-BODY, WERE YOU?
...
BLUSH

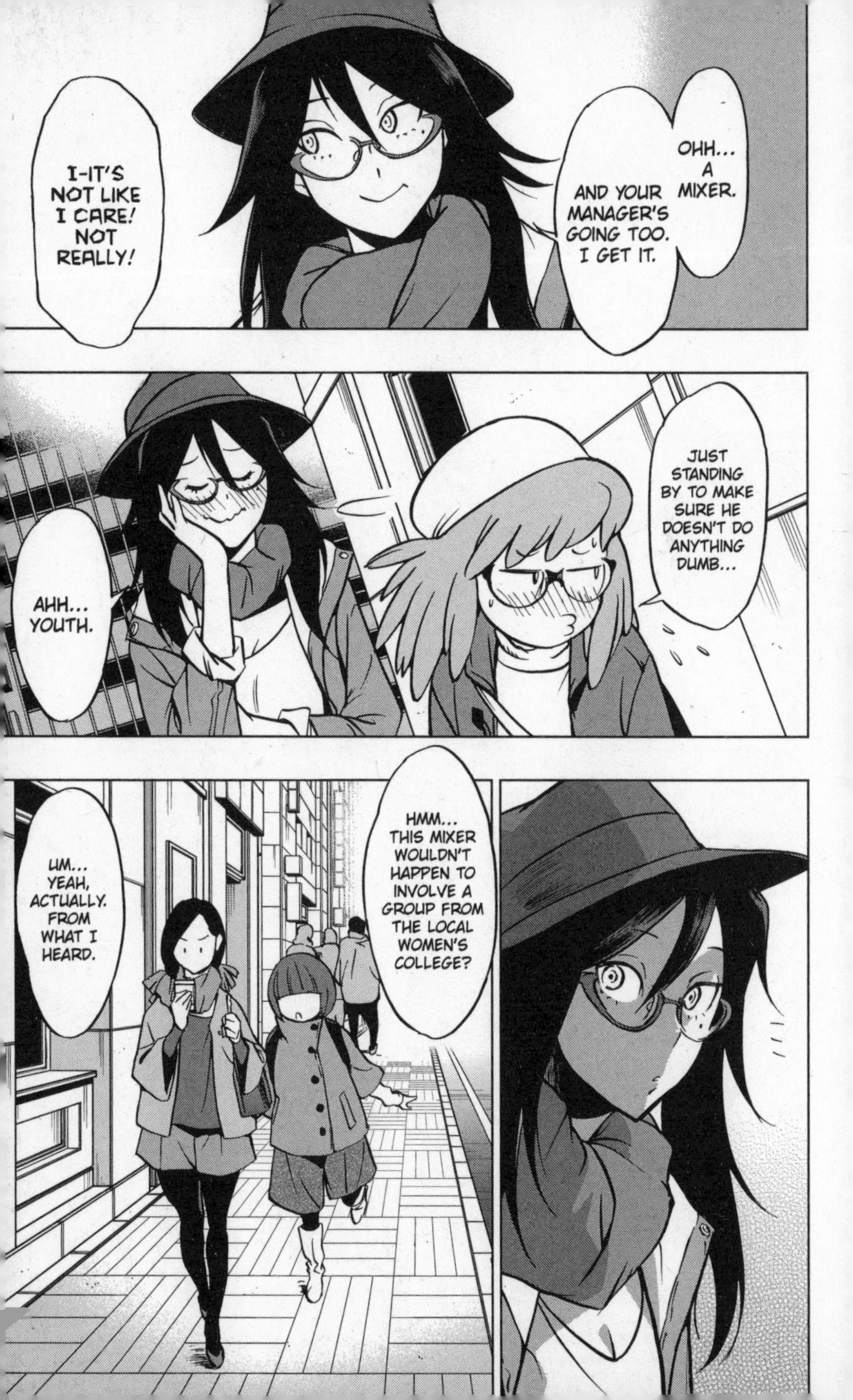
OHH... A MIXER.
AND YOUR MANAGER'S GOING TOO. I GET IT.
I-IT'S NOT LIKE I CARE! NOT REALLY!
JUST STANDING BY TO MAKE SURE HE DOESN'T DO ANYTHING DUMB...
AHH... YOUTH.
HMM... THIS MIXER WOULDN'T HAPPEN TO INVOLVE A GROUP FROM THE LOCAL WOMEN'S COLLEGE?
UM... YEAH, ACTUALLY. FROM WHAT I HEARD.

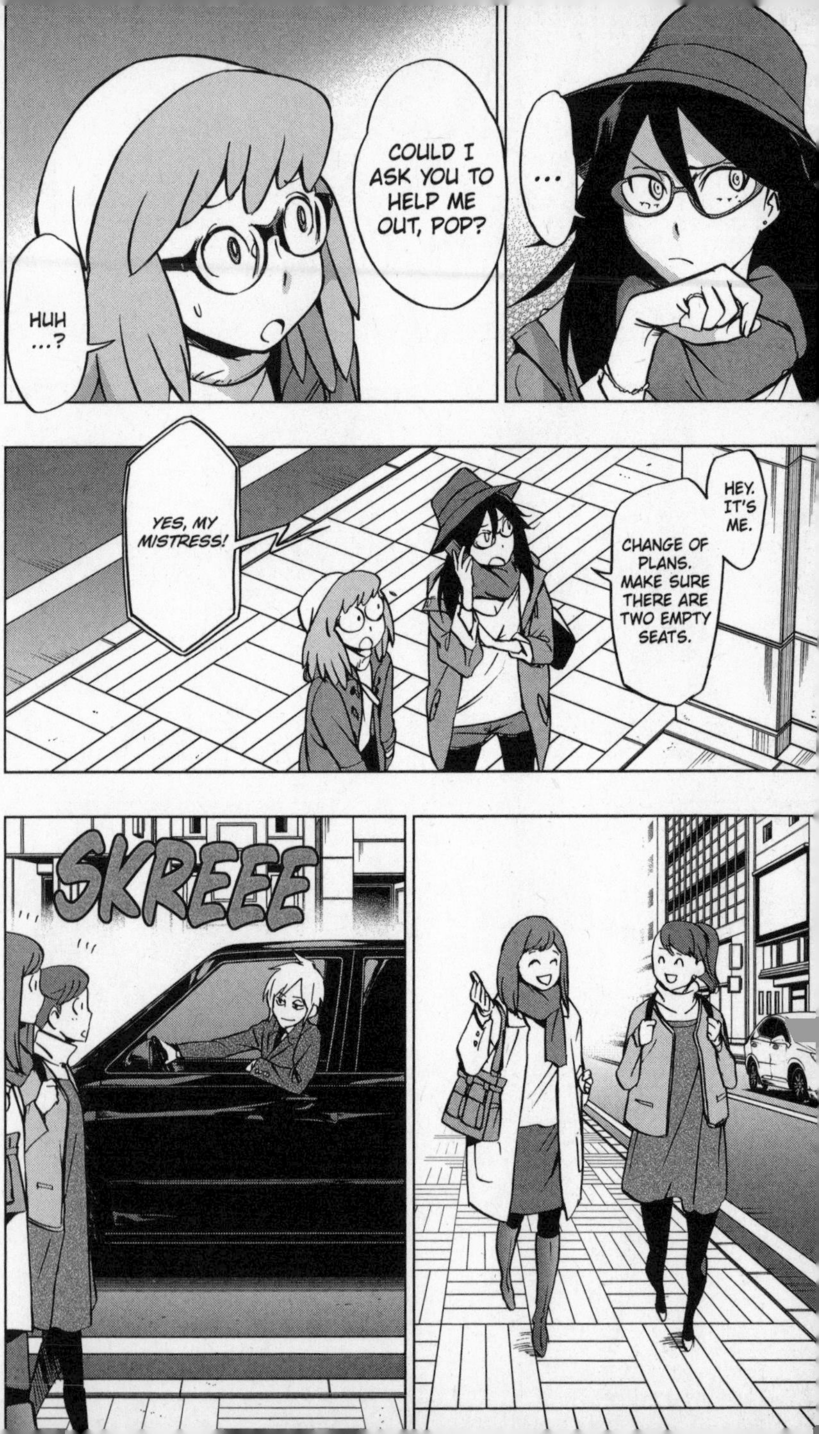
...
COULD I ASK YOU TO HELP ME OUT, POP?
HUH ...?
HEY. IT'S ME.
CHANGE OF PLANS. MAKE SURE THERE ARE TWO EMPTY SEATS.
...
YES, MY MISTRESS!
SKREEE

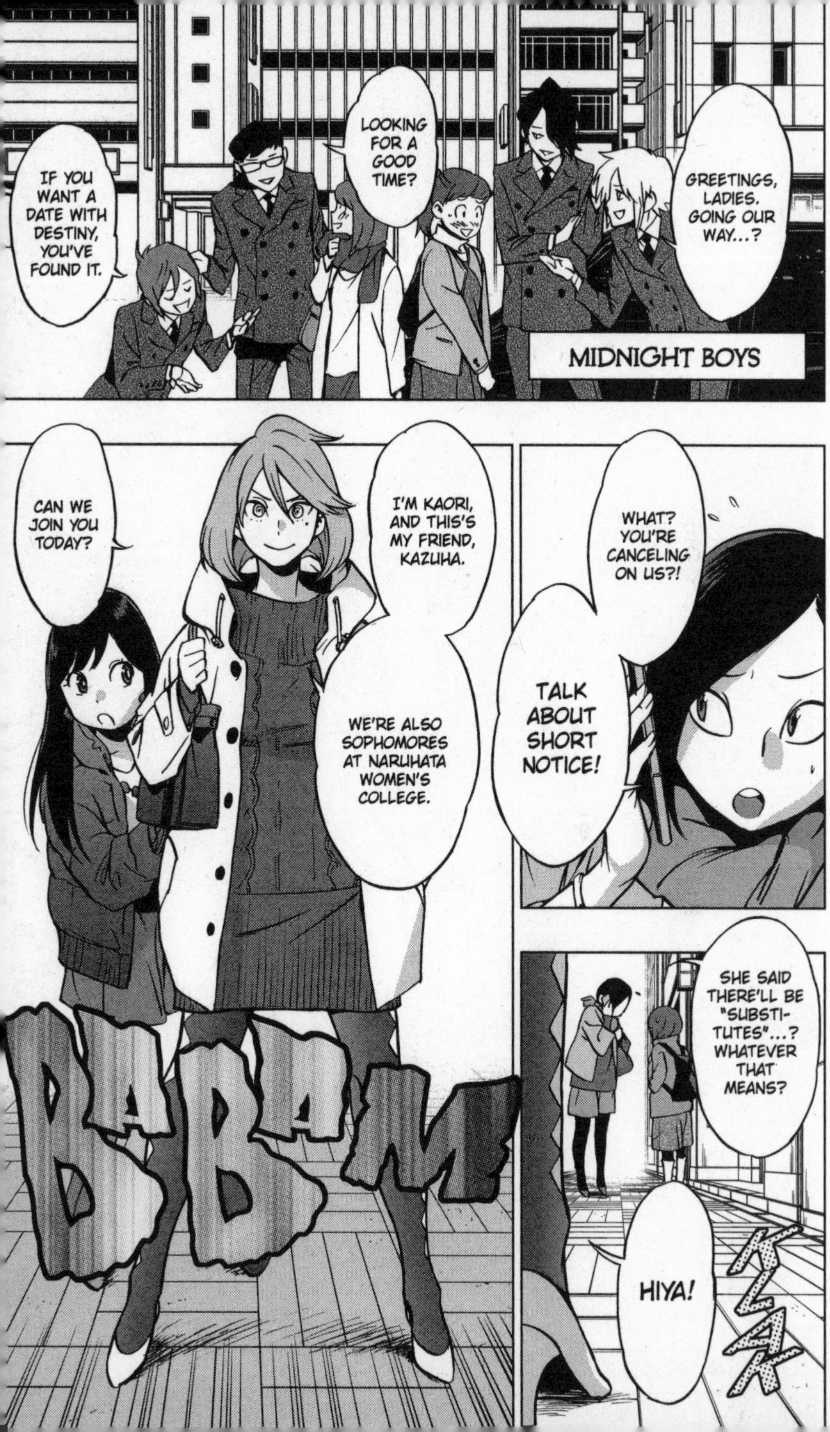
GREETINGS, LADIES. GOING OUR WAY...?
LOOKING FOR A GOOD TIME?
IF YOU WANT A DATE WITH DESTINY, YOU'VE FOUND IT.
MIDNIGHT BOYS
WHAT? YOU'RE CANCELING ON US?!
TALK ABOUT SHORT NOTICE!
SHE SAID THERE'LL BE "SUBSTI-TUTES"...? WHATEVER THAT MEANS?
HIYA!
KLAK
I'M KAORI, AND THIS'S MY FRIEND, KAZUHA.
CAN WE JOIN YOU TODAY?
WE'RE ALSO SOPHOMORES AT NARUHATA WOMEN'S COLLEGE.
BABAM

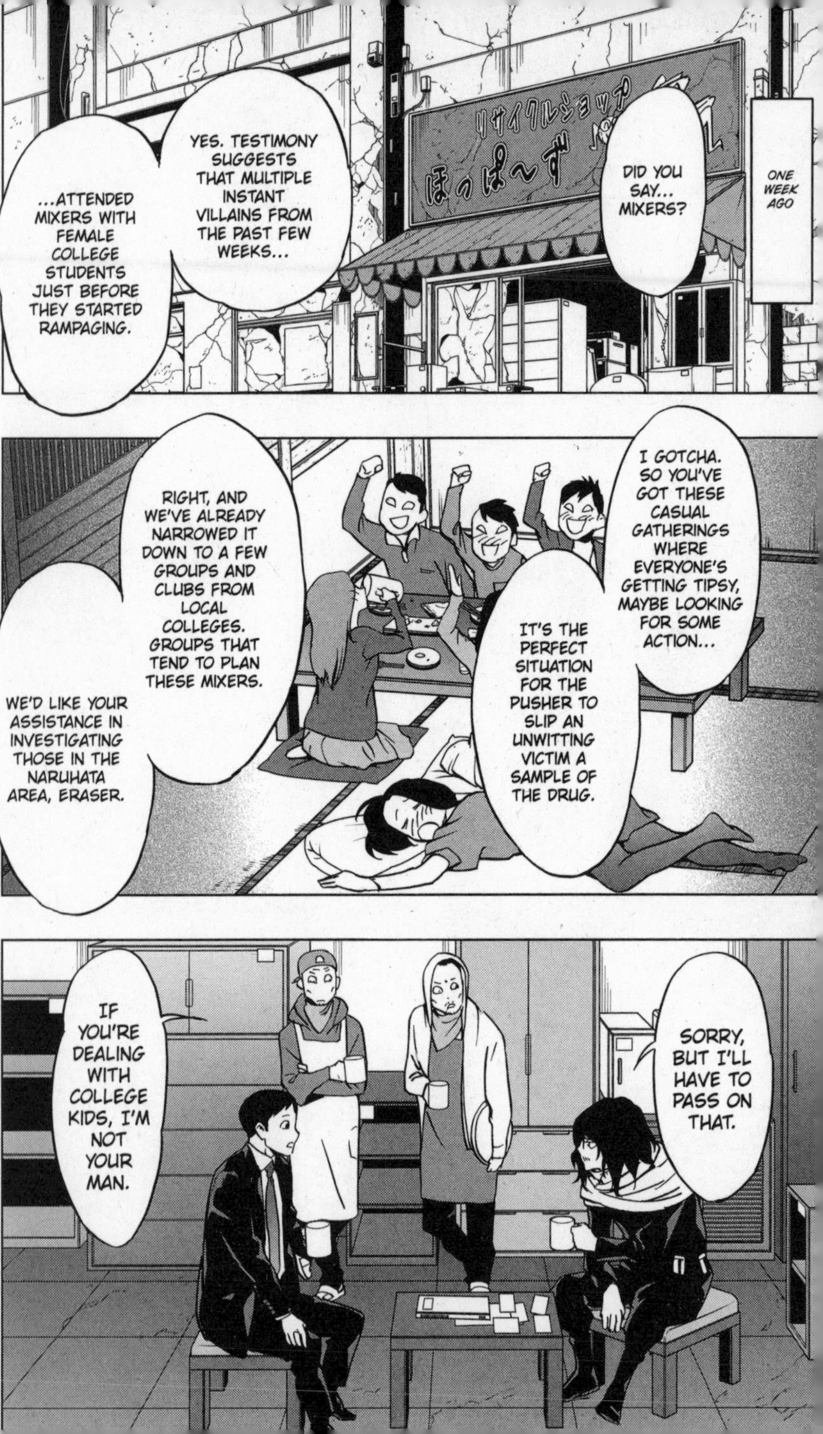
ONE WEEK AGO
リサイクルショップ
ほっぱ〜ず
DID YOU SAY... MIXERS?
YES. TESTIMONY SUGGESTS THAT MULTIPLE INSTANT VILLAINS FROM THE PAST FEW WEEKS...
...ATTENDED MIXERS WITH FEMALE COLLEGE STUDENTS JUST BEFORE THEY STARTED RAMPAGING.
I GOTCHA. SO YOU'VE GOT THESE CASUAL GATHERINGS WHERE EVERYONE'S GETTING TIPSY, MAYBE LOOKING FOR SOME ACTION...
IT'S THE PERFECT SITUATION FOR THE PUSHER TO SLIP AN UNWITTING VICTIM A SAMPLE OF THE DRUG.
RIGHT, AND WE'VE ALREADY NARROWED IT DOWN TO A FEW GROUPS AND CLUBS FROM LOCAL COLLEGES. GROUPS THAT TEND TO PLAN THESE MIXERS.
WE'D LIKE YOUR ASSISTANCE IN INVESTIGATING THOSE IN THE NARUHATA AREA, ERASER.
SORRY, BUT I'LL HAVE TO PASS ON THAT.
IF YOU'RE DEALING WITH COLLEGE KIDS, I'M NOT YOUR MAN.

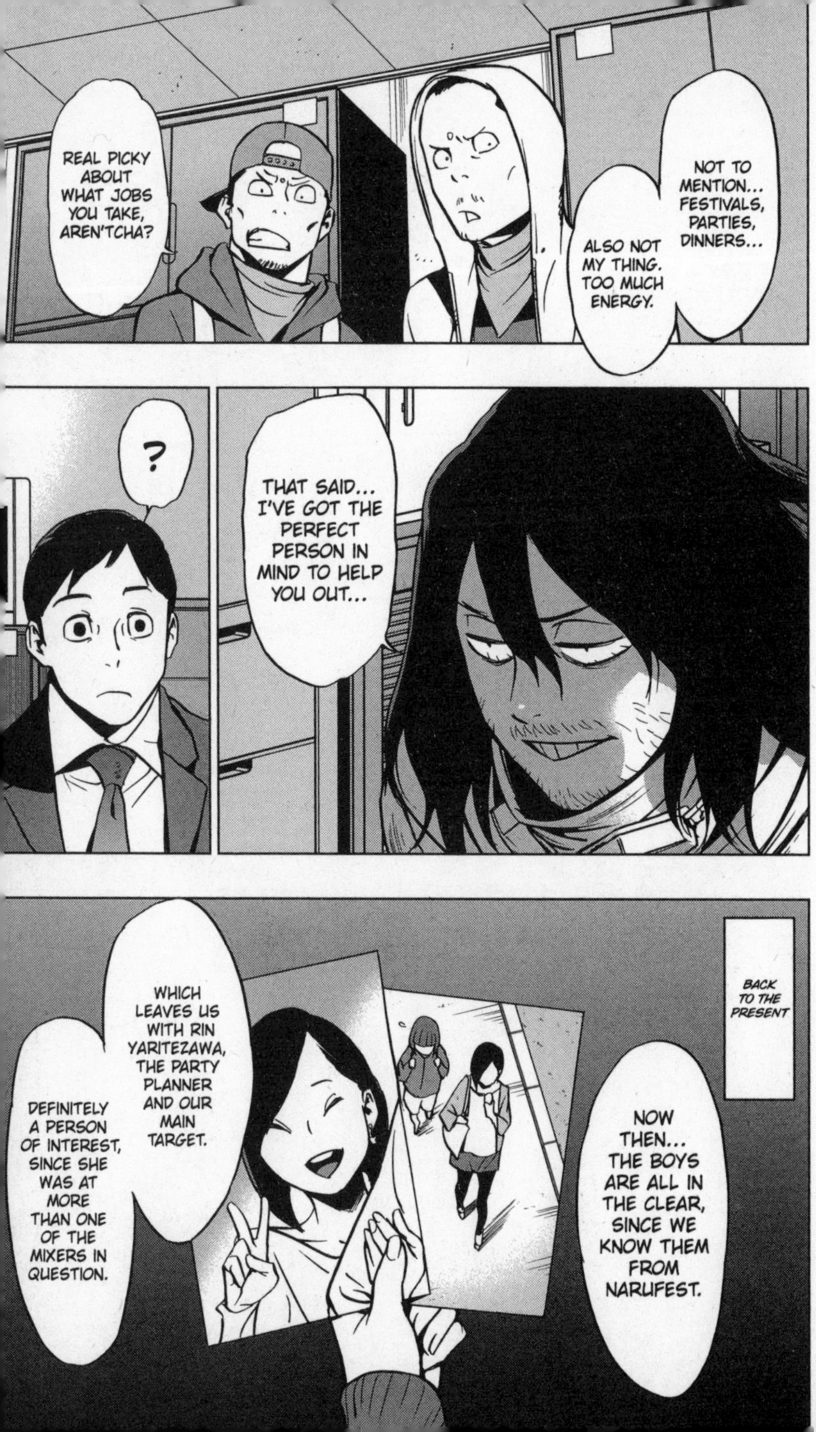
NOT TO MENTION... FESTIVALS, PARTIES, DINNERS...
ALSO NOT MY THING. TOO MUCH ENERGY.
REAL PICKY ABOUT WHAT JOBS YOU TAKE, AREN'TCHA?
THAT SAID... I'VE GOT THE PERFECT PERSON IN MIND TO HELP YOU OUT...
?
BACK TO THE PRESENT
NOW THEN... THE BOYS ARE ALL IN THE CLEAR, SINCE WE KNOW THEM FROM NARUFEST.
WHICH LEAVES US WITH RIN YARITEZAWA, THE PARTY PLANNER AND OUR MAIN TARGET.
DEFINITELY A PERSON OF INTEREST, SINCE SHE WAS AT MORE THAN ONE OF THE MIXERS IN QUESTION.

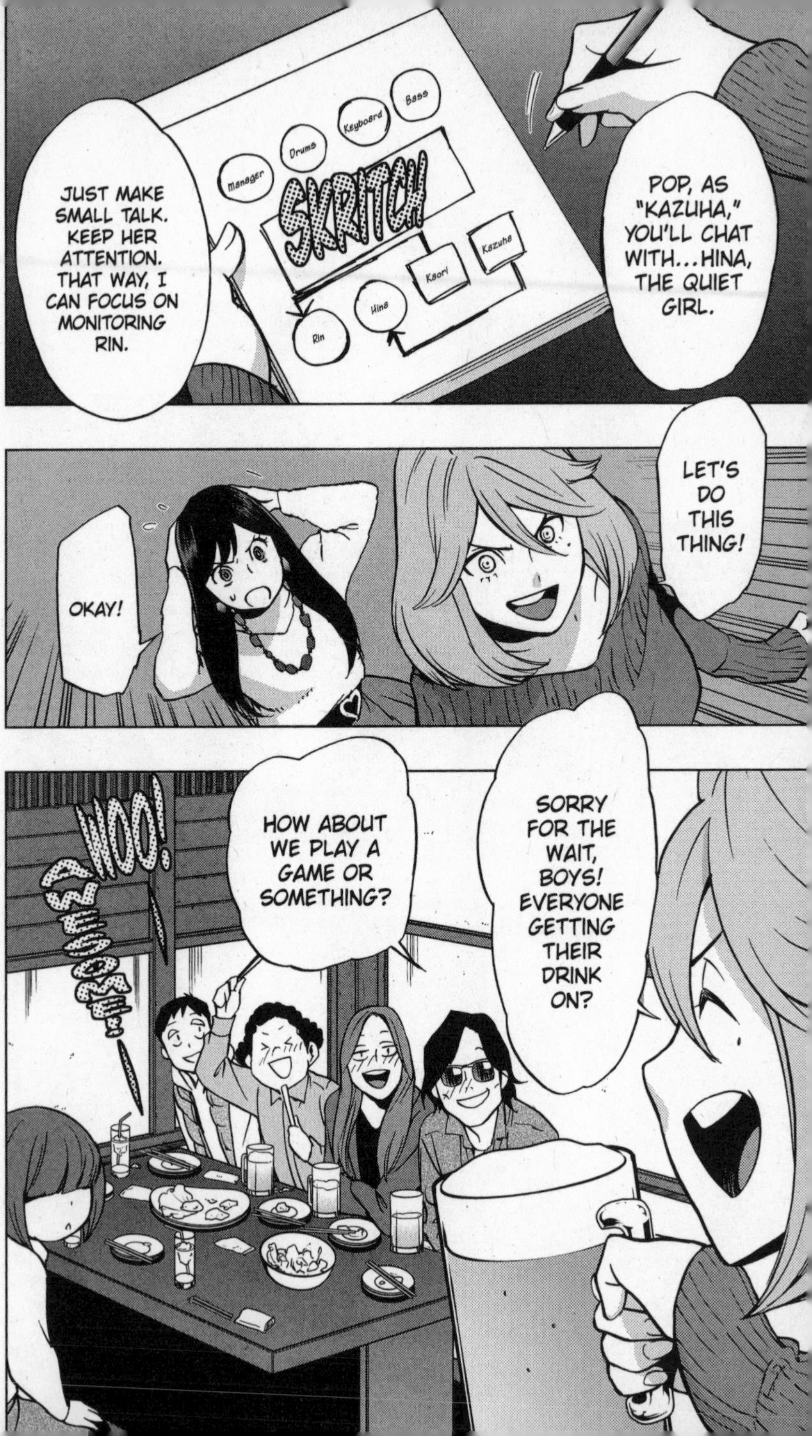
POP, AS "KAZUHA," YOU'LL CHAT WITH...HINA, THE QUIET GIRL.
SKRITCH
Bass
Keyboard
Drums
Manager
Kazuha
Kaori
Hina
Rin
JUST MAKE SMALL TALK. KEEP HER ATTENTION. THAT WAY, I CAN FOCUS ON MONITORING RIN.
LET'S DO THIS THING!
OKAY!
SORRY FOR THE WAIT, BOYS! EVERYONE GETTING THEIR DRINK ON?
HOW ABOUT WE PLAY A GAME OR SOMETHING?
WOO!

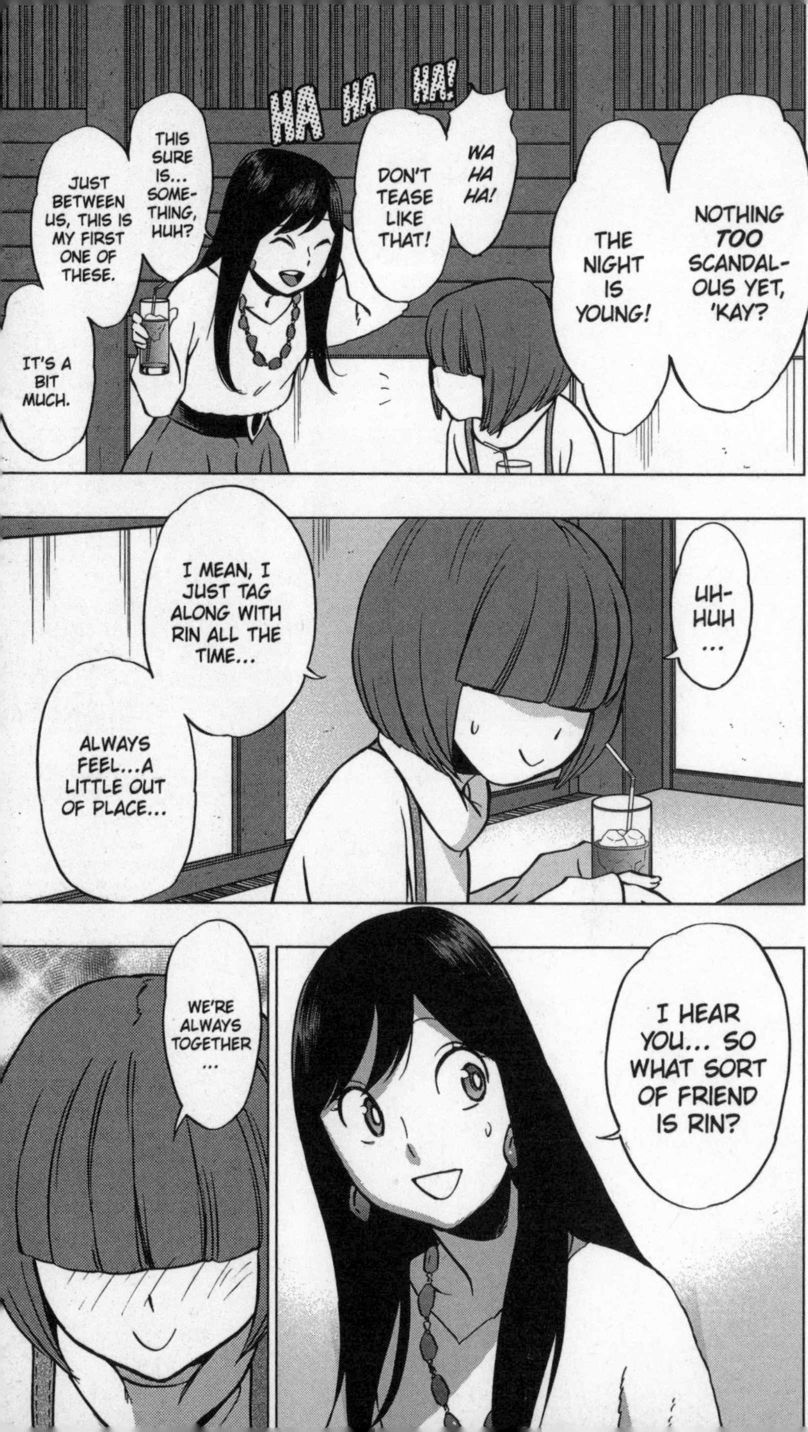
NOTHING *TOO* SCANDAL-OUS YET, 'KAY?
THE NIGHT IS YOUNG!
WA HA HA!
DON'T TEASE LIKE THAT!
HA HA HA!
THIS SURE IS... SOME-THING, HUH?
JUST BETWEEN US, THIS IS MY FIRST ONE OF THESE.
IT'S A BIT MUCH.
UH-HUH...
I MEAN, I JUST TAG ALONG WITH RIN ALL THE TIME...
ALWAYS FEEL...A LITTLE OUT OF PLACE...
I HEAR YOU... SO WHAT SORT OF FRIEND IS RIN?
WE'RE ALWAYS TOGETHER...

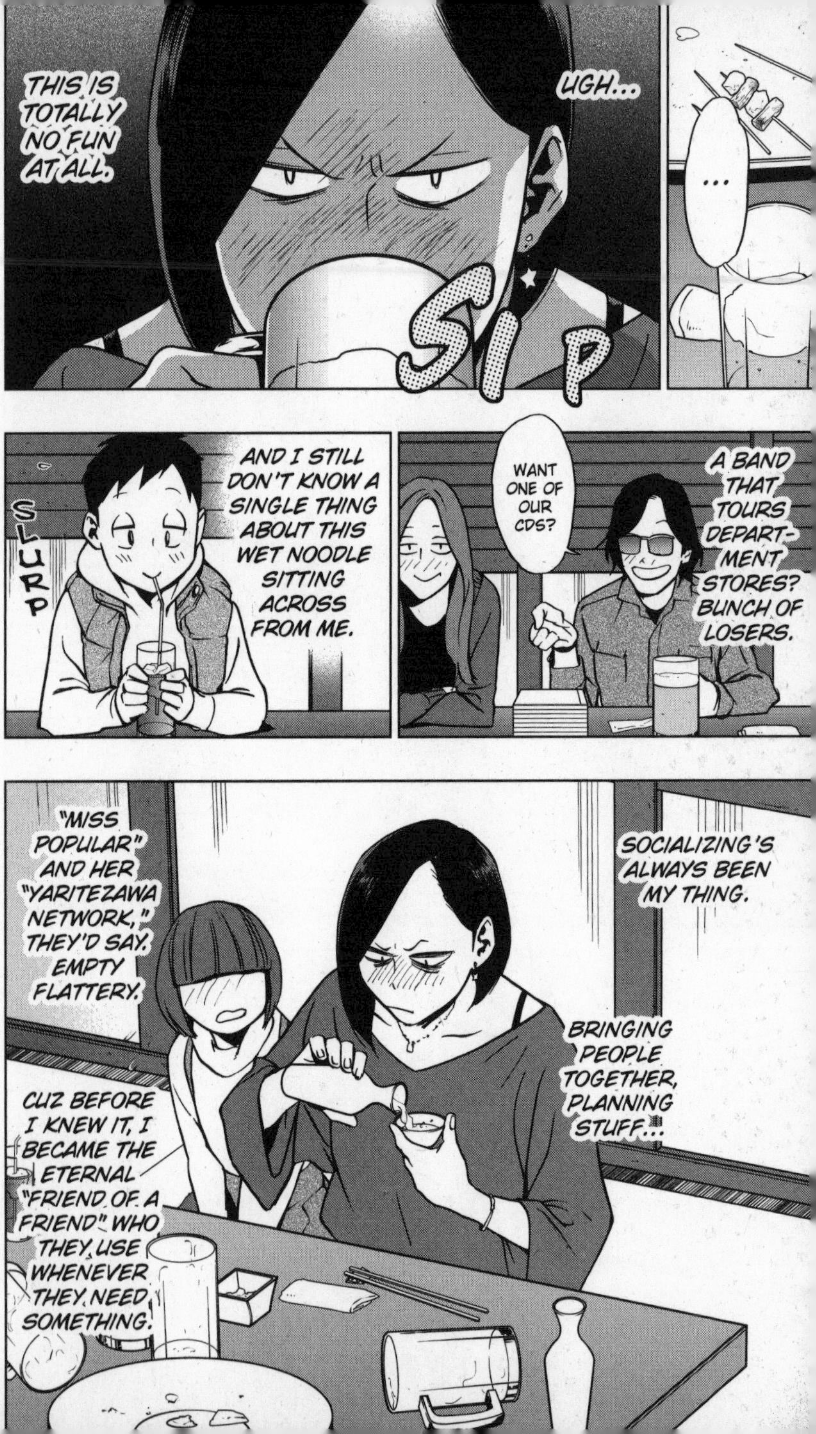
...
UGH...
THIS IS TOTALLY NO FUN AT ALL.
SIP
WANT ONE OF OUR CDS?
A BAND THAT TOURS DEPARTMENT STORES? BUNCH OF LOSERS.
AND I STILL DON'T KNOW A SINGLE THING ABOUT THIS WET NOODLE SITTING ACROSS FROM ME.
SLURP
SOCIALIZING'S ALWAYS BEEN MY THING.
"MISS POPULAR" AND HER "YARITEZAWA NETWORK," THEY'D SAY. EMPTY FLATTERY.
BRINGING PEOPLE TOGETHER, PLANNING STUFF...
CUZ BEFORE I KNEW IT, I BECAME THE ETERNAL "FRIEND OF A FRIEND" WHO THEY USE WHENEVER THEY NEED SOMETHING.

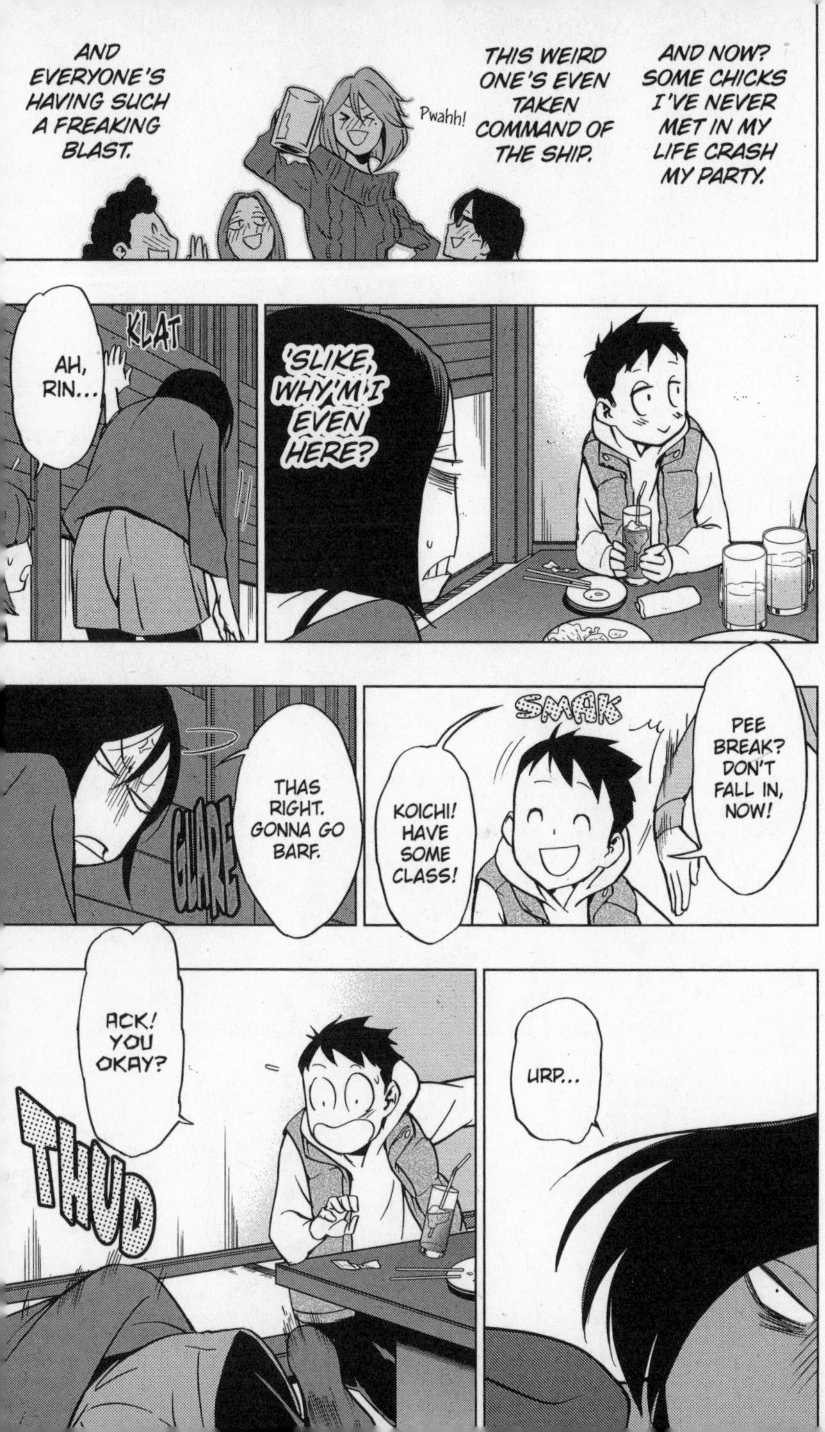
AND NOW? SOME CHICKS I'VE NEVER MET IN MY LIFE CRASH MY PARTY.
THIS WEIRD ONE'S EVEN TAKEN COMMAND OF THE SHIP.
Pwahh!
AND EVERYONE'S HAVING SUCH A FREAKING BLAST.
'SLIKE, WHY'M I EVEN HERE?
KLAT
AH, RIN...
PEE BREAK? DON'T FALL IN, NOW!
SMAK
KOICHI! HAVE SOME CLASS!
THAS RIGHT. GONNA GO BARF.
GLARE
URP...
ACK! YOU OKAY?
THUD

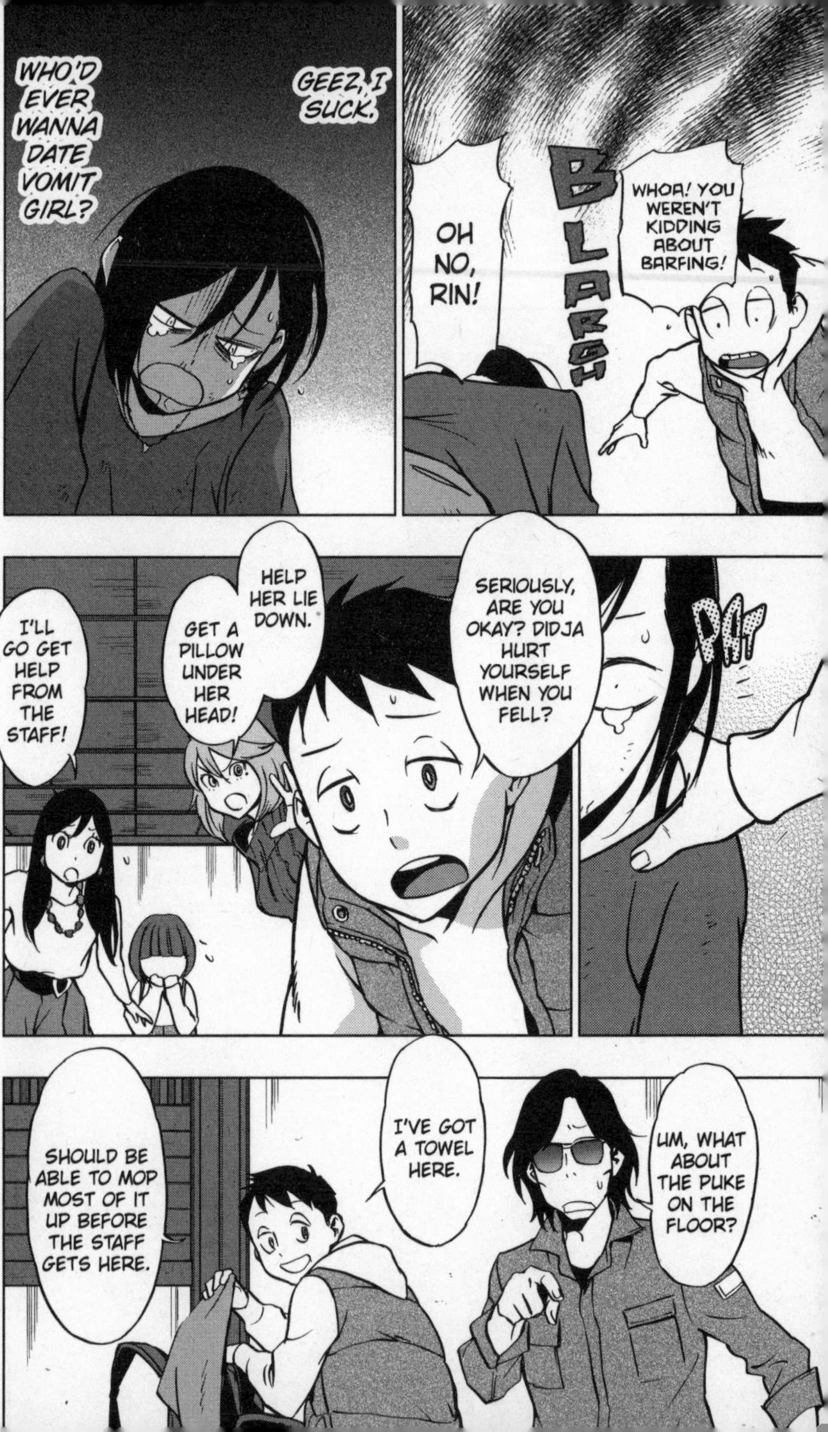
WHOA! YOU WEREN'T KIDDING ABOUT BARFING!
BLARGH
OH NO, RIN!
GEEZ, I SUCK.
WHO'D EVER WANNA DATE VOMIT GIRL?
PAT
SERIOUSLY, ARE YOU OKAY? DIDJA HURT YOURSELF WHEN YOU FELL?
HELP HER LIE DOWN.
GET A PILLOW UNDER HER HEAD!
I'LL GO GET HELP FROM THE STAFF!
UM, WHAT ABOUT THE PUKE ON THE FLOOR?
I'VE GOT A TOWEL HERE.
SHOULD BE ABLE TO MOP MOST OF IT UP BEFORE THE STAFF GETS HERE.

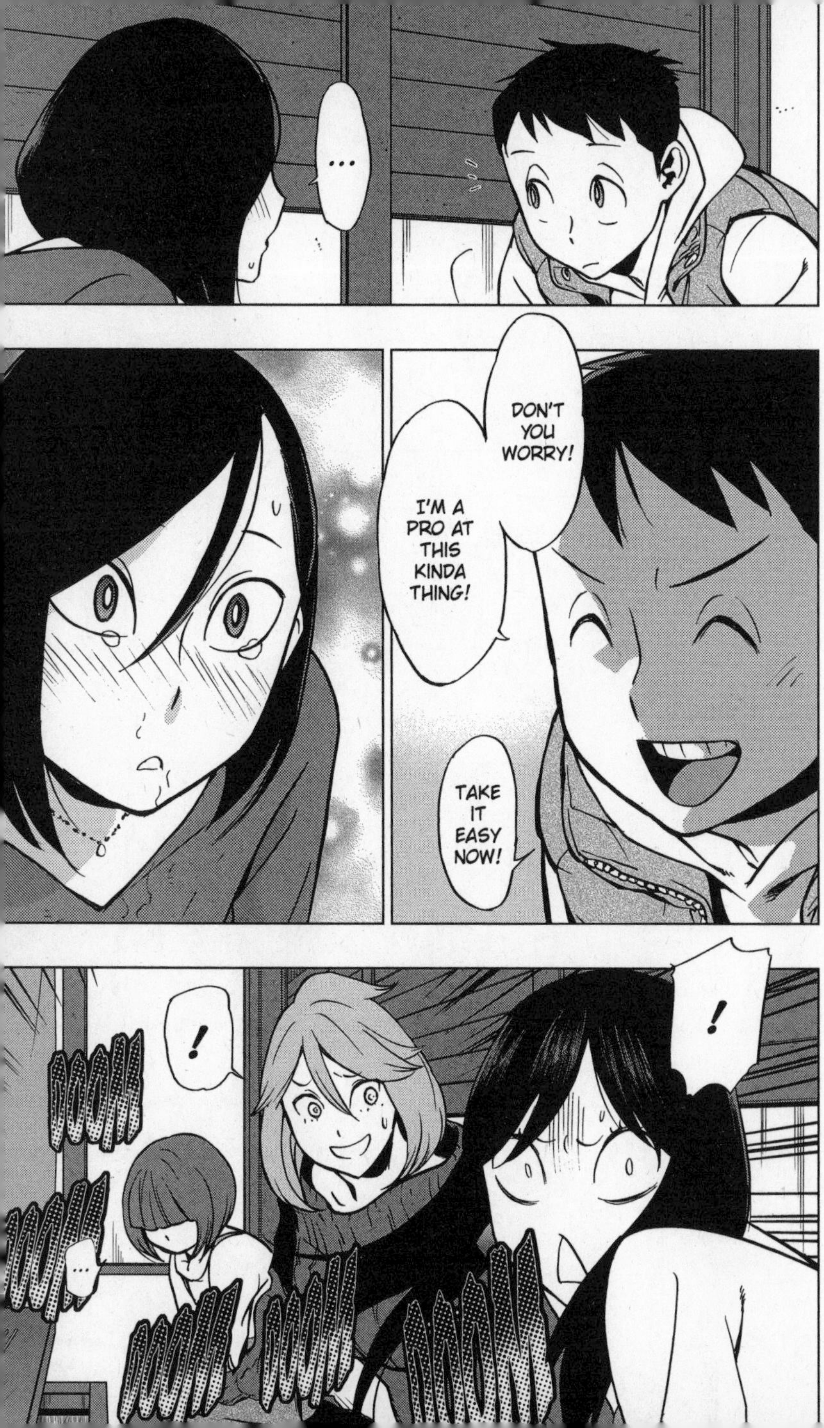
...
...
DON'T YOU WORRY!
I'M A PRO AT THIS KINDA THING!
TAKE IT EASY NOW!
!
!
...

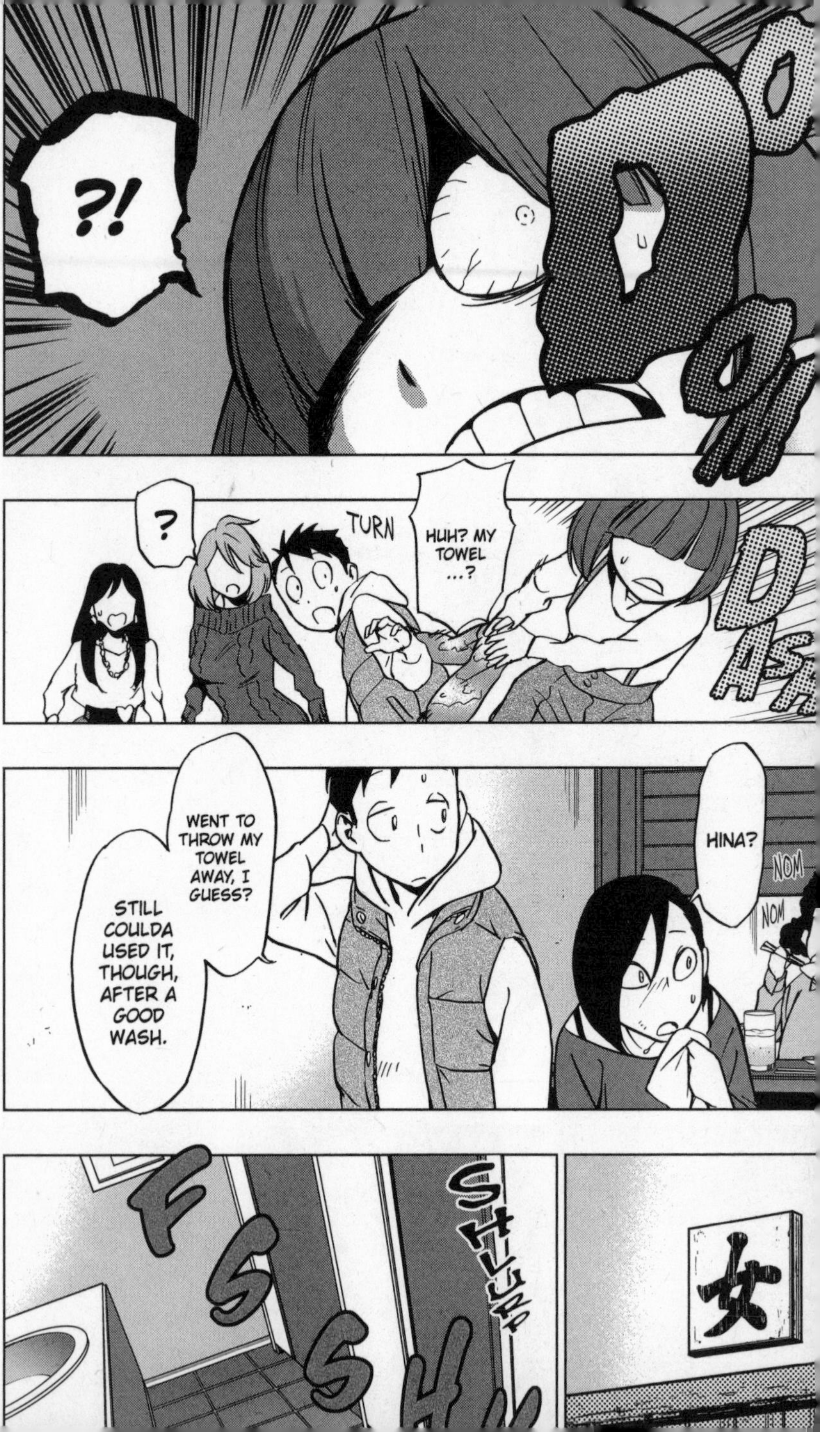
?!
DASH
HUH? MY TOWEL ...?
TURN
?
HINA?
NOM
NOM
WENT TO THROW MY TOWEL AWAY, I GUESS?
STILL COULDA USED IT, THOUGH, AFTER A GOOD WASH.
SHLURP
FSSSH

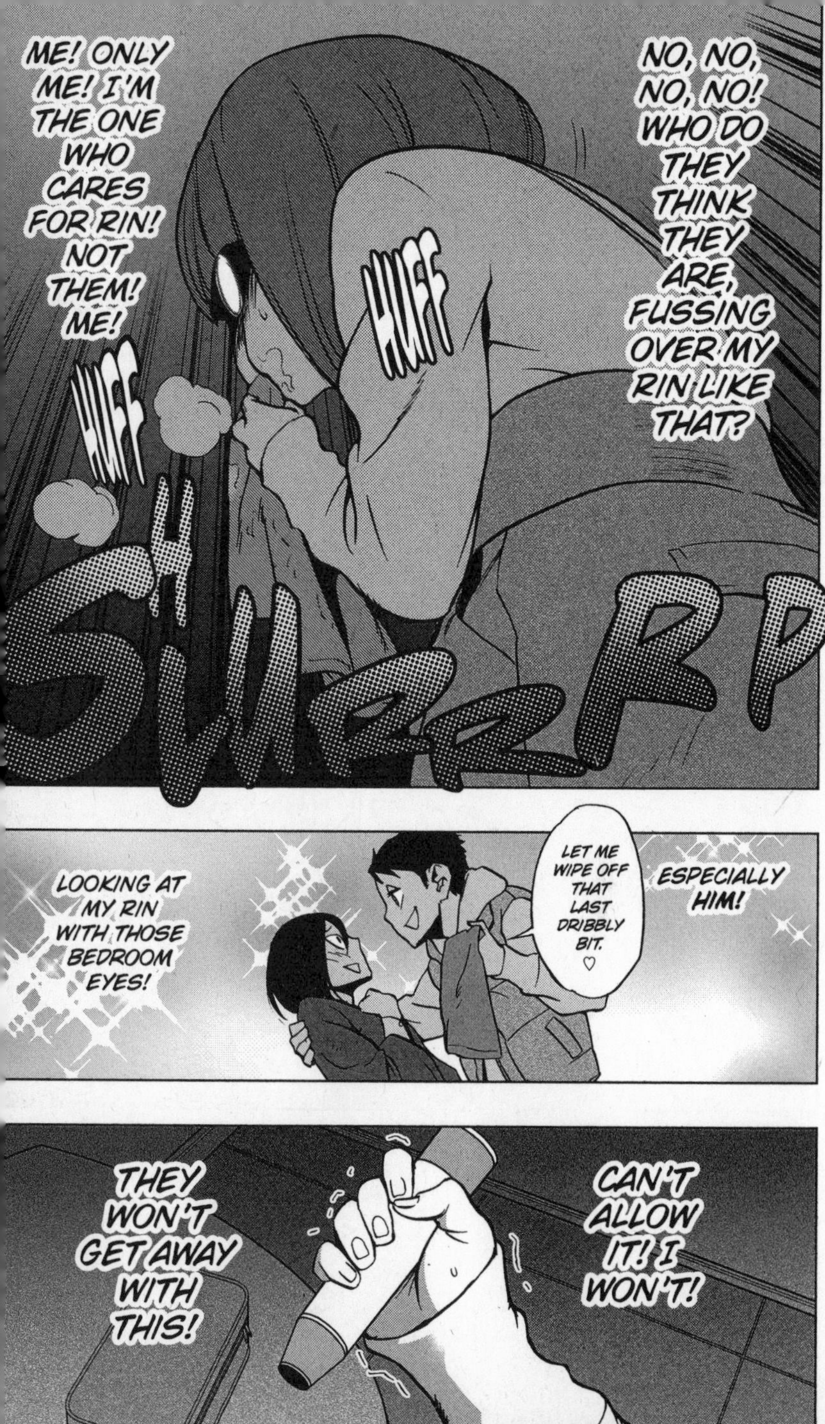
NO, NO, NO, NO! WHO DO THEY THINK THEY ARE, FUSSING OVER MY RIN LIKE THAT?
HUFF
ME! ONLY ME! I'M THE ONE WHO CARES FOR RIN! NOT THEM! ME!
HUFF
SHLURRP
ESPECIALLY HIM!
LET ME WIPE OFF THAT LAST DRIBBLY BIT. ♡
LOOKING AT MY RIN WITH THOSE BEDROOM EYES!
CAN'T ALLOW IT! I WON'T!
THEY WON'T GET AWAY WITH THIS!

KAORI AND KAZUHA

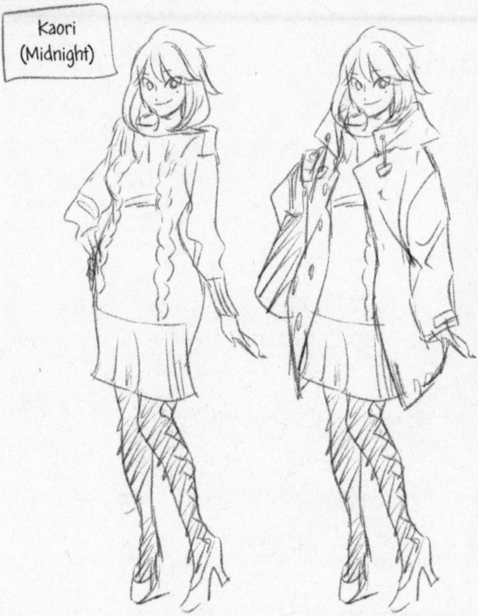
Kaori
(Midnight)

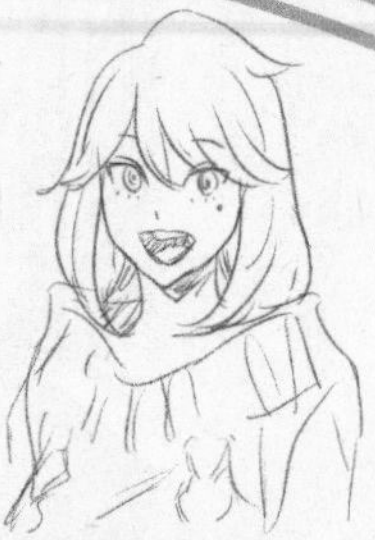
Like an office worker

BEHIND THE SCENES

The original plan was for these two not to realize the huge age gap between them and just think they were in the same year at college, but that would make Midnight seem more oblivious than she is and stall the flow of the scene, so I changed it to "they're working an undercover mission together."

I'm always happy with the results whenever I ask Betten-san to design a group of girls in street clothes. Show me all that fashion!

—Furuhashi

I don't mind coming up with street fashion now and then, but when I have to do it for a whole group of characters at once? Kill me, please! I was pleased to discover that when you give Pop a different hairstyle, she actually comes out looking cute in an ordinary way. (LOL)

—Betten

THE ROUGH DESIGNS

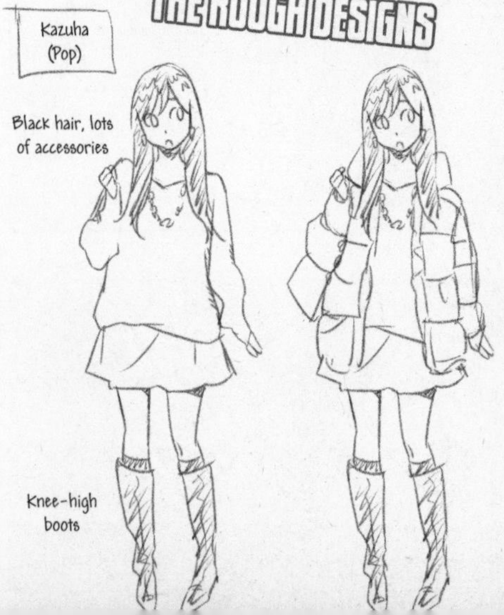
Kazuha
(Pop)
Black hair, lots
of accessories
Knee-high
boots

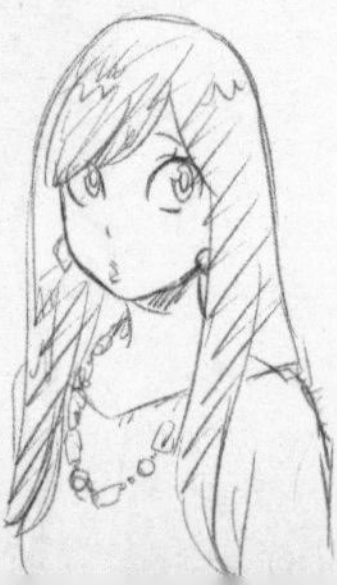

EP. 43 - CASANOVA

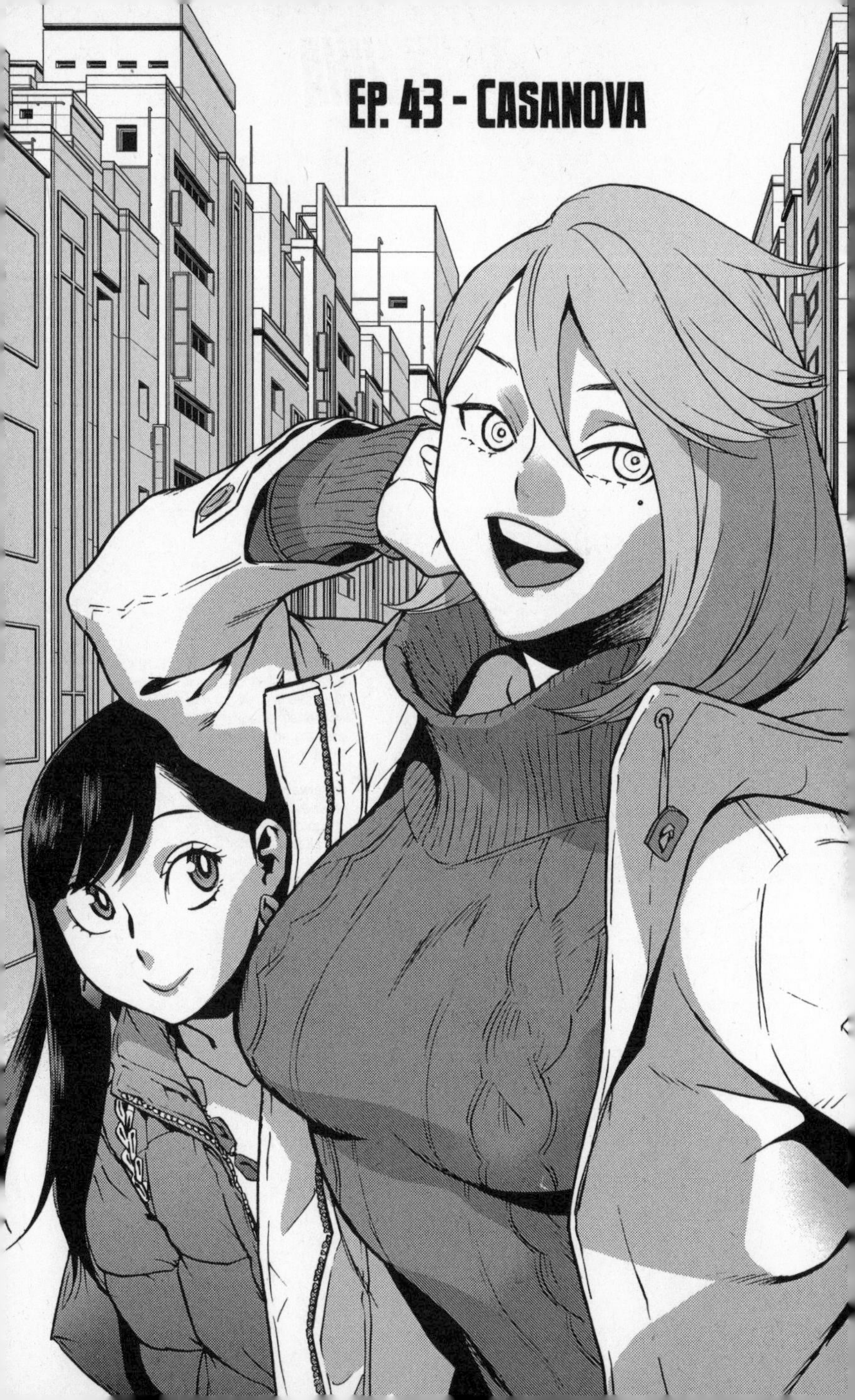

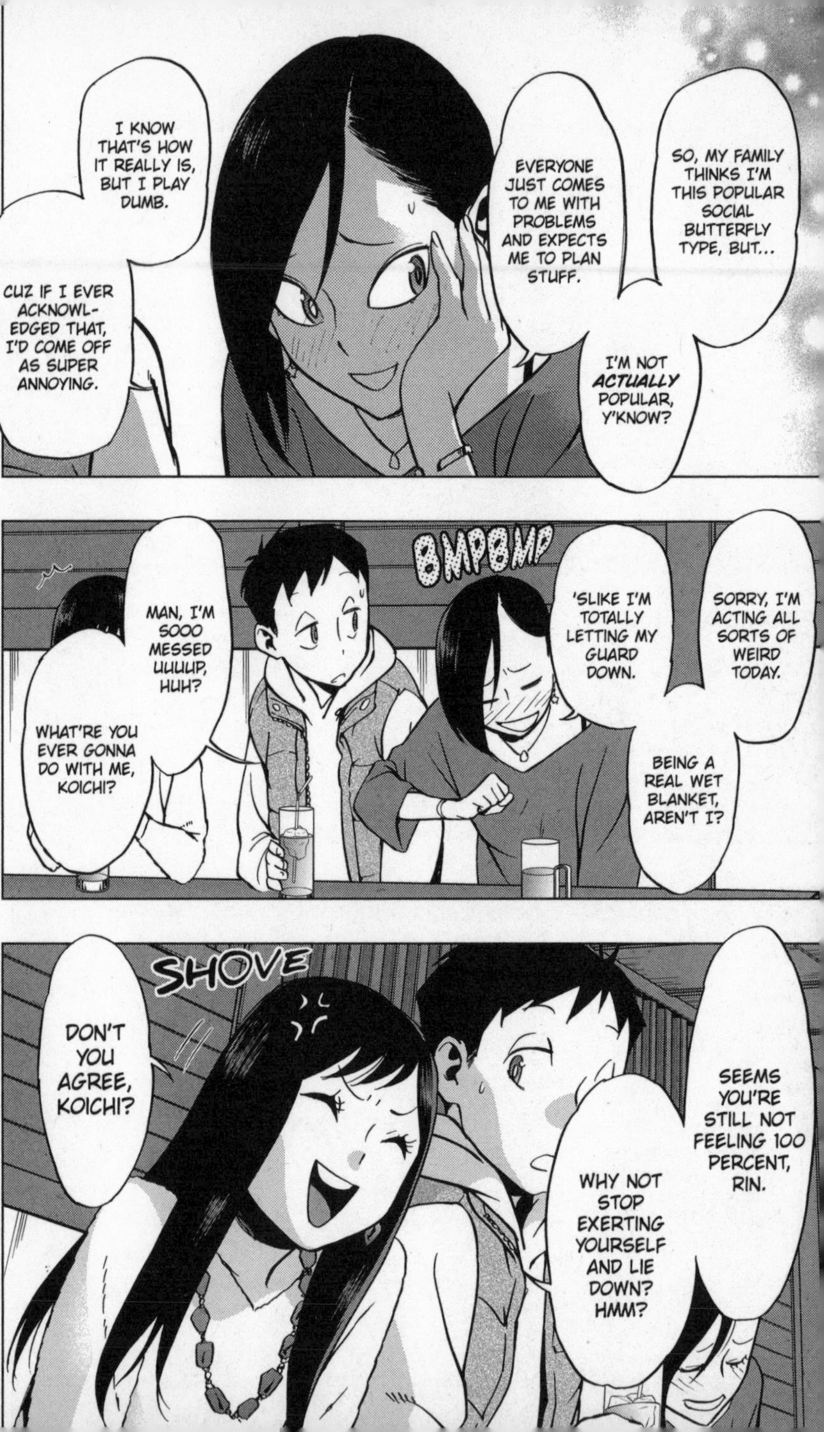
SO, MY FAMILY THINKS I'M THIS POPULAR SOCIAL BUTTERFLY TYPE, BUT...
EVERYONE JUST COMES TO ME WITH PROBLEMS AND EXPECTS ME TO PLAN STUFF.
I'M NOT *ACTUALLY* POPULAR, Y'KNOW?
I KNOW THAT'S HOW IT REALLY IS, BUT I PLAY DUMB.
CUZ IF I EVER ACKNOWL-EDGED THAT, I'D COME OFF AS SUPER ANNOYING.
SORRY, I'M ACTING ALL SORTS OF WEIRD TODAY.
'SLIKE I'M TOTALLY LETTING MY GUARD DOWN.
BEING A REAL WET BLANKET, AREN'T I?
BMPBMP
MAN, I'M SOOO MESSED UUUUP, HUH?
WHAT'RE YOU EVER GONNA DO WITH ME, KOICHI?
SEEMS YOU'RE STILL NOT FEELING 100 PERCENT, RIN.
WHY NOT STOP EXERTING YOURSELF AND LIE DOWN? HMM?
SHOVE
DON'T YOU AGREE, KOICHI?

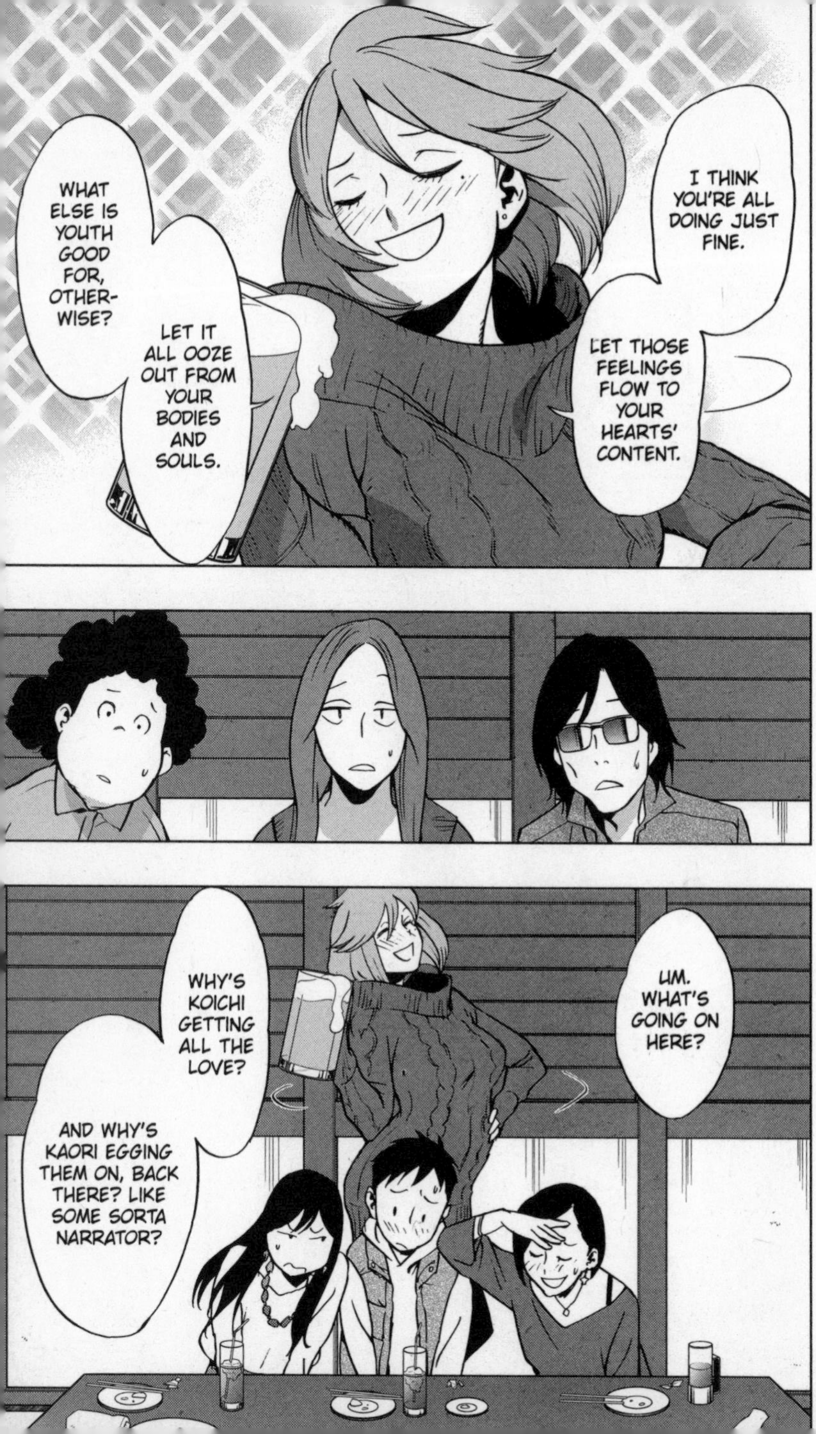
I THINK YOU'RE ALL DOING JUST FINE.
LET THOSE FEELINGS FLOW TO YOUR HEARTS' CONTENT.
WHAT ELSE IS YOUTH GOOD FOR, OTHER-WISE?
LET IT ALL OOZE OUT FROM YOUR BODIES AND SOULS.
UM. WHAT'S GOING ON HERE?
WHY'S KOICHI GETTING ALL THE LOVE?
AND WHY'S KAORI EGGING THEM ON, BACK THERE? LIKE SOME SORTA NARRATOR?

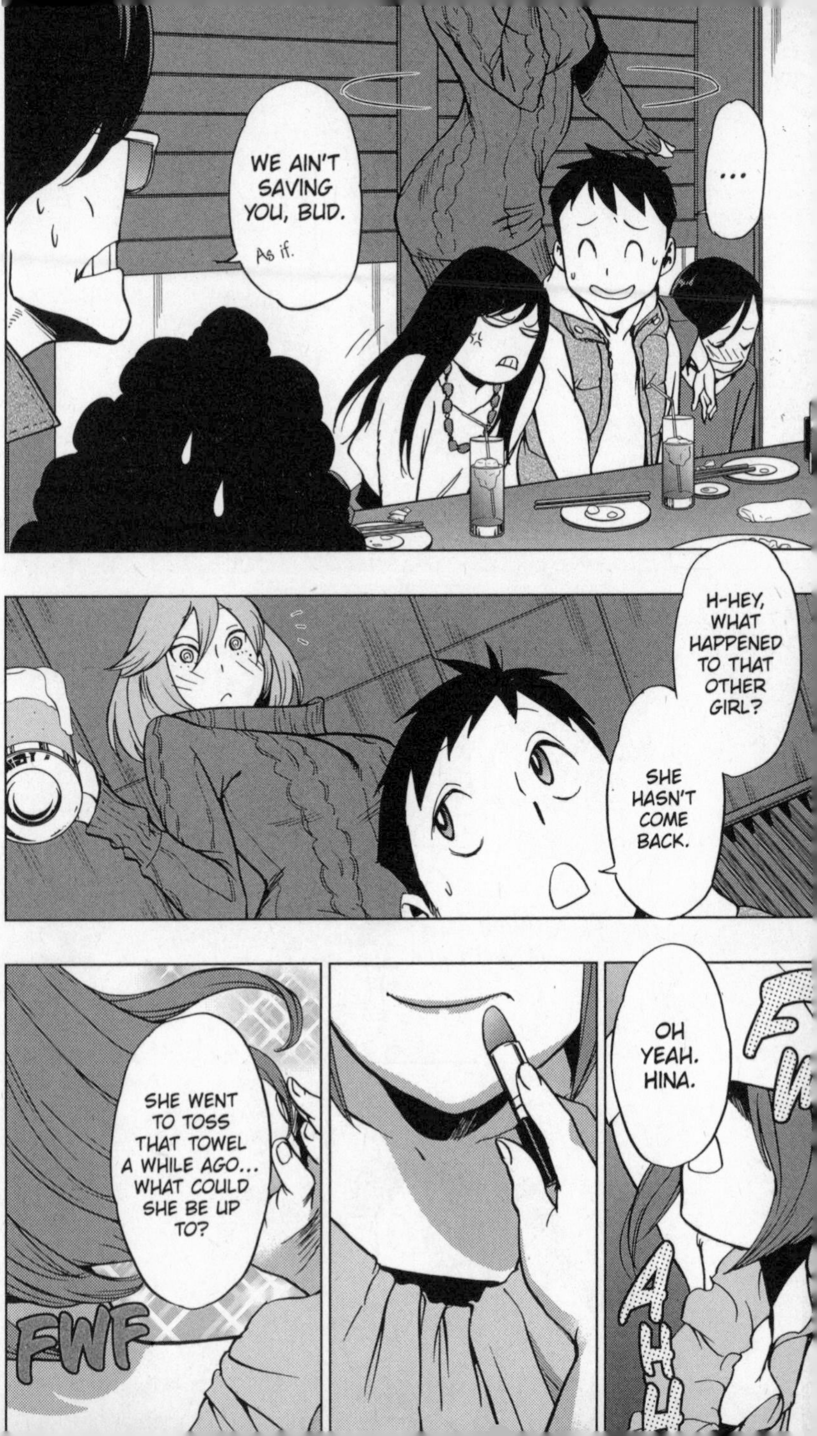
...
WE AIN'T SAVING YOU, BUD.
As if.
H-HEY, WHAT HAPPENED TO THAT OTHER GIRL?
SHE HASN'T COME BACK.
OH YEAH. HINA.
SHE WENT TO TOSS THAT TOWEL A WHILE AGO... WHAT COULD SHE BE UP TO?
FWF

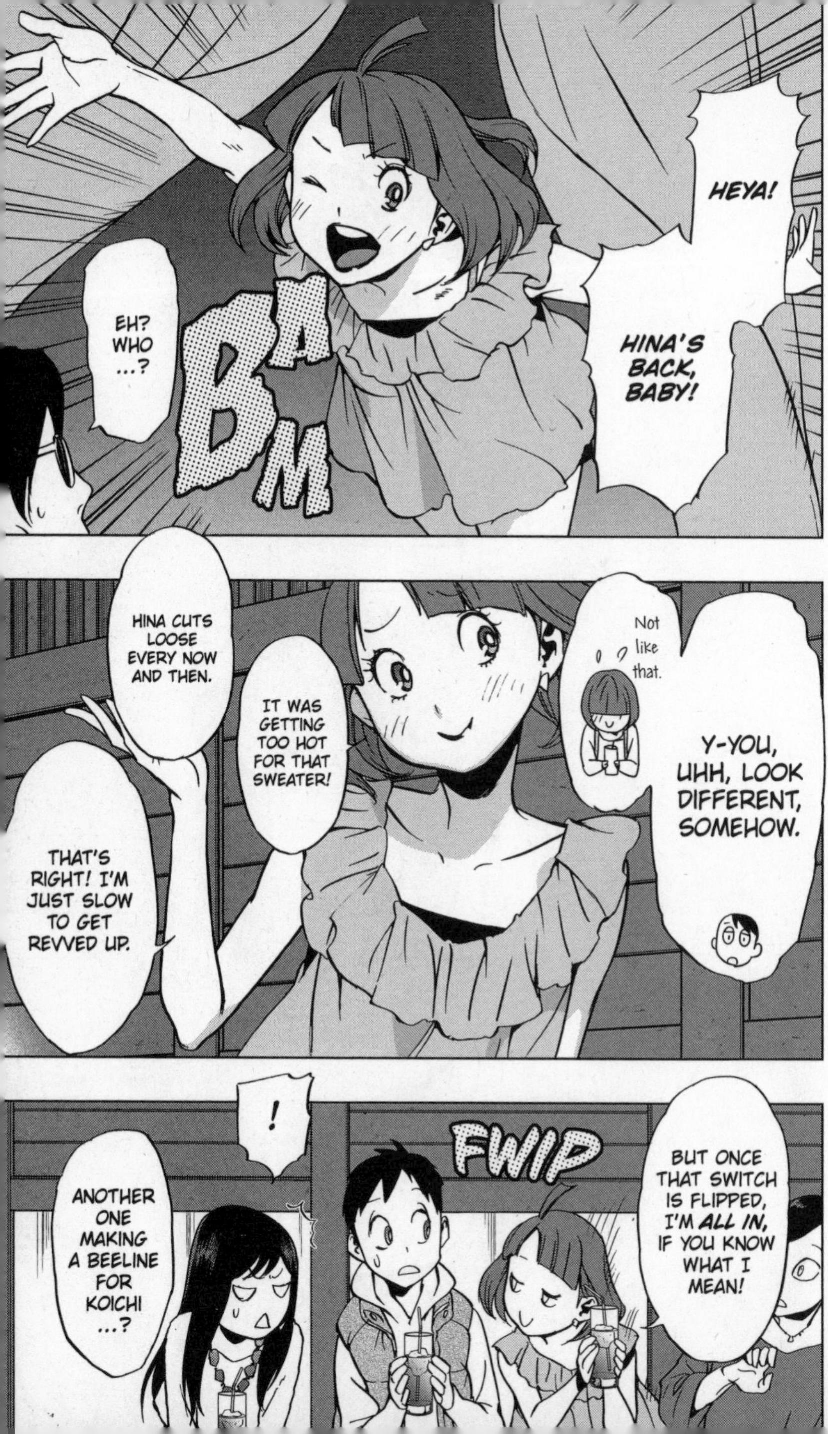
HEYA!
HINA'S BACK, BABY!
BAM
EH? WHO ...?
Y-YOU, UHH, LOOK DIFFERENT, SOMEHOW.
Not like that.
IT WAS GETTING TOO HOT FOR THAT SWEATER!
HINA CUTS LOOSE EVERY NOW AND THEN.
THAT'S RIGHT! I'M JUST SLOW TO GET REVVED UP.
BUT ONCE THAT SWITCH IS FLIPPED, I'M ALL IN, IF YOU KNOW WHAT I MEAN!
FWIP
!
ANOTHER ONE MAKING A BEELINE FOR KOICHI ...?

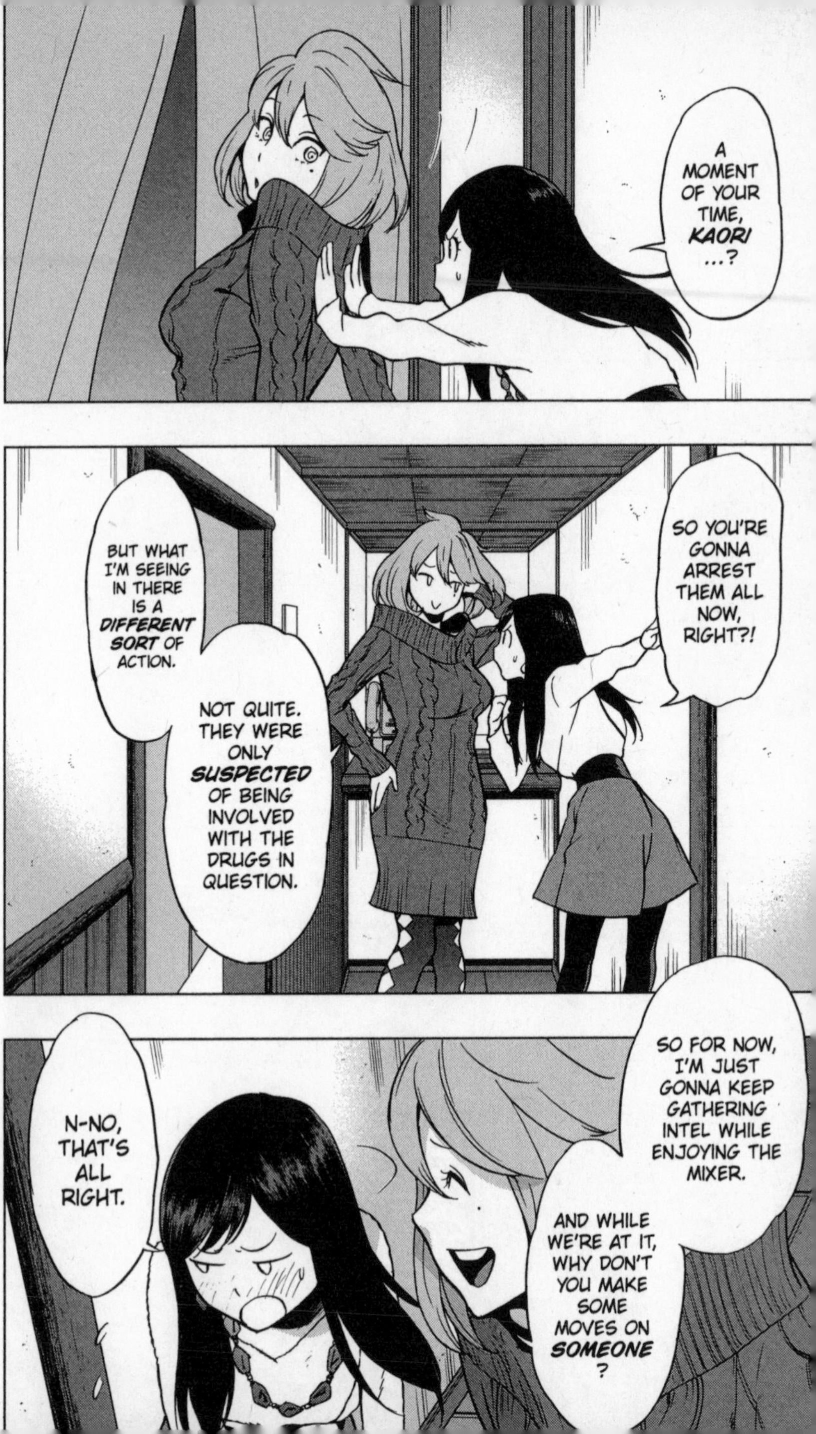
A MOMENT OF YOUR TIME, KAORI ...?
SO YOU'RE GONNA ARREST THEM ALL NOW, RIGHT?!
NOT QUITE. THEY WERE ONLY SUSPECTED OF BEING INVOLVED WITH THE DRUGS IN QUESTION.
BUT WHAT I'M SEEING IN THERE IS A DIFFERENT SORT OF ACTION.
SO FOR NOW, I'M JUST GONNA KEEP GATHERING INTEL WHILE ENJOYING THE MIXER.
AND WHILE WE'RE AT IT, WHY DON'T YOU MAKE SOME MOVES ON SOMEONE ?
N-NO, THAT'S ALL RIGHT.

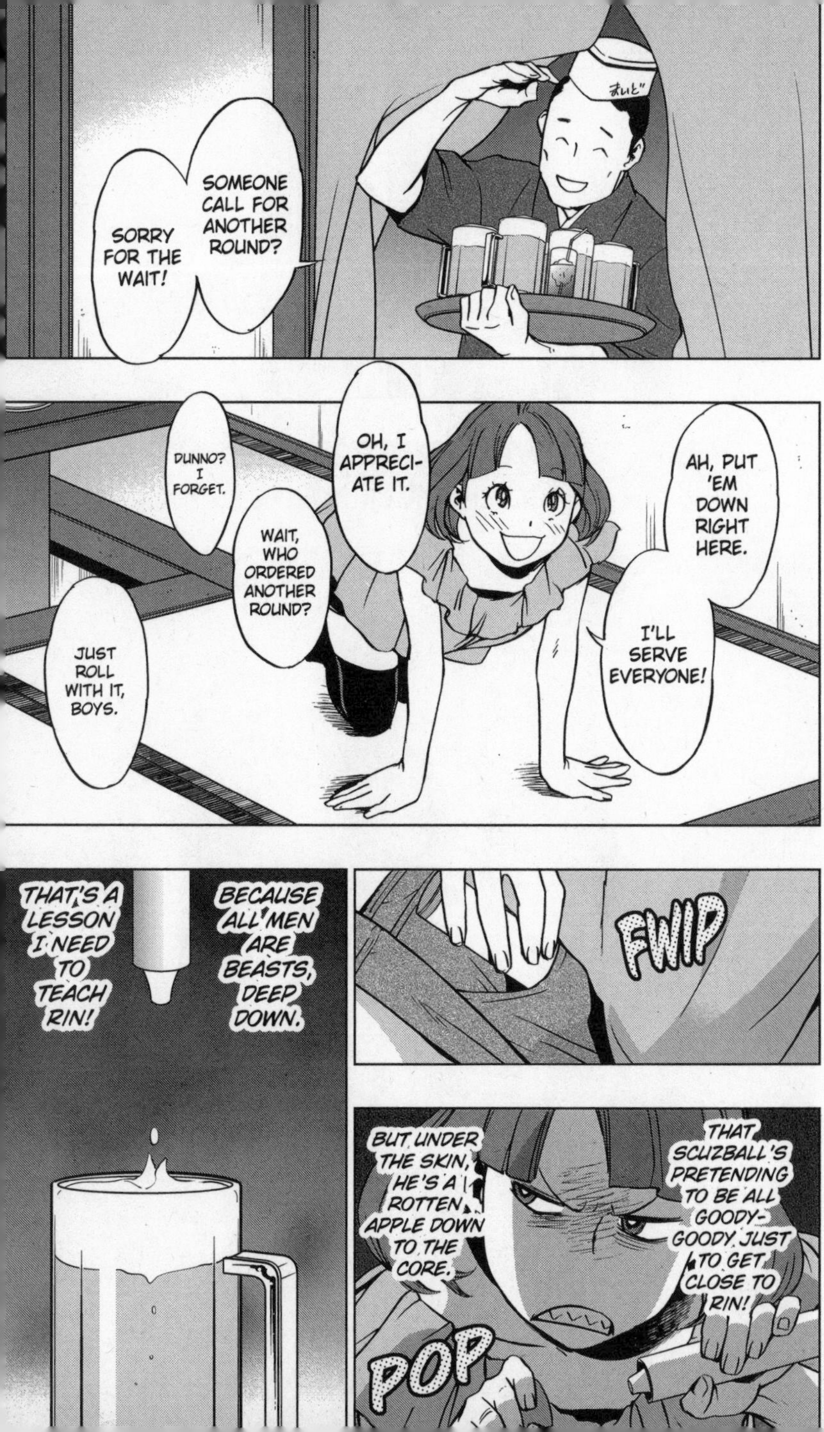
SOMEONE CALL FOR ANOTHER ROUND?
SORRY FOR THE WAIT!
AH, PUT 'EM DOWN RIGHT HERE.
I'LL SERVE EVERYONE!
OH, I APPRECIATE IT.
WAIT, WHO ORDERED ANOTHER ROUND?
DUNNO? I FORGET.
JUST ROLL WITH IT, BOYS.
FWIP
THAT SCUZBALL'S PRETENDING TO BE ALL GOODY-GOODY JUST TO GET CLOSE TO RIN!
BUT UNDER THE SKIN, HE'S A ROTTEN APPLE DOWN TO THE CORE.
POP
BECAUSE ALL MEN ARE BEASTS, DEEP DOWN.
THAT'S A LESSON I NEED TO TEACH RIN!

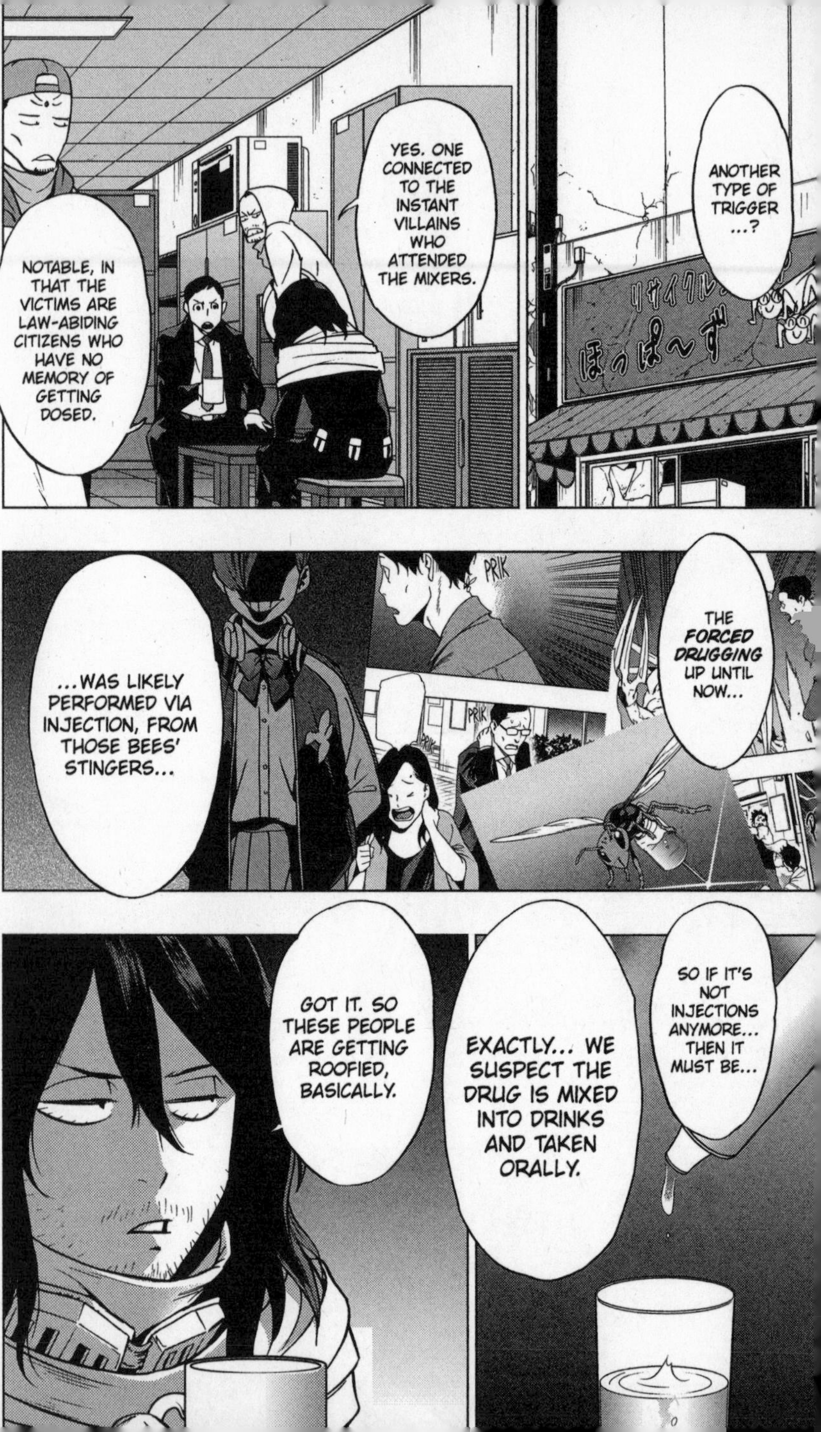
ANOTHER TYPE OF TRIGGER ...?
YES. ONE CONNECTED TO THE INSTANT VILLAINS WHO ATTENDED THE MIXERS.
NOTABLE, IN THAT THE VICTIMS ARE LAW-ABIDING CITIZENS WHO HAVE NO MEMORY OF GETTING DOSED.
THE FORCED DRUGGING UP UNTIL NOW...
PRIK
PRIK
PRIK
...WAS LIKELY PERFORMED VIA INJECTION, FROM THOSE BEES' STINGERS...
SO IF IT'S NOT INJECTIONS ANYMORE... THEN IT MUST BE...
GOT IT. SO THESE PEOPLE ARE GETTING ROOFIED, BASICALLY.
EXACTLY... WE SUSPECT THE DRUG IS MIXED INTO DRINKS AND TAKEN ORALLY.

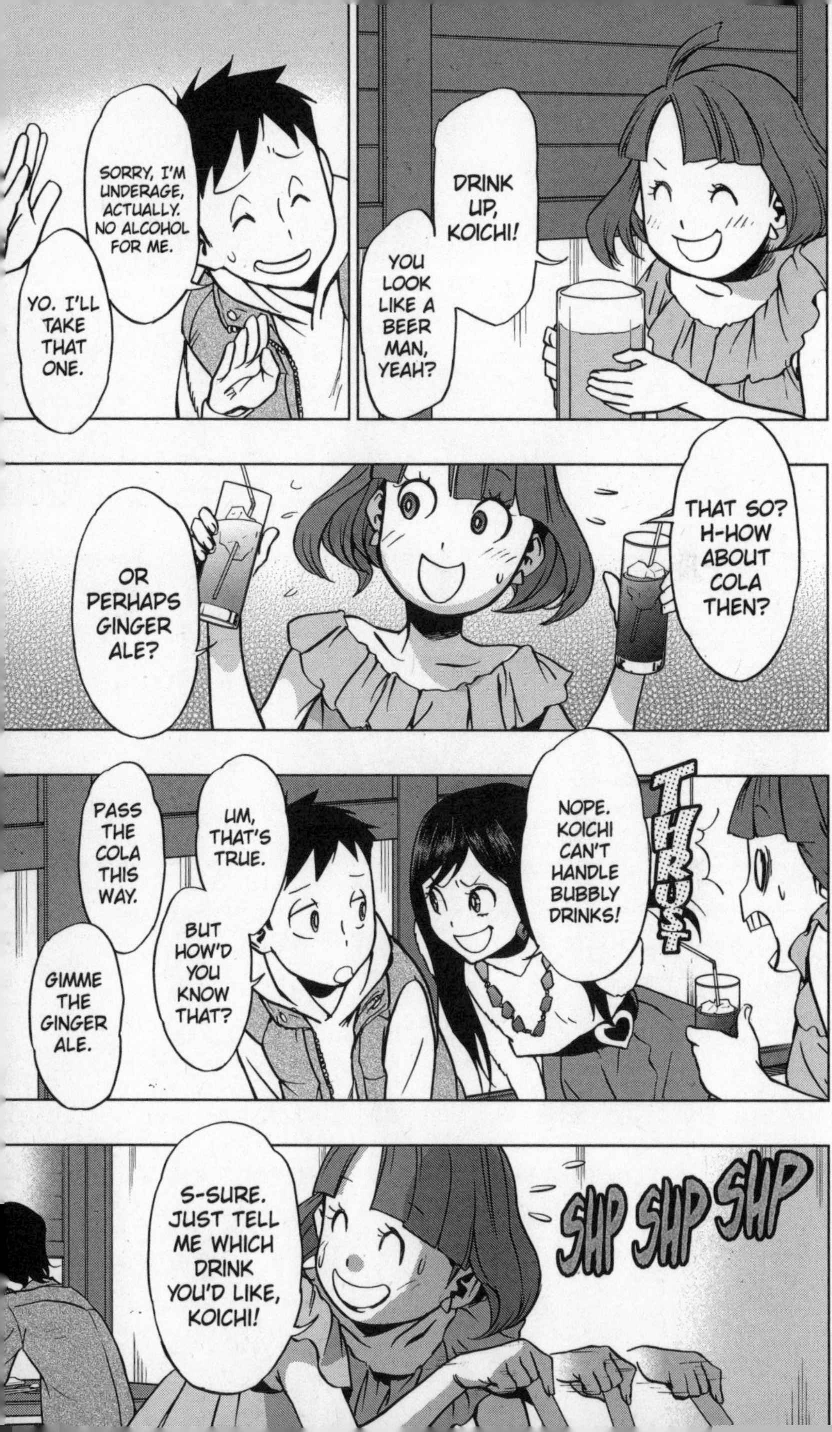
DRINK UP, KOICHI!
YOU LOOK LIKE A BEER MAN, YEAH?
SORRY, I'M UNDERAGE, ACTUALLY. NO ALCOHOL FOR ME.
YO. I'LL TAKE THAT ONE.
THAT SO? H-HOW ABOUT COLA THEN?
OR PERHAPS GINGER ALE?
THRUST
NOPE. KOICHI CAN'T HANDLE BUBBLY DRINKS!
UM, THAT'S TRUE.
BUT HOW'D YOU KNOW THAT?
PASS THE COLA THIS WAY.
GIMME THE GINGER ALE.
SHP SHP SHP
S-SURE. JUST TELL ME WHICH DRINK YOU'D LIKE, KOICHI!

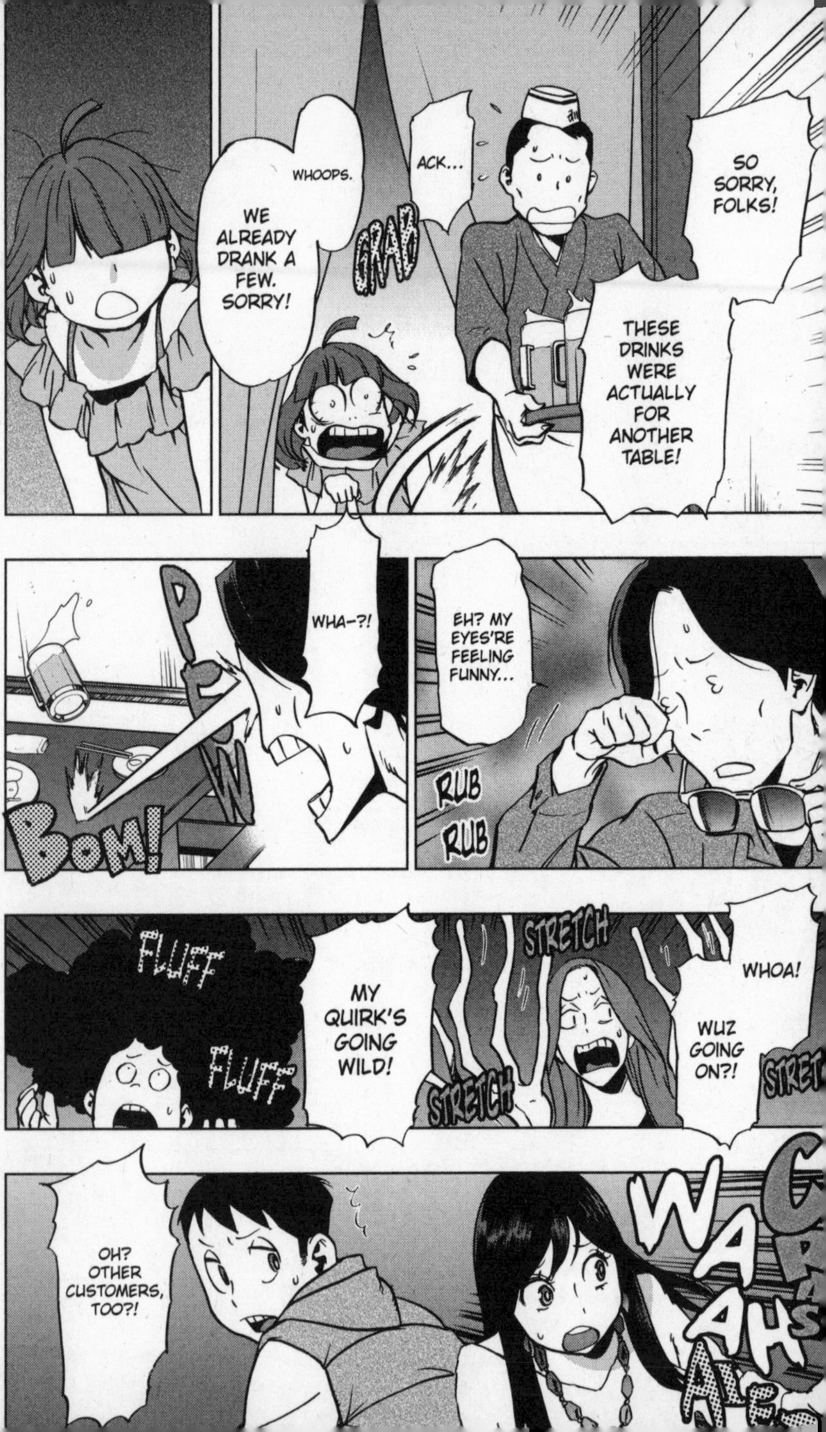
SO SORRY, FOLKS!
THESE DRINKS WERE ACTUALLY FOR ANOTHER TABLE!
ACK...
GRAB
WHOOPS.
WE ALREADY DRANK A FEW. SORRY!
EH? MY EYES'RE FEELING FUNNY...
RUB RUB
WHA-?!
POW
BOM!
WHOA!
WUZ GOING ON?!
STRETCH
STRETCH
MY QUIRK'S GOING WILD!
FLUFF
FLUFF
WAH
OH? OTHER CUSTOMERS, TOO?!

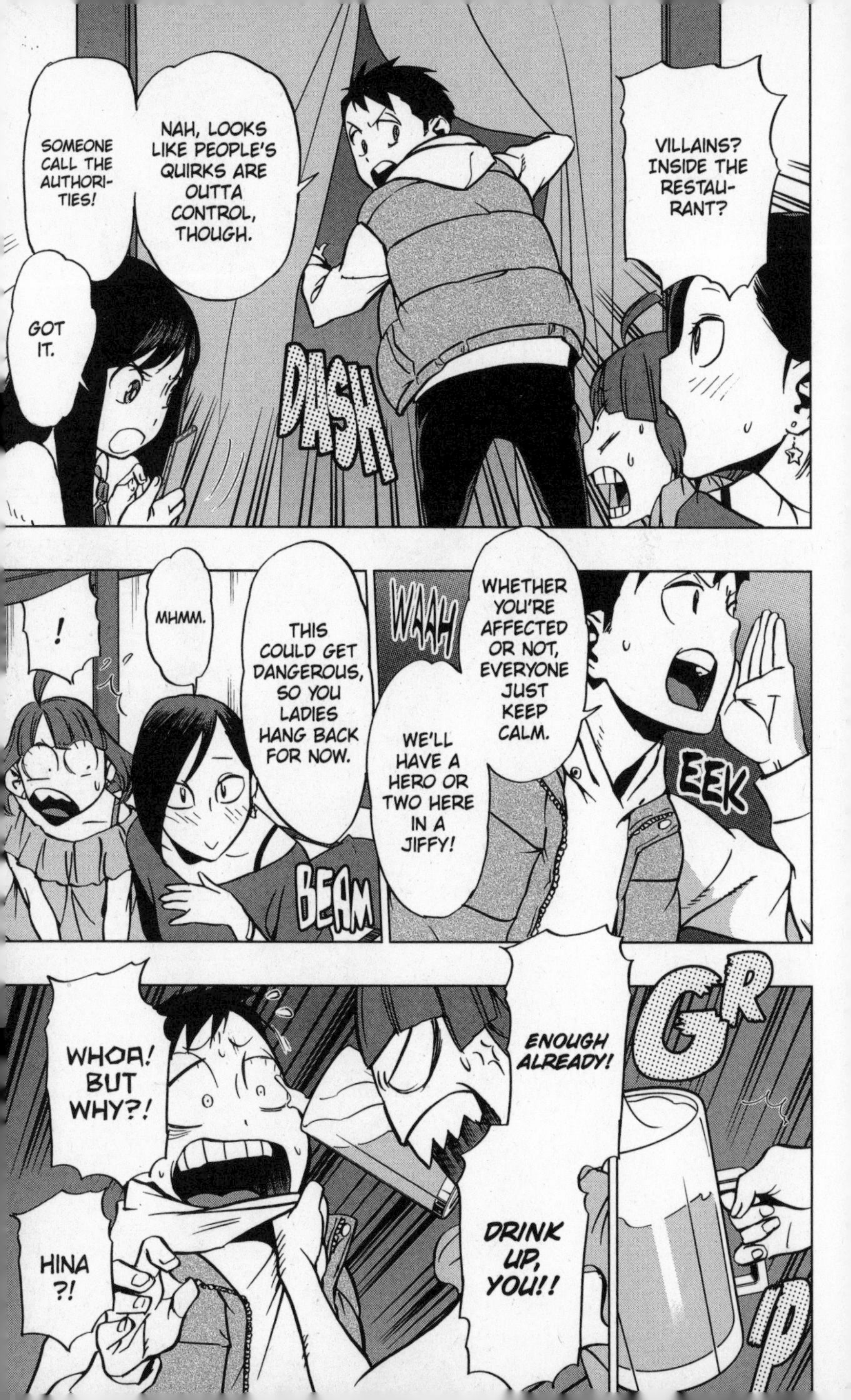
VILLAINS? INSIDE THE RESTAURANT?
NAH, LOOKS LIKE PEOPLE'S QUIRKS ARE OUTTA CONTROL, THOUGH.
SOMEONE CALL THE AUTHORITIES!
DASH
GOT IT.
WHETHER YOU'RE AFFECTED OR NOT, EVERYONE JUST KEEP CALM.
WAAH
EEK
WE'LL HAVE A HERO OR TWO HERE IN A JIFFY!
THIS COULD GET DANGEROUS, SO YOU LADIES HANG BACK FOR NOW.
MHMM.
!
BEAM
GR
ENOUGH ALREADY!
DRINK UP, YOU!!
IP
WHOA! BUT WHY?!
HINA?!

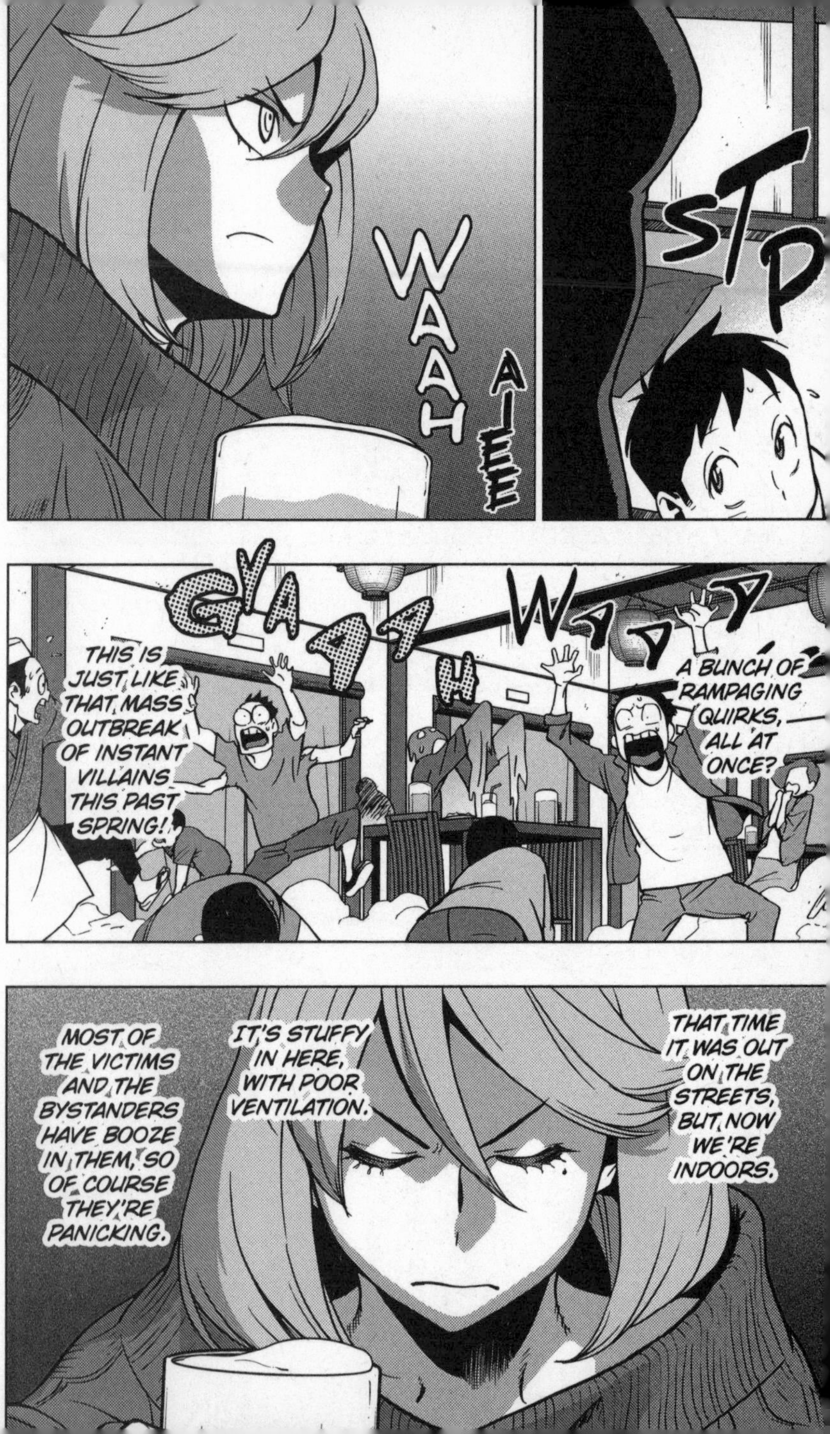
STP
WAAH
AIEEE
A BUNCH OF RAMPAGING QUIRKS, ALL AT ONCE?
WAAA
GYAAAH
THIS IS JUST LIKE THAT MASS OUTBREAK OF INSTANT VILLAINS THIS PAST SPRING!
THAT TIME IT WAS OUT ON THE STREETS, BUT NOW WE'RE INDOORS.
IT'S STUFFY IN HERE, WITH POOR VENTILATION.
MOST OF THE VICTIMS AND THE BYSTANDERS HAVE BOOZE IN THEM, SO OF COURSE THEY'RE PANICKING.

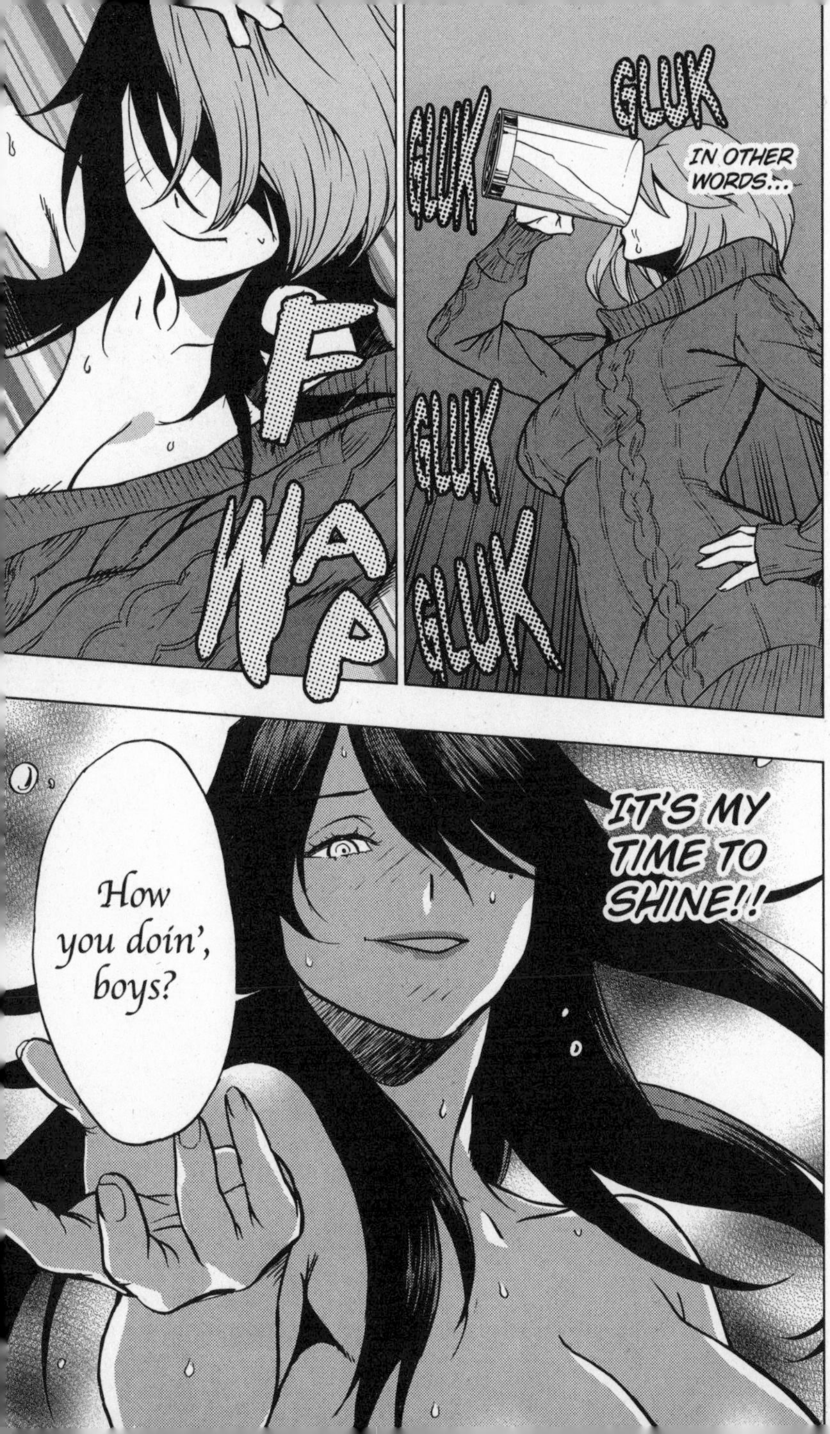
GLUK
IN OTHER WORDS...
GLUK
GLUK
GLUK
FWAP
IT'S MY TIME TO SHINE!!
How you doin', boys?

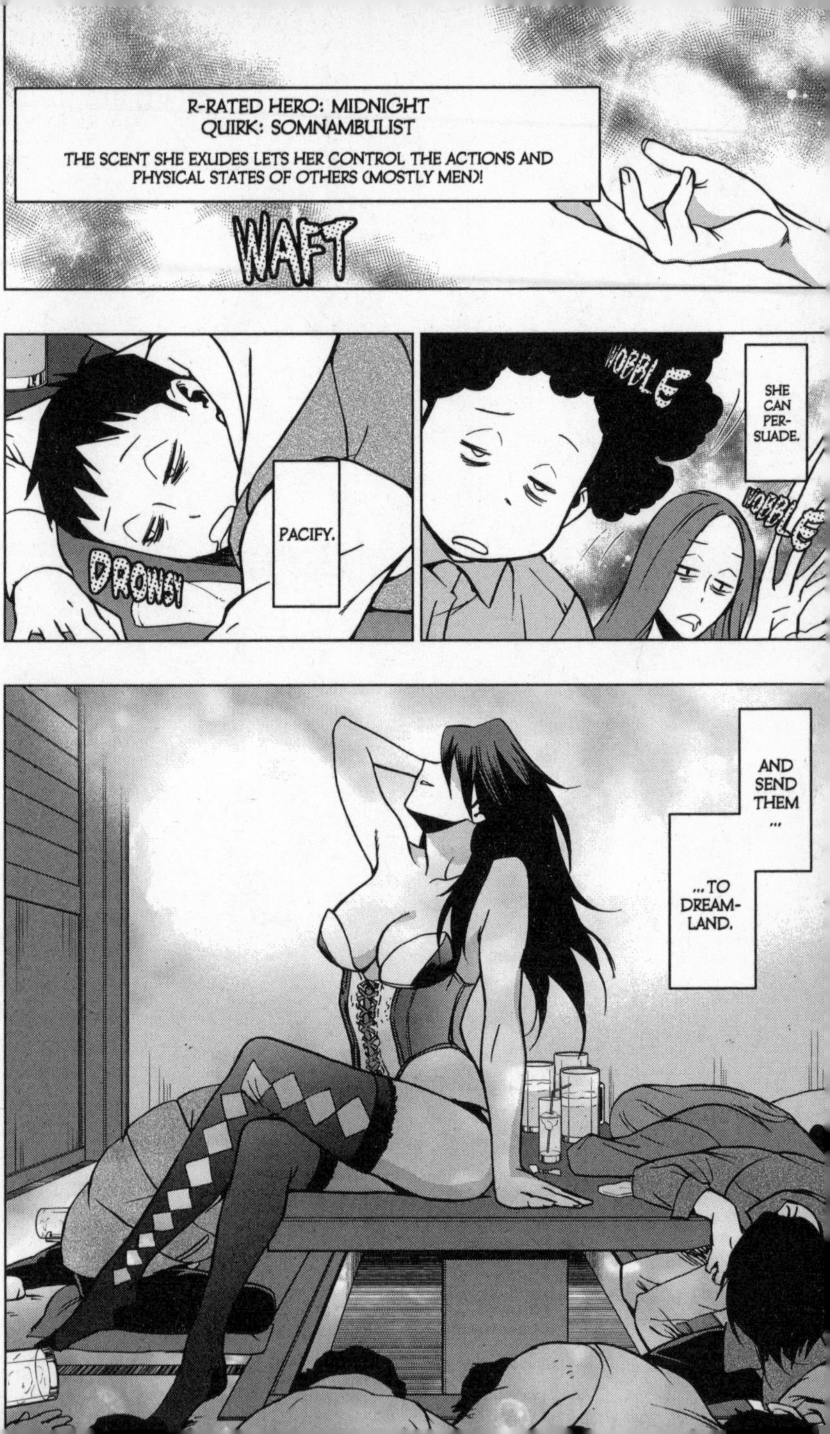
R-RATED HERO: MIDNIGHT
QUIRK: SOMNAMBULIST
THE SCENT SHE EXUDES LETS HER CONTROL THE ACTIONS AND PHYSICAL STATES OF OTHERS (MOSTLY MEN)!
WAFT
SHE CAN PER-SUADE.
WOBBLE
WOBBLE
PACIFY.
DROWSY
AND SEND THEM...
...TO DREAM-LAND.

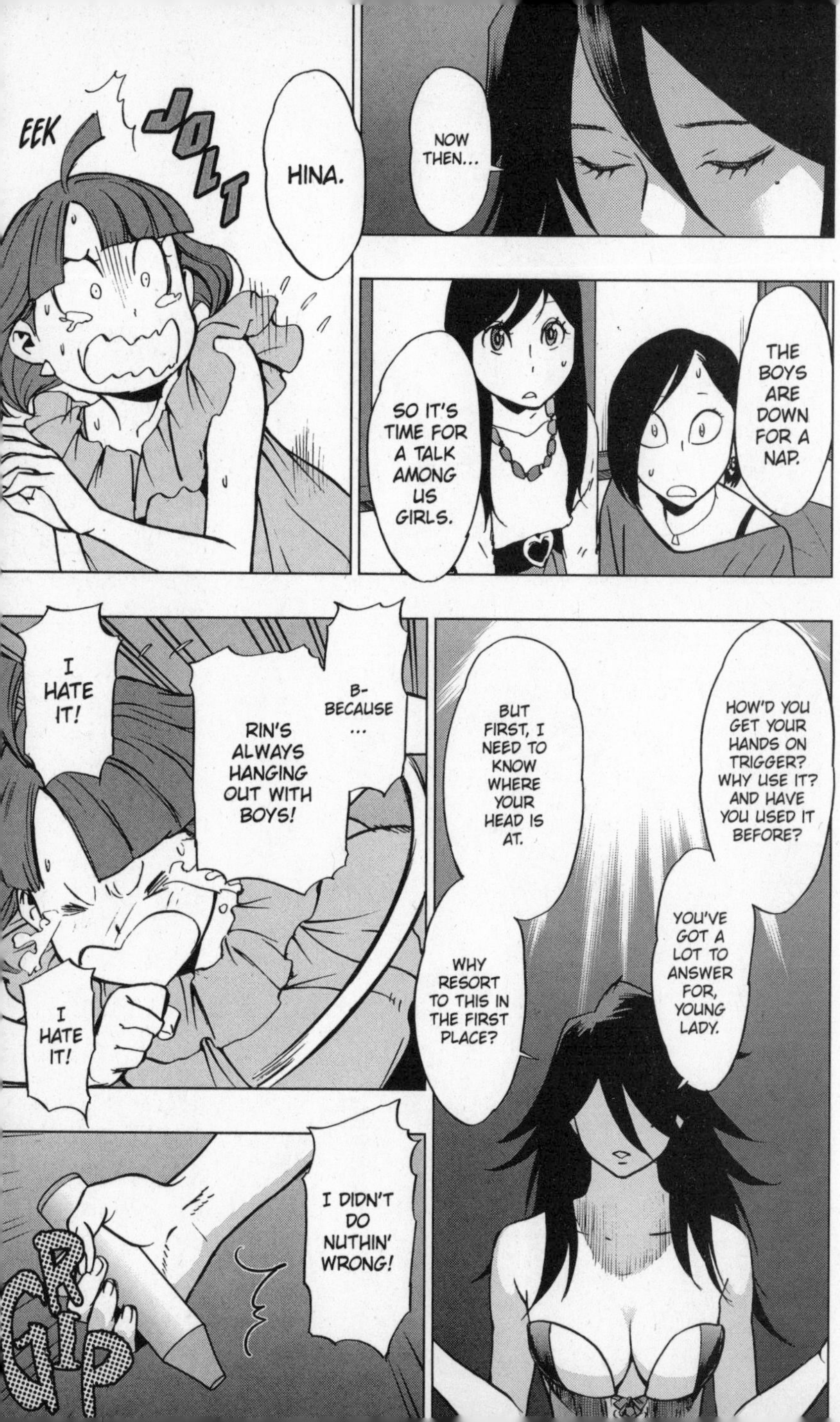
NOW THEN...
THE BOYS ARE DOWN FOR A NAP.
SO IT'S TIME FOR A TALK AMONG US GIRLS.
HINA.
JOLT
EEK
HOW'D YOU GET YOUR HANDS ON TRIGGER? WHY USE IT? AND HAVE YOU USED IT BEFORE?
BUT FIRST, I NEED TO KNOW WHERE YOUR HEAD IS AT.
YOU'VE GOT A LOT TO ANSWER FOR, YOUNG LADY.
WHY RESORT TO THIS IN THE FIRST PLACE?
B-BECAUSE...
RIN'S ALWAYS HANGING OUT WITH BOYS!
I HATE IT!
I HATE IT!
I DIDN'T DO NUTHIN' WRONG!
GRIP

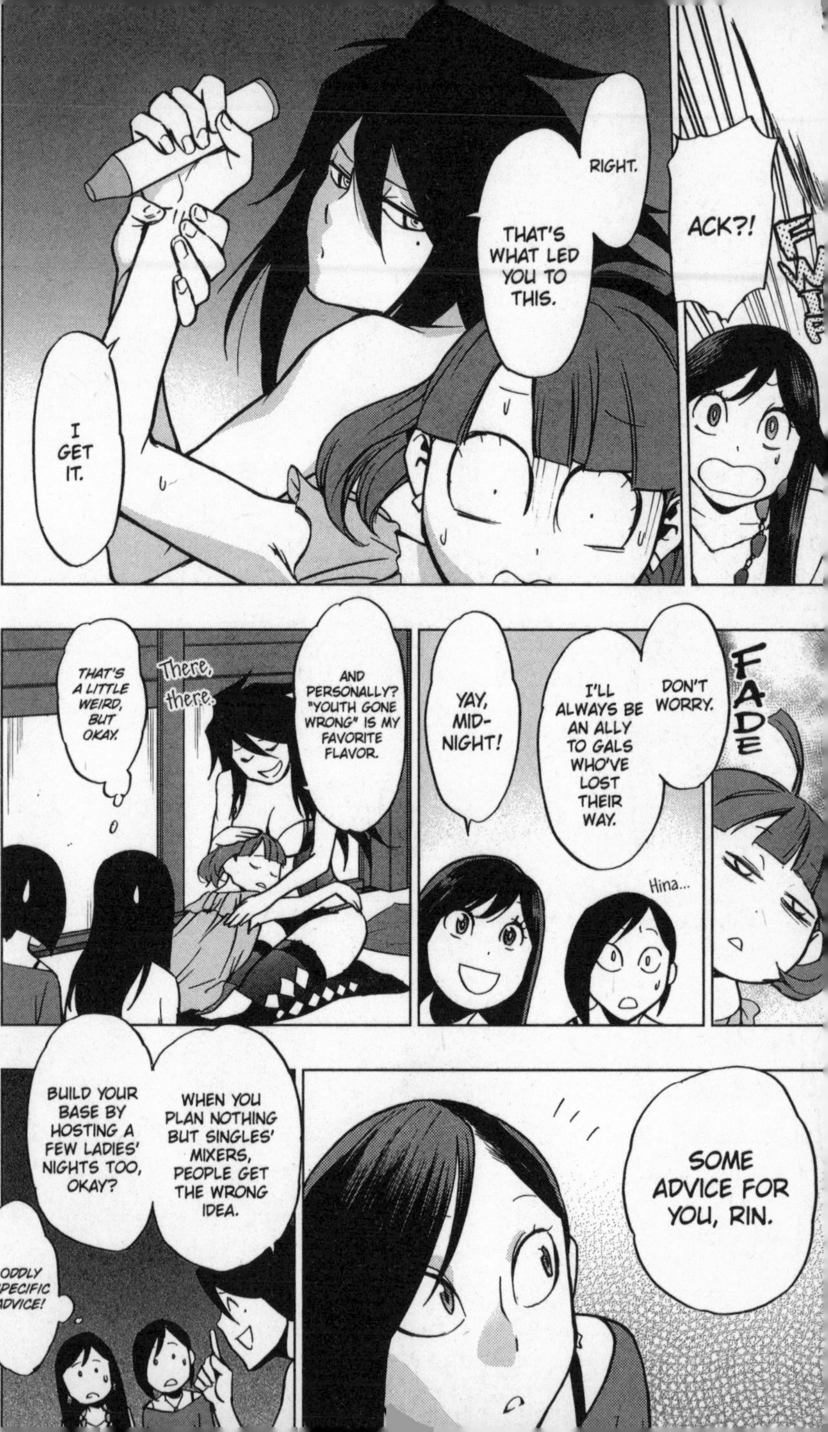
ACK?!
RIGHT.
THAT'S WHAT LED YOU TO THIS.
I GET IT.
FADE
DON'T WORRY.
I'LL ALWAYS BE AN ALLY TO GALS WHO'VE LOST THEIR WAY.
Hina...
YAY, MIDNIGHT!
AND PERSONALLY? "YOUTH GONE WRONG" IS MY FAVORITE FLAVOR.
There, there.
THAT'S A LITTLE WEIRD, BUT OKAY.
SOME ADVICE FOR YOU, RIN.
WHEN YOU PLAN NOTHING BUT SINGLES' MIXERS, PEOPLE GET THE WRONG IDEA.
BUILD YOUR BASE BY HOSTING A FEW LADIES' NIGHTS TOO, OKAY?
ODDLY SPECIFIC ADVICE!

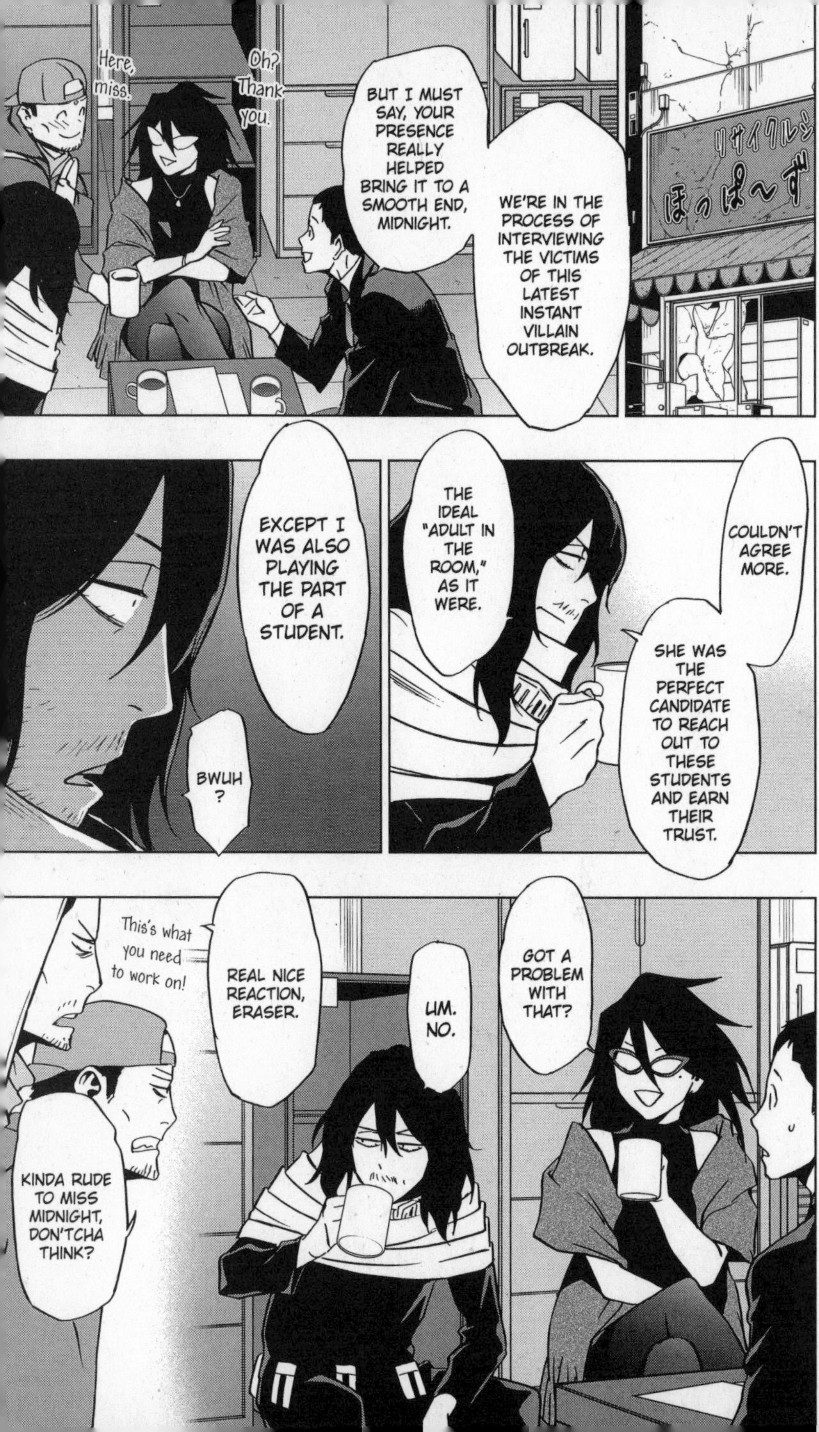
リサイクルシ
ほっぱ〜ず
WE'RE IN THE PROCESS OF INTERVIEWING THE VICTIMS OF THIS LATEST INSTANT VILLAIN OUTBREAK.
BUT I MUST SAY, YOUR PRESENCE REALLY HELPED BRING IT TO A SMOOTH END, MIDNIGHT.
Here, miss.
Oh? Thank you.
SHE WAS THE PERFECT CANDIDATE TO REACH OUT TO THESE STUDENTS AND EARN THEIR TRUST.
THE IDEAL "ADULT IN THE ROOM," AS IT WERE.
COULDN'T AGREE MORE.
EXCEPT I WAS ALSO PLAYING THE PART OF A STUDENT.
BWUH?
GOT A PROBLEM WITH THAT?
UM. NO.
REAL NICE REACTION, ERASER.
This's what you need to work on!
KINDA RUDE TO MISS MIDNIGHT, DON'TCHA THINK?

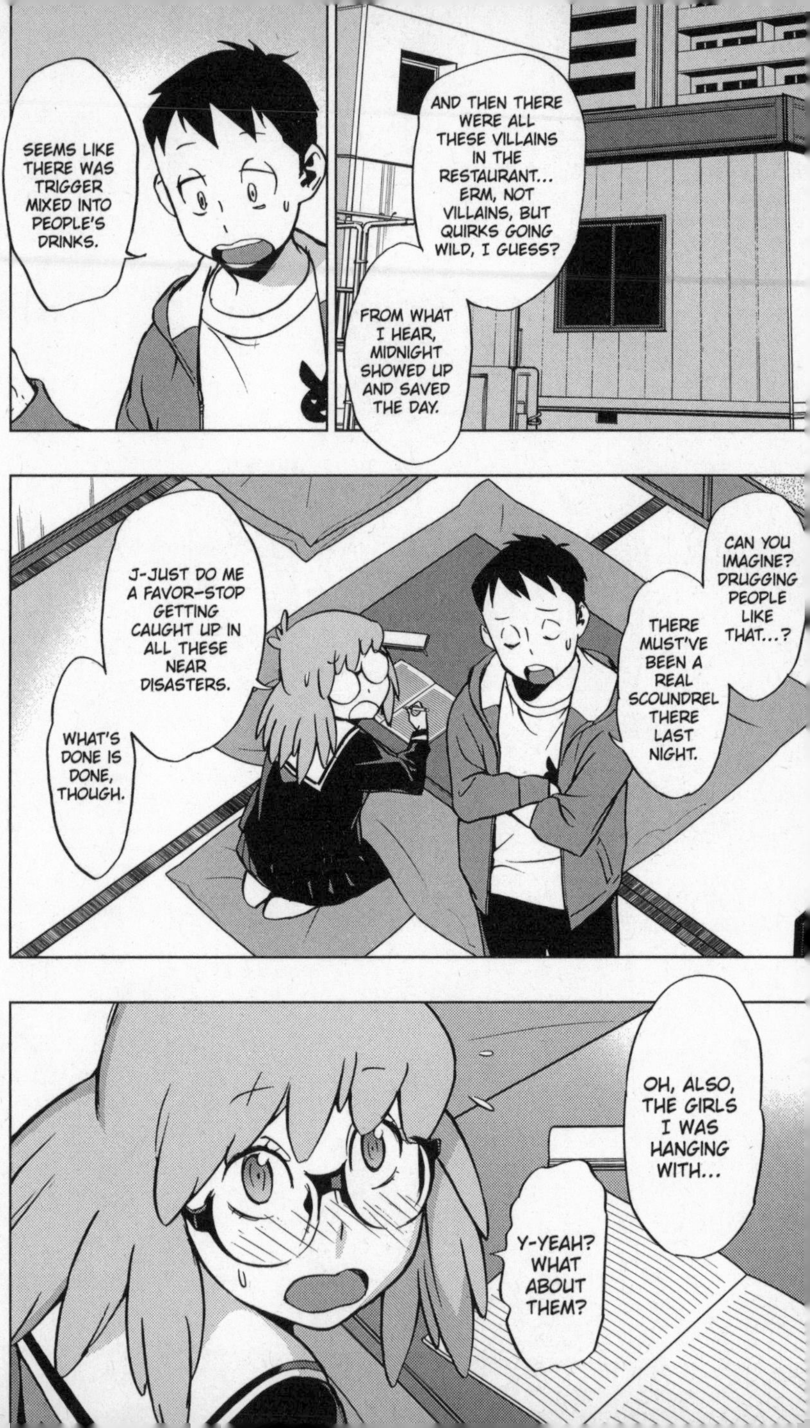
AND THEN THERE WERE ALL THESE VILLAINS IN THE RESTAURANT... ERM, NOT VILLAINS, BUT QUIRKS GOING WILD, I GUESS?
FROM WHAT I HEAR, MIDNIGHT SHOWED UP AND SAVED THE DAY.
SEEMS LIKE THERE WAS TRIGGER MIXED INTO PEOPLE'S DRINKS.
CAN YOU IMAGINE? DRUGGING PEOPLE LIKE THAT...?
THERE MUST'VE BEEN A REAL SCOUNDREL THERE LAST NIGHT.
J-JUST DO ME A FAVOR–STOP GETTING CAUGHT UP IN ALL THESE NEAR DISASTERS.
WHAT'S DONE IS DONE, THOUGH.
OH, ALSO, THE GIRLS I WAS HANGING WITH...
Y-YEAH? WHAT ABOUT THEM?

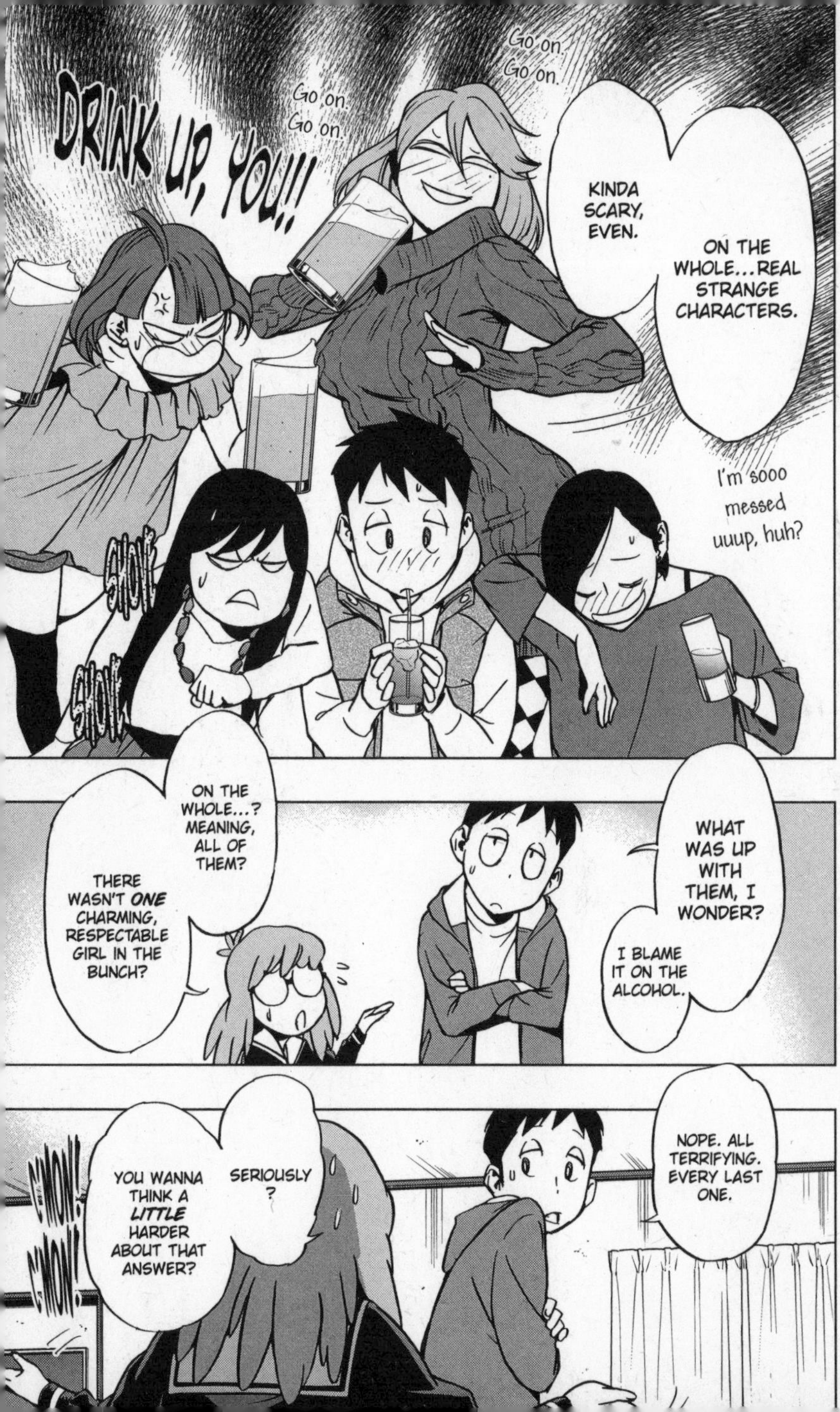
ON THE WHOLE...REAL STRANGE CHARACTERS.
KINDA SCARY, EVEN.
Go on. Go on.
DRINK UP, YOU!!
Go on. Go on.
I'm sooo messed uuup, huh?
SHOVE
SHOVE
WHAT WAS UP WITH THEM, I WONDER?
I BLAME IT ON THE ALCOHOL.
ON THE WHOLE...? MEANING, ALL OF THEM?
THERE WASN'T *ONE* CHARMING, RESPECTABLE GIRL IN THE BUNCH?
NOPE. ALL TERRIFYING. EVERY LAST ONE.
SERIOUSLY?
YOU WANNA THINK A *LITTLE* HARDER ABOUT THAT ANSWER?
C'MON! C'MON!

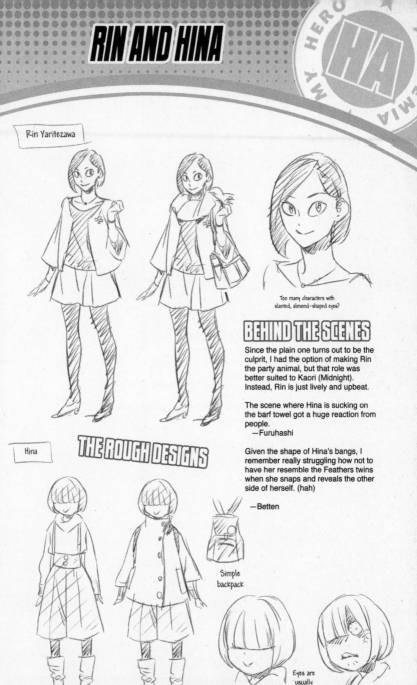

Rin Yaritezawa

Too many characters with slanted, almond-shaped eyes?

BEHIND THE SCENES

Since the plain one turns out to be the culprit, I had the option of making Rin the party animal, but that role was better suited to Kaori (Midnight). Instead, Rin is just lively and upbeat.

The scene where Hina is sucking on the barf towel got a huge reaction from people.
　—Furuhashi

Given the shape of Hina's bangs, I remember really struggling how not to have her resemble the Feathers twins when she snaps and reveals the other side of herself. (hah)

　—Betten

Hina

THE ROUGH DESIGNS

Simple backpack

Eyes are usually hidden

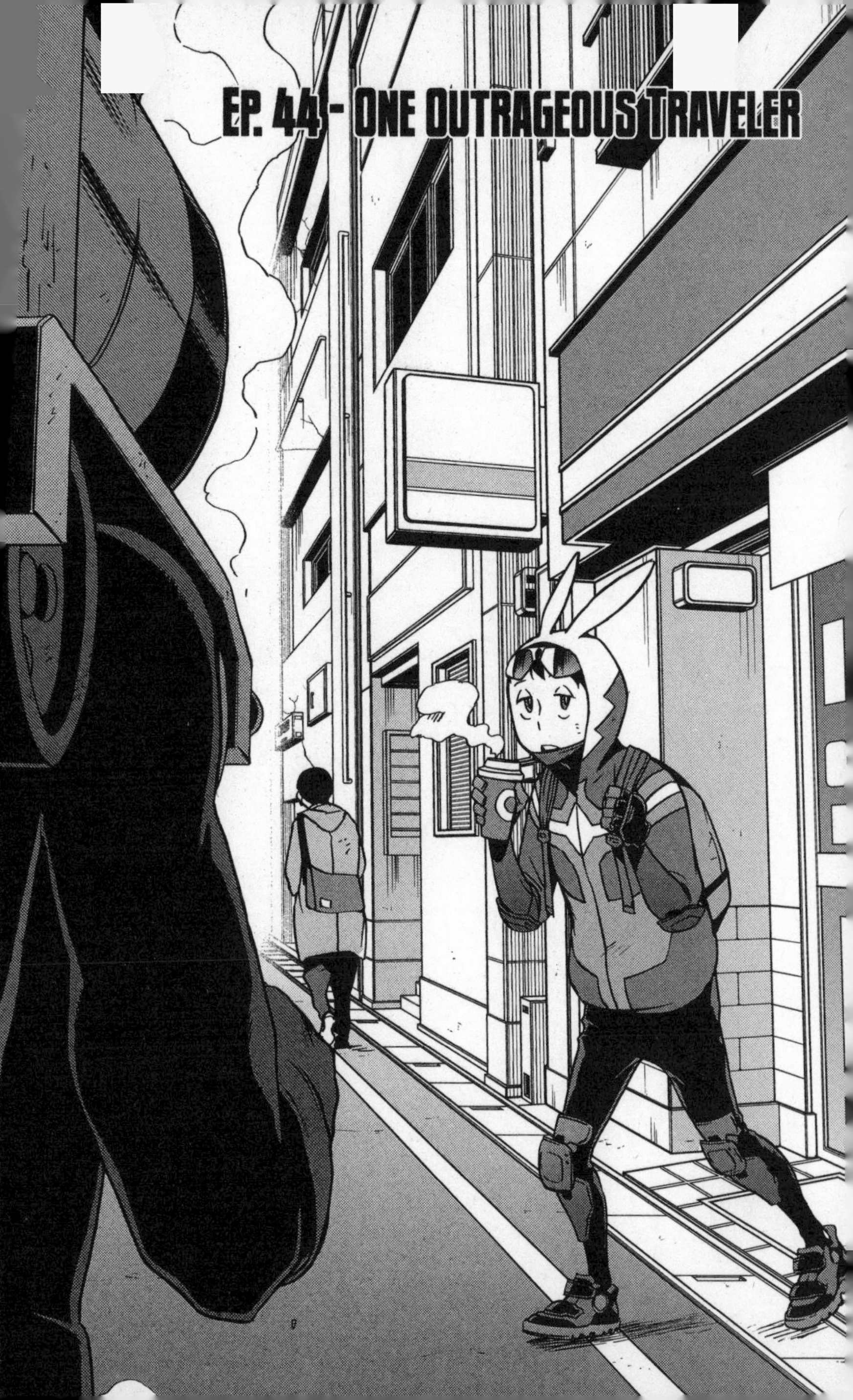
EP. 44 - ONE OUTRAGEOUS TRAVELER

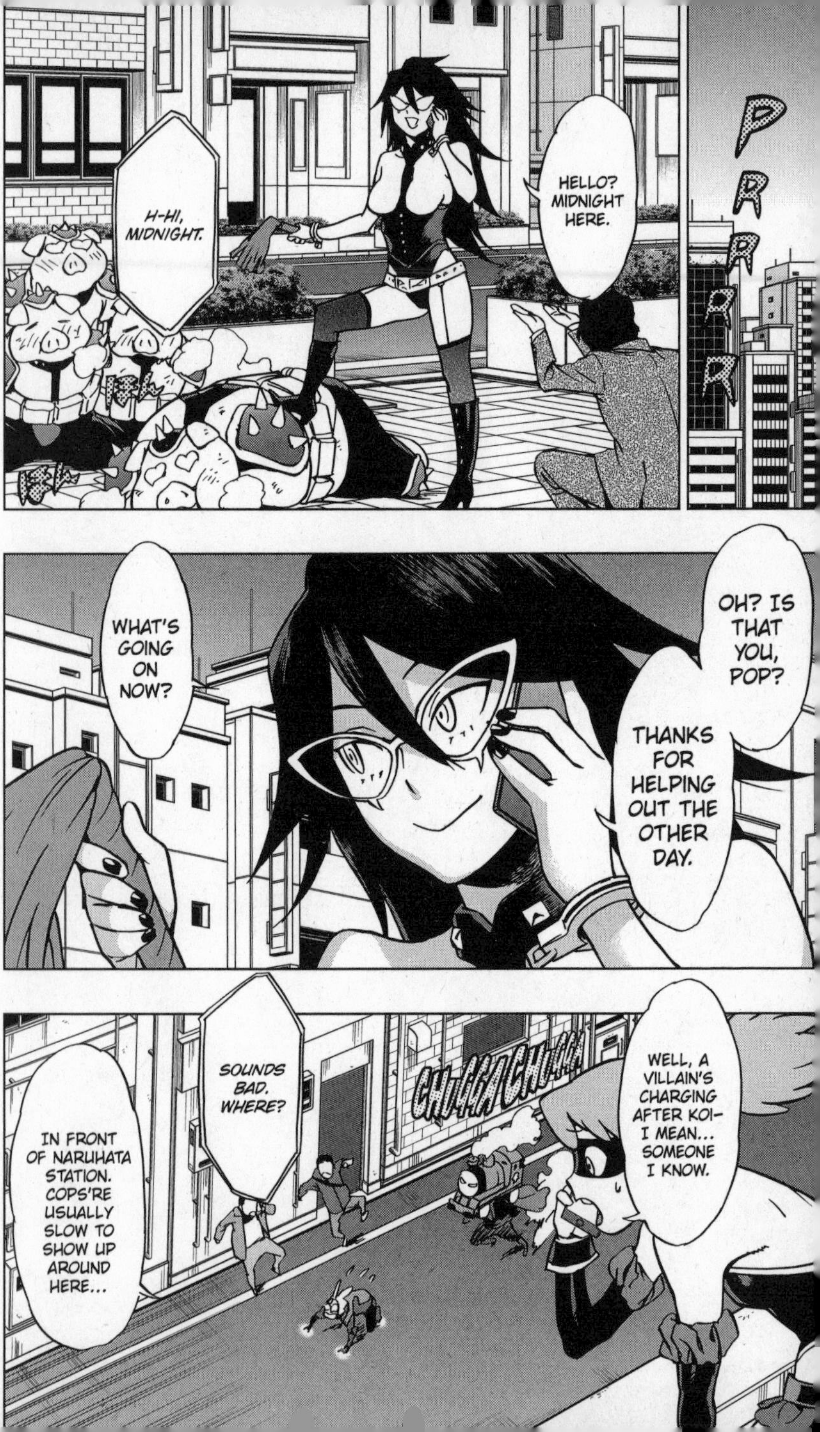
PRRRRR
HELLO? MIDNIGHT HERE.
H-HI, MIDNIGHT.
OH? IS THAT YOU, POP?
THANKS FOR HELPING OUT THE OTHER DAY.
WHAT'S GOING ON NOW?
WELL, A VILLAIN'S CHARGING AFTER KOI- I MEAN... SOMEONE I KNOW.
CHUGGA CHUGGA
SOUNDS BAD. WHERE?
IN FRONT OF NARUHATA STATION. COPS'RE USUALLY SLOW TO SHOW UP AROUND HERE...

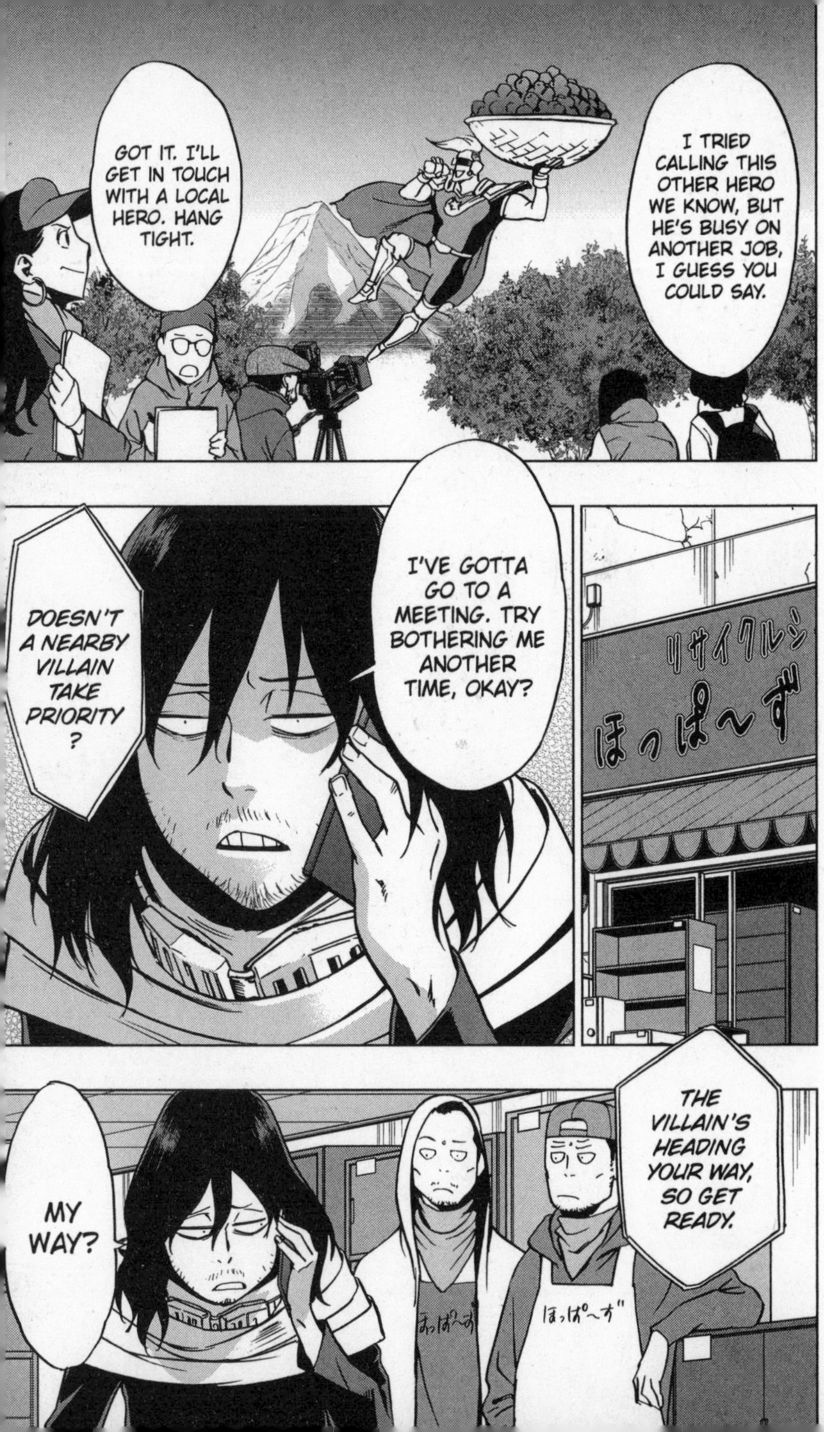
I TRIED CALLING THIS OTHER HERO WE KNOW, BUT HE'S BUSY ON ANOTHER JOB, I GUESS YOU COULD SAY.
GOT IT. I'LL GET IN TOUCH WITH A LOCAL HERO. HANG TIGHT.
リサイクルシ
ほっぱ〜ず
I'VE GOTTA GO TO A MEETING. TRY BOTHERING ME ANOTHER TIME, OKAY?
DOESN'T A NEARBY VILLAIN TAKE PRIORITY?
THE VILLAIN'S HEADING YOUR WAY, SO GET READY.
ほっぱ〜ず
ほっぱ〜ず
MY WAY?

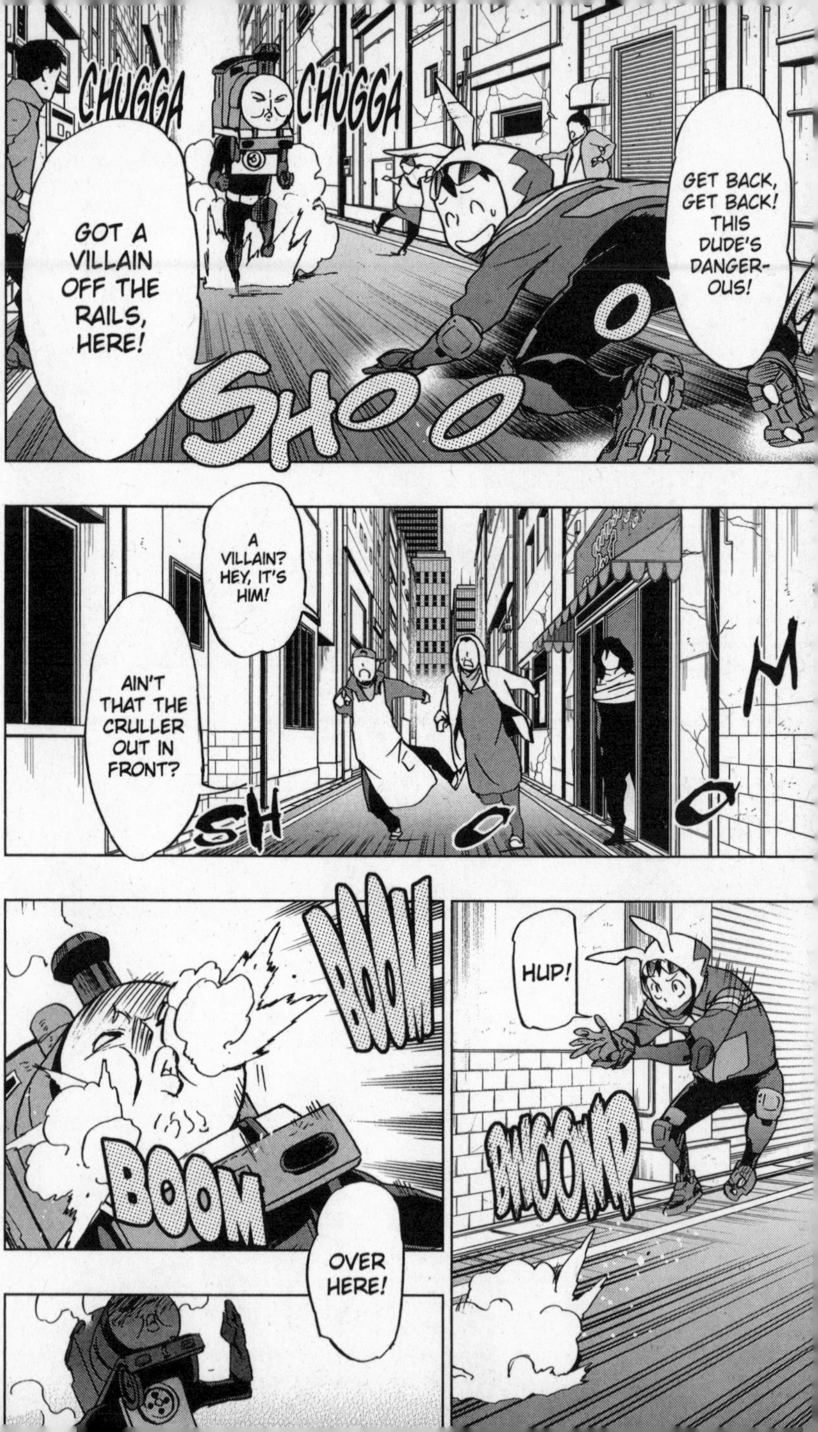
GET BACK, GET BACK! THIS DUDE'S DANGER-OUS!
CHUGGA CHUGGA
GOT A VILLAIN OFF THE RAILS, HERE!
SHOOOM
A VILLAIN? HEY, IT'S HIM!
AIN'T THAT THE CRULLER OUT IN FRONT?
SHOOOM
HUP!
BWOOMP
BOOM
BOOM
OVER HERE!

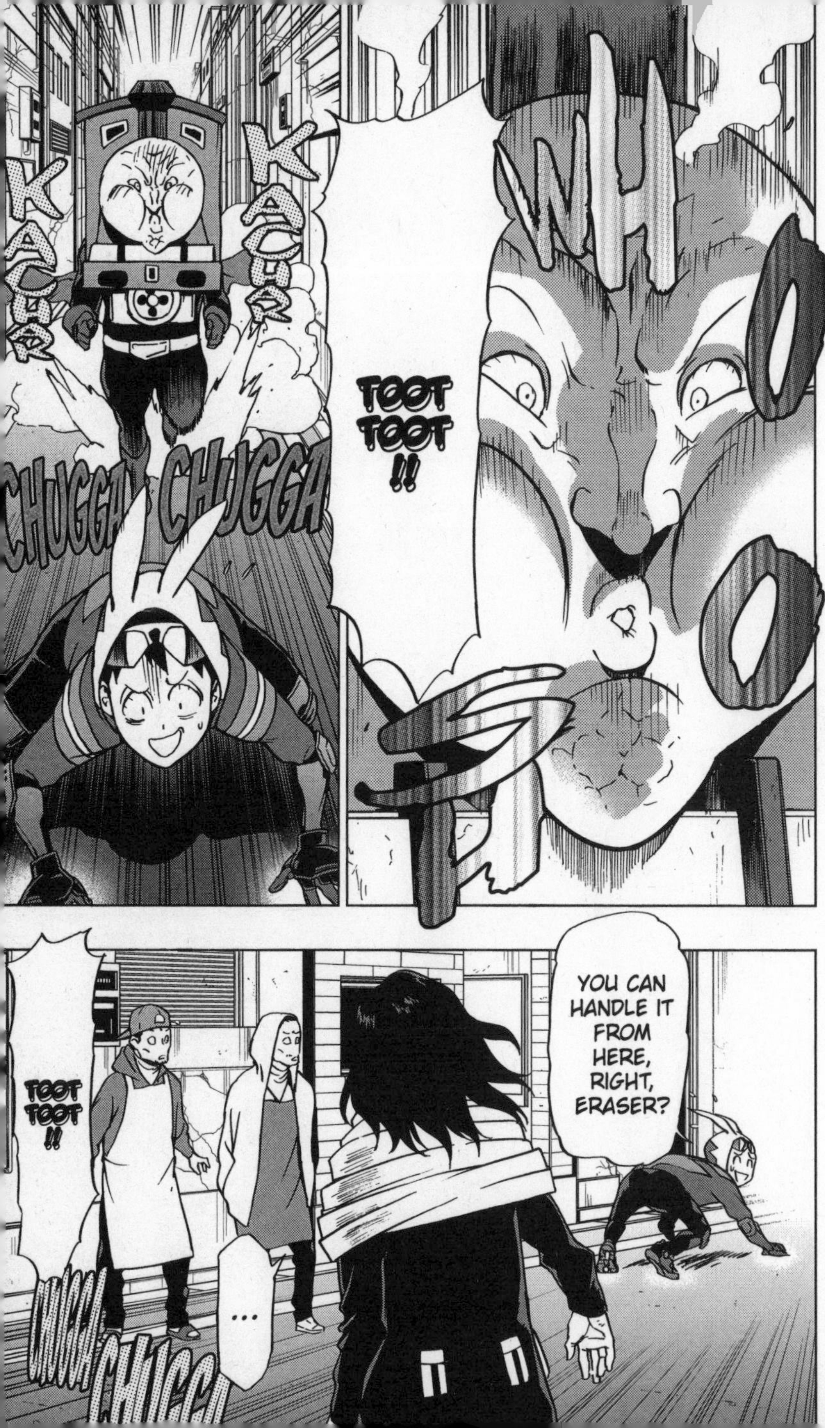
WHOO
TOOT TOOT !!
KACHA
KACHA
CHUGGA CHUGGA
YOU CAN HANDLE IT FROM HERE, RIGHT, ERASER?
TOOT TOOT !!
...
CHUGGA CHUGGA

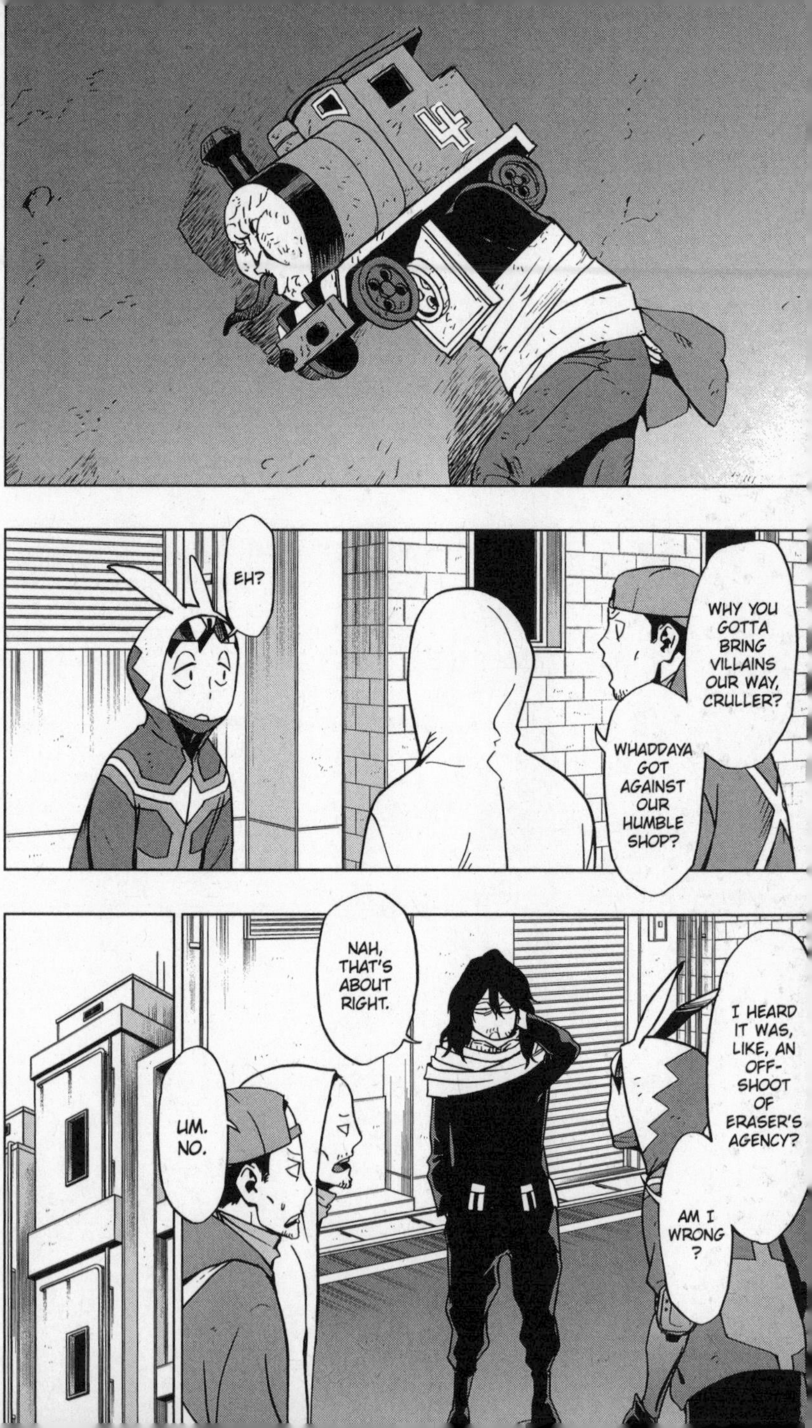
WHY YOU GOTTA BRING VILLAINS OUR WAY, CRULLER?
WHADDAYA GOT AGAINST OUR HUMBLE SHOP?
EH?
I HEARD IT WAS, LIKE, AN OFF-SHOOT OF ERASER'S AGENCY?
AM I WRONG?
NAH, THAT'S ABOUT RIGHT.
UM. NO.

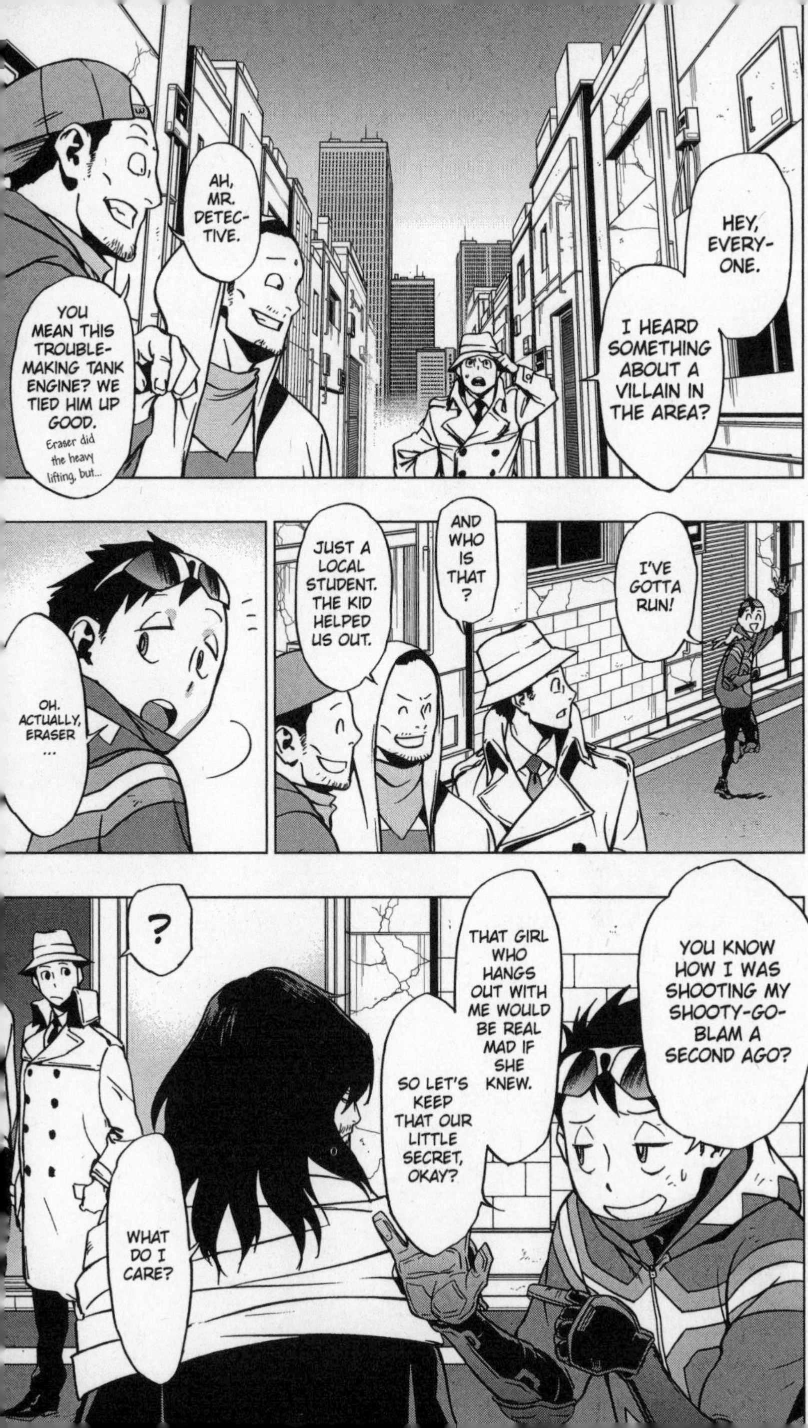
HEY, EVERY-ONE.
I HEARD SOMETHING ABOUT A VILLAIN IN THE AREA?
AH, MR. DETEC-TIVE.
YOU MEAN THIS TROUBLE-MAKING TANK ENGINE? WE TIED HIM UP GOOD.
Eraser did the heavy lifting, but...
I'VE GOTTA RUN!
AND WHO IS THAT?
JUST A LOCAL STUDENT. THE KID HELPED US OUT.
OH. ACTUALLY, ERASER ...
YOU KNOW HOW I WAS SHOOTING MY SHOOTY-GO-BLAM A SECOND AGO?
THAT GIRL WHO HANGS OUT WITH ME WOULD BE REAL MAD IF SHE KNEW.
SO LET'S KEEP THAT OUR LITTLE SECRET, OKAY?
?
WHAT DO I CARE?

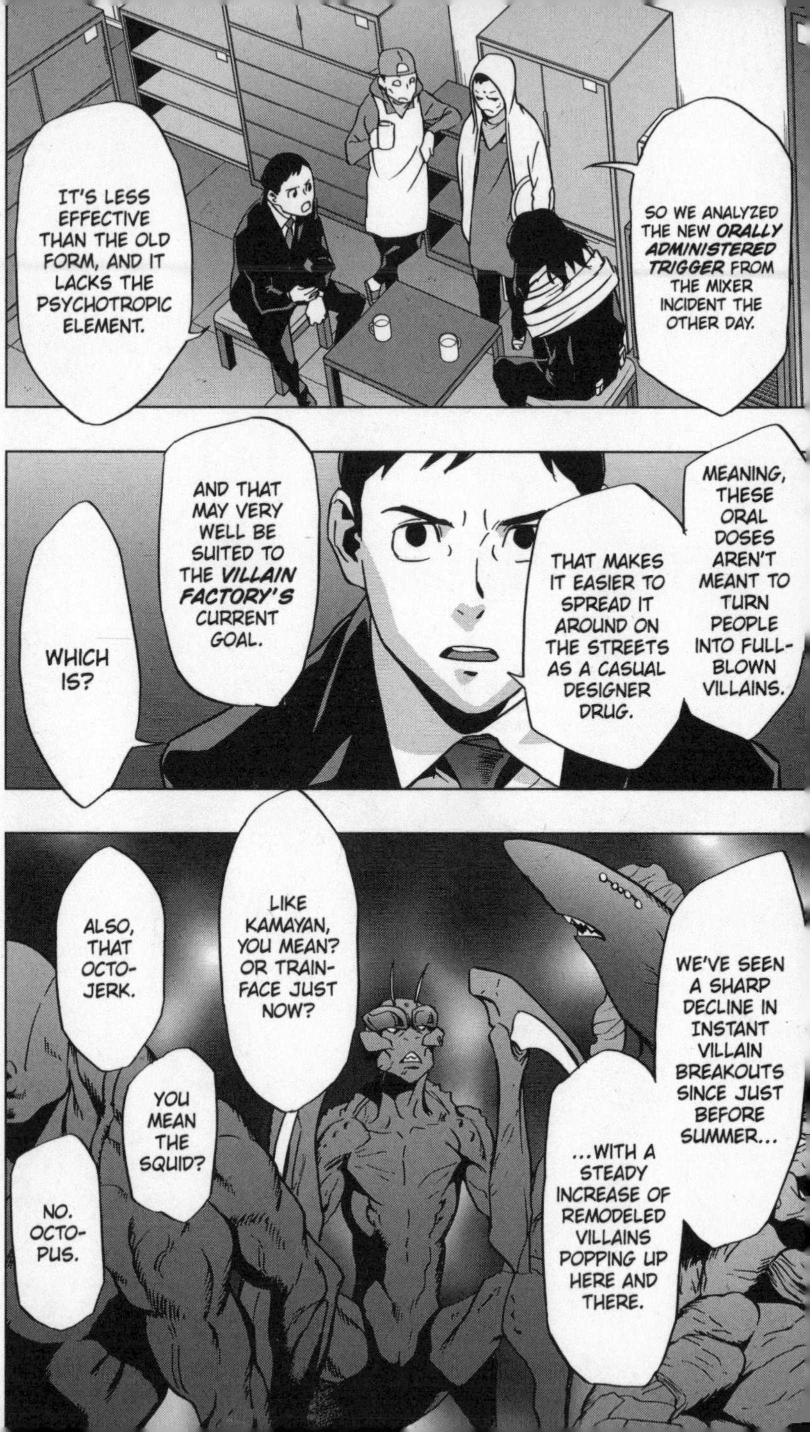
SO WE ANALYZED THE NEW ORALLY ADMINISTERED TRIGGER FROM THE MIXER INCIDENT THE OTHER DAY.
IT'S LESS EFFECTIVE THAN THE OLD FORM, AND IT LACKS THE PSYCHOTROPIC ELEMENT.
MEANING, THESE ORAL DOSES AREN'T MEANT TO TURN PEOPLE INTO FULL-BLOWN VILLAINS.
THAT MAKES IT EASIER TO SPREAD IT AROUND ON THE STREETS AS A CASUAL DESIGNER DRUG.
AND THAT MAY VERY WELL BE SUITED TO THE VILLAIN FACTORY'S CURRENT GOAL.
WHICH IS?
WE'VE SEEN A SHARP DECLINE IN INSTANT VILLAIN BREAKOUTS SINCE JUST BEFORE SUMMER...
...WITH A STEADY INCREASE OF REMODELED VILLAINS POPPING UP HERE AND THERE.
LIKE KAMAYAN, YOU MEAN? OR TRAIN-FACE JUST NOW?
ALSO, THAT OCTO-JERK.
YOU MEAN THE SQUID?
NO. OCTOPUS.

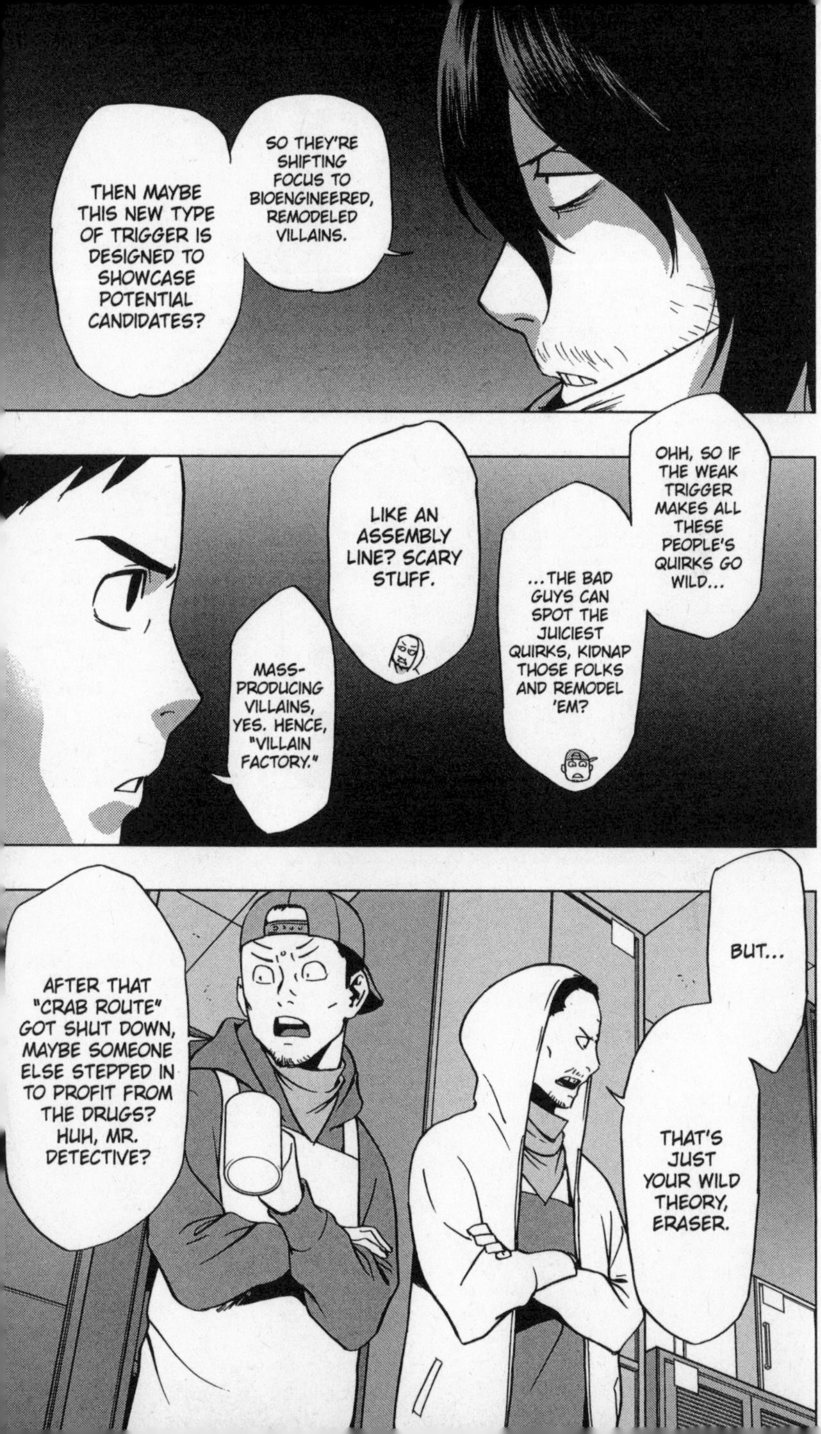
SO THEY'RE SHIFTING FOCUS TO BIOENGINEERED, REMODELED VILLAINS.
THEN MAYBE THIS NEW TYPE OF TRIGGER IS DESIGNED TO SHOWCASE POTENTIAL CANDIDATES?
OHH, SO IF THE WEAK TRIGGER MAKES ALL THESE PEOPLE'S QUIRKS GO WILD...
...THE BAD GUYS CAN SPOT THE JUICIEST QUIRKS, KIDNAP THOSE FOLKS AND REMODEL 'EM?
LIKE AN ASSEMBLY LINE? SCARY STUFF.
MASS-PRODUCING VILLAINS, YES. HENCE, "VILLAIN FACTORY."
BUT...
THAT'S JUST YOUR WILD THEORY, ERASER.
AFTER THAT "CRAB ROUTE" GOT SHUT DOWN, MAYBE SOMEONE ELSE STEPPED IN TO PROFIT FROM THE DRUGS? HUH, MR. DETECTIVE?

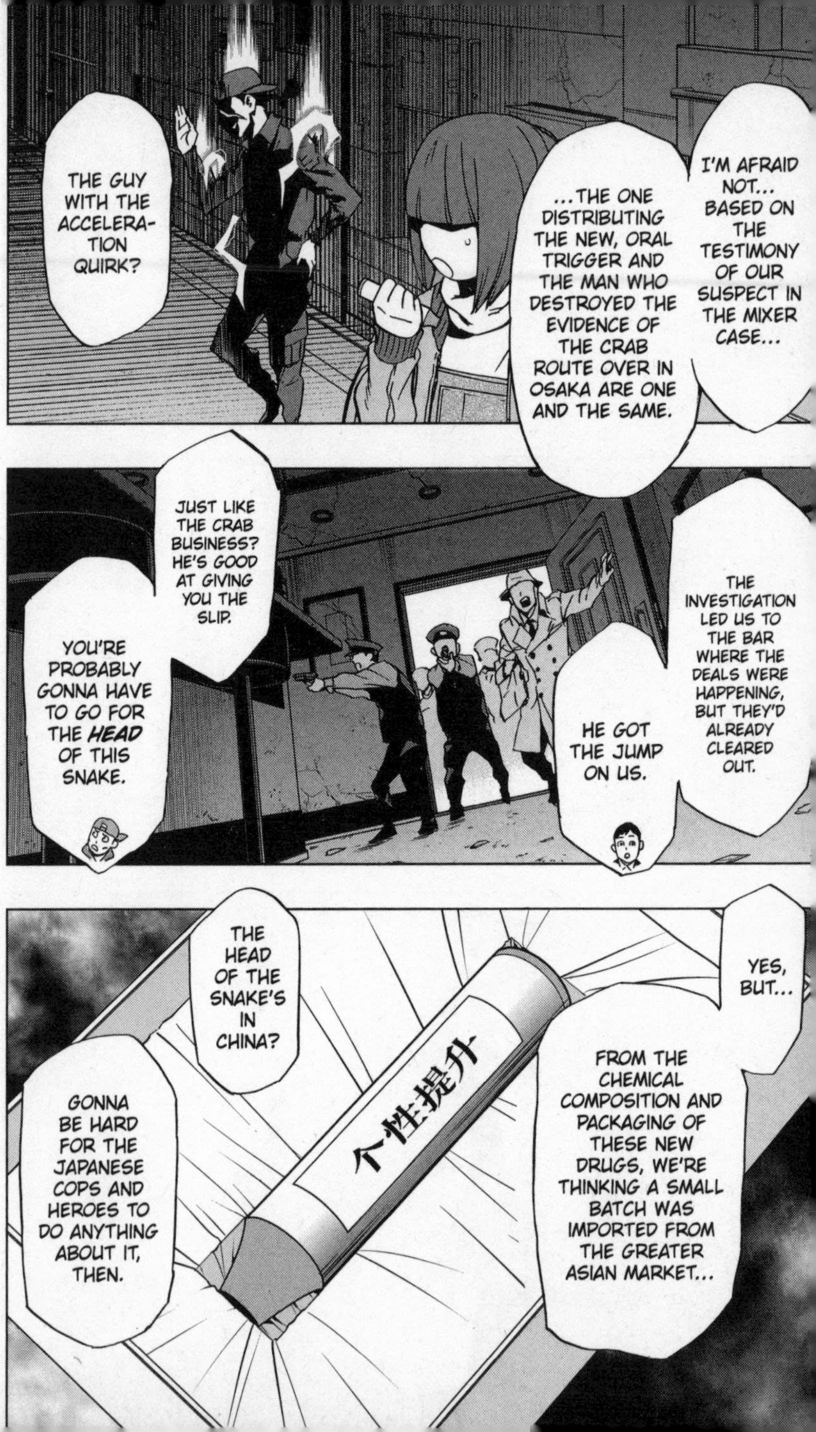
I'M AFRAID NOT... BASED ON THE TESTIMONY OF OUR SUSPECT IN THE MIXER CASE...
...THE ONE DISTRIBUTING THE NEW, ORAL TRIGGER AND THE MAN WHO DESTROYED THE EVIDENCE OF THE CRAB ROUTE OVER IN OSAKA ARE ONE AND THE SAME.
THE GUY WITH THE ACCELERATION QUIRK?
THE INVESTIGATION LED US TO THE BAR WHERE THE DEALS WERE HAPPENING, BUT THEY'D ALREADY CLEARED OUT.
HE GOT THE JUMP ON US.
JUST LIKE THE CRAB BUSINESS? HE'S GOOD AT GIVING YOU THE SLIP.
YOU'RE PROBABLY GONNA HAVE TO GO FOR THE *HEAD* OF THIS SNAKE.
YES, BUT...
FROM THE CHEMICAL COMPOSITION AND PACKAGING OF THESE NEW DRUGS, WE'RE THINKING A SMALL BATCH WAS IMPORTED FROM THE GREATER ASIAN MARKET...
个性提升
THE HEAD OF THE SNAKE'S IN CHINA?
GONNA BE HARD FOR THE JAPANESE COPS AND HEROES TO DO ANYTHING ABOUT IT, THEN.

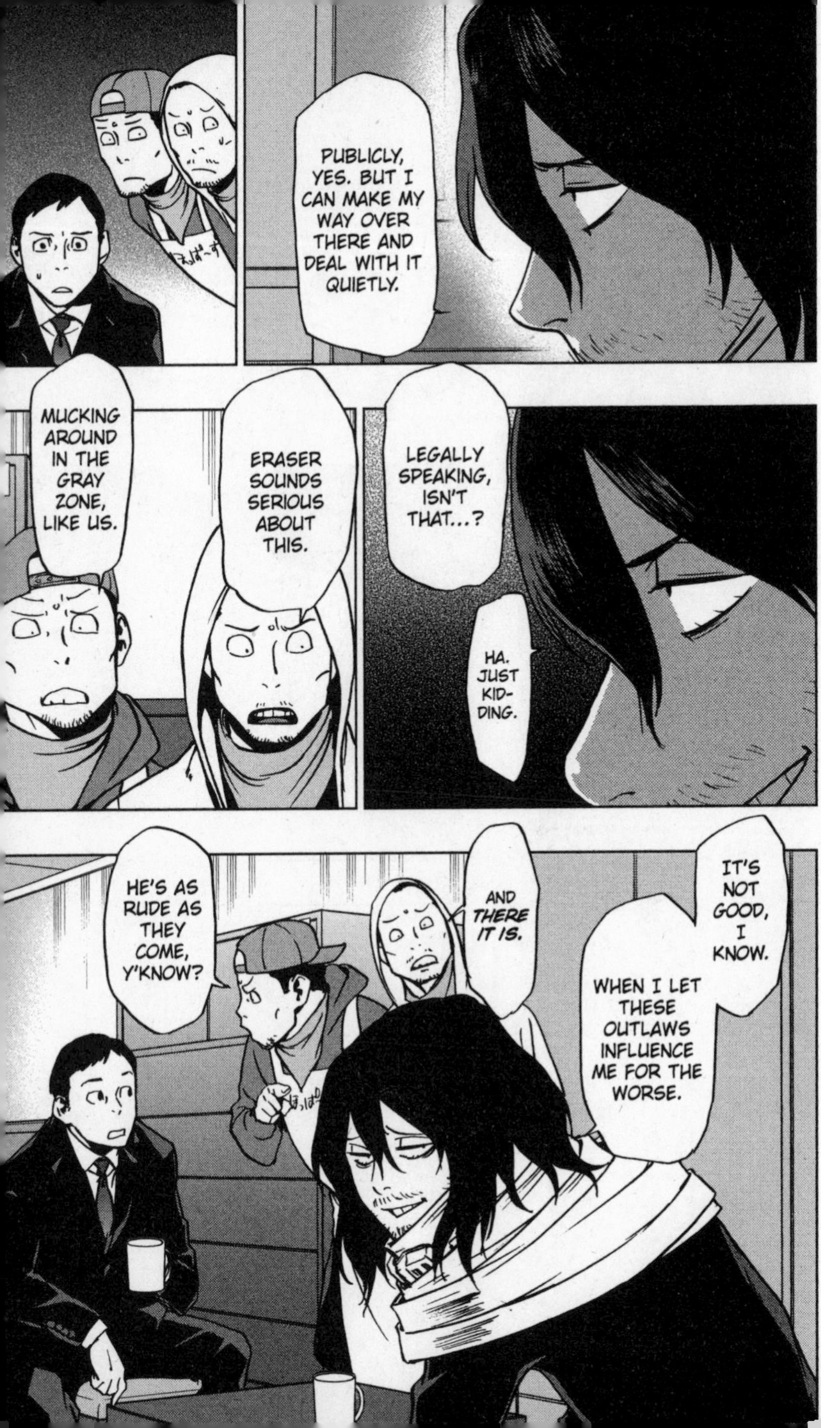
PUBLICLY, YES. BUT I CAN MAKE MY WAY OVER THERE AND DEAL WITH IT QUIETLY.
LEGALLY SPEAKING, ISN'T THAT...?
HA. JUST KID-DING.
ERASER SOUNDS SERIOUS ABOUT THIS.
MUCKING AROUND IN THE GRAY ZONE, LIKE US.
IT'S NOT GOOD, I KNOW.
WHEN I LET THESE OUTLAWS INFLUENCE ME FOR THE WORSE.
AND *THERE IT IS.*
HE'S AS RUDE AS THEY COME, Y'KNOW?

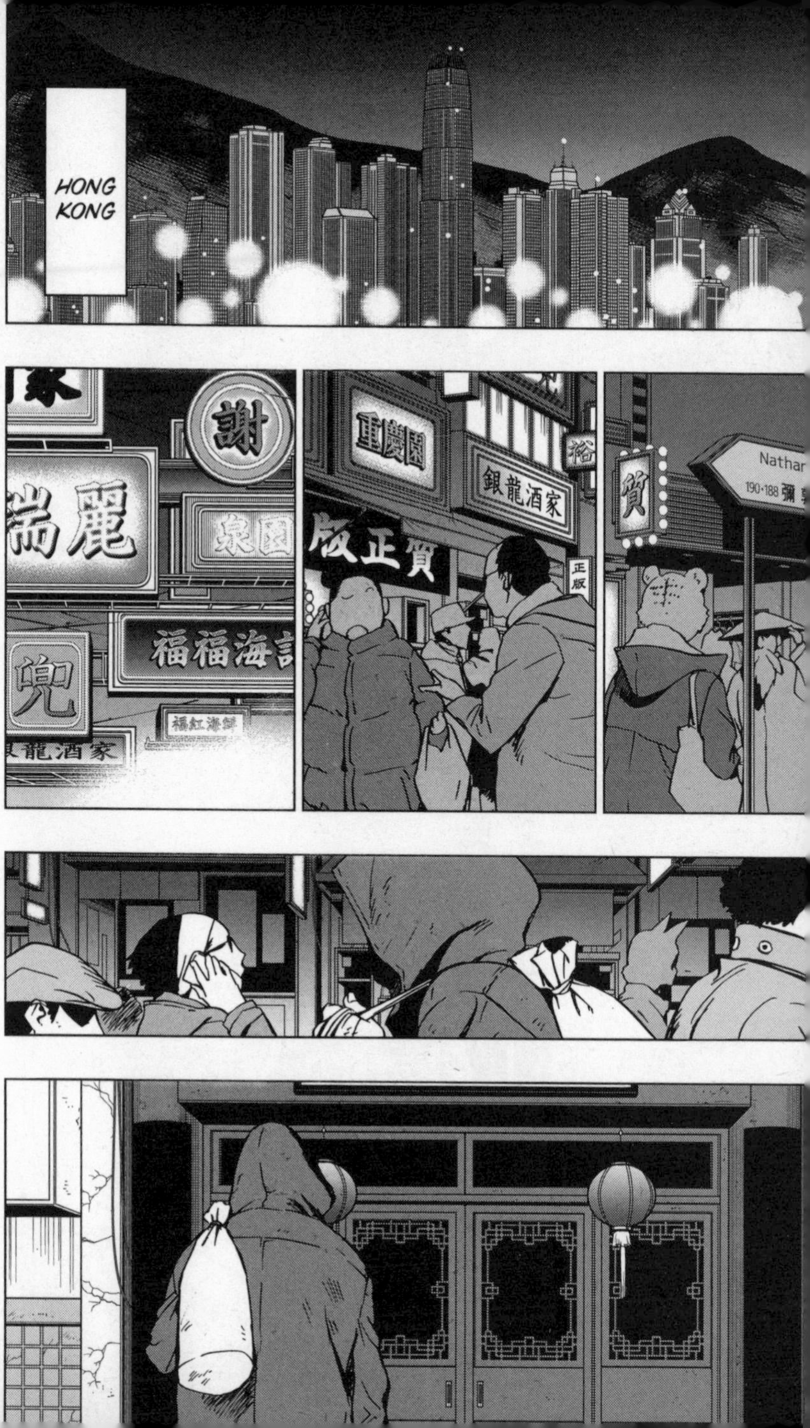
HONG KONG
謝
銀龍酒家
Nathar
190·188

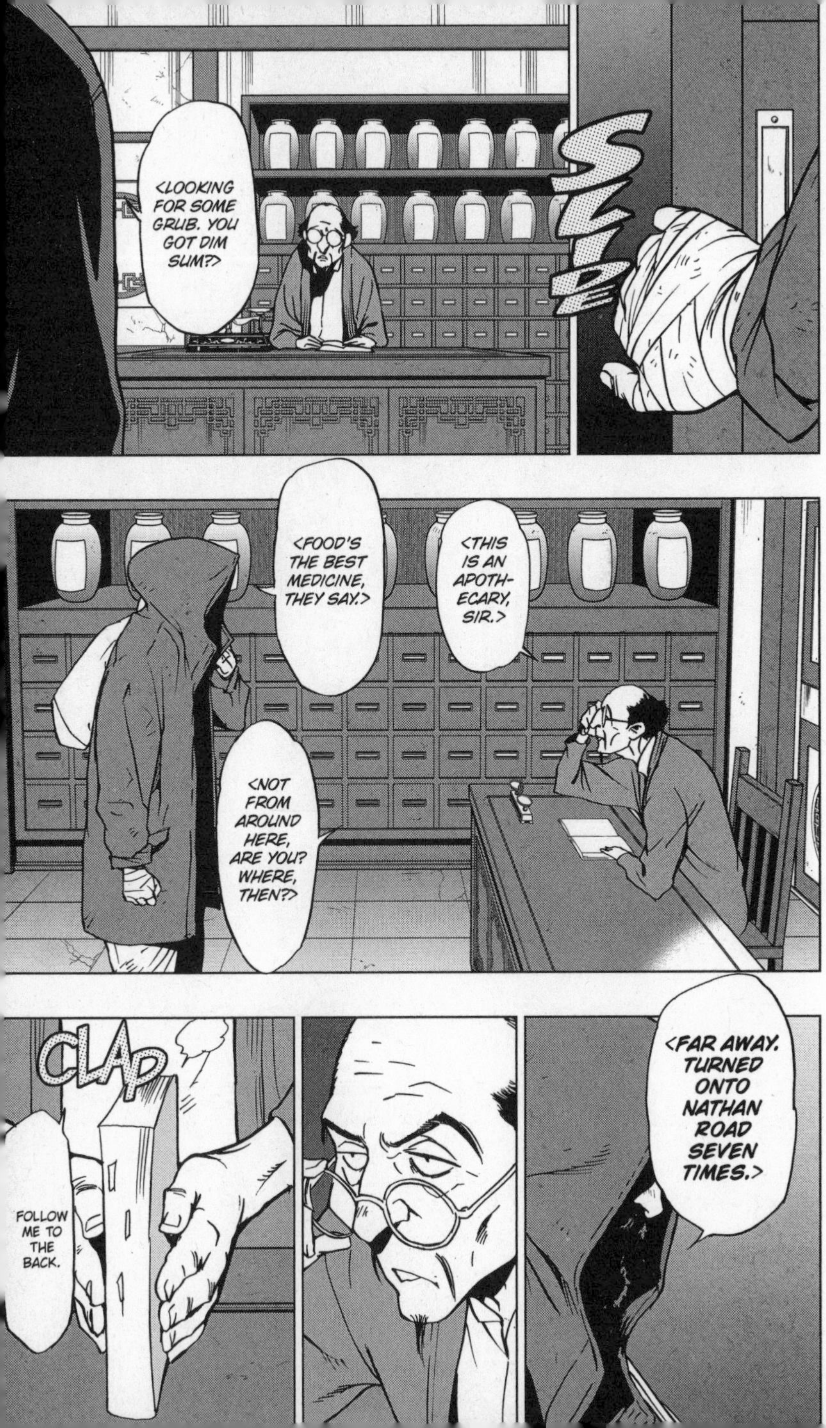
SLIDE
<LOOKING FOR SOME GRUB. YOU GOT DIM SUM?>
<THIS IS AN APOTHECARY, SIR.>
<FOOD'S THE BEST MEDICINE, THEY SAY.>
<NOT FROM AROUND HERE, ARE YOU? WHERE, THEN?>
<FAR AWAY. TURNED ONTO NATHAN ROAD SEVEN TIMES.>
CLAP
FOLLOW ME TO THE BACK.

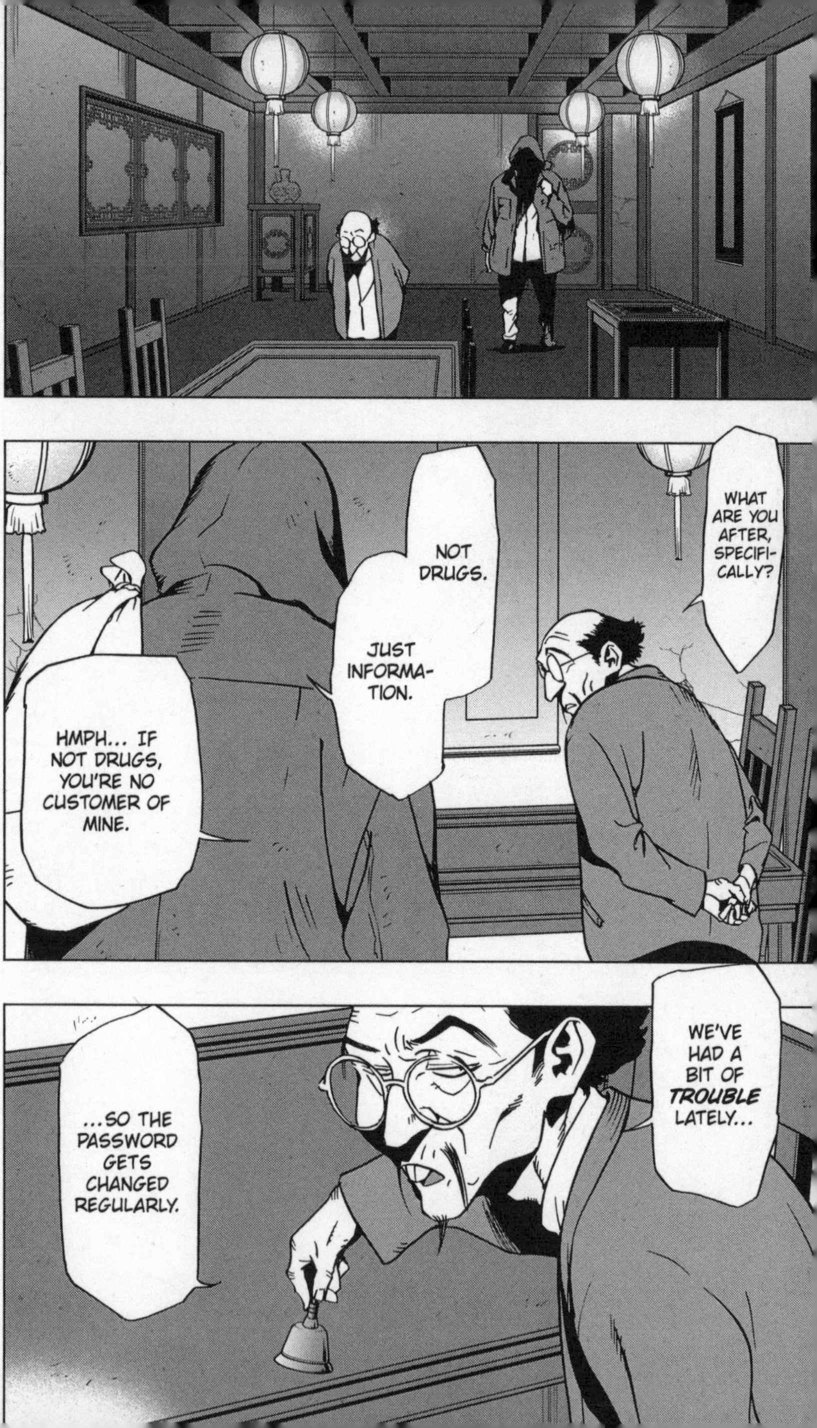
WHAT ARE YOU AFTER, SPECIFICALLY?
NOT DRUGS.
JUST INFORMATION.
HMPH... IF NOT DRUGS, YOU'RE NO CUSTOMER OF MINE.
WE'VE HAD A BIT OF ***TROUBLE*** LATELY...
...SO THE PASSWORD GETS CHANGED REGULARLY.

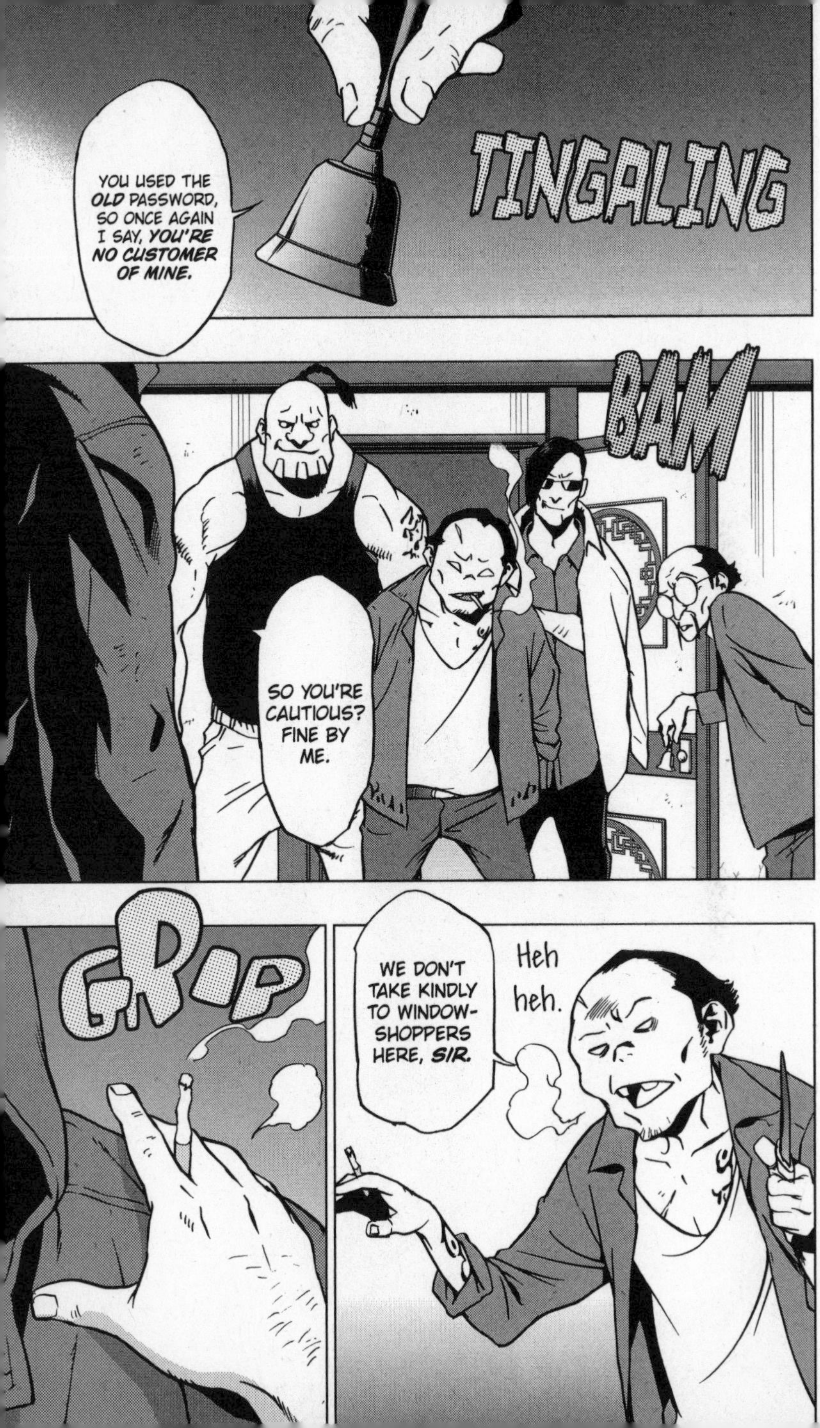
TINGALING
YOU USED THE *OLD* PASSWORD, SO ONCE AGAIN I SAY, ***YOU'RE NO CUSTOMER OF MINE.***
BAM
SO YOU'RE CAUTIOUS? FINE BY ME.
Heh heh.
WE DON'T TAKE KINDLY TO WINDOW-SHOPPERS HERE, ***SIR.***
GRIP

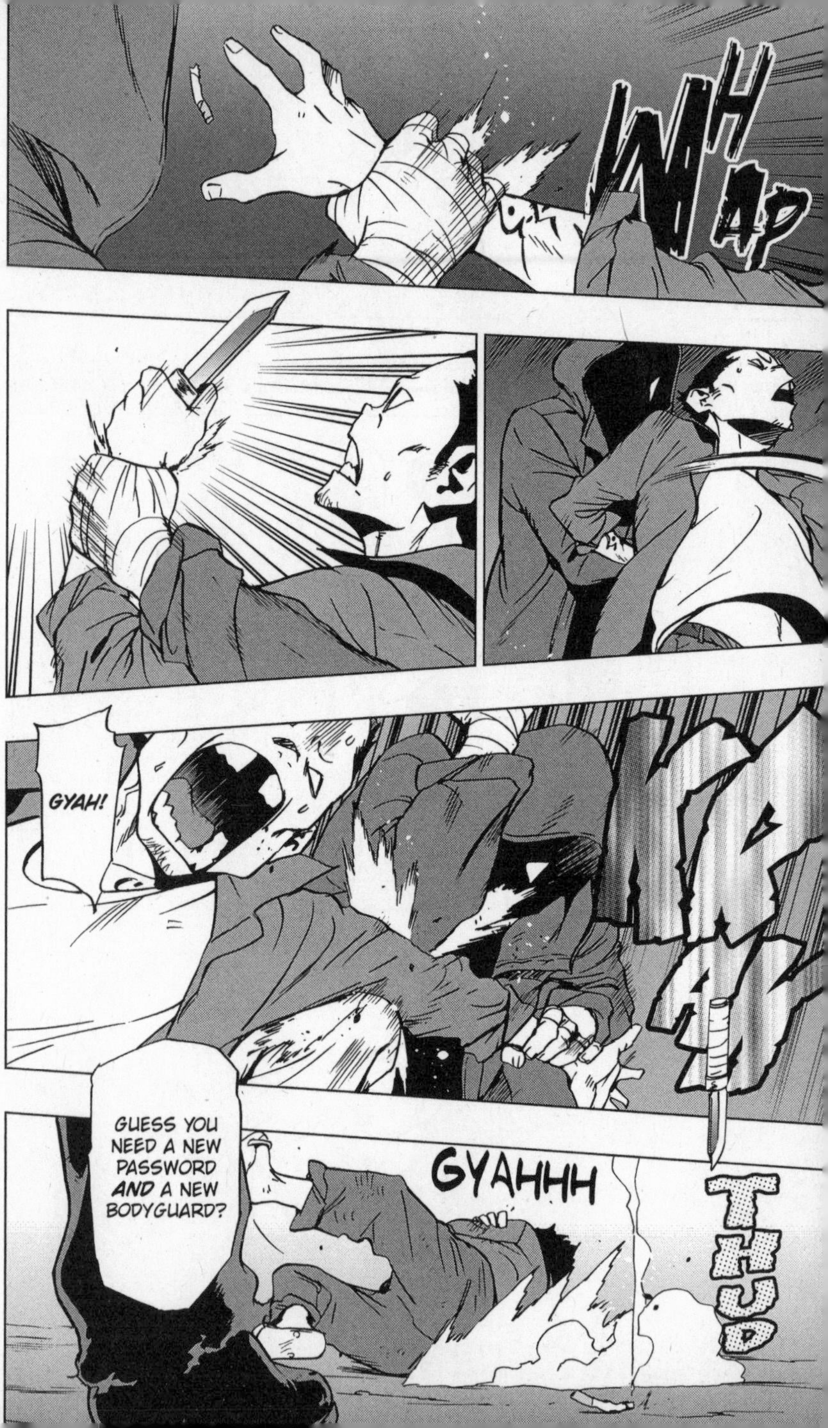
WHAP
GYAH!
THUD
GYAHHH
GUESS YOU NEED A NEW PASSWORD *AND* A NEW BODYGUARD?

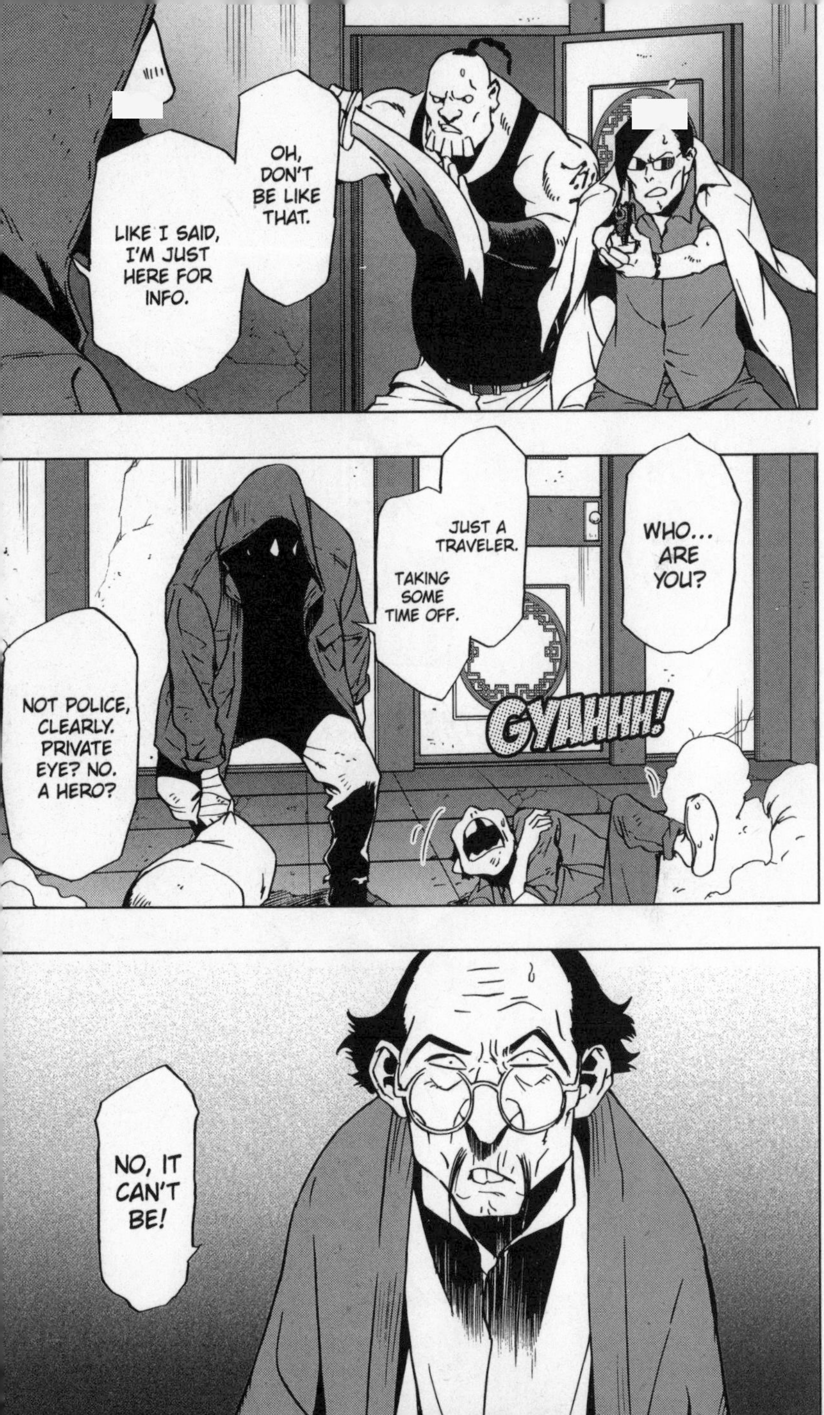
OH, DON'T BE LIKE THAT.
LIKE I SAID, I'M JUST HERE FOR INFO.
WHO... ARE YOU?
JUST A TRAVELER.
TAKING SOME TIME OFF.
GYAHHH!
NOT POLICE, CLEARLY. PRIVATE EYE? NO. A HERO?
NO, IT CAN'T BE!

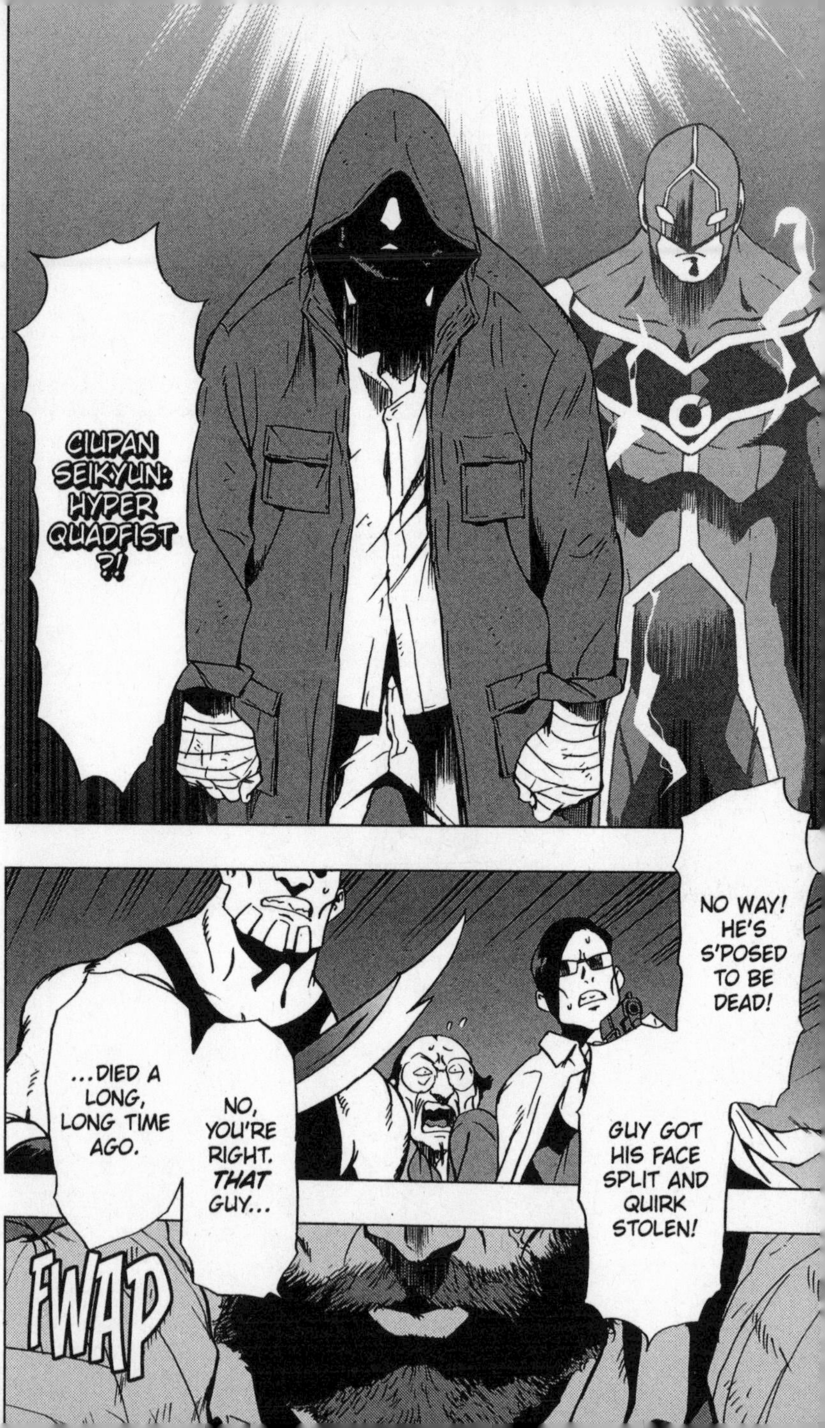
CIUPAN SEIKYUN: HYPER QUADFIST ?!
NO WAY! HE'S S'POSED TO BE DEAD!
GUY GOT HIS FACE SPLIT AND QUIRK STOLEN!
NO, YOU'RE RIGHT. THAT GUY...
...DIED A LONG, LONG TIME AGO.
FWAP

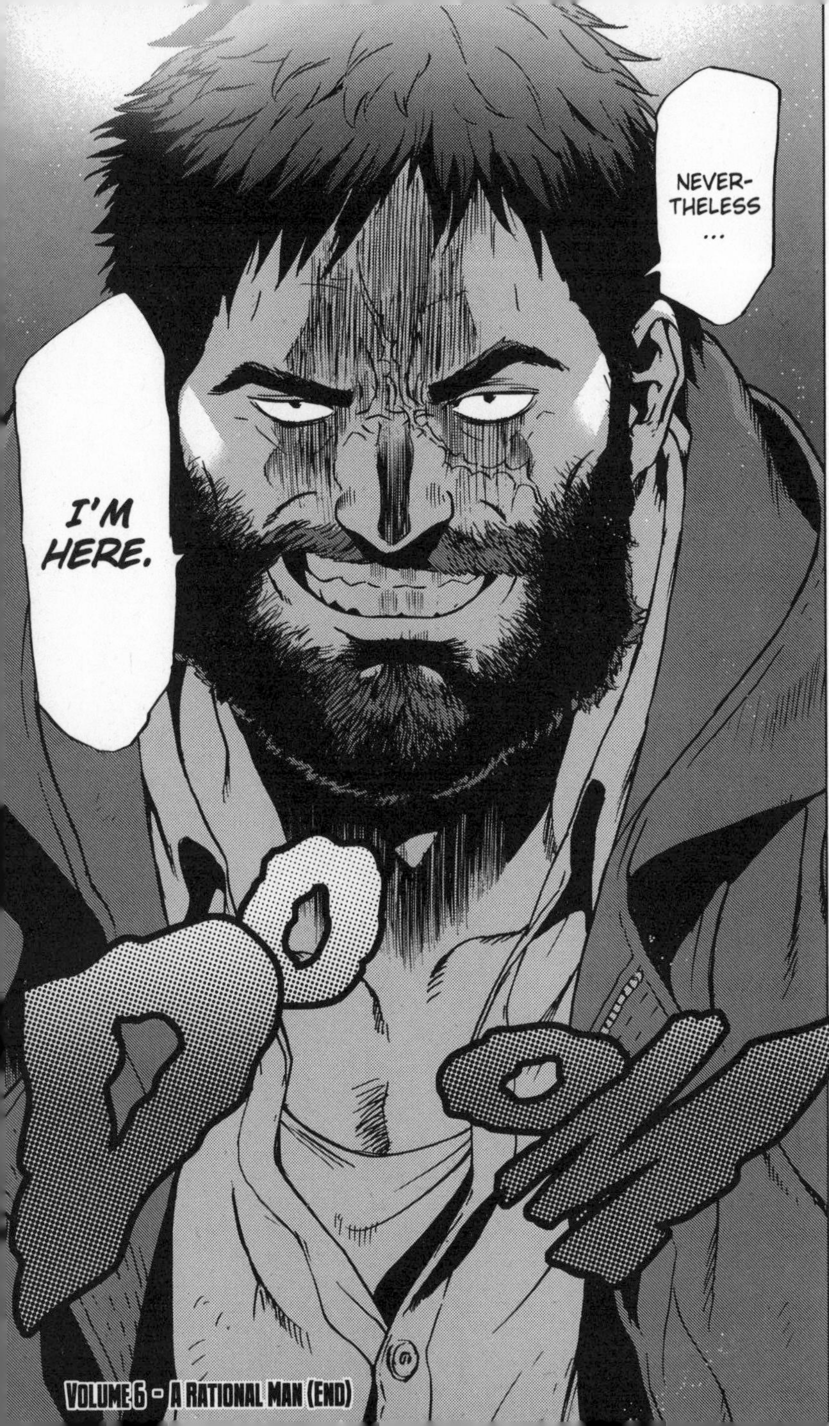
NEVER-THELESS...
I'M HERE.
VOLUME 6 - A RATIONAL MAN (END)

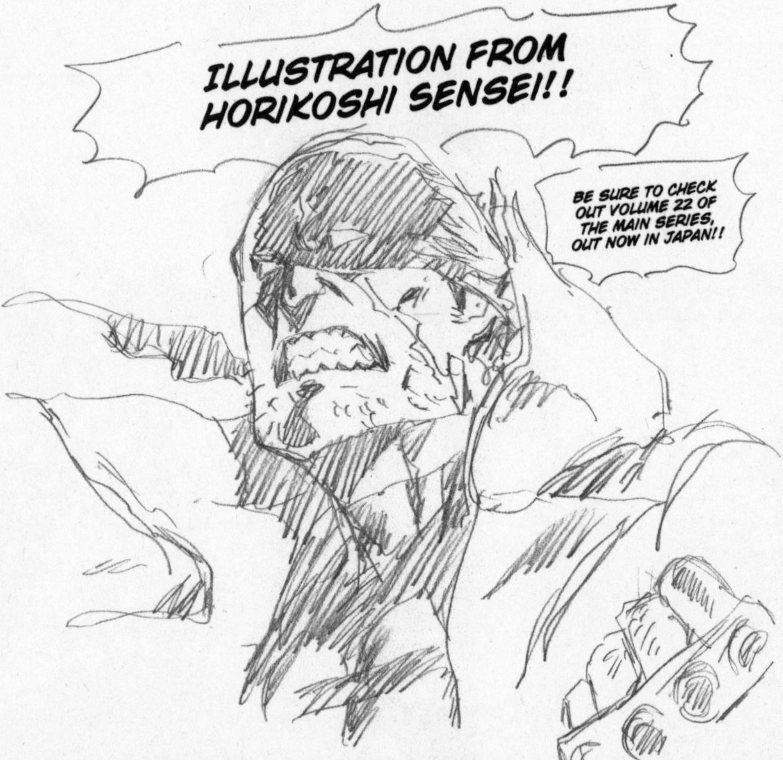
ILLUSTRATION FROM HORIKOSHI SENSEI!!
BE SURE TO CHECK OUT VOLUME 22 OF THE MAIN SERIES, OUT NOW IN JAPAN!!

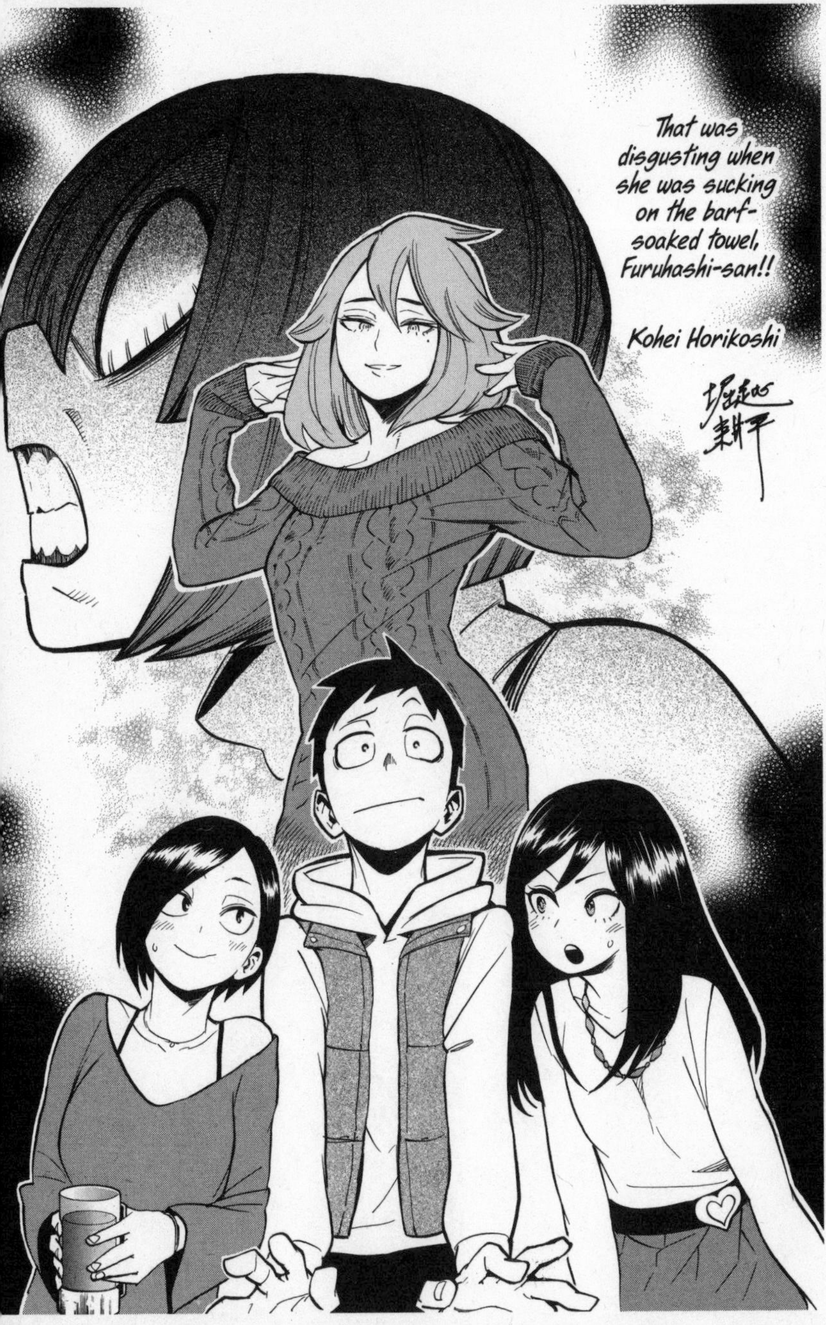
That was disgusting when she was sucking on the barf-soaked towel, Furuhashi-san!!
Kohei Horikoshi

Message from Kohei Horikoshi

HIDEYUKI FURUHASHI

Shota Aizawa, also known as Eraser Head, shows up a ton in this volume. I view underground heroes like him as being the closest thing to vigilantes, while still being licensed heroes. Since he's not a schoolteacher yet, I'm also thinking that he's not as much of a stickler about following the letter of the law…

BETTEN COURT

My son is getting old enough to understand the jobs that grown-ups do, so I'm dreading the day when one of his friends misunderstands and says, "Wait, so your dad's the guy who draws *MHA*? So cool!"

VOLUME 6
SHONEN JUMP Manga Edition

STORY: HIDEYUKI FURUHASHI
ART: BETTEN COURT
ORIGINAL CONCEPT: KOHEI HORIKOSHI

Translation & English Adaptation/Caleb Cook
Touch-Up Art & Lettering/John Hunt
Designer/Julian [JR] Robinson
Editor/Mike Montesa

VIGILANTE -BOKU NO HERO ACADEMIA ILLEGALS-
© 2016 by Hideyuki Furuhashi, Betten Court, Kohei Horikoshi
All rights reserved.
First published in Japan in 2016 by SHUEISHA Inc., Tokyo.
English translation rights arranged by SHUEISHA Inc.

The stories, characters and incidents mentioned in this publication
are entirely fictional.

Printed in the U.S.A.

Published by VIZ Media, LLC
P.O. Box 77010
San Francisco, CA 94107

10 9 8 7 6 5 4 3 2 1
First printing, October 2019

viz.com

shonenjump.com

PARENTAL ADVISORY
MY HERO ACADEMIA: VIGILANTES is rated
T for Teen and is recommended for ages
13 and up. This volume contains fantasy
violence.

MY HERO ACADEMIA

SCHOOL BRIEFS

ORIGINAL STORY BY
KOHEI HORIKOSHI

WRITTEN BY
ANRI YOSHI

Prose short stories
featuring the everyday
school lives of
My Hero Academia's
fan-favorite characters!

VIZ

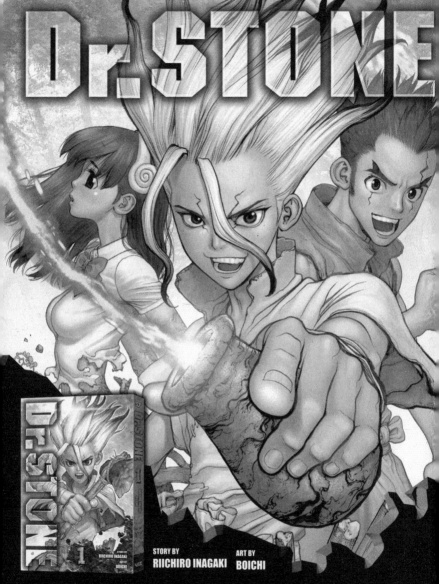

Dr.STONE

STORY BY
RIICHIRO INAGAKI

ART BY
BOICHI

One fateful day, all of humanity turned to stone. Many millennia later, Taiju frees himself from petrification and finds himself surrounded by statues. The situation looks grim—until he runs into his science-loving friend Senku! Together they plan to restart civilization with the power of science!

THE PROMISED NEVERLAND

STORY BY **KAIU SHIRAI**

ART BY **POSUKA DEMIZU**

Emma, Norman and Ray are the brightest kids
at the Grace Field House orphanage. And under
the care of the woman they refer to as "Mom,"
all the kids have enjoyed a comfortable life.
Good food, clean clothes and the perfect envi-
ronment to learn—what more could an orphan
ask for? One day, though, Emma and Norman
uncover the dark truth of the outside world
they are forbidden from seeing.

JoJo's

BIZARRE ADVENTURE

⬦⬦⬦⬦⬦⬦⬦   ◆   ⬦⬦⬦⬦⬦⬦⬦

★ PART 4 ★
DIAMOND IS UNBREAKABLE

Story & Art by
HIROHIKO ARAKI

A MULTIGENERATIONAL TALE OF THE HEROIC JOESTAR FAMILY AND THEIR NEVER-ENDING BATTLE AGAINST EVIL!

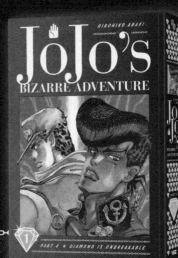

In April 1999, Jotaro Kujo travels to a town in Japan called Morioh to find a young man named Josuke Higashikata, the secret love child of his grandfather, Joseph Joestar. Upon finding him, Jotaro is surprised to learn that Josuke also possesses a Stand. After their strange meeting, the pair team up to investigate the town's proliferation of unusual Stands!

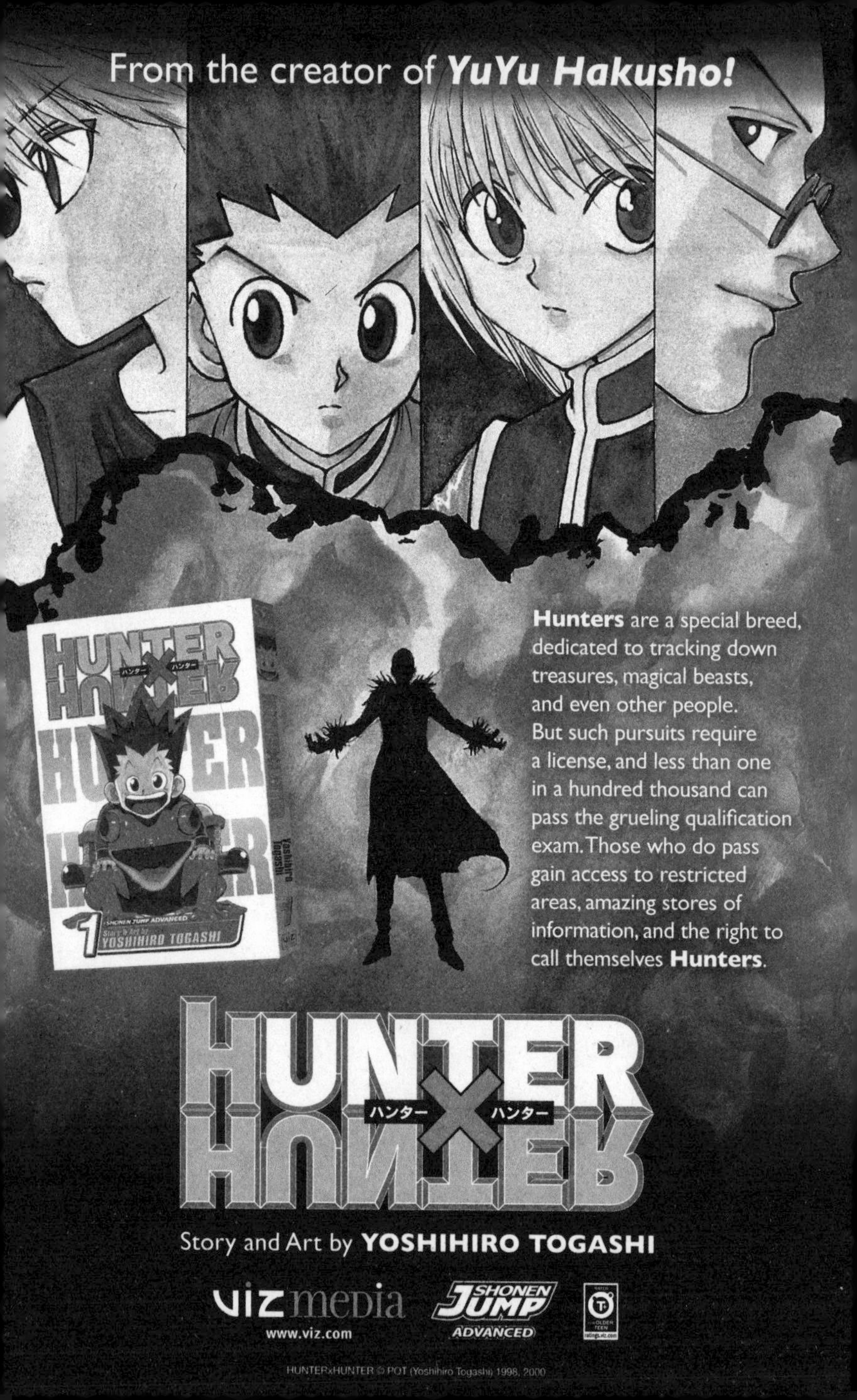
From the creator of YuYu Hakusho!
HUNTER × HUNTER
ハンター ハンター
SHONEN JUMP ADVANCED
1
Story & Art by
YOSHIHIRO TOGASHI
Yoshihiro Togashi
Hunters are a special breed, dedicated to tracking down treasures, magical beasts, and even other people. But such pursuits require a license, and less than one in a hundred thousand can pass the grueling qualification exam. Those who do pass gain access to restricted areas, amazing stores of information, and the right to call themselves Hunters.
HUNTER × HUNTER
ハンター ハンター
Story and Art by YOSHIHIRO TOGASHI
viz media
www.viz.com
SHONEN JUMP
ADVANCED
HUNTERxHUNTER © POT (Yoshihiro Togashi) 1998, 2000

DEATH NOTE

ALL-IN-ONE EDITION

Story by Tsugumi Ohba   Art by Takeshi Obata

Light Yagami is an ace student with great prospects—
and he's bored out of his mind. But all that changes
when he finds the Death Note, a notebook dropped by
a rogue Shinigami death god. Any human whose name
is written in the notebook dies, and now Light has
vowed to use the power of the Death Note to rid the
world of evil. But when criminals begin dropping dead,
the authorities send the legendary detective L to track
down the killer. With L hot on his heels, will Light lose
sight of his noble goal...or his life?

Includes a NEW epilogue chapter!

All 12 volumes in ONE monstrously large edition!

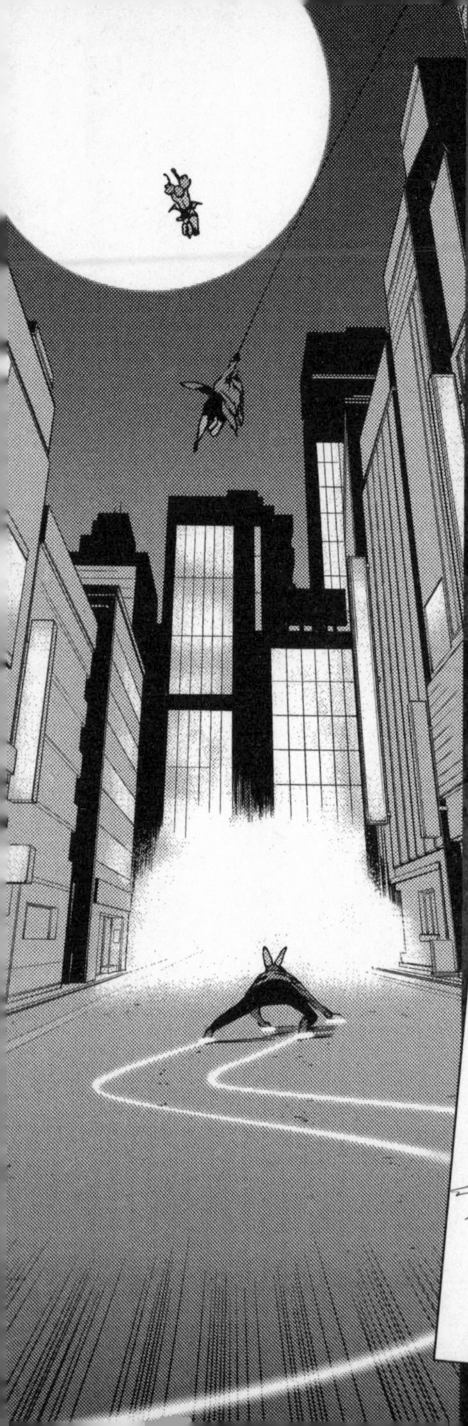

YOU'RE READING THE WRONG WAY!!

MY HERO ACADEMIA VIGILANTES

reads from right to left, starting in the upper-right corner. Japanese is read from right to left, meaning that action, sound effects and word-balloon order are completely reversed from English order.

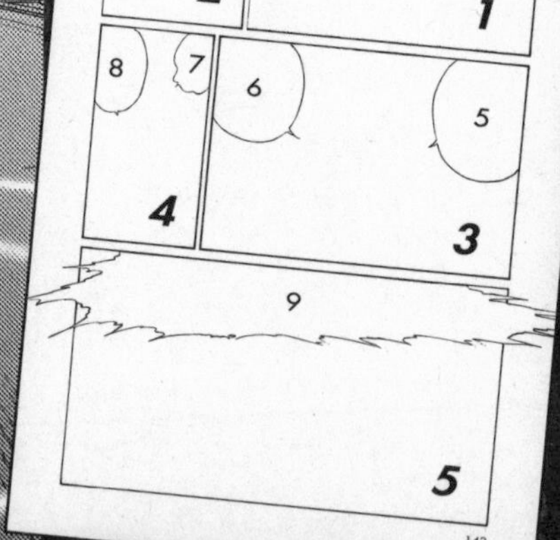

1
2
3
4
1
2
5
6
7
8
3
4
9
5
142

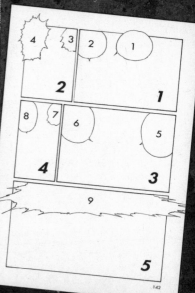